ExamMatrix™ CPA Review Textbook

ExamMatrix™

AUD

Auditing & Attestation

Sections 3000–3700

Year 2010

Matrix Learning Systems CPA Review Production Staff
Director of Accounting/Editorial: Pearl Zeiler, MBA
Coordinating Editor: James O'Leary
Desktop Publishing: Kimberli Mullen

Software Development Group:
Vice President of IT: Delmur Mayhak, Jr.
Testing Supervisor: Randy Morrow, MIS
Graphic Artist: Barry Schapiro

Printer: Corley Printing, Earth City, Missouri

This book contains material copyrighted © 1953 through 2010 by the American Institute of Certified Public Accountants, Inc., and is used or adapted with permission.

Portions of various FAF documents, copyrights by the Financial Accounting Standards Board and Governmental Accounting Standards Board, 401 Merritt 7, P.O. Box 5116, Norwalk, Connecticut 06856-5116, are reprinted with permission. Complete copies of these documents are available from the FASB and GASB.

This book contains material from Freeman/Shoulders/Allison, *Governmental & Nonprofit Accounting: Theory & Practice*. Reprinted by permission of Prentice Hall, Inc., Englewood Cliffs, NJ.

Material from Uniform CPA Examination Questions and Unofficial Answers, copyright © 1976 through 2010, American Institute of Certified Public Accountants, Inc., is used or adapted with permission.

The databanks contain material from Welsch/Newman/Zlatkovich, *Intermediate Accounting*. Reprinted by permission of Richard D. Irwin, Inc., Homewood, IL.

The databanks and textbooks contain quotations from *Governmental Accounting, Auditing, and Financial Reporting*, copyright © 2005 Government Finance Officers Association of the United States and Canada. Reprinted with permission.

This book is written to provide accurate and authoritative information concerning the covered topics. It is not meant to take the place of professional advice. **The content of this book has been updated to reflect relevant legislative and governing body modifications as of January 2010.**

Software copyright 2010, Matrix Learning Systems, Inc.

No part of this work may be reproduced or transmitted in any form or by any means, electronic or mechanical, including photocopying and recording, or by any information storage or retrieval system, except as may be expressly permitted by the 1976 Copyright Act or in writing by the Publisher. Requests for permission should be addressed in writing to Editor, Matrix Learning Systems, Inc; 8392 S. Continental Divide Rd., #105, Littleton, CO 80127.

Printed in the United States of America.

Preface

Congratulations on purchasing the ExamMatrix CPA Review. This powerful course is a complete system for success. It will teach you what you need to know, validate your readiness, and allow you to face the CPA Exams with confidence. It will guide you efficiently through your studies and help you achieve what thousands of other ExamMatrix accounting students and professionals before you have achieved—passing scores on the CPA Examination.

We use the power of your computer and our software to do the following:

- Provide you with your own personal instructor, who guides your customized study program.
- Prepare you for what to expect on the examination so there is no guesswork about what you need to know to pass.
- Coach you on ways to be physically, emotionally, and intellectually ready for the examination.
- Provide full printed text of examination preparation materials for you to study.
- Simulate the examination for you, drilling you with thousands of questions, weighted in accordance with the most current examination outlines.
- Give you instant help and guidance on every question, every step of the way, referring you back to the printed study materials when you need remedial help.
- Provide you with an Editorial Support Line to answer any questions that may arise while studying—call 877-272-7277.
- Provide a Pass Update or Pass Refund guarantee.
- Validate your readiness to pass each part of your examination.

You will pass with confidence.

The ExamMatrix CPA Review system components will help you reach that goal. The software portion of the ExamMatrix CPA Review is composed of the following:

- A database of over 4,000 categorized objective questions with immediate feedback to teach and review the points covered in the CPA testing process generated by the published weights from the AICPA Content Specification Outlines.
- Simulation format questions are contained in the following exam sections:

    Audit and Attestation

    Financial Accounting and Reporting

    Regulation

- The ExamMatrix CPA Review textbooks, which accompany your software, utilize a unique cross-referencing system to sections and paragraphs. The software targets your weak areas and, through the cross-referencing system, guides you directly to the section in the textbook that covers that material. Each Review textbook contains the following:

- Concise reviews of authoritative pronouncements needed to pass the CPA Examination in easy-to-understand paragraph form
- Learning aids such as charts, tables, and flowcharts to aid in remembering concepts and procedures

The Review textbooks are categorized as follows:
- Section 2000 Financial Accounting & Reporting (FAR)
- Section 3000 Auditing & Attestation (AUD)
- Section 4000 Regulation (REG)
- Section 5000 Business Environment and Concepts (BEC)

Our software and our CPA Review textbooks reflect all legislative changes and are in accordance with the AICPA Content Specification Outlines.

Thinking about achieving an additional designation? Matrix Learning Systems carries reviews for the following exams:
- Certified Management Accountant
- Certified Internal Auditor
- Certified Information Systems Auditor
- Chartered Financial Analyst
- Enrolled Agent

Matrix Learning Systems will be at your side throughout your professional career, meeting your educational needs every step of the way.

Acknowledgments

The ExamMatrix CPA Review was developed and written by a team of professionals who are experts in the fields of accounting, business law, and computer science, and are also experienced teachers in CPA Review programs and continuing professional education courses.

Matrix Learning Systems expresses its sincere appreciation to the many individual candidates, as well as accounting instructors, who took time to write to us about previous editions. The improvements in this edition are attributable to all of these individuals. Of course, any deficiencies are the responsibilities of the editors and authors. We very much appreciate and solicit your comments and suggestions about this year's edition.

The editors and authors are also indebted to the American Institute of Certified Public Accountants, the Financial Accounting Standards Board, and the Governmental Accounting Standards Board for permission to quote from their pronouncements. In addition, the AICPA granted us permission to use material from previous Uniform CPA Examination Questions and Answers. AICPA codification numbers are used throughout the Auditing portion of the Review to indicate the source of materials.

We recognize the work and dedication of our team of software designers and developers. Their vision has made this the best product possible. They contributed countless hours to deliver this package and are each fully dedicated to helping you pass the exam. Our thanks go out to the many individuals who have made contributions to both the software and textbook portions of the CPA Review. We extend our gratitude to our team of software testers who ensure that you receive only the highest quality product. Finally, we express appreciation to the editorial teams who have devoted their time to review this product. They have provided invaluable aid in the writing and production of the ExamMatrix CPA Review.

Good luck on the exam!

© 2010 ExamMatrix

Matrix Learning Systems

ExamMatrix CPA Review Textbook Authors

Raymond J. Clay, Jr., DBA, CPA, is the author of the ExamMatrix CPA Review Textbook: Auditing & Attestation. He holds the Internal Audit Professorship in Accounting at the University of North Texas. Prior to joining the University of North Texas, he served as Director of Professional Development at Union Pacific Corporation. Dr. Clay has held faculty positions in accounting at Indiana State University and Texas Tech University. He received his bachelor's and master's degrees from Northern Illinois University and his doctorate from the University of Kentucky. He has held significant committee appointments with professional organizations, including serving as a member of the AICPA Accounting and Review Services Committee for seven years. Dr. Clay is the author of 4 books, 10 continuing professional education courses, and numerous articles appearing in professional journals.

Ennis M. Hawkins, DBA, CPA, CMA, CIA, is a coauthor of the ExamMatrix CPA Review Textbook: Business Environment & Concepts and questions relative to this topic. He is currently a Professor of Accounting at Sam Houston State University in Huntsville, Texas. His teaching and research interests include environmental and cost accounting. Dr. Hawkins has served as the Program Co-Chairman and Vice President of the Southwest Region American Accounting Association. He is also a member of the AICPA, IMA, and IIA.

David G. Jaeger, JD, MST, MBA, is the author of the ExamMatrix CPA Review Textbook: Regulation. He is also the coauthor of the ExamMatrix CPA Review Textbook: Business Environment & Concepts. He is currently Associate Professor of Accounting and Taxation at the University of North Florida. He has taught numerous courses in taxation and business law at the undergraduate, MBA, Executive MBA, and Master of Accountancy levels, as well as in continuing education courses. His research has been published in such journals as *The Tax Advisor, TAXES, Tax Notes,* the *Journal of Accountancy,* and *Research in Accounting Regulation.* His work has also been cited by the U.S. Tax Court and several U.S. Federal Courts of Appeal.

Craig D. Shoulders, PhD, is a coauthor of the ExamMatrix CPA Review Textbook: Financial Accounting & Reporting. He joined the faculty at the University of North Carolina at Pembroke in 2004 after serving over 20 years on the accounting faculty at Virginia Tech. Dr. Shoulders has received the Cornelius E. Tierney/Ernst & Young Research Award from the Association of Government Accountants and has been recognized twice by the AICPA as an Outstanding Discussion Leader. He has recently completed a major research study on the financial reporting entity for the Governmental Accounting Standards Board and coauthors a Prentice Hall textbook on state and local government accounting as well as several continuing education courses on governmental accounting and financial reporting. Dr. Shoulders received his bachelor's degree from Campbellsville University, his master's degree from the University of Missouri-Columbia, and his PhD from Texas Tech University.

Jill Hazelbauer-Von der Ohe, MBA, CPA, CMA, CFM, CVA, is a coauthor of the ExamMatrix CPA Review Textbook: Business Environment Concepts and questions relative to this topic. She has her MBA from Rockford College and is currently a professor at Keller University, where she teaches accounting. She also has coauthored CPE courses with Robert Von der Ohe. In addition to a CPA, she holds CMA and CFM certifications, having received the Gold Award for the CFM exam during the 1997-98 winter exam cycle. She also holds a CVA (Certified Valuation Analyst) through NACVA, a professional organization that focuses on the valuation of closely held business for tax, estate, and other purposes. She has worked on accounting projects in Uganda and Poland.

Robert Von der Ohe, PhD, is a coauthor of the ExamMatrix CPA Review Textbook: Business Environment Concepts and questions relative to this topic. He earned his PhD in Economics from the University of Tennessee and currently holds the von Mises Chair in Economics at Rockford College in Rockford, Illinois, where he teaches economics and finance. He served 11 years as Chief Economist for the Credit Union National Association and has significant international consulting experience in the design and implementation of financial systems, working primarily in Latin America. He has undertaken numerous valuation projects, focusing on valuation of financial institutions and business entities.

Matrix Learning Systems

ExamMatrix CPA Review Question Database Contributors

William V. Allen, Jr., CPA, is currently a Principal in Making Auditors Proficient, Inc. (MAP). MAP provides training, technical assistance, peer reviews, and other services to local CPA firms throughout the United States and Canada. Their specialty and what gives them a unique approach to the various services, including peer reviews, is their proficiency in audit effectiveness and efficiency using a risk-based approach. He is also a recognized expert in Single Audits (Government and Nonprofit). He was the Audit Partner for the City of Los Angeles audit from 1985 to 1991. He was a Partner in a local firm in northern California with responsibility for over 50 small- and medium-sized audit engagements. He is also a contributing editor to the *Single Audit Information Service* published by Thompson Publishing Group.

Paul N. Brown, CPA, is the Director of Technical Services for the Florida Institute of CPAs (FICPA). One of his main duties is to serve as the technical reviewer in Florida for the AICPA Peer Review Program, which administers approximately 600 reviews annually in Florida. Paul has previously been an instructor for the AICPA Advanced Reviewers Training Course and writes and instructs his own course in Florida on peer review called Peer Review Forum for Reviewers, for which he has received several outstanding discussion leader and author awards. He has also served on the AICPA's Technical Reviewers Advisory Task Force to the Peer Review Board and serves as staff liaison to various committees of the Florida Institute of CPAs. Prior to joining the FICPA, Paul was an audit manager with a regional firm in Florida. He holds a BS in Accounting and Finance from Florida State University.

Annhenrie Campbell, PhD, CPA, CMA, CGFM, is a Professor of Accounting at California State University, Stanislaus. While working as a municipal accountant, Dr. Campbell taught governmental and not-for-profit accounting as an adjunct lecturer for several years. She completed her MBA at Humboldt State University in California and her PhD at the University of Colorado in Boulder. After earning a CPA and CMA and starting her university career, Dr. Campbell became a Certified Government Financial Manager at the start of the CGFM program. She has maintained her interest in students' professional preparation for governmental and not-for-profit careers, starting with her MBA thesis topic and a joint publication on the topic in the *Government Accountants' Journal,* and continuing now in teaching both graduate and undergraduate students. In addition to numerous presentations, Dr. Campbell and her colleagues have published additional articles on educational issues in the *Journal of Business and Management, The Accounting Educators' Journal, Accounting Perspectives,* and the *Journal of the Academy of Business Education* (forthcoming).

Anthony P. Curatola, PhD, is the Joseph F. Ford Professor of Accounting at Drexel University. He holds a BS in Accounting and an MBA in Finance from Drexel University, an MA in Accounting from the Wharton Graduate School of the University of Pennsylvania, and a PhD in Accounting from Texas A&M University. Dr. Curatola joined the faculty of Louisiana State University in 1981 and returned to Drexel University in 1989 by accepting the appointment to the Joseph F. Ford Professor of Accounting Chair. Dr. Curatola's findings have appeared in media such as *Forbes,* the *Washington Post, Money* magazine, the *Wall Street Journal,* and the *New York Times,* to name a few. Currently he serves on the Foundation of Academic Research. Most recently, he was awarded the R. Lee Brummet Award in Academic Excellence from the IMA.

Donna Hogan, CPA, CFP, is a shareholder in Hogan & Co., CPA, PC, in Fort Collins, Colorado, where she focuses on the areas of taxation and financial planning. She also often advises individuals who are starting businesses (on tax and other issues). She received her bachelor's degree in Accountancy from New Mexico State University and was a partner in charge of the tax department at an Albuquerque firm.

Taylor S. Klett, CPA, JD, is of counsel for the firm of Havins & Associates, LLP. He is currently an Associate Professor at Sam Houston State University and was an administrator and on the adjunct faculty there. His teaching and research interests include taxation, estate planning, ethics, and business law. He is an attorney and CPA in Texas and a member of the American Bar Association, Texas Bar Association, and AICPA. He graduated from the University of Texas and attended law school at the University of Houston Law Center (JD, with honors).

Tabitha McCormick, CPA, CFE, is the owner of Cornerstone Accounting in Millville, Pennsylvania. Cornerstone Accounting concentrates on training small business owners and financial employees to keep accurate accounting records, create efficient and effective policies and procedures, and institute strong internal controls. Cornerstone also assists businesses with implementing accounting software packages. She is a Certified Advanced QuickBooks® and QuickBooks Point of Sale® ProAdvisor and enjoys teaching QuickBooks classes for Bloomsburg University's Magee Center and other training institutions. Tabitha is also the author of two CPE courses on Identity Theft for MicroMash. She is a member of the Pennsylvania Institute of Certified Public Accountants (PICPA) and the Association of Certified Fraud Examiners (ACFE).

Robert J. Nieschwietz, a Visiting Assistant Professor at Seattle University, received his PhD in Accountancy from Arizona State University in 2001. He received a BBA and MS in Accounting from Texas A&M University in 1991 and 1996, respectively. Dr. Nieschwietz's primary research and teaching interests are within the area of auditing. His research has been published in various journals, including the *Journal of Accounting Literature, International Journal of Accounting Information Systems, International Journal of Auditing, Journal of Accounting Education, Journal of Applied Business Research, Academy of Accounting and Financial Studies Journal,* and *Journal of Risk Research.*

Paul Pierson is Director of Technical Services for the Illinois CPA Society. In this capacity, he oversees the administration of the AICPA Peer Review Program for approximately 1,300 CPA firms in Illinois. Paul has served as a discussion leader at the AICPA's Annual Peer Review Conference and its Advanced Reviewer Training Course, and is editor for the Society's peer review newsletter. He is also responsible for monitoring the continuing professional education and licensing rules in the state and responding to member inquiries regarding those matters. He currently serves on the Technical Reviewers' Advisory Task Force of the AICPA, having previously served a three-year term, and is the staff liaison for the Illinois CPA Society's Peer Review Report Acceptance and Governmental Accounting Executive Committees. Paul graduated from Illinois State University with a BS in Accounting and was an audit manager with a large, local CPA firm in East Peoria, Illinois, prior to joining the Society.

Cheryl L. Prachyl, PhD, is an Adjunct Assistant Professor of Accounting at the University of Texas at Arlington. She is a CPA licensed in the state of Texas. Dr. Prachyl holds a BBA in Marketing and an MS in Accounting from Texas A&M University. She holds a PhD in Accounting with a minor in Information Systems from the University of Texas at Arlington. In addition to her teaching experience, Dr. Prachyl has worked for NCR Corporation and Bosque County Bank and as an accounting systems consultant for numerous small businesses.

Darlene A. Pulliam, PhD, CPA, joined the faculty of West Texas A&M in 1997. A native of eastern New Mexico, Dr. Pulliam received a BS in Mathematics in 1976 and an MBA in 1978 from Eastern New Mexico University and joined the accounting firm of Peat Marwick and Mitchell and Co. (now KPMG) in Albuquerque. After five years in public accounting, she completed her PhD at the University of North Texas and joined the faculty of the University of Tulsa in 1987. During her 10 years in Tulsa, she taught primarily in the University of Tulsa's Master of Taxation program. Her publications include many articles appearing in *Tax Advisor;* the *Journal of Accountancy; Practical Tax Strategies; Oil, Gas and Energy Quarterly;* and the *Journal of Forensic Accounting* as an author or coauthor.

Marianne Rexer, PhD, CPA, is currently an Associate Professor of Accounting at Wilkes University. She has also taught at Drexel University and Johnson & Wales University. She received her PhD in Accounting at Drexel in 1997, her MS in Taxation at Bryant College in 1989, and her BS in Accounting from Wilkes University in 1985. Dr. Rexer has worked at a national CPA firm. She is a member of the American Accounting Association, the AICPA, the AICPA Audit Division, and the Pennsylvania Institute of CPAs.

Bob Thomas, PhD, is an Assistant Professor of Accounting at West Texas A&M University. He holds a PhD from Texas Tech University and a BBA from Midwestern State University, both with specializations in Management Information Systems and Accounting. Dr. Thomas' current teaching areas include auditing, governmental accounting, nonprofit accounting, accounting principles, and accounting information systems. His current research interests include assessment/improvement of information system success, accounting information systems, knowledge management, petroleum accounting, and social capital. Dr. Thomas has published in *Information & Management* and *Oil, Gas, and Energy Quarterly*. He is a member of the Association for Information Systems, Institute of Management Accountants, and Texas Society of Certified Public Accountants.

Table of Contents

Auditing & Attestation

Section 3000	Overview of the Auditing & Attestation Examination	1
Section 3100	The Auditing Function, the General Standards, and Planning the Audit	13
Section 3200	Auditing Aspects of EDP	63
Section 3300	Audit Evidence	77
Section 3400	Audit Sampling	123
Section 3500	Report on Audited Financial Statements	147
Section 3600	Other Reporting Standards	187
Section 3700	Standards of the Public Company Accounting Oversight Board (PCAOB)	245
	Index	275

This page intentionally left blank.

Section 3000
Overview of the Auditing & Attestation Examination

3010 **The Auditing & Attestation Examination**
   3011 Purpose of the Examination
   3012 General Content of the Examination
   3013 Study Suggestions for the Auditing & Attestation Portion of the CPA Examination
   3014 Index of Official Pronouncements
   3015 Suggested Readings and References

3010 The Auditing & Attestation Examination

3011 Purpose of the Examination

3011.01   The Auditing & Attestation exam covers knowledge of auditing procedures, and standards generally accepted in the United States and the skills needed to apply that knowledge in auditing and other attestation engagements. This section tests such knowledge and skills in the context of the five broad engagement tasks:

- Plan the engagement, evaluate the prospective client and engagement, decide whether to accept or continue the client and the engagement, and enter into an agreement with the client

- Consider internal control in both manual and computerized environments

- Obtain and document information to form a basis for conclusions

- Review the engagement to provide reasonable assurance that objectives are achieved and evaluate information obtained to reach and to document engagement conclusions

- Prepare communications to satisfy engagement objectives

Source: *AICPA Uniform CPA Examination Content Specifications*, October 19, 2005

3012 General Content of the Examination

3012.01   The multiple-choice questions in this portion of the Examination are presented in random order of topics, requiring the candidate to shift from topic to topic while working through the examination. The multiple-choice questions will be given in three separate testlets with each testlet containing approximately 25-30 questions. There will also be two simulation questions which will compliment the multiple-choice portion of the exam. Simulations are condensed case studies that will test candidates' auditing knowledge using real life work-related situations. Each simulation is approximately 30 minutes in length.

3012.02 The key to passing the auditing portion of the CPA Examination is a thorough knowledge of the authoritative auditing literature, especially the Statements on Auditing Standards (SASs). A common misconception is that the CPA candidate must have practical auditing experience to pass the auditing examination. This may have been true 10 years ago, but today concepts and their application are clearly more important on the examination than highly technical practice considerations, such as lengthy audit programs.

3013 Study Suggestions for the Auditing & Attestation Portion of the CPA Examination

3013.01 According to the AICPA Content Specification Outlines (starting in section **1600** of your ExamMatrix Intro Volume found in the software under "Tools"), it appears that the content of future exams will basically follow this outline. All of the topics are covered in this review. For your convenience, this text is organized according to these topics. The text reference numbers are provided as follows:

Planning the Engagement (section **3100**):

a. Preengagement Acceptance Activities

b. Staffing and Supervision Requirements

c. Understanding the Entity's Business and its Industry

d. Analytical Procedures

e. Audit Risk and Materiality

f. Errors and Illegal Acts

g. Documentation and Audit Programs

h. Engagement Responsibilities

(1) Attestation (section **3682**)

(2) Audit (section **3645**)

(3) Review (section **3644**)

(4) Compilation (section **3643**)

(5) Prospective Financial Statements (section **3684**)

i. Quality Control Considerations

3013.02 Considering the Internal Control Structure:

a. Definitions and Basic Concepts

b. Understanding and Documenting the Structure

(1) Control Environment

(2) Risk Assessment

(3) Activities

(4) Information and Communications

(5) Monitoring

       c. Assessing Control Risk

       d. Testing Controls

       e. Other Considerations

           (1) Reportable Conditions

           (2) Reports on Internal Control

           (3) Special-Purpose Reports on Internal Control Structure of Service Organizations

3013.03 Obtaining Evidence and Applying Procedures:

       a. Audit Evidence

           (1) Nature, Competence, and Sufficiency of Audit Evidence

           (2) Audit Evidence for Financial Statement Assertions and Objectives

           (3) Confirmations

           (4) Analytical Procedures and Related Inquiries

           (5) Audit Sampling

           (6) Accounting Estimates

       b. Tests of Details of Transactions and Balances

           (1) Sales, Receivables, and Cash Receipts

           (2) Purchases, Payables, and Cash Disbursements

           (3) Inventories and Production

           (4) Personnel and Payroll

           (5) Financing and Investing

           (6) Other

       c. Other Specific Audit Topics

           (1) Substantive Tests Prior to the Balance Sheet Date

           (2) Effect of the Internal Audit Function

           (3) Using the Work of a Specialist

           (4) Inquiry of a Client's Lawyer

           (5) Subsequent Events

           (6) Client Representations

           (7) Related Parties and Related Party Transactions

           (8) Using the Computer in Performing the Audit

           (9) Going Concern

           (10) Workpapers

       d. Review and Compilation Procedures

           (1) Understanding of Accounting Principles and Practices of the Industry

           (2) Inquiry and Analytical Procedures

           (3) Other Procedures

3013.04 Preparing Reports:

    a. Reports on Audited Financial Statements

        (1) Reporting Responsibilities

        (2) Presentation in Conformity with Generally Accepted Accounting Principles

        (3) Standard Report

        (4) Departures from Unqualified Opinions

        (5) Explanatory Language Added to the Standard Report

        (6) Uncertainties

        (7) Going Concern

        (8) Consistency

        (9) Comparative Financial Statements

        (10) Part of the Audit Performed by Other Independent Auditors

        (11) Dating and Addressing the Auditor's Report

        (12) Disclosure

    b. Reports on Reviewed and Compiled Financial Statements

    c. Other Reporting Considerations

        (1) Attestation Engagements

        (2) Prospective Financial Statements

        (3) Special Reports

        (4) Review of Interim Financial Information

        (5) Compliance with Laws and Regulations

        (6) Subsequent Discovery of Facts Existing at the Date of the Auditor's Report

        (7) Consideration of Omitted Procedures after the Report Date

        (8) Letters for Underwriters

        (9) Filings under Federal Securities Statutes

        (10) Other Information in Documents Containing Audited Financial Statements

        (11) Required Supplementary Information

        (12) Reporting on Information Accompanying the Basic Financial Statements

        (13) Reporting on Condensed Financial Statements

        (14) Reporting on Financial Statements Prepared for Use in Other Countries

        (15) Reports on the Application of Accounting Principles

        (16) Communication with Audit Committees

        (17) Governmental Reporting Responsibilities

3014 Index of Official Pronouncements

3014.01 This reference manual covers all relevant pronouncements needed to prepare for the auditing portion of the CPA Examination. The information contained in the 3,000-plus pages of pronouncements has been distilled down to essential points and then arranged in an order conducive to classroom or self-study in this reference manual. All references refer to AICPA Codification numbers and use the following abbreviations:

AU	Auditing	Statements on Auditing Standards
AR	Accounting and Review	Statements on Standards for Accounting and Review Services
AT	Attestation	Statements on Standards for Attestation Engagements (SSAEs)

Thus, *AU 508.04* means that the source of the referenced materials is **Section 508**, paragraph .04, of the AICPA's Codification of Statements on Auditing Standards. We do not use SAS numbers because they are in chronological order (not a logical topic order), and they are not used in the student's basic reference, which is the AICPA codification.

3014.02 For those who want to find where we cover a particular SAS or other pronouncement, the following index cross-references SASs, codification numbers, and section numbers in this reference.

Statement	Codification Number	Topic	Section Number
SAS 1	AU 110 (AU 110.05-.08 superseded by SAS 16)	Responsibilities and Function of the Independent Auditor	3112
	AU 210	Training and Proficiency of the Independent Auditor	3141
	AU 220	Independence	3142
	AU 230	Due Professional Care in the Performance of Work	3144
	(AU 310 superseded by SAS 108)		
	(AU 320 superseded by SAS 55)		
	AU 331	Inventories	3363, 3365
	AU 332	Auditing Derivative Instruments, Hedging Activities, and Investments in Securities	3367
	(AU 338 superseded by SAS 41)		
	AU 410	Adherence to GAAP	3522
	(AU 410.03–.04 superseded by SAS 5)		
	AU 420 (See AU 508 for opinion)	Consistency of Application to GAAP	3523 (Modified by SAS 58)
	AU 431	Adequacy of Disclosure in Financial Statements	3524
	(AU 510–515 superseded by SAS 2)		
	(AU 516, 517, and 518 superseded by SAS 26)		
	AU 530	Dating of the Independent Auditor's Report	3534
	(AU 535, 540, and 541 superseded by SAS 2)		
	(AU 542 superseded by SAS 58)		
	AU 543	Part of Audit Performed by Other Independent Auditors	3521
	(AU 543.18 superseded by SAS 7)		
	AU 544	Lack of Conformity with GAAP	3522
	(AU 544.01 superseded by SAS 2)		
	(AU 545 superseded by SAS 58)		
	(AU 546 superseded by SAS 53)		

Statement	Codification Number	Topic	Section Number
	(AU 547 superseded by SAS 2)		
	AU 560	Subsequent Events	3531
	AU 561	Subsequent Discovery of Facts Existing at the Date of the Auditor's Report	3532
	(AU 610 superseded by SAS 29)		
	(AU 620 superseded by SAS 14)		
	(AU 630 superseded by SAS 38)		
	(AU 640 superseded by SAS 30)		
	(AU 641 superseded by SAS 30)		
	(AU 710 superseded by SAS 37)		
SAS 2	(AU 509 superseded by SAS 58)		
SAS 3	(AU 321 superseded by SAS 48)		
SAS 4	(AU 160 superseded by SAS 25)		
SAS 5	(AU 411 superseded by SAS 69)		
SAS 6	(AU 335 superseded by SAS 45)		
SAS 7	AU 315 (AU 315.11 superseded by SAS 58) (AU 315 superseded by SAS 84)		
SAS 8	AU 550	Other Information in Documents Containing Audited Financial Statements	3550
SAS 9	(AU 322 superseded by SAS 65)		
SAS 10	(AU 720 superseded by SAS 24)		
SAS 11	(AU 336 superseded by SAS 73)		
SAS 12	AU 337	Inquiry of a Client's Lawyer Concerning Litigation, Claims, and Assessments	3343
SAS 13	(AU 519 superseded by SAS 24)		
SAS 14	(AU 621 superseded by SAS 62)		
SAS 15	(AU 505 superseded by SAS 58)		
SAS 16	(AU 327 superseded by SAS 53)		
SAS 17	(AU 328 superseded by SAS 54)		
SAS 18	(AU 330 superseded by SAS 67)		
SAS 19	(AU 333 superseded by SAS 85)		
SAS 20	(AU 323 superseded by SAS 60)		
SAS 21	(AU 435 rescinded by Auditing Standards Board)		
SAS 22	(AU 311 superseded by SAS 108)		
SAS 23	(AU 318 superseded by SAS 56)		
SAS 24	(AU 721 superseded by SAS 71)		
SAS 25	AU 161 (supersedes AU 160)	The Relationship of Generally Accepted Auditing Standards to Quality Control Standards	3145
SAS 26	AU 504 (supersedes AU 516, 517, and 505.13–15)	Association with Financial Statements	3630, 3633
SAS 27	(AU 553 superseded by SAS 52)		
SAS 28	(AU 554 withdrawn by SAS 52)		
SAS 29	AU 551 (supersedes AU 610)	Reporting on Information Accompanying the Basic Financial Statements in Auditor-Submitted Documents	3570
SAS 30	(AU 642 superseded by SSAE 2)		
SAS 31	(AU 326 superseded by SAS 106)		
SAS 32	AU 431	Adequacy of Disclosure	3524
SAS 33	(AU 555 superseded by SAS 45)		
SAS 34	(AU 340 superseded by SAS 59)		
SAS 35	(AU 622 superseded by SAS 75)	Special Reports for Applying Agreed-Upon Procedures	3683
SAS 36	(AU 722 superseded by SAS 71)		

Statement	Codification Number	Topic	Section Number
SAS 37	AU 711 (supersedes AU 710)	Filing under Federal Securities Laws	3664
SAS 38	(AU 631 superseded by SAS 49)		
SAS 39	AU 350 (supersedes AU 320A and AU 320B)	Audit Sampling	3400
SAS 40	(AU 556 superseded by SAS 52)		
SAS 41	(AU 339 superseded by SAS 96)		
SAS 42	AU 552	Reporting on Condensed Financial Statements and Selected Financial Data	3581
SAS 43	Amends various SASs (integrated in many sections)	Omnibus Statement on Auditing Standards	3513, 3514
SAS 44	(AU 324 superseded by SAS 70)		
SAS 45	(AU 313 and 334 superseded by SAS 110)		
SAS 46	AU 390	Consideration of Omitted Procedures after the Report Date	3533
SAS 47	(AU 312 superseded by SAS 107)		
SAS 48	Amends various SASs (integrated into many sections)	Effects of Computer Processing on the Examination of Financial Statements	3200
SAS 49	(AU 634 superseded by SAS 72)		
SAS 50	AU 625	Reports on the Application of Accounting Principles	3582
SAS 51	AU 534	Reports on Financial Statements Prepared for Use in Other Countries	3583
SAS 52	AU 411.05–.08, 551.15, 558	Omnibus SAS 1987	3513, 3560
SAS 53	(AU 316 superseded by SAS 82)		
SAS 54	AU 317	Illegal Acts by Clients	3600
SAS 55	(AU 319 superseded by SAS 109 and 110)		
SAS 56	AU 329	Analytical Procedures	3339
SAS 57	AU 342	Auditing Accounting Estimates	3344
SAS 58	AU 508	Reports on Audited Financial Statements	3510–3520, 3622
SAS 59	AU 341	The Auditor's Consideration of an Entity's Ability to Continue as a Going Concern	3526
SAS 60	(AU 325 superseded by SAS 112)		
SAS 61	(AU 380 superseded by SAS 114)		
SAS 62	AU 623	Special Reports	3620
SAS 63	(AU 801 superseded by SAS 68)		
SAS 64	AU 341.12, 508.83, 543.16	Omnibus SAS 1990	3510, 3521, 3526
SAS 65	AU 322	The Auditor's Consideration of the Internal Audit Function in an Audit of Financial Statements	3130
SAS 66	(AU 722 superseded by SAS 71)		
SAS 67	AU 330	The Confirmation Process	3333
SAS 68	(AU 801 superseded by SAS 74)		
SAS 69	AU 411	The Meaning of *Presents Fairly in Conformity with Generally Accepted Accounting Principles* in the Independent Auditor's Report	3513
SAS 70	AU 324	Reports on the Processing of Transactions by Service Organizations	3696
SAS 71	(AU 722 superseded by SAS 100)		
SAS 72	AU 634	Letters for Underwriters and Certain Other Requesting Parties	3662
SAS 73	AU 336	Using the Work of a Specialist	3342

Statement	Codification Number	Topic	Section Number
SAS 74	AU 801	Compliance Auditing Considerations in Audits of Governmental Entities and Recipients of Governmental Financial Assistance	3345
SAS 75	(AU 622 superseded by SAS 98)		
SAS 76	AU 634	Amendments to Statement on Auditing Standards No. 72, *Letters for Underwriters and Certain Other Requesting Parties*	3662
SAS 77	AU 311, AU 544, AU 623	Amendments to Statements on Auditing Standards No. 22, *Planning and Supervision*, No. 59, *The Auditor's Consideration of an Entity's Ability to Continue As a Going Concern*, and No. 62, *Special Reports*	3150, 3526, 3620
SAS 78	(AU 319 superseded by SAS 109 and 110)		
SAS 79	AU 508	Amendment to Statement on Auditing Standards No. 58, *Reports on Audited Financial Statements*	3525
SAS 80	AU 326	Amendment to Statement on Auditing Standards No. 31, *Evidential Matter*	3300
SAS 81	(AU 332 superseded by SAS 92)		
SAS 82	(AU 316 superseded by SAS 99)		
SAS 83	AU 310	Establishing an Understanding With the Client	3154, 3600
SAS 84	AU 315	Communicating Between Predecessor and Successor Auditor	3153
SAS 85	AU 333	Management Representations	3336
SAS 86	AU 634	Amendment to Statement on Auditing Standards No. 72, *Letters for Underwriters and Certain Other Parties*	3662
SAS 87	AU 532	Restricting the Use of an Auditor's Report	3584
SAS 88	AU 324, 420	Service Organizations & Reporting Consistency	3523, 3696
SAS 89	AU 380, 722	Audit Adjustments	3174, 3540
SAS 90	AU 310, 333, 380	Audit Committee Communications	3540, 3615
SAS 91	AU 411	Federal GAAP Hierarchy	3513
SAS 92	AU 332	Auditing Derivative Instruments, Hedging Activities, and Investments in Securities	3347
SAS 93	AU 508	Omnibus Statement on Auditing Standards—2000	3510, 3520
SAS 94	(AU 319 superseded by SAS 109 and 110)		
SAS 95	AU 150	Generally Accepted Auditing Standards	3120
SAS 96	AU 339	Audit Documentation	3314
SAS 97	AU 625	Amendment to Statement on Auditing Standards No. 50, *Reports on the Application of Accounting Principles*	3582
SAS 98	Amends Various SASs (Integrated into many sections)	Omnibus Statement on Auditing Standards—2002	3100, 3510, 3696
SAS 99	AU 316	Consideration of Fraud in a Financial Statement Audit	3170

Statement	Codification Number	Topic	Section Number
SAS 100	AU 722	Interim Financial Information	3610
SAS 101	AU 328	Auditing Fair Value Measurements and Disclosures	3346
SAS 102	AU 120	Defining Professional Requirements in Statements on Auditing Standards	3120
SAS 103	AU 339	Audit Documentation	
SAS 104	AU 230	Amendment to SAS No. 1, On Due Care	3144
SAS 105	AU 150	Amendment to SAS No. 95, *Generally Accepted Auditing Standards*	3120
SAS 106	AU 326	Audit Evidence	3330
SAS 107	AU 312	Audit Risk and Materiality in Conducting an Audit	3130
SAS 108	AU 311	Planning and Supervision	3155–3156
SAS 109	AU 314	Understanding the Entity and Its Environment and Assessing the Risks of Material Misstatement	3160
SAS 110	AU 318	Performing Audit Procedures in Response to Assessed Risks and Evaluating the Audit Evidence Obtained	3320
SAS 111	AU 350	Amendment to SAS No. 39, *Audit Sampling*	3400
SAS 112	(AU 325 superseded by SAS 115)		
SAS 113		Omnibus SAS 2006	3120
SAS 114	AU 380	The Auditor's Communication with Those Charged with Governance	3540
SAS 115	AU 325	Communicating Internal Control Related Matters Identified in an Audit	3697
SAS 116	AU 722	Interim Financial Information	3610
PCAOB Audit Standard 1		References in Auditor's Reports to the Standards of the Public Company Accounting Oversight Board	3714
PCAOB Audit Standard 2	(superseded)		
PCAOB Audit Standard 3		Audit Documentation	3720
PCAOB Audit Standard 4		Reporting on Whether a Previously Reported Material Weakness Continues to Exist	3730
PCAOB Audit Standard 5		An Audit of Internal Control Over Financial Reporting That Is Integrated with An Audit of Financial Statements	3740
PCAOB Audit Standard 6		Evaluating Consistency of Financial Statements	3750
PCAOB Rule 3100		Compliance with Auditing and Related Professional Practice Standards	3712
PCAOB Rule 3101		Certain Terms Used in Auditing and Related Professional Practice Standards	3713
PCAOB Rule 3501, 3502, 3520–3524, and 3526		Ethics and Independence Rules and Related Information	3700
PCAOB Rule 3525		Audit Committee Pre-approval of Non-audit Services Related to Internal Control Over Financial Reporting	3700
PCAOB Rule 3526		Communication with Audit Committees Concerning Independence	3700
SSAE 1	(superseded by SSAE 10)		
SSAE 2	(superseded by SSAE 10)		

Statement	Codification Number	Topic	Section Number
SSAE 3	(superseded by SSAE 10)		
SSAE 4	(superseded by SSAE 10)		
SSAE 5	(superseded by SSAE 10)		
SSAE 6	(superseded by SSAE 10)		
SSAE 7	(superseded by SSAE 10)		
SSAE 8	(superseded by SSAE 10)		
SSAE 9	(superseded by SSAE 10)		
SSAE 10	AT 101	Attestation Engagements	3682
SSAE 11	AT 101	Attest Documentation	3682
	AT 201	Agreed-Upon Procedures Engagements	3683
	AT 301	Financial Forecasts and Projections	3684
	AT 401	Reporting on Pro Forma Financial Information	3685
	AT 501	Reporting on an Entity's Internal Control	3690
	AT 601	Compliance Attestation	3686
	AT 701	Management's Discussion and Analysis	3687
SSAE 12	AT 101	Amendment to SSAE No. 10	3682
SSAE 13	AT 101	Defining Professional Requirements in Statements on Standards for Attestation Engagements	3681
SSARS 1	AR 100	Compilation and Review of Financial Statements	3642–3645
SSARS 2	AR 200	Reporting on Comparative Financial Statements	3646
SSARS 3	AR 300	Compilation Reports on Financial Statements Included in Certain Prescribed Forms	3647
SSARS 4	AR 400	Communication between Predecessor and Successor Accountants	3648
SSARS 5	(deleted by SSARS 7)		
SSARS 6	AR 600	Reporting on Personal Financial Statements Included in Personal Financial Plans	3649
SSARS 7	(amends SSARS 1)	Omnibus SSARS—1992	3641, 3642
SSARS 8	AR 100	Amendment to Statement on Standards for Accounting Review Services 1, *Compilation and Review of Financial Statements*	3642–3645
SSARS 9	(amends SSARS 1 & 4)	Omnibus Statement on Standards for Accounting and Review Services	3642, 3648
SSARS 10	(amends SSARS 1)	Performance of Review Engagements	3644
SSARS 11	AR 50	Standards for Accounting and Review Services	3641
SSARS 12	(amends SSARS 1 & 2)	Omnibus Statement on Standards for Accounting and Review Services	3642, 3646
SSARS 13	AR 110	Compilation of Specified Elements, Accounts, or Items of a Financial Statement	3652
SSARS 14	AR 120	Compilation of Pro Forma Financial Information	3653
SSARS 15	(amends AR 100)	Elimination of Certain References to SASs and Incorporation of Appropriate Guidance into SSARS	3642–3645
SSARS 16		Defining Professional Requirements in Statements on Standards for Accounting and Review Services	3654
SSARS 17	(amends AR 100)	Omnibus SSARS	3642–3645
SSARS 18	(amends AR 100)	Applicability of Statements on Standards for Accounting and Review Services	3610

Statement	Codification Number	Topic	Section Number
SQCS 2	(superseded by SQCS 7)		
SQCS 3	(superseded by SQCS 7)		
SQCS 4	(superseded by SQCS 7)		
SQCS 5	(superseded by SQCS 7)		
SQCS 6	(superseded by SQCS 7)		
SQCS 7		A Firm's System of Quality Control	3146
Statements of Position	82–1	Accounting and Financial Reporting for Personal Financial Statements	3649

3014.03 This reference also covers many important topics that frequently appear on the CPA Examination but are not covered specifically in the authoritative literature listed in section **3014.02**. The following are some of these topics:

— Section 3200, Auditing Aspects of EDP

— Section 3320, Types of Audit Evidence

— Section 3340, General Audit Procedures

— Section 3660, SEC Reporting

— Section 3670, Government Auditing Standards (Issued by Government Accountability Office)

— Section 3684, Financial Forecasts and Projections

3015 Suggested Readings and References

3015.01 In addition to the careful reading and study of this reference manual, a CPA candidate should refer to other literature resources when necessary. Suggested supplementary readings are listed as follows.

3015.02 Authoritative pronouncements and other professional publications:

— AICPA *Professional Standards, Volume I,* latest edition

— AICPA *Professional Standards, Volume II,* latest edition

— AICPA Industry Audit Guides

— AICPA Statements on Quality Control Standards

— U.S. Government Accountability Office *Government Auditing Standards*

— AICPA Audit and Accounting Guides:

  (1) Audit Sampling

  (2) Consideration of Internal Control in a Financial Audit

— AICPA Auditing Procedure Studies

— AICPA Audit and Accounting Manual

— AICPA Top 10 Technologies and Their Impact on CPAs

— AICPA Risk Alerts

— SECPS Practice Alerts

— Single Audit Act, as amended

— Information on auditing and other assurance services on the AICPA website

3015.03 Journal articles:

— *Journal of Accountancy,* last 18 months

3015.04 General textbooks.

— **Arens,** Elder, and Beasley. *Auditing and Assurance Services: An Integrated Approach.* Prentice Hall.

— **Boynton** and Johnson. *Modern Auditing: Assurance Services and The Integrity of Financial Reporting.* Wiley.

— **Louwers,** Ramsay, Sinason, and Strawser. *Auditing and Assurance Services.* McGraw-Hill/Irwin.

— **O'Reilly,** Winograd, Gerson, and Jaenicke. *Montgomery's Auditing.* Wiley.

— **Rittenberg,** Schwieger, and Johnson. *Auditing: A Business Risk Approach.* Cengage Learning (Thomson Learning), South-Western.

— **Whittington** and Pany. *Principles of Auditing and Other Assurance Services.* McGraw-Hill/Irwin.

Section 3100
The Auditing Function, the General Standards, and Planning the Audit

3110 The Audit
- 3111 Independent Audit Defined
- 3112 Objectives of the Audit Summarized
- 3113 The Public Benefit of Audits
- 3114 Responsibilities of the CPA and Entity Management

3120 Generally Accepted Auditing Standards (AU 150)
- 3121 Auditing Standards and Procedures
- 3122 The General Standards
- 3123 The Standards of Fieldwork
- 3124 The Standards of Reporting
- 3125 Interpretive Publications and Other Auditing Publications
- 3126 Types of Auditor's Reports
- 3127 Meaning of Terminology Imposed on Auditors

3130 Audit Risk and Materiality in Conducting an Audit (AU 312)
- 3131 Understanding Audit Risk and Materiality
- 3132 The Concept of Misstatements
- 3133 Audit Risk at the Financial Statement Level
- 3134 Risk at the Account Balance, Class of Transactions, or Disclosure Level
- 3135 Planning Materiality for the Financial Statements
- 3136 Other Considerations by the Auditor
- 3137 Evaluating Audit Findings

3140 The General Standards
- 3141 Technical Training and Proficiency (AU 210)
- 3142 Independence (AU 220)
- 3143 Audit Committees
- 3144 Due Care (AU 230)
- 3145 The Relationship of Generally Accepted Auditing Standards to Quality Control Standards
- 3146 Quality Control Standard 7, "A Firm's System of Quality Control"

3150 Planning and Supervising the Audit
- 3151 Steps in an Audit Engagement Summarized
- 3152 Appointment of the Independent Auditor
- 3153 Communication Between Predecessor and Successor Auditors (AU 315)
- 3154 Engagement Letters
- 3155 Planning the Audit (AU 311)
- 3156 Supervision (AU 311)
- 3157 Ratio Analysis

- 3160 Understanding the Entity and Its Environment and Assessing the Risk of Material Misstatement (AU 314)
  - 3161 Sources of Information About the Entity and Its Environment, Including Its Internal Control
  - 3162 Discussion Among the Audit Team
  - 3163 The Entity and Its Environment
  - 3164 Objectives, Strategies, Related Business Risks, and the Entity's Financial Performance
  - 3165 Internal Control
  - 3166 Effect of Information Technology (IT)
  - 3167 Components of Internal Control
  - 3168 Assessing the Risks of Material Misstatement
  - 3169 Documentation

- 3170 Consideration of Fraud in a Financial Statement Audit (AU 316)
  - 3171 Description and Characteristics of Fraud
  - 3172 Discussion Among Engagement Personnel Regarding the Risks of Material Misstatement Due to Fraud
  - 3173 Identifying Risks That May Result in Material Misstatement Due to Fraud
  - 3174 Responding to the Results of Fraud Risk Assessment
  - 3175 Evaluating Audit Evidence
  - 3176 Communicating About Possible Fraud to Management, the Audit Committee, and Others
  - 3177 Documenting the Auditor's Consideration of Fraud

3110 The Audit

3111 Independent Audit Defined

3111.01 Financial statement auditing is defined as a systematic process of objectively obtaining and evaluating evidence regarding assertions about economic actions and events to ascertain the degree of correspondence between those assertions and established criteria and communicating the results to interested users.

3111.02 An independent auditor plans, conducts, and reports the results of an audit in accordance with generally accepted audit standards (GAAS).

3112 Objectives of the Audit Summarized

3112.01 **Systematic process:** Auditing involves a structured and disciplined approach carried out by the auditor in forming an opinion on the financial statements being audited.

3112.02 **Objectively obtaining and evaluating evidence:** In an audit, evidence is any information used by the auditor in arriving at the conclusions on which the audit opinion is based. This evidence is obtained and evaluated in an objective manner to insure an independent approach to the audit.

3112.03 **Assertions about economic actions:** An economic assertion is a positive statement about an entity's economic activities made by those responsible for the preparation of the financial statements (entity management).

3112.04 **Correspondence between assertions and established criteria:** Generally accepted accounting principles (GAAP) represent the established criteria upon which assertions are evaluated. Thus, the auditor must determine whether the economic assertions made by management have been recorded in the account balances in accordance with GAAP.

3112.05 **Communicating the results to interested users:** The results of an audit are communicated to interested users in the form of an auditor's report, commonly referred to as the auditor's opinion.

3113 The Public Benefit of Audits

3113.01 **Credibility:** The independent audit lends credibility to the financial statements and, thus, third-party investors and creditors may make investing and lending decisions with the confidence that they have reliable information.

3113.02 **Capital formation and flow:** The capital markets in our society depend substantially on audited financial statements to determine the riskiness of alternative investments or loans.

3113.03 **Freedom from bias:** The independent audit is objective and thwarts the natural tendency of management to bias the financial statements toward a particular viewpoint or conclusion.

3113.04 **Freedom from material error:** The independent audit provides reasonable assurance that the financial statements are free from material misstatement, either inadvertent or deliberate.

3114 Responsibilities of the CPA and Entity Management

3114.01 Entity management is responsible for the following:

   a. The entity's financial statements and the selection and application of accounting principles

   b. Establishing and maintaining effective internal control over financial reporting

   c. Designing and implementing programs and controls to prevent and detect fraud

   d. Identifying and ensuring that the entity complies with the laws and regulations applicable to its activities

   e. Making all financial records and related information available to the auditor

   f. At the conclusion of the engagement, providing the auditor with a letter that confirms certain representations made during the audit

3114.02 The auditor is responsible for the following:

   a. Establishing an understanding with the client regarding the services to be performed for each engagement and documenting the communication through a written communication with the client

   b. Conducting the audit in accordance with generally accepted auditing standards (GAAS)

   c. Ensuring that those charged with governance are aware of any significant deficiencies that come to their attention

   d. Either expressing an opinion regarding the financial statements, taken as a whole, or stating that an opinion cannot be expressed

3120 Generally Accepted Auditing Standards (AU 150)

3121 Auditing Standards and Procedures

3121.01 **Auditing standards** are related to the *quality* of the CPA's work and to the *objectives* of the audit. They are concerned not only with the auditor's professional qualities, but also with the auditor's judgment exercised in the performance of the audit.

3121.02 **Auditing procedures** are *acts* that the auditor performs during the course of an audit to comply with auditing standards.

3121.03 GAAS apply to the performance of an independent audit and, to the extent that they are relevant, to all other services governed by statements on auditing standards.

3122 The General Standards

3122.01 The three general standards pertain to the personal qualifications of the CPA and apply to all phases of the audit.

3122.02 **1st General Standard:** The auditor must have adequate technical training and proficiency to perform the audit.

3122.03 **2nd General Standard:** The auditor must maintain independence in mental attitude in all matters relating to the audit.

3122.04 **3rd General Standard:** The auditor must exercise due professional care in the performance of the audit and the preparation of the report.

3123 The Standards of Fieldwork

3123.01 These three standards apply to the process of obtaining and evaluating evidence for the purpose of forming an opinion on the financial statements.

3123.02 **1st Standard of Fieldwork:** The auditor must adequately plan the work and must properly supervise any assistants.

3123.03 **2nd Standard of Fieldwork:** The auditor must obtain a sufficient understanding of the entity and its environment, including its internal control, to assess the risk of material misstatement of the financial statements whether due to error or fraud, and to design the nature, timing, and extent of further audit procedures.

3123.04 **3rd Standard of Fieldwork:** The auditor must obtain sufficient appropriate audit evidence by performing audit procedures to afford a reasonable basis for an opinion regarding the financial statements under audit.

3124 The Standards of Reporting

3124.01 These standards apply to the preparation and communication of the auditor's report.

3124.02 **1st Standard of Reporting:** The auditor must state in the auditor's report whether the financial statements are presented in accordance with generally accepted accounting principles (GAAP).

3124.03 **2nd Standard of Reporting:** The auditor must identify in the auditor's report those circumstances in which such principles have not been consistently observed in the current period in relation to the preceding period.

3124.04 **3rd Standard of Reporting:** When the auditor determines that informative disclosures are not reasonably adequate, the auditor must so state in the auditor's report.

3124.05 **4th Standard of Reporting:** The auditor must either express an opinion regarding the financial statements taken as a whole or state that an opinion cannot be expressed in the auditor's report. When the auditor cannot express an overall opinion, the auditor should state the reasons therefore in the auditor's report. In all cases where an auditor's name is associated with financial statements, the auditor should clearly indicate the character of the auditor's work, if any, and the degree of responsibility the auditor is taking in the auditor's report.

3125 Interpretive Publications and Other Auditing Publications

3125.01 **Statements on Auditing Standards (SASs)** are pronouncements of the Auditing Standards Board (ASB) and are authoritative interpretations of the 10 generally accepted auditing standards, and departures therefrom must be justified (ET 202.01).

3125.02 *Interpretive publications* consist of auditing interpretations of the SASs, appendixes to the SASs, auditing guidance included in AICPA Audit and Accounting Guides, and AICPA Auditing Statements of Position. Interpretive publications are not auditing standards. Interpretive publications are recommendations on the application of the SASs in specific circumstances, including engagements for entities in specialized industries.

3125.03 The auditor should be aware of and consider interpretive publications applicable to his or her audit. If the auditor does not apply the auditing guidance included in an applicable interpretive publication, the auditor should be prepared to explain how he or she complied with the SAS provisions addressed by such auditing guidance.

3125.04 *Other auditing publications* include AICPA auditing publications not referred to above; auditing articles in the *Journal of Accountancy* and other professional journals; auditing articles in the AICPA *CPA Letter*; continuing professional education programs and other instruction materials, textbooks, guide books, audit programs, and checklists; and other auditing publications from state CPA societies, other organizations, and individuals. Other auditing publications have no authoritative status; however, they may help the auditor understand and apply the SASs.

3125.05 If an auditor applies the auditing guidance included in another auditing publication, he or she should be satisfied that, in his or her judgment, it is both relevant to the circumstances of the audit, and appropriate.

3125.06 On July 30, 2002, the Sarbanes-Oxley Act was signed into law. The Act created the Public Company Accounting Oversight Board (PCAOB). This Board is empowered to establish auditing standards for the audits of publicly traded companies. The auditing standards established by the AICPA Auditing Standards Board will remain in effect until they are superseded by any standards issued by the PCAOB.

3126 Types of Auditor's Reports

3126.01 When a CPA has audited the financial statements of a company, the CPA must issue one of the following:

    a. Unqualified opinion (section **3512**)

    b. Qualified opinion (section **3515**)

    c. Adverse opinion (section **3516**)

    d. Disclaimer of opinion (section **3517**)

3126.02 When a CPA is not independent with respect to the audit of a public company, a nonindependent disclaimer should be issued (see section **3632**). When not independent with respect to a nonpublic company, a CPA may issue only a compilation report (see section **3643**).

3126.03 For discussion of types of reports for review engagements, see sections **3642** and **3644**.

3127 Meaning of Terminology Imposed on Auditors

3127.01 **Unconditional requirements:** The auditor is required to comply with an unconditional requirement in all cases in which the circumstances exist to which the unconditional requirement applies. An unconditional requirement is indicated by the words *must* or *is required*.

3127.02 **Presumptively mandatory requirements:** The auditor is also required to comply with a presumptively mandatory requirement in all cases in which the circumstances exist to which the presumptively mandatory requirement applies; however, in rare circumstances the auditor may depart from a presumptively mandatory requirement provided he/she documents the justification for departure and how alternative procedures performed in the circumstances were sufficient to achieve the objectives of the presumptively mandatory requirement. The word *should* indicates a presumptively mandatory requirement.

3130 Audit Risk and Materiality in Conducting an Audit (AU 312)

3131 Understanding Audit Risk and Materiality

3131.01 Audit risk and materiality affect the application of generally accepted auditing standards, especially the standards of fieldwork and reporting, and are reflected in the auditor's standard report.

3131.02 Audit risk and materiality, among other matters, need to be considered together in designing the nature, timing, and extent of audit procedures and in evaluating the results of those procedures.

3131.03 **Audit risk** is the risk that the auditor may unknowingly fail to appropriately modify his/her opinion on financial statements that are materially misstated. The auditor's responsibility is to plan and perform the audit to obtain reasonable assurance that material misstatements, whether caused by errors or fraud, are detected.

3131.04 The auditor's consideration of materiality is a matter of professional judgment and is influenced by the auditor's perception of the needs of users who will rely on the financial statements.

3131.05 The perceived needs of users are recognized in the discussion of materiality in Financial Accounting Standards Board (FASB) Statement of Financial Accounting Concepts No. 2, *Qualitative Characteristics of Accounting Information*, which defines **materiality** as "the magnitude of an omission or misstatement of accounting information that, in the light of surrounding circumstances, makes it probable that the judgment of a reasonable person relying on the information would have been changed or influenced by the omission or misstatement."

3131.06 The auditor's judgment as to matters that are material to users of financial statements is based on consideration of the needs of users as a group; the auditor does not consider the possible effect of misstatements on specific individual users, whose needs vary widely. The evaluation of whether a misstatement could influence economic decisions of users, and therefore be material, involves consideration of the characteristics of those users. Users are assumed to:

   a. have an appropriate knowledge of business and economic activities and accounting and a willingness to study the information in the financial statements with an appropriate diligence;

   b. understand that financial statements are prepared and audited to levels of materiality;

   c. recognize the uncertainties inherent in the measurement of amounts based on the use of estimates, judgment, and the consideration of future events; and

   d. make appropriate economic decisions on the basis of the information in the financial statements.

3132 The Concept of Misstatements

3132.01 Misstatements can result from errors or fraud and may consist of any of the following:

   a. An inaccuracy in gathering or processing data from which financial statements are prepared

   b. A difference between the amount, classification, or presentation of a reported financial statement element, account, or item and the amount, classification, or presentation that would have been reported under generally accepted accounting principles

   c. The omission of a financial statement element, account, or item

   d. A financial statement disclosure that is not presented in conformity with generally accepted accounting principles

   e. The omission of information required to be disclosed in conformity with generally accepted accounting principles

   f. An incorrect accounting estimate arising, for example, from an oversight or misinterpretation of facts

   g. Differences between management's and the auditor's judgments concerning accounting estimates, or the selection and application of accounting policies that the auditor considers inappropriate

3132.02 The term *errors* refers to unintentional misstatements of amounts or disclosures in financial statements. The term *fraud* refers to an intentional act by one or more individuals among management, those charged with governance, employees, or third parties, involving the use of deception to obtain an unjust or illegal advantage. The two types of misstatements resulting from fraud that are relevant to an auditor are (a) fraudulent financial reporting and (b) misappropriation of assets.

3132.03 Misstatements may be of two types: **known** and **likely**. Known misstatements consist of the amount of misstatements specifically identified. Likely misstatements represent the auditor's best estimate of the total misstatements in the account balances or classes of transactions that the auditor has examined.

3133 Audit Risk at the Financial Statement Level

3133.01 The auditor must consider audit risk and must determine a materiality level for the financial statements as a whole for the purpose of:

    a. determining the extent and nature of risk assessment procedures.

    b. identifying and assessing the risks of material misstatement.

    c. determining the nature, timing, and extent of further audit procedures.

    d. evaluating whether the financial statements as a whole are presented fairly, in conformity with generally accepted accounting principles.

3133.02 The auditor should perform the audit to reduce audit risk to a low level that is, in the auditor's judgment, appropriate for expressing an opinion on the financial statements. Audit risk may be assessed in quantitative or nonquantitative terms.

3133.03 In considering audit risk at the overall financial statement level, the auditor should consider risks of material misstatement that relate pervasively to the financial statements as a whole and potentially affect many relevant assertions. Risks of this nature often relate to the entity's control environment and are not necessarily identifiable with specific relevant assertions at the class of transactions, account balance, or disclosure level.

3133.04 In an audit of an entity with operations in multiple locations or with multiple components, the auditor should consider the extent to which audit procedures should be performed at selected locations or components. The factors an auditor should consider regarding the selection of a particular location or component include:

    a. the nature and amount of assets and transactions executed at the location or component.

    b. the degree of centralization of records or information processing.

    c. the effectiveness of the control environment, particularly with respect to management's direct control over the exercise of authority delegated to others and its ability to effectively supervise activities at the location or component.

    d. the frequency, timing, and scope of monitoring activities by the entity or others at the location or component.

    e. judgments about materiality of the location or component.

3134 Risk at the Account Balance, Class of Transactions, or Disclosure Level

3134.01 In determining the nature, timing, and extent of audit procedures to be applied to a specific account balance, class of transactions, or disclosure, the auditor should design audit procedures to obtain reasonable assurance of detecting misstatements that the auditor believes, based on the judgment about materiality, could be material, when aggregated with misstatements in other balances, classes, or disclosures, to the financial statements taken as a whole.

3134.02 At the account balance, class of transactions, or disclosure level, audit risk consists of:

a. the risk (consisting of inherent risk and control risk) that the balance, class, or disclosure and relevant assertions contain misstatements (whether caused by error or fraud) that could be material to the financial statements when aggregated with misstatements in other balances, classes, or disclosures and

b. the risk (detection risk) that the auditor will not detect such misstatements.

3134.03 The risk that the account balance, class of transactions, or disclosure and relevant assertions are misstated consists of the following two components:

1. **Inherent risk** is the susceptibility of a relevant assertion to a misstatement that could be material, either individually or when aggregated with other misstatements, assuming that there are no related controls.

2. **Control risk** is the risk that a misstatement that could occur in a relevant assertion and that could be material, either individually or when aggregated with other misstatements, will not be prevented or detected on a timely basis by the entity's internal control.

3134.04 Inherent risk and control risk are the entity's risks, that is, they exist independently of the audit of the financial statements. SAS 109 and other SASs describe the risk of material misstatement as the auditor's combined assessment of inherent risk and control risk; however, the auditor may make separate assessments of inherent risk and control risk.

3134.05 **Detection risk** is the risk that the auditor will not detect a misstatement that exists in a relevant assertion that could be material, either individually or when aggregated with other misstatements. Detection risk is a function of the effectiveness of an audit procedure and its application by the auditor.

3134.06 Detection risk relates to the substantive audit procedures and is managed by the auditor's response to risk of material misstatement. The greater the risk of material misstatement, the less the detection risk that can be accepted by the auditor.

3135 Planning Materiality for the Financial Statements

3135.01 The determination of what is material to the users is a matter of professional judgment. The auditor often applies a percentage to a chosen benchmark as a step in determining materiality for the financial statements as a whole. When identifying an appropriate benchmark, the auditor considers factors such as:

a. the elements of the financial statements and the financial statement measures defined in generally accepted accounting principles (for example, financial position, financial performance, and cash flows) or other specific requirements,

b. whether there are financial statement items on which, for the particular entity, users' attention tends to be focused,

c. the nature of the entity and the industry in which it operates, and

d. the size of the entity, nature of its ownership, and the way it is financed.

3135.02 When determining materiality, the auditor should consider prior periods' financial results and financial positions, the period-to-date financial results and financial position, and budgets or forecasts for the current period, taking account of significant changes in the entity's circumstances and any relevant changes of conditions in the economy as a whole or the industry in which the entity operates.

3135.03 Once materiality is established, the auditor considers materiality when planning and evaluating the same way regardless of the inherent business characteristics of the entity being audited. Materiality is determined based on the auditor's understanding of the user needs and expectations.

3135.04 When establishing the overall strategy for the audit, the auditor should consider whether misstatements of lesser amounts than the financial statement materiality level could reasonably be expected to influence economic decisions of users. In making this judgment, the auditor should consider factors such as the following:

a. Whether accounting standards, laws, or regulations affect users' expectations regarding the measurement or disclosure of certain items

b. The key disclosures in relation to the industry and the environment in which the entity operates

c. Whether attention is focused on the financial performance of a particular business segment that is separately disclosed in the financial statements.

3136 Other Considerations by the Auditor

3136.01 **Tolerable misstatement** is the maximum error in a population that the auditor is willing to accept. This term may be referred to as *tolerable error* in other standards. The auditor should determine one or more levels of tolerable misstatements for classes of transactions, account balances, and disclosures.

3136.02 Because it is not feasible for the auditor to anticipate all the circumstances that may ultimately influence judgments about materiality in evaluating the audit findings at the completion of the audit, the auditor's judgment about materiality for planning purposes may differ from the judgment about materiality used in evaluating the audit findings.

3136.03 If the aggregate of the misstatements (known and likely) that the auditor has identified approaches the materiality level, the auditor should consider whether there is a greater than acceptably low level of risk that undetected misstatements, when taken with the aggregate identified misstatements, could exceed the materiality level and, if so, the auditor should reconsider the nature and extent of further audit procedures.

3136.04 The auditor must accumulate all known and likely misstatements identified during the audit, other than those that the auditor believes are trivial, and communicate them to appropriate management.

3136.05 When communicating details of misstatements, the auditor should distinguish between the following:

a. **Known misstatements.** These are specific misstatements arising from the incorrect selection or misapplication of accounting principles or misstatements of facts identified during the audit, including, for example, those arising from mistakes in gathering or processing data and the overlooking of misinterpretations of facts.

    b. **Likely misstatements.** These are misstatements that:

        (1) arise from differences between management's and the auditor's judgments concerning accounting estimates (for example, because an estimate included in the financial statements by management is outside of the reasonable range of outcomes the auditor has determined).

        (2) the auditor considers likely to exist based on an extrapolation from audit evidence obtained; for example, the amount obtained by projecting known misstatements identified in an audit sample to the entire population from which the sample was drawn.

3136.06   The auditor should request management to correct all known misstatements, other than those that the auditor believes are trivial. If management refuses to correct some or all of the misstatements communicated to it by the auditor, the auditor should obtain an understanding of management's reasons for not making the corrections and should take that into account when considering the qualitative aspects of the entity's accounting principles.

3137 Evaluating Audit Findings

3137.01   In evaluating whether the financial statements are presented fairly in conformity with GAAP, the auditor must consider the effects, both individually and in the aggregate, of misstatements (known and likely) that are not corrected by the entity.

3137.02   Before considering the aggregate effect of identified uncorrected misstatements, the auditor should consider each misstatement separately to evaluate:

    a. its effect in relation to the relevant individual classes of transactions, account balances, or disclosures, including whether materiality levels for particular items of lesser amounts than the materiality level for the financial statements as a whole have been exceeded.

    b. whether, in considering the effect of the individual misstatement on the financial statements as a whole, it is appropriate to offset misstatements.

    c. the effect of misstatements related to prior periods.

3137.03   When an auditor uses audit sampling to test a relevant assertion for an account balance or a class of transactions, he/she should project the amount of known misstatements identified in the sample to the items in the balance or class from which the sample was selected. That projected misstatement, along with the results of other substantive procedures, contributes to the auditor's assessment of likely misstatement in the balance or class.

3137.04   Qualitative considerations also influence the auditor in reaching a conclusion about whether misstatements are material. Qualitative factors that the auditor may consider relevant to his or her consideration of whether misstatements are material include the following:

    a. The potential effect of the misstatement on trends, especially trends in profitability

    b. A misstatement that changes a loss into income or vice versa

    c. The potential effect of the misstatement on the entity's compliance with loan covenants, other contractual agreements, and regulatory provisions

    d. The existence of statutory or regulatory reporting requirements that affect materiality thresholds

    e. Masks a change in earnings or other trends, especially in the context of general economic and industry conditions

    f. A misstatement that has the effect of increasing management's compensation; for example, by satisfying the requirements for the award of bonuses or other forms of incentive compensation

    g. The sensitivity of the circumstances surrounding the misstatement; for example, the implications of misstatements involving fraud and possible illegal acts, violations of contractual provisions, and conflicts of interest

    h. The significance of the financial statement elements affected by the misstatement

    i. The effects of misclassifications

    j. The significance of the misstatement relative to reasonable user needs; for example, earnings to investors and the equity amounts to creditors

    k. The definitive character of the misstatement; for example, the precision of an error that is objectively determinable as contrasted with a misstatement that unavoidably involves a degree of subjectivity through estimation, allocation, or uncertainty

    l. The motivation of management with respect to the misstatement; for example, (1) an indication of a possible pattern of basis by management when developing and accumulating accounting estimates, (2) a misstatement precipitated by management's continued unwillingness to correct weaknesses in the financial reporting process, or (3) an international decision not to follow GAAP

    m. The existence of offsetting effects of individually significant but different misstatements

    n. The likelihood that a misstatement that is currently immaterial may have a material effect in future periods because of a cumulative effect; for example, that builds over several periods

    o. The cost of making the correction. It may not be cost beneficial for the client to develop a system to calculate a basis to record the effect of an immaterial misstatement

    p. The risk that possible additional undetected misstatements would affect the auditor's evaluation

3137.05 The auditor must evaluate whether the financial statements as a whole are free of material misstatement. In making this evaluation, the auditor should consider both the evaluation of the uncorrected (known and likely) misstatements and the qualitative considerations noted in section **3137.04**.

3137.06 If the auditor believes that the financial statements as a whole are materially misstated, the auditor should request management to make the necessary corrections. If management refuses to make the corrections, the auditor must determine the implications for his/her report.

3137.07 The auditor can reduce audit risk by modifying the nature, timing, and extent of planned audit procedures in performing the audit. If the auditor believes that such risk is unacceptably high, the auditor should perform additional audit procedures or satisfy himself/herself that the entity has adjusted the financial statement to reduce the risk of material misstatement to an appropriate level.

3137.08 The auditor should document:

    a. the levels of materiality and tolerable misstatement, including any changes thereto, used in the audit and the basis on which those levels were determined;

    b. a summary of uncorrected misstatements, other than those that are trivial, related to known and likely misstatements; and

c. the auditor's conclusion as to whether uncorrected misstatements, individually or in the aggregate, do or do not cause the financial statements to be materially misstated, and the basis for that conclusion.

3137.09 Uncorrected misstatements should be documented in a manner that allows the auditor to:

a. separately consider the effects of known and likely misstatements;

b. consider the aggregate effect of misstatements on the financial statements; and

c. consider the qualitative factors that are relevant to the auditor's consideration of whether misstatements are material.

3140 The General Standards

3141 Technical Training and Proficiency (AU 210)

3141.01 A person, no matter how capable in other fields such as business and finance, cannot meet the requirements of this standard without proper education and experience in the field of auditing.

3141.02 Proficiency as an auditor requires both formal education and experience.

3141.03 The auditor must be aware of current developments in business and auditing and must study, understand, and apply new pronouncements in accounting and auditing.

3142 Independence (AU 220)

3142.01 The independent CPA must be without bias with respect to the client under audit. The CPA's attitude is to be one of judicial impartiality. The CPA recognizes an obligation for fairness not only to management and owners but also to creditors. The CPA's attitude should not be the accusatory attitude of a prosecutor.

3142.02 To be independent, the CPA must *in fact* be intellectually honest and be recognized *in appearance* as independent by third parties. The CPA must be free from any obligation to or interest in the client, its management, or owners. (For interpretations of independence under the Code of Professional Conduct, see Regulation section **4101**.)

3142.03 To strengthen the CPA's appearance of independence, many public corporations have established audit committees on the board of directors to whom the independent CPA reports (section 3143).

3143 Audit Committees

3143.01 An *audit committee* is a standing committee of the board of directors of a public corporation composed mainly of nonofficer directors. Its major responsibilities are to deal with the company's financial reports, its external audit, and its system of internal accounting control and internal audit.

3143.02 Audit committees have been formed for the following reasons:

a. To enable directors to carry out their fiduciary responsibility to the stockholders

b. To carry out the board's overall responsibility for the financial statements of the company

c. To protect the board from civil and criminal actions related to the financial statements

   d. To enhance the external audit function

3143.03 The functions of a typical audit committee include the following:

   a. Recommend the selection, retention, or termination of the company's external auditors.

   b. Review the overall scope of the audit with the external auditors.

   c. Review the financial statements and external audit results, including communication of material weaknesses in internal accounting control.

   d. Handle unforeseen problems when the external auditor needs access to the board.

   e. Prepare the committee's report to the board.

   f. Approve the budget and audit plan of the company's internal audit activities.

   g. Approve the selection or termination of the director of internal auditing.

3143.04 See section **3534** for a discussion of AU 380, *Communications with Audit Committees*.

3144 Due Care (AU 230)

3144.01 **Due care** concerns what the independent CPA does and how well the CPA does it. It imposes an obligation on each person within a CPA's organization to observe the standards of fieldwork and reporting.

3144.02 While exercising due professional care, the auditor must plan and perform the audit to obtain sufficient appropriate evidence so that audit risk will be limited to a low level that is, in his/her professional judgment, appropriate for expressing an opinion on the financial statements. The high level of assurance that is intended to be obtained by the auditor is expressed in the auditor's report as obtaining reasonable assurance about whether the financial statements are free of material misstatement (whether caused by error or fraud). Absolute assurance is not attainable because of the nature of audit evidence and the characteristics of fraud. Therefore, an audit conducted in accordance with generally accepted auditing standards may not detect a material misstatement.

3145 The Relationship of Generally Accepted Auditing Standards to Quality Control Standards

3145.01 The independent auditor is responsible for compliance with generally accepted auditing standards in an audit engagement.

3145.02 A firm of independent auditors has a responsibility to adopt a system of quality control in conducting an audit practice. Thus, a firm should establish quality control policies and procedures to provide it with reasonable assurance that its personnel comply with generally accepted auditing standards in audit engagements.

3145.03 The nature and extent of a firm's quality control policies and procedures depend on factors such as its size, the degree of operating autonomy allowed its personnel and its practice offices, the nature of its practice, its organization, and appropriate cost versus benefit considerations.

3145.04 Generally accepted auditing standards relate to the conduct of individual audit engagements; quality control standards relate to the conduct of a firm's audit practice.

3145.05 Deficiencies in or instances of noncompliance with a firm's quality control policies and procedures do not, in and of themselves, indicate that a particular audit engagement was not performed in accordance with generally accepted auditing standards.

3146 Quality Control Standard 7, "A Firm's System of Quality Control"

3146.01 The purpose of Statement on Quality Control Standards (SQCS) 7 is to establish standards and provide guidance for a CPA firm's responsibilities for its system of quality control for its accounting and auditing practice.

3146.02 The firm must establish a system of quality control designed to provide the firm with reasonable assurance that the firm and its personnel comply with professional standards and applicable regulatory and legal requirements, and that the firm or engagement partners issue reports that are appropriate in the circumstances.

3146.03 The system of quality control should be designed to provide the firm with reasonable assurance that the segments of the firm's engagements performed by its foreign member firms or offices or by its domestic or foreign affiliates, if any, are performed in accordance with professional standards in the United States when such standards are applicable.

3146.04 The definitions that are presented in the next four paragraphs are important to an understanding of Statement on Quality Control Standards 7.

3146.05 An *engagement quality control review* is a process designed to provide an objective evaluation, by an individual or individuals who are not members of the engagement team, of the significant judgments the engagement team made and the conclusions reached in formulating the report.

3146.06 An *engagement quality control reviewer* is a partner, other person in the firm, qualified external person, or a team made up of such individuals, none of whom is part of the engagement team, with sufficient and appropriate experience and authority to perform the engagement quality control review.

3146.07 A *qualified external person* is an individual outside the firm with the capabilities and competence to act as an engagement partner.

3146.08 *Relevant ethical requirements* refer to ethical requirements to which the firm and its personnel are subject, which consist of the AICPA Code of Professional Conduct together with rules of state boards of accountancy and applicable regulatory agencies, which may be more restrictive.

3146.09 The firm should document its quality control policies and procedures and communicate them to its personnel. Even though communication is enhanced if it is in writing, the communication can be either written or oral.

3146.10 The firm's system of quality control should include policies and procedures addressing each of the following elements:

   a. Leadership responsibilities for quality within the firm (tone at the top)
   b. Relevant ethical requirements
   c. Acceptance and continuance of client relationships and specific engagements
   d. Human resources
   e. Engagement performance
   f. Monitoring

3146.11 The firm should promote an internal culture based on the recognition that quality is essential in performing engagements and should establish policies and procedures to support that culture. Such policies and procedures should require the firm's leadership to assume ultimate responsibility for the firm's system of quality control.

3146.12 Of particular importance in promoting an internal culture based on quality is the need for the firm's leadership to recognize that the firm's business strategy is subject to the overreaching requirements for the firm to achieve the objectives of the system of quality control in all engagements that the firm performs. Accordingly, the firm should establish policies to:

   a. assign management responsibilities so that commercial considerations do not override the quality of work performed;
   b. address performance evaluation, compensation, and advancement with regard to personnel, to demonstrate the firm's overreaching commitment to the objectives of the system of quality control; and
   c. devote sufficient and appropriate resources for the development, communication, and support of its quality control policies and procedures.

3146.13 At least annually, the firm should obtain written confirmation of compliance with its policies and procedures on independence from all firm personnel required to be independent.

3146.14 The firm should establish policies and procedures for the acceptance and continuance of client relationships and specific engagements, designed to provide the firm with reasonable assurance that it will undertake or continue relationships and engagements only where the firm:

   a. has considered the integrity of the client, including the identity and business reputation of the client's principal owners, key management, related parties, and those charged with governance, and the risks associated with providing professional services in the particular circumstances;
   b. is competent to perform the engagement and has the capabilities and resources to do so; and
   c. can comply with legal and ethical requirements.

3146.15 Matters to consider in accepting or continuing the client engagement include whether:

   a. firm personnel have knowledge of relevant industries or subject matters or the ability to effectively gain the necessary knowledge;
   b. firm personnel have experience with relevant regulatory or reporting requirements, or the ability to effectively gain the necessary competencies;
   c. the firm has sufficient personnel with the necessary capabilities and competence;

d. specialists are available, if needed;

e. individuals meeting the criteria and eligibility requirements to perform an engagement quality control review are available, where applicable; and

f. the firm is able to complete the engagement within the reporting deadline.

3146.16 Policies and procedures on withdrawal from an engagement or from both the engagement and the client relationship should include documenting significant issues, consultations, conclusions, and the basis for conclusions.

3146.17 The firm should establish policies and procedures designed to provide it with reasonable assurance that it has sufficient personnel with the capabilities, competence, and commitment to ethical principles necessary to:

a. perform its engagement in accordance with professional standards and regulatory and legal requirements, and

b. enable the firm to issue reports that are appropriate in the circumstances.

3146.18 Capabilities and competencies are the knowledge, skills, and abilities that qualify personnel to perform an engagement covered by the quality control standards.

3146.19 A firm's quality control policies and procedures should provide reasonable assurance that an engagement partner possesses the competencies necessary to fulfill his/her engagement responsibilities.

3146.20 In practice, the competency requirements necessary for the engagement partner are broad and varied in both their nature and number. Required competencies include the following, as well as other competencies as necessary in the circumstances:

a. Understanding of the role of a system of quality control and the Code of Professional Conduct

b. Understanding of the service to be performed

c. Technical proficiency

d. Familiarity with the industry

e. Professional judgment

f. Understanding the organization's information technology system

3146.21 The continuing competence of the firm's personnel depends to a significant extent on an appropriate level of continuing professional development so that personnel maintain their knowledge and capabilities.

3146.22 Effective policies and procedures emphasize the need for levels of firm personnel to participate in general and industry-specific continuing professional education and other professional development activities that enable them to fulfill responsibilities assigned, and to satisfy applicable continuing professional education requirements.

3146.23 The firm's policies and procedures should provide that personnel selected for advancement have the qualifications necessary for fulfillment of the responsibilities they will be called on to assume.

3146.24 Effective performance evaluation, compensation, and advancement procedures give due recognition and reward to the development and maintenance of competence and commitment to ethical principles.

3146.25 The firm should establish policies and procedures designed to provide it with reasonable assurance that engagements are consistently performed in accordance with professional standards and regulatory and legal requirements, and that the firm or the engagement partner issues reports that are appropriate in the circumstances. Required policies and procedures should address:

    a. engagement performance,

    b. supervision responsibilities, and

    c. review responsibilities.

3146.26 The firm should establish policies and procedures designed to maintain the confidentiality, safe custody, integrity, accessibility, and retrievability of engagement documentation.

3146.27 Whether engagement documentation is in paper, electronic, or other media, the integrity, accessibility, and retrievability of the underlying data may be compromised if the documentation could be altered, added to, or deleted without the firm's knowledge, or could be permanently lost or damaged.

3146.28 The firm should establish policies and procedures for the retention of engagement documentation for a period sufficient to meet the needs of the firm, professional standards, laws, and regulations.

3146.29 The firm should establish policies and procedures designed to provide it with reasonable assurance that:

    a. consultation takes place when appropriate (for example, when dealing with complex, unusual, unfamiliar, difficult, or contentious issues);

    b. sufficient and appropriate resources are available to enable appropriate consultation to take place;

    c. all the relevant facts known to the engagement team are provided to those consulted;

    d. the nature and scope of such consultations are documented, and are understood by both the individual seeking consultation and the individual consulted; and

    e. the conclusions resulting from such consultations are documented and implemented.

3146.30 The firm should establish policies and procedures for dealing with and resolving differences of opinion within the engagement team, with those consulted, and, where applicable, between the engagement partner and engagement quality control reviewer. Such policies and procedures should require that:

    a. conclusions reached be documented and implemented, and

    b. the report not be released until the matter is resolved.

3146.31 The firm should establish criteria against which all engagements covered by Statement on Quality Control Standards 7 are to be evaluated to determine whether an engagement quality control review should be performed.

3146.32 The firm's policies and procedures should require that if an engagement meets the criteria established, an engagement quality control review be performed for that engagement, and that the review be completed before the report is released.

3146.33   The structure and nature of the firm's practice are important considerations in establishing criteria to consider when determining which engagements are to be subject to an engagement quality control review. Such criteria may include:

   a. the nature of the engagement, including the extent to which it involves a matter of public interest;

   b. the identification of unusual circumstances or risks in an engagement or class of engagements; and

   c. whether laws or regulations require an engagement quality control review.

3146.34   The engagement quality control review should include an objective evaluation of the significant judgments made by the engagement team and the conclusions reached in formulating the report.

3146.35   An engagement quality control review also should include a review of selected engagement documentation relating to the significant judgments the engagement team made and the conclusions reached, and should include a discussion with the engagement partner regarding significant findings and issues.

3146.36   When the engagement quality control reviewer makes recommendations that the engagement partner does not accept and the matter is not resolved to the reviewer's satisfaction, the firm's procedures for dealing with differences of opinion apply.

3146.37   The firm's policies and procedures on the technical qualifications of engagement quality control reviewers may address the technical expertise, experience, and authority necessary to fulfill the role.

3146.38   The firm should establish policies and procedures designed to maintain the objectivity of the engagement quality control reviewer. Such policies and procedures should provide that while the engagement quality control reviewer is not a member of the engagement team, he/she should satisfy the independence requirements relating to the engagements reviewed.

3146.39   The engagement partner may consult the engagement quality control reviewer at any stage during the engagement; for example, to establish that a judgment made by the engagement partner will be acceptable to the engagement quality reviewer. Such consultation need not impair the engagement quality control reviewer's eligibility to perform the role.

3146.40   However, when the nature and extent of such consultations become significant, the reviewer's objectivity may be impaired unless both the engagement team and the reviewer are careful to maintain the reviewer's objectivity.

3146.41   The firm should establish policies and procedures that provide for appropriate documentation of the engagement quality control review, including documentation that:

   a. the procedures required by the firm's policies on engagement quality control review have been performed;

   b. the engagement quality control review has been completed before the report is released; and

   c. the reviewer is not aware of any unresolved matters that would cause the reviewer to believe that the significant judgments the engagement team made and the conclusions reached were not appropriate.

3146.42 The firm should establish policies and procedures designed to provide the firm and its engagement partners with reasonable assurance that the policies and procedures relating to the system of quality control are relevant, adequate, operating effectively, and complied with in practice.

3146.43 The purpose of monitoring compliance with quality control policies and procedures is to provide an evaluation of:

    a. adherence to professional standards and regulatory and legal requirements;

    b. whether the quality control system has been appropriately designed and effectively implemented; and

    c. whether the firm's quality control policies and procedures have been operating effectively, so that reports that are issued by the firm are appropriate in the circumstances.

3146.44 The firm's policies should require the performance of monitoring procedures that are sufficiently comprehensive to enable the firm to assess compliance with all applicable professional standards and regulatory requirements, and the firm's quality control policies and procedures.

3146.45 In small firms with a limited number of persons with sufficient and appropriate experience and authority in the firm, monitoring procedures may need to be performed by some of the same individuals who are responsible for compliance with the firm's quality control policies and procedures.

3146.46 To effectively monitor one's own compliance with the firm's policies and procedures, it is necessary that an individual be able to critically review his/her own performance, assess his/her own strengths and weaknesses, and maintain an attitude of continual improvement.

3146.47 When one individual inspects his/her own compliance, the firm has a higher risk that noncompliance with policies and procedures will not be detected. Accordingly, a firm with a limited number of persons with sufficient and appropriate experience and authority in the firm may find it beneficial to engage a qualified individual from outside the firm to perform inspection procedures.

3146.48 A peer review does not substitute for all monitoring procedures. However, since the objective of a peer review is similar to that of inspection procedures, a firm's quality control policies and procedures may provide that a peer review conducted under the standards established by the AICPA may substitute for the inspection of engagement working papers, reports, and client's financial statements for some or all engagements covered by the peer review.

3146.49 Complaints and allegations of noncompliance with the firm's system of quality control may originate from within or outside the firm. The firm should require that investigations of such complaints and allegations in accordance with established policies and procedures be supervised by a person with sufficient and appropriate experience and authority who is not otherwise involved in the engagement.

3146.50 The firm should establish policies and procedures requiring appropriate documentation to provide evidence of the operation of each element of its system of quality control.

3150 Planning and Supervising the Audit

3151 Steps in an Audit Engagement Summarized

3151.01 Evaluate the client and, if possible, accept the engagement (section **3152**). In the case of a new client, communicate with the predecessor CPA (section **3153**).

3151.02 Prepare the engagement letter (section **3154**).

3151.03 Perform planning procedures considering the following factors:

    a. Gain an understanding of the internal control structure.

    b. Perform analytical procedure (section **3339**).

    c. Assess audit risk (section **3130**).

3151.04 Assess control risk and perform control risk assessment procedures only if internal controls appear reliable (section **3213**).

3151.05 Design audit tests for areas where audit procedures will be performed (section **3300**).

3151.06 Perform analytical procedures in the overall review stage (section **3339**).

3151.07 Supervise and review the work of audit assistants continuously (section **3156**).

3151.08 Form conclusions on the basis of evidence obtained and issue the audit report (sections **3500** and **3600**).

3152 Appointment of the Independent Auditor

3152.01 Early appointment of the CPA enables the CPA to plan work so that it can be done expeditiously, and the extent of the audit can be determined before the balance sheet date (SAS 108).

3152.02 In accepting an engagement near or after the close of the fiscal year, the CPA should determine if the circumstances will prevent an adequate examination and expression of an unqualified opinion. The CPA should discuss with the client the possibility of a qualified opinion or a disclaimer. Sometimes the audit limitations may be remedied by such methods as postponing or retaking the physical inventory (SAS 108).

3152.03 When the CPA cannot be satisfied with regard to opening inventories, the CPA should qualify or disclaim an opinion.

3152.04 The auditor should establish an understanding with the client regarding the services to be performed for each engagement. The understanding should include the objectives of the engagement, management's responsibilities, the auditor's responsibilities, and limitations of the engagement.

3152.05 The auditor should document the understanding in the workpapers, preferably through a written communication with the client. If the auditor believes an understanding with the client has not been established, the auditor should decline to accept or perform the engagement.

3152.06 An understanding with the client regarding an audit of the financial statements generally includes the following matters:

   a. The objective of the audit is the expression of an opinion on the financial statements.

   b. Management is responsible for the entity's financial statements.

   c. Management is responsible for establishing and maintaining effective internal control over financial reporting.

   d. Management is responsible for designing and implementing programs and controls to prevent and detect fraud.

   e. Management is responsible for the entity's compliance with laws and regulations applicable to its activities.

   f. Management is responsible for making financial records available to the auditor.

   g. Management will provide the auditor with a representation letter at the conclusion of the audit.

   h. The auditor is responsible for conducting the audit in accordance with GAAS.

   i. An audit includes obtaining an understanding of internal controls sufficient to plan the audit and to determine the nature, extent, and timing of audit procedures to be performed.

   j. Management is responsible for adjusting the financial statements to correct material misstatements and for affirming to the auditor in the representation letter that the effects of any uncorrected misstatements aggregated by the auditor during the current engagement and pertaining to the latest period presented are immaterial, both individually and in the aggregate, to the financial statements taken as a whole.

3152.07 An understanding with the client also may include other matters, such as the following:

   a. Arrangements regarding the conduct of the engagement

   b. Arrangements regarding the involvement of specialists

   c. Arrangements regarding fees and billing

   d. Any limitations of or other arrangements regarding the liability of the auditor or the client

   e. Conditions under which access to the auditor's workpapers may be granted to others

   f. Additional services to be provided relating to regulatory requirements

   g. Arrangements regarding other services to be provided in connection with the engagement

3152.08 These matters may be communicated in the form of an engagement letter. See section **3154** for a sample engagement letter.

3153 Communication Between Predecessor and Successor Auditors (AU 315)

3153.01 The successor auditor must communicate with the predecessor auditor before accepting an engagement, because the predecessor may provide information regarding disagreements about important accounting and auditing matters that will bear on the decision of whether or not to accept the engagement.

3153.02 The successor auditor and predecessor auditor are defined as follows:

   a. *Successor auditor*: An auditor who has accepted an engagement or an auditor who has been invited to make a proposal for an engagement

   b. *Predecessor auditor*: An auditor who (1) has reported on the most recent financial statements or was engaged to perform and did not complete an audit of the financial statements, and (2) has resigned, declined to stand for reappointment, or been notified that these services have been, or may be, terminated

3153.03 Since the Code of Professional Conduct precludes an auditor from disclosing confidential information obtained in an audit unless the client consents, the successor auditor must ask the prospective client to authorize the predecessor auditor to respond fully to the successor's inquiries. Once the engagement is accepted, a second inquiry may be made to allow the successor to view the predecessor auditor's workpapers.

3153.04 The successor should inquire of the predecessor regarding the following:

   a. Information that might bear on the integrity of management

   b. Disagreements with management as to accounting principles, auditing procedures, or other similarly significant matters

   c. The predecessor's understanding as to the reasons for the change of auditors

   d. Communications to audit committees or others with equivalent authority and responsibility regarding fraud, illegal acts by clients, and internal control related matters

3153.05 When more than one auditor is considering accepting an engagement, the predecessor auditor should not be expected to be available to respond to inquires until a successor auditor has been selected by the client and has accepted the engagement subject to the evaluation of the communications with the predecessor auditor as provided in section **3153.04**.

3153.06 An auditor should not finalize formal acceptance of an engagement until the communications noted are completed. However, an auditor may make a proposal for an engagement before communicating with the predecessor auditor and can tentatively accept the engagement as long as the client is aware that acceptance cannot be finalized until the inquiries of the predecessor have been completed.

3153.07 If the inquiry or response is limited, such limitations should be considered when deciding to accept the engagement.

3153.08 Once an engagement has been accepted, the successor may do the following:

   a. Make specific inquiries of the predecessor as to matters that affect the conduct of the audit.

   b. Review the predecessor's workpapers.

3153.09 The successor auditor's review of the predecessor's workpapers may affect the nature, extent, and timing of the successor's procedures with respect to the opening balances and consistency of accounting principles. However, the nature, extent, and timing of audit work performed and the conclusions reached in both these areas are the responsibility of the successor auditor.

3153.10 In reporting on the audit, the successor auditor should not make reference to the report or work of the predecessor auditor as the basis, in part, of the successor's own opinion.

3153.11 An auditor may be asked to perform a "reaudit"—an audit of financial statements that have been audited and reported on previously. In addition to the communications described previously, the successor auditor should state that the purpose of the inquiries of the predecessor is to obtain information about whether to accept an engagement to perform a reaudit.

3153.12 The successor auditor may consider the information obtained from the predecessor auditor if the successor auditor accepts the reaudit. Information obtained and a review of the predecessor auditor's report and workpapers are not sufficient to afford a basis for expressing an opinion. Nature, extent, and timing of the audit work performed and conclusions reached in the reaudit are solely the responsibility of the successor auditor performing the reaudit.

3153.13 The successor auditor should:

    a. plan and perform the reaudit in accordance with GAAS,

    b. not assume responsibility for the predecessor auditor's work, and

    c. not issue a report that reflects divided responsibility.

3153.14 The results of the audit in the current period performed by the successor auditor may be considered in planning and performing the reaudit of the preceding period or periods.

3153.15 The successor auditor should qualify or disclaim an opinion if the auditor is:

    a. unable to obtain sufficient appropriate audit evidence to express an opinion or

    b. unable to perform procedures considered necessary in the circumstances.

3153.16 The successor auditor generally will be unable to observe inventory or make physical counts at the reaudit date or dates. In such cases, the successor auditor:

    a. may consider the knowledge obtained from inquiries of the predecessor auditor and the review of the predecessor auditor's workpapers,

    b. should, if material, observe or perform some physical counts of inventory at a date subsequent to the period of the reaudit, or

    c. should apply appropriate tests of intervening transactions.

3153.17 The successor auditor should request the client to inform the predecessor auditor when the successor auditor becomes aware of information that leads them to believe the financial statements reported on by the predecessor auditor may require revision. If the client refuses to inform the predecessor auditor, or if the successor auditor is not satisfied with the resolution of the matter, the successor auditor should evaluate:

    a. implications on the current engagement,

    b. whether to resign from the engagement, and

    c. whether to consult with legal counsel in determining an appropriate course of further action.

3154 Engagement Letters

3154.01 The engagement letter is written by the CPA and constitutes the CPA's understanding of the work to be done in an audit.

3154.02 The engagement letter is a contract between the CPA and the client, and a copy of it signed by the client should be requested and retained by the CPA.

3154.03 The engagement letter should be addressed to the client and dated as soon as an understanding of the engagement is reached.

Sample Engagement Letter

Auditor's letterhead	TURNER and MATHEWS Certified Public Accountants March 1, 20X5
Addressed to client	Mr. Tom Client, Secretary Melville Doll Co., Inc. Route 32 Melville, New York 11746
	Dear Mr. Client:
Objective of engagement	This will confirm our understanding of the engagement arrangements for our examination of the financial statements of Melville Doll Co., Inc., for the year ending March 31, 20X5.
Scope	We will examine the Company's balance sheet at March 31, 20X5, and the related statements of income, retained earnings, and statement of cash flows for the year then ended, for the purpose of expressing an opinion on them.
In accordance with GAAS	Our examination will be in accordance with generally accepted auditing standards as we consider necessary to accomplish this purpose.
	These procedures will include tests (by statistical sampling, if feasible) of documentary evidence supporting the transactions recorded in the accounts, tests of the physical existence of inventories, and direct confirmation of receivables and certain other assets and liabilities by correspondence with selected customers, creditors, legal counsel, and banks.
Management letter	We will, of course, report to you anything that appears to us during our examination to be unusual or abnormal.
Other work	We will review the Company's federal and state (identify states) income tax returns for the fiscal year ended March 31, 20X5. These returns, we understand, will be personally prepared by you. Further, we will be available during the year to consult with you on the tax effects of any proposed transactions or contemplated changes in business policies.
Engagement fee	Our fee for this examination will be at our regular per diem rates, plus travel and other out-of-pocket costs. Invoices will be rendered every two weeks and are payable on presentation.
	We are pleased to have this opportunity to serve you. If this letter correctly expresses your understanding, please sign the enclosed copy where indicated and return to us.

>   Signed by CPA   Very truly yours,
>   TURNER and MATHEWS, CPAs
>
> Signed by client and returned to CPA   APPROVED:
>
>   By: _____
>   Date: _____

3154.04 The engagement letter should contain statements regarding the following:

    a. The objective of the engagement

    b. The scope of the audit work to be performed (in accordance with GAAS)

    c. The fact that the purpose of the audit is not to detect fraud but to enable the auditor to express an opinion as to the fairness of the financial statements

    d. A management letter (if any)

    e. Additional work to be performed, such as tax, consulting, or other services (if any)

    f. Any limitations or restrictions on the scope of the study

    g. Work to be performed by the client's staff (if any)

    h. The basis of the auditor's fee

    i. Audit work schedule and estimated date of completion

3155 Planning the Audit (AU 311)

3155.01 Audit planning involves developing an overall audit strategy for the expected conduct, organization, and staffing of the audit. Obtaining an understanding of the entity and its environment, including its internal control, is an essential part of planning and performing an audit.

3155.02 Although early appointment of the independent auditor is preferable, an independent auditor may accept an engagement near or after the close of the fiscal year. In such instances, before accepting the engagement, the auditor should ascertain whether circumstances are likely to permit an adequate audit and expression of an unqualified opinion. If an unqualified opinion does not appear likely, the auditor should discuss with the client the possible necessity for a qualified or disclaimer of opinion.

3155.03 The auditor **should** establish an understanding with the client regarding the services to be performed for each engagement. The understanding should include the objectives of the engagement, management's responsibilities, the auditor's responsibilities, and limitations of the engagement. The auditor should document this understanding, preferably through a written communication with the client.

3155.04 The understanding with the client may be in the form of an engagement letter and should generally include the following matters:

    a. The objective of the audit is the expression of an opinion on the financial statements.

    b. Management is responsible for the entity's financial statements and the selection and application of accounting principles.

    c. Management is responsible for establishing and maintaining effective internal controls over financial reporting.

d. Management is responsible for designing and implementing programs and controls to prevent and detect fraud.

e. Management is responsible for identifying and ensuring that the entity complies with the laws and regulations applicable to its activities.

f. Management is responsible for making all financial records and related information available to the auditor.

g. At the conclusion of the engagement, management will provide the auditor with a letter that confirms certain representations made during the audit.

h. The auditor is responsible for conducting the audit in accordance with GAAS. (A brief indication of what these standards require should be included.)

i. An audit includes obtaining an understanding of the entity and its environment, including its internal control, sufficient to assess the risks of material misstatement of the financial statements and to design the nature, extent, and timing of further audit procedures.

j. Management is responsible for adjusting the financial statements to correct material misstatements and for affirming to the auditor in the representation letter that the effects of any uncorrected misstatements aggregated by the auditor during the current engagement and pertaining to the latest period presented are immaterial, both individually and in the aggregate, to the financial statements taken as a whole.

3155.05 In addition to the procedures related to the appointment of the auditor and establishing an understanding, the auditor should perform the following activities at the beginning of the current audit engagement:

a. Perform procedures regarding the continuance of the client relationship and the specific audit engagement.

b. Evaluate the auditor's compliance with ethical requirements, including independence.

3155.06 The auditor should establish the overall audit strategy. The overall audit strategy involves:

a. determining the characteristics of the engagement that define its scope, such as the basis for reporting, industry-specific reporting requirements, and the locations of the entity;

b. ascertaining the reporting objectives of the engagement to plan the timing of the audit and the nature of the communications required, such as deadlines for interim and final reporting, and key dates for expected communications with management and those charged with governance; and

c. considering the important factors that will determine the focus of the audit team's efforts, such as determination of appropriate materiality levels, preliminary identification of areas where there may be higher risks of material misstatement, financial reporting developments, etc.

3155.07 The purpose of performing these preliminary engagement activities is to consider any events or circumstances that may either adversely affect the auditor's ability to plan and perform the audit engagement to reduce audit risk to an acceptably low level or that may pose an unacceptable level of risk to the auditor.

3155.08 Once the audit strategy has been established, the auditor is able to start the development of a more detailed audit plan to address the various matters identified in the audit strategy, taking into account the need to achieve the audit objectives through the efficient use of the auditor's resources.

3155.09 The auditor must develop an audit plan for the audit in order to reduce audit risk to an acceptably low level. The audit plan is more detailed than the audit strategy and includes the nature, extent, and timing of audit procedures to be performed by audit team members.

3155.10 The audit plan should include:

    a. a description of the nature, extent, and timing of planned risk assessment procedures sufficient to assess the risks of material misstatement.

    b. a description of the nature, extent, and timing of planned further audit procedures at the relevant assertion level for each material class of transactions, account balance, and disclosure.

    c. a description of other audit procedures to be carried out for the engagement in order to comply with GAAS.

3155.11 The auditor should consider whether specialized skills are needed in performing the audit. If specialized skills are needed, the auditor should seek the assistance of a professional possessing such skills, who may be either on the auditor's staff or an outside professional.

3155.12 The use of professionals possessing information technology (IT) skills to determine the effect of IT on the audit, to understand IT controls, or to design and perform tests of IT controls or substantive procedures is a significant aspect of many audit engagements. In determining whether such a professional is needed on the audit team, the auditor should consider such factors as the following:

    a. The complexity of the entity's systems and IT controls and the manner in which they are used in conducting the entity's business

    b. The significance of changes made to existing systems, or the implementation of new systems

    c. The extent to which data is shared among systems

    d. The extent of the entity's participation in electronic commerce

    e. The entity's use of emerging technologies

    f. The significance of audit evidence that is available only in electronic form

3155.13 Audit procedures that the auditor may assign to the IT professional include inquiring of the entity's IT personnel about how data and transactions are initiated, recorded, processed, and reported and how IT controls are designed; inspecting systems documentation; observing the operation of IT controls; and planning and performing tests of IT controls.

3155.14 The auditor may discuss elements of planning with those charged with governance and the entity's management. These discussions may be a part of overall communications made to those charged with governance of the entity or may be made to improve the effectiveness and efficiency of the audit.

3155.15 The purpose and objective of planning the audit are the same whether the audit is an initial or recurring engagement. However, for an initial audit, the auditor may need to expand the planning activities because the auditor does not ordinarily have the previous experience with the entity that is considered when planning recurring engagements.

3155.16 For initial audits, additional matters the auditor should consider in developing the overall audit strategy and audit plan include the following:

    a. Arrangements to be made with the previous auditor, for example, to review the previous auditor's audit documentation

    b. Any major issues discussed with management in connection with the initial selection as auditors, the communication of these matters to those charged with governance, and how these matters affect the overall audit strategy and audit plan

    c. The planned audit procedures to obtain sufficient appropriate audit evidence regarding opening balances

    d. The assignment of firm personnel with appropriate levels of capabilities and competence to respond to anticipated significant risks

    e. Other personnel required by the firm's system of quality control for initial audit engagements

3156 Supervision (AU 311)

3156.01 Supervision involves directing the efforts of assistants who are involved in accomplishing the objectives of the audit and determining whether those objectives were accomplished. Elements of supervision include instructing assistants, keeping informed of significant issues encountered, reviewing the work performed, and dealing with differences of opinion among firm personnel.

3156.02 The auditor with final responsibility for the audit should communicate with members of the audit team regarding the susceptibility of the entity's financial statements to material misstatement due to error or fraud, with special emphasis on fraud. In addition, assistants should be informed of their responsibilities and the objectives of the audit procedures they are to perform.

3156.03 The work performed by each assistant, including the audit documentation, should be reviewed to determine whether it was adequately performed and documented and to evaluate the results, relative to the conclusions to be presented in the auditor's report.

3156.04 Each assistant has a professional responsibility to bring to the attention of appropriate individuals in the firm disagreements or concerns with respect to accounting and auditing issues that the assistant believes are of significance to the financial statements or auditor's report, however those disagreements or concerns may have arisen.

3156.05 The auditor with final responsibility for the audit and assistants should be aware of the procedures to be followed when differences of opinion concerning accounting and auditing issues exist among firm personnel involved in the audit. Such procedures should enable an assistant to document his/her disagreement with the conclusions reached if, after appropriate consultation, he/she believes it necessary to disassociate him/herself from the resolution of the matter. In this situation, the basis for the final resolution should also be documented.

3157 Ratio Analysis

3157.01 The analysis and interpretation of financial statements is carried out in part through ratio analysis, which relates different financial statement elements in a meaningful way. Ratios are computed and analyzed on a comparative basis by:

  a. comparing operating characteristics of an enterprise over a series of successive years and

  b. comparing operating characteristics of the enterprise with other similar enterprises, preestablished standards (target ratios), or legal requirements.

3157.02 Many different ratios are computed and used to analyze the operating characteristics of enterprises, primarily by investors and creditors, both present and potential. Several of the frequently encountered ratios are presented in the next paragraph in the illustration of the Ratio Company, whose income statement (year 20X2) and balance sheets (years 20X1 and 20X2) are presented. The ratios are computed as of December 31, 20X2.

Ratio Company
Comparative Balance Sheets
At December 31, 20X1, and 20X2

	12/31/X2	12/31/X1
Assets		
Cash and marketable securities	$ 250,000	$ 200,000
Net accounts receivable	200,000	100,000
Inventories	100,000	150,000
Total current assets	550,000	450,000
Net plant and equipment	400,000	450,000
Goodwill	100,000	100,000
	$1,050,000	$1,000,000
Liabilities and Equities		
Accounts payable	$ 200,000	$ 150,000
Long-term debt	450,000	500,000
Preferred stock, $100 par	100,000	100,000
Common stock, $10 par (market price $17.00)	200,000	200,000
Retained earnings	100,000	50,000
	$1,050,000	$1,000,000

Ratio Company Income Statement For Year Ended December 31, 20X2

Net sales (all credit)	$1,000,000
Cost of goods sold ($25,000 depreciation)	600,000
Gross profit on sales	$ 400,000
Selling and administrative expenses	225,000
Income from operations	$ 175,000
Interest on long-term debt	50,000
Income before taxes	$ 125,000
Taxes, 40%	50,000
Net income	$ 75,000
Dividends declared on common stock	10,000
Dividends declared on preferred stock	15,000
Net income to retained earnings	$ 50,000
Net earnings per common share*	$ 3

*(75,000 - 15,000) ÷ 20,000 shares = $3

Ratio Company Statement of Cash Flows For Year Ended December 31, 20X2

Cash flows from operating activities:		
Cash received from customers	$1,100,000	
Cash paid to purchase inventory	(675,000)	
Cash paid for selling and administrative expenses	(225,000)	
Cash paid for interest	(50,000)	
Cash paid for taxes	(50,000)	
Net cash provided by operating activities		$100,000
Cash from investing activities:		
Cash paid for plant and equipment		(75,000)
Cash from financing activities:		
Proceeds from long-term debt	$50,000	
Cash paid for dividends on common stock	(10,000)	
Cash paid for dividends on preferred stock	(15,000)	
Net cash provided by financing activities		25,000
Net increase in cash		$ 50,000
Cash, beginning of 20X2		200,000
Cash, end of 20X2		$250,000

3157.03 These ratios should be understood in terms of the following:

    a. Definition (i.e., how is the ratio computed?)

    b. Significance (i.e., what does the ratio tell you?)

    c. Limitations (i.e., what care should be taken in the use of the ratio?)

Ratios Used in Financial Statement Analysis

Ratio	Definition	Significance	Computation	Limitations
a. Current ratio	$\dfrac{\text{Current assets}}{\text{Current liabilities}}$	Measures ability to discharge currently maturing obligations from existing current assets.	$\dfrac{\$550,000}{\$200,000} = 2.75$	Balance sheet account totals based on historical cost do not necessarily represent market values. A sizable amount of the current asset total might be tied up in inventory which is less liquid. Implies liquidation of assets and elimination of liabilities (neither of which is likely in a "going concern").
b. Quick (acid test) ratio	$\dfrac{\text{Current assets less inventories and prepaid assets}}{\text{Current liabilities}}$	Measures ability to discharge currently maturing obligations based on most liquid (quick) assets.	$\dfrac{\$550,000 - \$100,000}{\$200,000} = 2.25$	Receivables may be subject to a lengthy collection period and might have to be factored at less than carrying value if cash is needed immediately. Securities are subject to fluctuating market conditions which affect their liquidation amount.
c. Inventory turnover	$\dfrac{\text{Cost of goods sold}}{\text{Average inventory}}$	Measures relative control over inventory investment. May provide basis for determining the presence of obsolete inventory or pricing problems (in case of low turnover).	$\dfrac{\$600,000}{\left(\dfrac{\$150,000 + \$100,000}{2}\right)} = 4.80$	Different inventory cost flow assumptions can produce widely different inventory valuations and thus turnover ratios.
d. Receivables turnover	$\dfrac{\text{Net credit sales}}{\text{Average receivables}}$	Confirms the fairness of the receivable balance. May indicate presence of possible collection problems (in case of low turnover).	$\dfrac{\$1,000,000}{\left(\dfrac{\$200,000+\$100,000}{2}\right)} = 6.67$	Affected by significant seasonal fluctuations unless denominator is a weighted-average. Poor collection policy can understate this ratio by increasing average receivables.
e. Cash from operating activities to current liabilities	$\dfrac{\text{Net cash provided by operating activities}}{\text{Current liabilities}}$	Shows extent to which a company has covered its current liabilities by generating cash from normal operations.	$\dfrac{\$100,000}{\$200,000} = 0.50$	Current liabilities may understate short-term demands on cash.

Ratio	Definition	Significance	Computation	Limitations
f. Total asset turnover	$$\frac{\text{Net sales}}{\text{Average total assets}}$$	Measures how efficiently assets are used to produce sales.	$$\frac{\$1,000,000}{\left(\frac{\$1,050,000 + \$1,000,000}{2}\right)} = 0.98$$	Does not take into account that certain assets make no tangible contribution to sales. Assumes that an asset's participation in generating sales is relative to its recorded amount. Rate of return is based on historical asset cost which does not reflect current values.
g. Rate of return on total assets	$$\frac{\text{Net income plus interest expense (net-of-tax effect)}}{\text{Average total assets}}$$	Measures the productivity of assets in terms of producing income.	$$\frac{\$75,000 + (\$50,000 - \$20,000)}{\left(\frac{\$1,050,000 + \$1,000,000}{2}\right)} = 0.10 \text{ or } 10\%$$	Similar to total asset turnover ratio. Accrual net income subject to estimates and does not reflect actual cash return. Rate of return is based on historical asset cost which does not reflect current values.
h. Return on common stockholders' equity	$$\frac{\text{Net income less preferred dividends}}{\text{Average common stockholders' equity}}$$	Measures return to common stockholders in aggregate.	$$\frac{\$75,000 - \$15,000}{\left(\frac{\$300,000 + \$250,000}{2}\right)} = 0.22 \text{ or } 22\%$$	Book value of common stockholders' equity reflects historical cost and not current value. Accrual net income involves estimations and does not reflect actual cash return.
i.(1) Debt ratio	$$\frac{\text{Total liabilities}}{\text{Total assets}}$$	Indicates extent of leverage used and creditor protection in case of insolvency.	$$\frac{\$200,000 + \$450,000}{\$1,050,000} = 0.62 \text{ or } 62\%$$	Denominator reflects historical costs and not current values.
i.(2) Debt/equity ratio	$$\frac{\text{Total liabilities}}{\text{Stockholders' equity}}$$	Determine the equity's long-term debt-paying ability.	$$\frac{\$200,000 + \$450,000}{\$100,000 + \$200,000 + \$100,000} = 1.62$$	There is a lack of uniformity in calculating this ratio.
j. Equity ratio	$$\frac{\text{Total stockholders' equity}}{\text{Total assets}}$$	Measures total asset investment provided by stockholders.	$$\frac{\$100,000 + \$200,000 + \$100,000}{\$1,050,000} = 0.38$$	Assets are recorded at historical cost and not at current value.
k. Times interest earned	$$\frac{\text{Income before interest expenses and taxes}}{\text{Interest expense}}$$	Measures ability to cover interest charges.	$$\frac{\$175,000}{\$50,000} = 3.50$$	Accrual income does not necessarily indicate availability of cash to pay interest charges.
l. Price-earnings ratio	$$\frac{\text{Market price per common share}}{\text{Earnings per share}}$$	Indicates relationship of common stock to net earnings.	$$\frac{\$17.00}{\$3.00} = 5.67$$	Earnings per share computation subject to arbitrary assumptions and accrual income. EPS is not the only factor affecting market prices.

Ratio	Definition	Significance	Computation	Limitations
m. Dividend yield	$$\frac{\text{Dividend per common share}}{\text{Market price per common share}}$$	Shows return to stockholders based on current market price of stock.	$$\frac{\$10{,}000 \div 20{,}000 \text{ shares}}{\$17.00} = 0.03$$	Dividend payments to stockholders are subject to many variables. The relationship between dividends paid and market prices is a reciprocal one.
n. Profit margin on sales	$$\frac{\text{Net income}}{\text{Sales}}$$	Measures efficiency of earning income from sales.	$$\frac{\$75{,}000}{\$1{,}000{,}000} = 0.08$$	Accrual income includes estimations. Income includes costs over which management has little or no control (e.g., taxes).
o. Book value per common share	$$\frac{\text{Common stockholders' equity}}{\text{Common shares outstanding}}$$	Measures net assets applicable to each common share.	$$\frac{\$200{,}000 + \$100{,}000}{20{,}000 \text{ shares}} = \$15.00$$	Assets are recorded at historical cost and not at current value.
p. Cash flow per common share	$$\frac{\text{Income plus noncash adjustments}}{\text{Common shares outstanding}}$$	Measures resources (i.e., cash) generated per common share.	$$\frac{\$75{,}000 + \$25{,}000}{20{,}000 \text{ shares}} = \$5.00$$	This ratio is the least understood and therefore the most likely to mislead an investor. SFAS 95 strongly recommends against the isolated disclosure of this ratio.
q. Payout ratio to common shareholders	$$\frac{\text{Common dividends}}{\text{Net income less preferred dividends}}$$	Measures portion of net income to common shareholders paid out in dividends.	$$\frac{\$10{,}000}{\$75{,}000 - \$15{,}000} = 0.17$$	Income does not necessarily measure cash available for dividend payment. Heavily influenced by management policy, nature of business, and stage of development, all of which diminish comparability.
r. Cash from operating activities to net income	$$\frac{\text{Net cash provided by operating activities}}{\text{Net income}}$$	Shows cash flow effects of the company's net income for the period.	$$\frac{\$100{,}000}{\$75{,}000} = 1.33$$	Net income includes noncash revenues and expenses recognized by accrual accounting principles.

3157.04 For analytical purposes, the ratios presented in this table can be grouped as follows:

    a. Measures of liquidity (i.e., ability to meet current debt):

        (1) Current ratio

        (2) Quick ratio

        (3) Inventory turnover

        (4) Receivables turnover

        (5) Cash from operating activities to current liabilities

    b. Measures of return on investment:

        (1) Total asset turnover

        (2) Rate of return on total assets

        (3) Return on common stockholders' equity

        (4) Price-earnings ratio

        (5) Dividend yield

(6) Profit margin on sales

(7) Payout ratio to common shareholders

c. Measures of solvency (i.e., long-term financing and debt-paying ability):

(1) Debt to equity ratio

(2) Equity ratio

(3) Times interest earned

(4) Book value per common share

(5) Cash flow per common share

(6) Cash from operating activities to net income

3157.05 Care must be taken in the use of ratios, as can be seen by the specific limitations stated previously. In summary, several of the critical considerations of which one must be continually mindful in ratio analysis include the following:

a. Accounting methods used to state assets, liabilities, stockholders' equity, revenues, and expenses are not necessarily designed to produce the most useful numbers for the purposes for which the ratios are intended.

b. Differences in the underlying economic events, the types of enterprises involved, the stage of development of enterprises, and other factors affect comparability between enterprises.

c. Several ratios include the use of external market values of stock, which are influenced by numerous variables over which management has little influence or control.

d. Management policy may influence many ratios.

3160 Understanding the Entity and Its Environment and Assessing the Risk of Material Misstatement (AU 314)

3161 Sources of Information About the Entity and Its Environment, Including Its Internal Control

3161.01 Obtaining an understanding of the entity and its environment is an essential aspect of performing an audit in accordance with GAAS. In particular, that understanding establishes a frame of reference within which the auditor plans the audit and exercises professional judgment about assessing risks of material misstatement of the financial statements and responding to those risks throughout the audit.

3161.02 The auditor should use professional judgment to determine the extent of the understanding required of the entity and its environment, including its internal control. The auditor's primary consideration is whether the understanding that has been obtained is sufficient to assess risks of material misstatement of the financial statements and to design and perform further audit procedures.

3161.03 Obtaining an understanding of the entity and its environment, including its internal control, is a continuous, dynamic process of gathering, updating, and analyzing information throughout the audit.

3161.04 The auditor should perform the following risk assessment procedures to obtain an understanding of the entity and its environment, including its internal control:

  a. Inquiries of management and others within the entity

  b. Analytical procedures

  c. Observation and inspection

3161.05 In addition, the auditor might perform other procedures where the information obtained may be helpful in identifying risks of material misstatement. For example, the auditor may consider making inquiries of others outside the entity such as the entity's external legal counsel or of valuation experts that the entity has used.

3161.06 Although much of the information the auditor obtains by inquiries can be obtained from management and those responsible for financial reporting, inquiries of others within the entity, such as production and internal audit personnel, and other employees with different levels of authority, may be useful in providing the auditor with a different perspective in identifying risks of material misstatement.

3162 Discussion Among the Audit Team

3162.01 The members of the audit team should discuss the susceptibility of the entity's financial statements to material misstatements. This discussion could be held concurrently with the discussion among the audit team that is specified by SAS 99 to discuss the susceptibility of the entity's financial statements to fraud.

3162.02 The objective of this discussion is for members of the audit team to gain a better understanding of the potential for material misstatements of the financial statements resulting from fraud or error in the specific areas assigned to them, and to understand how the results of the audit procedures that they perform may affect other aspects of the audit, including the decisions about the nature, extent, and timing of further audit procedures.

3162.03 The discussion provides an opportunity for more experienced team members, including the engagement partner, to share their insights based on their knowledge of the entity and for the team members to exchange information about the business risks to which the entity is subject and about how and where the financial statements may be susceptible to material misstatement.

3162.04 Professional judgment should be used to determine which members of the audit team should be included in the discussion, how and when it should occur, and the extent of the discussion. The key members of the audit team are ordinarily involved in the discussion; however, it is not necessary for all team members to have a comprehensive knowledge of all aspects of the audit.

3163 The Entity and Its Environment

3163.01 The auditor's understanding of the entity and its environment consists of an understanding of the following aspects:

   a. Industry, regulatory, and other external factors

   b. Nature of the entity, including the entity's selection and application of accounting policies

   c. Objectives and strategies and the related business risks that may result in a material misstatement and review of the entity's financial statements

   d. Measurements and review of the entity's financial performance

   e. Internal control

3163.02 The auditor should obtain an understanding of relevant industry, regulatory, and other external factors. The industry in which the entity operates may be subject to specific risks of material misstatement arising from the nature of the business, the degree of regulation, or other external forces (such as political, economic, social, technical, and competitive).

3163.03 The auditor should obtain an understanding of the nature of the entity. The nature of an entity refers to the entity's operations, its ownership, governance, the types of investments that it is making and plans to make, the way that the entity is structured and how it is financed. This understanding enables the auditor to understand the classes of transactions, account balances, and disclosures to be expected in the financial statements.

3163.04 The auditor should obtain an understanding of the entity's selection and application of accounting policies and should consider whether they are appropriate for its business and consistent with GAAP and accounting policies used in the relevant industry.

3164 Objectives, Strategies, Related Business Risks, and the Entity's Financial Performance

3164.01 The auditor should obtain an understanding of the entity's objectives and strategies, and the related business risks that may result in material misstatement of the financial statements. Strategies are the operational approaches by which management intends to achieve its objectives.

3164.02 Business risk is broader than the risk of material misstatement of the financial statements, although it includes the latter. Most business risks will eventually have financial consequences and, therefore, an effect on the financial statements. However, not all business risks give rise to risks of material misstatement. The auditor's consideration of whether a business risk may result in material misstatement is made in light of the entity's circumstances.

3164.03 Smaller entities often do not set their objectives and strategies, or manage the related business risks, through formal plans or processes. In many cases, there may be no documentation of such matters. In such entities, the auditor's understanding is ordinarily obtained through inquiries of management and observation of how the entity responds to such matters.

3164.04 The auditor should obtain an understanding of the measurement and review of the entity's financial performance. Performance measures and their review indicate to the auditor aspects of the entity's performance that management and others consider to be important.

3164.05 Performance measures, whether external or internal, create pressures to the entity that, in turn, may motivate management to take action to improve the business performance or to misstate the financial statements. Obtaining an understanding of the entity's performance measures assists the auditor in considering whether such pressures result in management actions that may have increased the risks of material misstatement.

3164.06 Much of the information used in performance measurement may be produced by the entity's information system. If management assumes that data used for reviewing the entity's performance are accurate without having a basis for that assumption, errors may exist in the information, potentially leading management to incorrect conclusions about performance.

3164.07 When the auditor intends to make use of the performance measures for the purpose of the audit (for example, in performing analytical procedures), the auditor should consider whether the information related to management's review of the entity's performance provides a reliable basis and is sufficiently precise for such a purpose.

3164.08 Smaller entities ordinarily do not have formal processes to measure and review the entity's financial performance. Management nevertheless often relies on certain key indicators which knowledge and experience of the business suggest are reliable bases for evaluating financial performance and taking appropriate action.

3165 Internal Control

3165.01 The information on internal control included in SAS 109 is quite extensive. The Standard also includes a detailed discussion of the five components of internal control in Appendix B. The information presented in this outline of the Standard includes far less detail than is found in the final version of the Standard. If you need further information on the particulars of the data presented in this section, you should refer to the actual text of SAS 109.

3165.02 The auditor should obtain an understanding of the five components of internal control sufficient to assess the risk of material misstatement of the financial statements whether due to error or fraud, and to design the nature, extent, and timing of further audit procedures. (The five components are (a) control environment, (b) risk assessment, (c) information and communication, (d) control activities, and (e) monitoring.)

3165.03 The division of internal control into five components provides a useful framework for auditors to consider how different aspects of an entity's internal control may affect the audit. However, the division does not necessarily reflect how an entity considers and implements internal control.

3165.04 The auditor's primary consideration is whether, and how, a specific control prevents, or detects and corrects, material misstatements in classes of transactions, account balances, or disclosures, and their relevant assertions, rather than its classification into any particular component.

3165.05 The way in which internal control is designed and implemented varies with an entity's size and complexity. Specifically, smaller entities may use less formal means and simpler processes and procedures to achieve their objectives.

3165.06 Ordinarily, controls that are relevant to an audit pertain to the entity's objective of preparing financial statements that are fairly presented in conformity with GAAP, including the management of risk that may give rise to a risk of material misstatement in those financial statements.

3165.07 It is not necessary to assess all controls in connection with assessing the risks of material misstatement and designing and performing further audit procedures in response to assessed risks. It is a matter of the auditor's professional judgment as to the controls or combination of controls that should be assessed.

3165.08 Obtaining an understanding of internal control involves evaluating the design of a control and determining whether it has been implemented. Evaluating the design of a control involves considering whether the control, individually or in combination with other controls, is capable of effectively preventing or detecting and correcting material misstatements.

3165.09 Implementation of a control means that the control exists and that the entity is using it. The auditor should consider the design of a control in determining whether to consider its implementation. An improperly designed control may represent a material weakness in the entity's internal control and the auditor should consider whether to communicate this to those charged with governance and management.

3166 Effect of Information Technology (IT)

3166.01 An entity's use of IT may affect any of the five components of internal control relevant to the achievement of the entity's financial reporting, operations, or compliance objectives, and its operating units or business functions.

3166.02 Generally, IT provides potential benefits of effectiveness and efficiency for an entity's internal control because it enables an entity to:

   a. consistently apply predefined business rules and perform complex calculations in processing large volumes of transactions or data.

   b. enhance the timeliness, availability, and accuracy of information.

   c. facilitate the additional analysis of information.

   d. enhance the ability to monitor the performance of the entity's activities and its policies and procedures.

   e. reduce the risk that controls will be circumvented.

   f. enhance the ability to achieve effective segregation of duties by implementing security controls in applications, databases, and operating systems.

3166.03 IT also poses specific risks to an entity's internal control, including:

   a. reliance on systems or programs that are processing data inaccurately, processing inaccurate data, or both.

   b. unauthorized access to data that may result in destruction of data or improper changes to data, including the recording of unauthorized or nonexistent transactions or inaccurate recording of transactions.

   c. unauthorized changes to data in master files.

   d. unauthorized changes to systems or programs.

   e. failure to make necessary changes to systems or programs.

   f. inappropriate manual intervention.

   g. potential loss of data or inability to access data as required.

3166.04 Internal control, no matter how well designed and operated, can provide an entity with reasonable assurance, but not absolute assurance, about achieving an entity's objectives. The likelihood of achievement is affected by limitations inherent to internal control.

3166.05 Internal control limitations include realities that human judgment in decision making can be faulty and that breakdowns in internal control can occur because of human failures such as simple errors or mistakes. Additionally, controls, whether manual or automated, can be circumvented by the collusion of two or more people or inappropriate management override of internal control.

3166.06 Smaller entities often have fewer employees, which may limit the extent to which segregation of duties is practicable. However, for key areas, even in a very small entity, it can be practicable to implement some degree of segregation of duties or other form of unsophisticated but effective controls.

3167 Components of Internal Control

3167.01 The **control environment** sets the tone of an organization, influencing the control consciousness of its people. It is the foundation for all other components of internal control, providing discipline and structure.

3167.02 In evaluating the design of the entity's control environment, the auditor should consider the following elements and how they have been incorporated into the entity's processes:

   a. Communication and enforcement of integrity and ethical values
   b. Commitment to competence
   c. Participation of those charged with governance
   d. Management's philosophy and operating style
   e. Organizational structure
   f. Assignment of authority and responsibility
   g. Human resource policies and practices

3167.03 An entity's **risk assessment process** for financial reporting purposes is its identification, analysis, and management of risks relevant to the preparation of financial statements that are fairly presented in conformity with GAAP.

3167.04 The **information system** relevant to financial reporting objectives, which includes the accounting system, consists of the procedures, whether automated or manual, and records established to initiate, record, process, and report entity transactions and to maintain accountability for the related assets, liabilities, and equity.

3167.05 An entity's **communication** involves providing an understanding of individual roles and responsibilities pertaining to internal control over financial reporting.

3167.06 The auditor should obtain an understanding of those **control activities** relevant to the audit. Control activities are the policies and procedures that help ensure that management directives are carried out and necessary actions are taken to address risks that threaten the achievement of the entity's objectives. Examples of specific control activities include the following:

   a. Authorization

   b. Segregation of duties

   c. Safeguarding

   d. Asset accountability

3167.07 The auditor should obtain an understanding of the major types of activities that the entity uses to monitor control over financial reporting, including the sources of the information related to those activities, and how those activities are used to initiate corrective actions to its controls.

3167.08 **Monitoring** of controls is a process to assess the quality of internal control performance over time. It involves assessing the design and operation of controls on a timely basis and taking necessary corrective actions.

3168 Assessing the Risks of Material Misstatement

3168.01 The auditor should identify and assess the risks of material misstatement at the financial statement level and at the relevant assertion level for classes of transactions, account balances, and disclosures. For this purpose, the auditor should:

   a. identify risks throughout the process of obtaining an understanding of the entity and its environment, including relevant controls that relate to the risks, and by considering the classes of transactions, account balances, and disclosures in the financial statements.

   b. relate the identified risks to what can go wrong at the relevant assertion level.

   c. consider whether the risks are of a magnitude that could result in a material misstatement of the financial statements.

   d. consider the likelihood that the risks could result in a material misstatement of the financial statements.

3168.02 The auditor should use information gathered by performing risk assessment procedures, including the audit evidence obtained in evaluating the design of controls and determining whether they have been implemented, as audit evidence to support the risk assessment. The auditor should use the risk assessment to determine the nature, extent, and timing of future audit procedures to be performed.

3168.03 When the risk assessment is based on an expectation that controls are operating effectively to prevent or detect material misstatement, individually or when aggregated, at the relevant assertion level, the auditor should perform tests of the controls that the auditor has determined to be suitably designed to prevent or detect a material misstatement in the relevant assertion to obtain audit evidence that the controls are operating effectively.

3168.04 The nature of the risks arising from a weak control environment is such that they are not likely to be confined to specific individual risks of material misstatement in particular classes of transactions, account balances, and disclosures. Rather, weaknesses such as management's lack of competence may have a more pervasive effect on the financial statements and may require an overall response by the auditor.

3168.05 As part of the risk assessment process, the auditor should determine which of the risks identified are, in the auditor's judgment, risks that require special audit consideration (such risks are defined as "significant risks"). The determination of significant risks, which arise on most audits, is a matter for the auditor's professional judgment.

3168.06 Significant risks are often derived from business risks that may result in a material misstatement. In considering the nature of the risks, the auditor should consider a number of matters, including the following:

    a. Whether the risk is a risk of fraud

    b. Whether the risk is related to recent significant economic, accounting, or other developments and, therefore, requires specific attention

    c. The complexity of transactions

    d. Whether the risk involves significant transactions with related parties

    e. The degree of subjectivity in the measurement of financial information related to the risks, especially those involving a wide range of measurement uncertainty

    f. Whether the risk involves significant non-routine transactions that are outside the normal course of business of the entity, or that otherwise appear to be unusual

3168.07 Significant risks often relate to significant non-routine transactions and judgmental matters. Non-routine transactions are transactions that are unusual, either due to size or nature and that therefore occur infrequently. Judgmental matters may include the development of accounting estimates for which there is significant measurement uncertainty.

3168.08 For significant risks, to the extent the auditor has not already done so, the auditor should evaluate the design of the entity's related controls, including relevant control activities, and determine whether they have been implemented. An understanding of the entity's controls related to significant risks should provide the auditor with adequate information to develop an effective audit approach.

3168.09 If management has not adequately responded by implementing controls over significant risks and if, as a result, the auditor judges that there is a material weakness in the entity's internal control, the auditor should communicate this matter to those charged with governance. In these circumstances, the auditor also should consider the implications for the auditor's risk assessment.

3169 Documentation

3169.01 The auditor should document:

    a. the discussion among the audit team regarding the susceptibility of the entity's financial statements to material misstatement due to error or fraud, including how and when the discussion occurred, the subject matter discussed, the audit team members who participated, and significant decisions reached concerning planned responses at the financial statement and relevant assertion levels.

    b. key elements of the understanding obtained regarding each of the aspects of the entity and its environment, including each of the components of internal control to assess the risks of material misstatements of the financial statements; sources of information from which the understanding was obtained; and the risk assessment procedures.

  c. the assessment of the risks of material misstatement both at the financial statement level and at the relevant assertion level and the basis for the assessment.

  d. the risks identified and related controls evaluated as a result of the significant risks that require special audit consideration.

3169.02 The manner in which these matters are documented is for the auditor to determine using professional judgment. See SAS 96 and AU 339, *Audit Documentation,* for general guidance.

3170 Consideration of Fraud in a Financial Statement Audit (AU 316)

3171 Description and Characteristics of Fraud

3171.01 An auditor has a responsibility to plan and perform the audit to obtain reasonable assurance about whether the financial statements are free of material misstatements, whether caused by fraud or error. Although fraud is a broad legal concept, the auditor's interest specifically relates to fraudulent acts that cause material misstatements of financial statements.

3171.02 Two types of misstatements are relevant to the auditor's consideration in a financial statement audit—misstatements arising from fraudulent financial reporting and misstatements arising from misappropriation of assets.

3171.03 Fraudulent financial reporting and misappropriation of assets differ in that fraudulent financial reporting is committed, usually by management, to deceive financial statement users while misappropriation of assets is committed against an entity, most often by employees.

3171.04 Fraudulent financial reporting may be accomplished by the following:

  a. Manipulation, falsification, or alteration of accounting records or supporting documents from which financial statements are prepared

  b. Misrepresentation in or intentional omission from the financial statements of events, transactions, or other significant information

  c. Intentional misapplication of accounting principles relating to amounts, classification, manner of presentation, or disclosure

3171.05 Misappropriation of assets involves the theft of assets that result in the financial statements not being presented in conformity with GAAP. Misappropriation of assets includes acts such as embezzling receipts, stealing assets, or causing an entity to pay for goods or services that have not been received.

3171.06 Three conditions are generally present in an organization when fraud occurs:

1. Employees have pressure or incentive to commit fraud.

2. A perceived opportunity to commit fraud exists.

3. Those involved in the fraudulent act are able to rationalize committing the fraud.

3171.07 Although fraud usually is concealed and management's intent is difficult to determine, the presence of certain conditions may suggest to the auditor the possibility that fraud may exist. However, absolute assurance is not attainable and thus even a properly planned and performed audit may not detect a material misstatement resulting from fraud.

3171.08 Due professional care requires the auditor to exercise professional skepticism. Professional skepticism is an attitude that includes a questioning mind and a critical assessment of audit evidence.

3172 Discussion Among Engagement Personnel Regarding the Risks of Material Misstatement Due to Fraud

3172.01 Prior to or in conjunction with the information-gathering procedures performed during an audit, members of the audit engagement team are required to discuss the potential for material misstatement due to fraud.

3172.02 This discussion should include:

   a. an exchange of ideas or a brainstorming among the audit team members, including the auditor with final responsibility for the audit.

   b. the exchange should include a discussion of how and where team members believe the entity's financial statements might be susceptible to material misstatement due to fraud, how management could perpetrate and conceal fraud, and how assets of the entity could be misappropriated.

   c. emphasizing the importance of maintaining a proper state of mind throughout the audit regarding the potential for material misstatement due to fraud.

3172.03 The discussion among the audit team members about the susceptibility of the entity's financial statements to material misstatement due to fraud should include consideration of the known external and internal factors affecting the entity.

3172.04 The discussion among the audit team members should emphasize the need to maintain a questioning mind and to exercise professional skepticism in gathering and evaluating evidence throughout the audit.

3172.05 Although professional judgment should be used in determining which audit team members should be included in the discussion, the discussion ordinarily should involve the key members of the audit team.

3173 Identifying Risks That May Result in Material Misstatement Due to Fraud

3173.01 SAS 22, *Planning and Supervision*, provides guidance about how the auditor obtains knowledge about the entity's business and the industry in which it operates. As part of that work, the auditor should perform the following procedures to obtain information that is used to identify the risks of material misstatement due to fraud.

   a. Make inquiries of management and others within the entity to obtain their views about the risks of fraud and how they are addressed.

   b. Consider any unusual or unexpected relationships that have been identified in performing analytical procedures in planning the audit.

c. Consider whether one or more fraud risk factors exist.

d. Consider other information that may be helpful in the identification of risks of material misstatement due to fraud.

3173.02 In identifying risks of material misstatement due to fraud, it is helpful for the auditor to consider the information that has been gathered in the context of the three conditions present when a material misstatement due to fraud occurs; that is, *incentive/pressures, opportunities, and attitudes/rationalizations.*

3173.03 Certain accounts, classes of transactions, and assertions that have high inherent risk because they involve a high degree of management judgment and subjectivity may also present risks of material misstatement due to fraud because they are susceptible to manipulation by management.

3173.04 The identification of a risk of material misstatement due to fraud involves the application of professional judgment and includes the consideration of the attributes of the risk, including:

a. the **type** of risk that may exist, that is, whether it involves fraudulent financial reporting or misappropriation of assets.

b. the **significance** of the risk, that is, whether it is of a magnitude that could result in a possible material misstatement of the financial statements.

c. the **likelihood** of the risk, that is, the likelihood that it will result in a material misstatement in the financial statements.

d. the **pervasiveness** of the risk, that is, whether the potential risk is pervasive to the financial statements as a whole or specifically related to a particular assertion, account, or class of transactions.

3173.05 Material misstatements due to fraudulent financial reporting often result from an overstatement or understatement of revenues. Therefore, the auditor should ordinarily presume that there is a risk of material misstatement due to fraud relating to revenue recognition.

3173.06 Even if specific risks of material misstatement due to fraud are not identified by the auditor, there is a possibility that management override of controls could occur, and accordingly, the auditor should address that risk apart from any conclusions regarding the existence of more specifically identifiable risks.

3173.07 As a part of the understanding of internal control sufficient to plan the audit (SAS 55), the auditor should evaluate whether the entity's programs and controls that address identified risks of material misstatement due to fraud have been suitably designed and placed in operation.

3174 Responding to the Results of Fraud Risk Assessment

3174.01 The auditor responds to risks of material misstatement due to fraud in the following three ways:

1. A response that has an overall effect on how the audit is conducted, including (1) assignment of personnel and supervision, (2) management's selection of accounting principles, and (3) using audit procedures that include an element of unpredictability.

2. A response to identified risks involving the nature, extent, and timing of the auditing procedures to be performed. The auditor should consider changing the nature, extent, and timing of audit procedures to address specifically identified risks.

3. A response involving the performance of certain procedures to further address the risk of material misstatement due to fraud involving management override of controls. Because management override of controls can occur in unpredictable ways, the auditor must be inventive in developing audit procedures.

3174.02 In modifying the nature, extent, and timing of audit procedures in response to identified risks of material misstatements due to fraud, the auditor should consider the following:

a. Performing procedures at locations on a surprise or unannounced basis

b. Requesting that inventories be counted at the end of the reporting period or on a date closer to period end to minimize the risk of manipulation of balances

c. Making oral inquiries of major customers and suppliers in addition to sending written confirmations, or sending confirmations to a specific party within an organization

d. Performing substantive analytical procedures using disaggregated data, for example, comparing gross profit or operating margins by location, line of business, or month to auditor-developed expectations

e. Interviewing personnel involved in activities in areas where a risk of material misstatement due to fraud has been identified to obtain their insights about the risk and how controls address the risk

3174.03 The auditor's response to a risk of material misstatement due to fraud relating to misappropriation of assets usually will be directed toward certain account balances, such as cash or merchandise inventory.

3174.04 The auditor should use professional judgment in determining the nature, extent, and timing of the testing of journal entries and other adjustments. In determining the appropriate method of examining the underlying support for such items, the auditor should consider:

a. the auditor's assessment of the risk of material misstatement due to fraud.

b. the effectiveness of controls that have been implemented over journal entries and other adjustments.

c. the entity's financial reporting process and the nature of the evidence that can be examined.

d. the characteristics of fraudulent entries or adjustments.

e. the nature and complexity of accounts.

f. journal entries or other adjustments processed outside the normal course of business.

3174.05 The auditor should also perform a retrospective review of significant accounting estimates reflected in the financial statements of the prior year to determine whether management judgments and assumptions relating to the estimates indicate a possible bias on the part of management.

3174.06 If the auditor identifies a possible bias on the part of management in making accounting estimates, the auditor should evaluate whether circumstances producing such a bias represent a risk of a material misstatement due to fraud.

3174.07 During the course of an audit, an auditor may become aware of business transactions that are outside the normal course of business for the entity. The auditor should gain an understanding of the business rationale for such transactions and whether that rationale suggests that the transactions may have been entered into to engage in fraudulent financial reporting or conceal misappropriation of assets.

3174.08 In understanding the business rationale for an entity's transactions, the auditor should consider:

   a. whether the form of such transactions is overly complex.

   b. whether management has discussed the nature of and accounting for such transactions with the audit committee or board of directors.

   c. whether management is placing more emphasis on the need for a particular accounting treatment than on the underlying economics of the transaction.

   d. whether transactions that involve unconsolidated related parties, including special purpose entities, have been properly reviewed and approved by the audit committee or board of directors.

   e. whether the transactions involve previously unidentified related parties or parties that do not have the substance or the financial strength to support the transaction without assistance from the entity under audit.

3175 Evaluating Audit Evidence

3175.01 Analytical procedures performed in the overall review stage of an audit may indicate a previously unrecognized risk of material misstatement due to fraud. When these procedures identify an unusual or unexpected relationship that may indicate the potential for fraud the auditor should use judgment in deciding on the extent of any additional procedures to be performed.

3175.02 At or near the completion of fieldwork, the auditor should evaluate whether the accumulated results of auditing procedures and other observations affect the assessment of the risks of material misstatement due to fraud made earlier in the audit. This evaluation primarily is a qualitative matter based on the auditor's judgment.

3175.03 When audit test results identify misstatements in the financial statements, the auditor should consider whether such misstatements may be indicative of fraud.

3175.04 If the auditor believes that the misstatement is or may be the result of fraud, and either has determined that the effect could be material to the financial statements or has been unable to evaluate whether the effect is material, the auditor should:

   a. attempt to obtain additional audit evidence to determine whether material fraud has occurred or is likely to have occurred, and, if so, its effect on the financial statements and the auditor's report thereon.

   b. consider the implications for other aspects of the audit.

   c. discuss the matter and the approach for further investigation with an appropriate level of management that is at least one level above those involved, and with senior management and the audit committee.

   d. if appropriate, suggest that the client consult with legal counsel.

3176 Communicating About Possible Fraud to Management, the Audit Committee, and Others

3176.01 Whenever the auditor has determined that there is evidence that fraud may exist, that matter should be brought to the attention of an appropriate level of management. This is appropriate even if the matter might be considered inconsequential, such as a minor defalcation by an employee at a low level in the entity's organization.

3176.02 Fraud involving senior management and fraud that causes a material misstatement of the financial statements should be reported directly to the audit committee.

3176.03 If the auditor has identified risks of material misstatement due to fraud that have continuing control implications, the auditor should consider whether these risks represent reportable conditions that should be communicated to senior management and the audit committee.

3176.04 The disclosure of possible fraud to parties other than the client's senior management and its audit committee ordinarily is not part of the auditor's responsibility and ordinarily would be precluded by the auditor's ethical or legal obligations of confidentiality unless the matter is reflected in the auditor's report.

3176.05 The auditor should recognize, however, that in the following circumstances a duty to disclose to parties outside the entity may exist:

a. To comply with legal and regulatory requirements

b. To a successor auditor when the successor makes inquiries in accordance with SAS 84

c. In response to a subpoena

d. To a funding agency or other specified agency in accordance with requirements for the audits of entities that receive governmental financial assistance

3177 Documenting the Auditor's Consideration of Fraud

3177.01 The auditor should document, in the audit working papers, information related to the assessment of the risk of material misstatement due to fraud.

3177.02 The auditor should document the following:

a. The discussion among engagement personnel in planning the audit regarding the susceptibility of the entity's financial statement to material misstatement due to fraud, including how and when the discussion occurred, the audit team members who participated, and the subject matter discussed

b. The procedures performed to obtain information necessary to identify and assess the risks of material misstatement due to fraud

c. Specific risks of material misstatement due to fraud that were identified and a description of the auditor's response to those risks

d. The reasons supporting the auditor's conclusion, if the auditor has not identified in a particular circumstance, improper revenue recognition as a risk of material misstatement due to fraud

e. The results of the procedures performed to further address the risk of management override of controls

- **f.** Other conditions and analytical relationships that caused the auditor to believe that additional auditing procedures or other responses were required and any further responses the auditor concluded were appropriate, to address such risks or other conditions
- **g.** The nature of the communications about fraud made to management, the audit committee, and others

This page intentionally left blank.

Section 3200
Auditing Aspects of EDP

3210 EDP and Its Effect upon Audits
    3211 The Effects of Computer Processing on the Examination of Financial Statements
    3212 Audit Approaches to EDP Systems
    3213 The Effect of EDP on Internal Control

3220 The Effect of EDP on the Auditor's Assessment of Control Risk
    3221 Preliminary Review of EDP
    3222 Purpose of the Preliminary Review

3230 Audit Approaches to EDP
    3231 Auditing Around the Computer
    3232 Auditing Through the Computer
    3233 Auditing with the Computer

3240 Auditing Advanced Computer Systems
    3241 Unique Controls
    3242 Advanced Audit Techniques

3210 EDP and Its Effect upon Audits

3211 The Effects of Computer Processing on the Examination of Financial Statements

3211.01   **Audit objectives:** The auditor's specific audit objectives do not change whether accounting data is processed manually or by computer. However, the methods of applying audit procedures to gather evidence may be influenced by the method of data processing.

3211.02   **Planning:** The extent to which computer processing is used in accounting and the complexity of that processing will influence the design of the accounting system and the nature of the internal control structure, and may influence the nature, extent, and timing of audit procedures. Accordingly, the auditor should consider such matters as the following:

    a. The extent to which the computer is used in significant accounting applications

    b. The complexity of the entity's computer operations, including the use of an outside service center

    c. The organizational structure of the computer processing activities

    d. The availability of data

    e. The possible use of computer-assisted audit techniques

3211.03   The auditor should consider whether specialized skills in the computer area are needed in light of the listed matters.

3211.04 The increased availability of computer-generated data may also affect the auditor's planning with regard to the use of analytical review procedures.

3211.05 **Internal control:** From an audit perspective, there are several characteristics that distinguish computer processing from manual processing.

    a. **Transaction trails:** In some computer systems, the audit trail may exist only for a short period of time or only in machine-readable form.

    b. **Uniform processing of transactions:** Computer processing virtually eliminates the occurrence of clerical error.

    c. **Segregation of functions:** An individual who has access to a computer may be in a position to perform incompatible functions that would be separated in a manual system. As a result, other control procedures may be necessary. In an accounting system that uses computer processing, the auditor's concern over the interdependence of control procedures may be greater than in a manual system because of the increased concentration of functions within the operations of computer processing.

    d. **Potential for errors and fraud:** The potential for individuals to gain unauthorized access to data and/or assets without visible evidence is greater in a computerized system than in a manual system.

    e. **Potential for increased management supervision:** The system of internal accounting control is enhanced in a computerized system by management's increased ability to use analytical tools to review and supervise the operations of the company. Examples are use and monitoring of budgets, reconciliations, ratios, and other statistics.

    f. **Initiation or subsequent execution of transactions by computer:** The computer system may be designed in such a way as to permit certain transactions to be initiated or executed automatically. The authorization of these transactions may be implied by the design of the system or otherwise accomplished differently than in a manual system.

    g. **Dependence of other controls on computer processing:** Computer processing may produce reports and other output used in performing manual control procedures. An example is an exception report.

3211.06 There are two basic types of EDP accounting control procedures.

    1. **General controls** relate to all EDP activities.

    2. **Application controls** are designed to achieve specific control objectives related to specific accounting tasks.

3211.07 **General controls** are classified as follows:

    a. Organization and operations controls

    b. System design, documentation, and testing controls

    c. Hardware controls

    d. Access and security controls

    e. Data and procedural controls

3211.08 **Application controls** are classified as follows:

    a. Input controls

    b. Processing controls

    c. Output controls

3211.09 Application controls are often dependent on general controls. It may be more efficient to review the design of internal control procedures that are essential to the operation of several specific control procedures before reviewing those specific control procedures. For example, if an application control procedure, such as matching shipping information with billing information, were to be performed by a customer-billing program, the auditor might review the controls over the access to and changing of computer programs before reviewing this programmed control procedure.

3212 Audit Approaches to EDP Systems

3212.01 There are three alternatives available to the CPA for performing audit procedures when records are computerized:

1. Auditing around the computer (see section **3231**)
2. Auditing through the computer (see section **3232**)
3. Auditing with the computer (see section **3233**)

3212.02 **Auditing around the computer** means the auditor performs manual audit procedures on computer-produced records.

3212.03 **Auditing through the computer** means tracing the processing of transactions through the computer system to arrive at conclusions about operation of controls (generally, program controls).

3212.04 **Auditing with the computer,** which some CPAs feel is a variation of auditing through the computer, involves using a computer program to access client data and to perform audit tests.

3213 The Effect of EDP on Internal Control

3213.01 Section **3200** includes a detailed discussion of internal control and its impact on an audit engagement. In that section, the five components of internal control were presented along with the audit requirements related to those components.

3213.02 The presence of computer processing for significant accounting applications affects how an entity implements its internal control and, accordingly, how the auditor approaches the audit examination.

3213.03 Certain factors related to each of the five components of internal control must be considered by the auditor in planning the audit and assessing control risk in an EDP environment. The information in the following sections (**3213.04–3213.08**) provides an analysis of the factors related to each of the internal control components and examples of control considerations that should be made by the auditor.

3213.04 The factors related to **control environment** that impact an auditor's consideration of the effect of EDP on internal control are as follows:

   a. **Assignment of authority and responsibility.** Clear lines of authority and responsibility are important in an EDP environment due to the potential access to data by multiple users. When multiple users have access to a particular database, the potential for manipulation increases. If manipulation does occur, management may have problems determining responsibility.

   b. **Human resource policies and practices.** One of the basic concepts of good internal control is competent and trustworthy employees. In a computerized environment, the need for skilled employees operating with a high degree of integrity is of great importance.

3213.05 **Risk assessment** requires the inclusion of a strict policy of control over changes in programs and inappropriate access to data. The greatest risks in an EDP environment are that the programs that process the data will be altered to generate fraudulent results or data will be manipulated by unauthorized data entry.

3213.06 The following factors related to **control activities** impact an auditor's consideration of the effect of EDP on internal control.

   a. **Information processing.** Two areas in which control activities can be affected by computer processing are authorization of transactions and the maintenance of adequate documents and records. Authorization procedures in many computer systems are a part of the computer program. Thus, there is increased potential for unauthorized individuals to gain access to sensitive accounting information. Concerning the maintenance of adequate documentary evidence, auditors must be aware that the traditional audit trail may not be available due to the fact that the EDP system does not provide a hard copy of source documents.

   b. **Segregation of duties.** Adequate controls must be established within the EDP department to compensate for the lack of segregation of duties that would normally be available in a manual system. So many functions are combined in an EDP department that segregation of duties is often difficult to achieve.

   c. **Physical controls.** In an EDP department, access to assets is often possible through the computer system. As such, the need for enhanced physical controls is of great importance in an EDP environment. It is also important to have adequate backup for computer files, as their destruction or damage could result in significant problems for a business entity.

3213.07 The **information and communication** component of internal control has a direct impact on the quality of the system-generated information provided to management. The quality of the information has a direct relationship to the relevance and appropriateness of the decision making process. Controls embedded in the software and hardware must be utilized by the system and be acted on by personnel in the EDP department. The decisions are only as good as the information on which those decisions are based. The integrity of the information used by management is of great concern to the auditor.

3213.08 Management is responsible for establishing and maintaining proper internal controls. Management must **monitor** controls to consider whether they are operating as intended and that they are modified as appropriate for changes in conditions. An important consideration for the auditor is that the knowledge base and skill level of those responsible for monitoring the system is adequate to identify problems encountered and seek corrective action.

3213.09 Once an auditor has a thorough understanding of internal control and has documented that understanding, the next step is to assess control risk. If, in the opinion of the auditor, control risk cannot be reduced and the assessment is at the maximum, the auditor must expand substantive tests. If the auditor concludes that the controls in the EDP area do not appear to be effective, an in-depth review of internal control should be conducted along with extensive testing of controls. In many cases, clients have a complex computer system. Where a complex computer system exists, the auditor should strongly consider the need for a computer audit specialist to assist in performing tests of controls.

3220 The Effect of EDP on the Auditor's Assessment of Control Risk

3221 Preliminary Review of EDP

3221.01 When EDP is used in significant accounting applications (i.e., those relating to accounting information that can materially affect the financial statements the CPA is examining), the CPA *should consider the EDP activity* in the assessment of control risk.

This assessment can be divided into the following two phases:

1. The preliminary phase of the review
2. The completion of the review (detailed tests of controls)

3221.02 *Both* general and application controls should be considered by the auditor in each of the two phases in section **3221.01**. The depth and level to which these controls are reviewed will, however, vary significantly between the two phases.

3221.03 The CPA's preliminary understanding of the accounting system is obtained by inquiry, but it may also be obtained by observing client personnel and reviewing documentation. The preliminary phase of the review covers both the EDP and non-EDP portions of the accounting system.

3221.04 If the client uses EDP in its accounting system, *whether the application is simple or complex,* the CPA needs to perform a preliminary review.

a. Complex EDP applications will require that the CPA apply specialized expertise in EDP in the performance of the necessary procedures.

b. Examples of complex applications include on line computerized systems, large-scale EDP installations, and advanced file management systems.

3222 Purpose of the Preliminary Review

3222.01 The purpose of the preliminary review is to enable understanding of the accounting system, including both EDP and non-EDP segments. Understanding includes the following:

   a. The flow of transactions and significance of output

   b. The extent to which EDP is used in significant accounting applications

   c. The basic structure of accounting control, including both EDP and user controls

3222.02 After completing the preliminary phase of the review for each significant accounting application, the CPA should be in a position to assess the significance of the accounting control within EDP in relation to the entire control structure; therefore, the CPA can determine the extent of the detailed review of EDP accounting control. Options available include the following:

   a. Test and rely on EDP control procedures.

   b. Do not test EDP controls, but test and rely on user controls.

   c. Do not test controls, but carry out other audit tests to achieve audit satisfaction.

3222.03 When an auditor follows a strategy of relying on EDP controls, detailed tests of general and application controls must be employed. In testing general controls, the auditor will normally rely on such procedures as inquiry of client personnel, observation, and documentary evidence. In testing application controls, the auditor will rely on computer-assisted audit techniques.

3222.04 In many situations, an auditor decides not to rely on controls in an EDP environment to limit the nature, extent, and timing of audit procedures. The normal procedure would be to carry out extended substantive audit tests to achieve audit satisfaction. However, paragraph 14 of AU 326 (*Audit Evidence,* under the heading "The Use of Assertions in Obtaining Audit Evidence") points out that where significant information is processed, transmitted, maintained, or accessed electronically, the auditor may determine that it is not practical or possible to reduce detection risk to an acceptable level by performance of only substantive tests. In such situations, the auditor should perform tests of controls to gather audit evidence to use in assessing control risk. Thus, even in circumstances where the auditor is not going to rely on EDP controls, the auditor may still need to test controls in assessing control risk.

3230 Audit Approaches to EDP

3231 Auditing Around the Computer

3231.01 The practice of *auditing around the computer* began in the early days of computer usage, when the typical CPA was unfamiliar with computers. Auditing around the computer views the computer as a black box. The audit is performed by selecting a sample of transactions that have already been processed. These transactions are traced from their points of origin as source documents to the output records and vice versa.

3231.02 Auditing around the computer may be illustrated as follows:

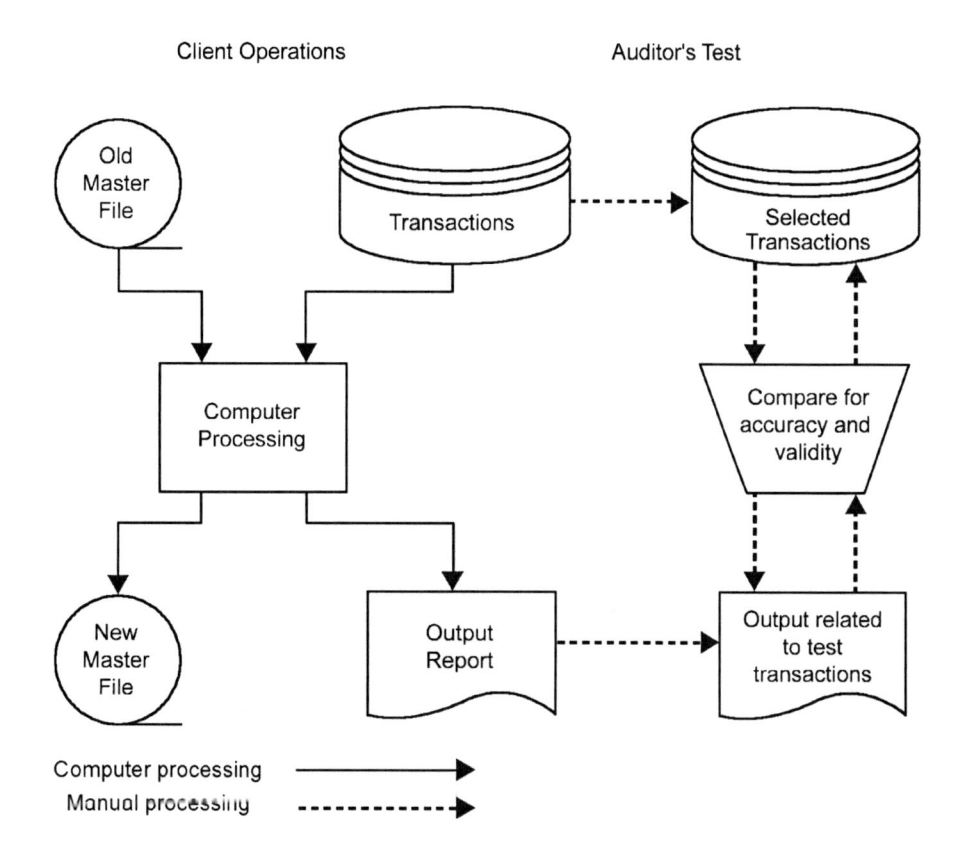

3231.03 Advantages associated with auditing around the computer are that it:

a. requires little technical training,

b. is simple and straightforward, and

c. entails no risk of tampering with live client data.

3231.04 Disadvantages associated with auditing around the computer are that it:

    a. requires file dumps and costly hard-copy printouts that sometimes only the CPA needs and

    b. is not adequate for advanced EDP systems.

3231.05 In auditing around the computer, the CPA still must document an understanding of the control environment and accounting system, including EDP and non-EDP aspects.

3232 Auditing Through the Computer

3232.01 There are four primary approaches used to *audit through the computer*.

1. Test deck
2. Controlled reprocessing
3. Integrated test facility
4. Parallel simulation

3232.02 The *test deck* requires the preparation of a series of test transactions. The test deck is run on the computer system using the same program used to operate the application being tested.

3232.03 The test deck approach is illustrated as follows:

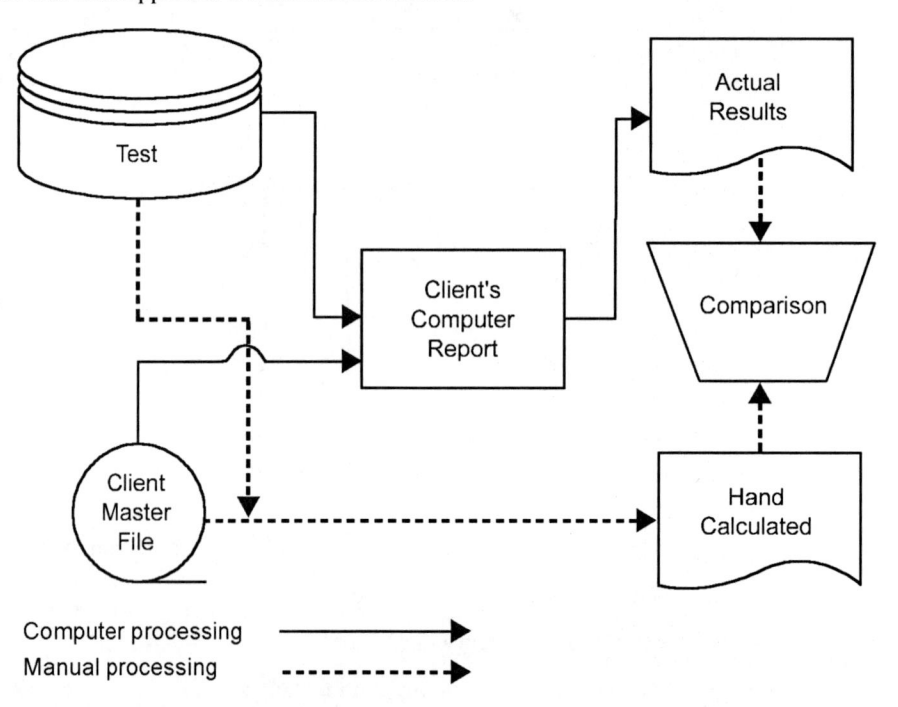

[Diagram: Test file and Client Master File feed into Client's Computer Report (computer processing) producing Actual Results; Client Master File also feeds into Hand Calculated (manual processing); Actual Results and Hand Calculated go into Comparison.

Computer processing ⟶
Manual processing ┈┈⟶]

3232.04 Advantages of the test deck are that it:

    a. provides objective assessment of the computer program and

    b. provides a good opportunity for the CPA to review the client's system and test compliance with programming controls.

3232.05 Disadvantages of the test deck include that it:

    a. is difficult to establish that the program being tested is the one the client uses regularly,

    b. requires careful and time-consuming planning,

    c. is costly to prepare and maintain,

    d. requires a higher degree of expertise from the CPA, and

    e. is valid only if there has been adequate control over program changes.

3232.06 In **controlled processing,** the CPA uses a controlled program copy (secured by the CPA earlier) that is known to be adequate to process real client data. An output report produced by running the controlled program is then compared with output of the regular client-supervised processing.

3232.07 An **integrated test facility** (ITF) is the establishment of a dummy entity through which data can be processed (e.g., a fictitious employee or customer). After the entity is established, the CPA can process test transactions against this entity, using the client's regular program. The ITF data is entered into the system with live data, and it is processed in the same way. The CPA compares what is in the ITF entity at a point in time with what should be there. Of course, the ITF transactions have to be removed from the system at some point.

3232.08 ITF processing can be illustrated as follows:

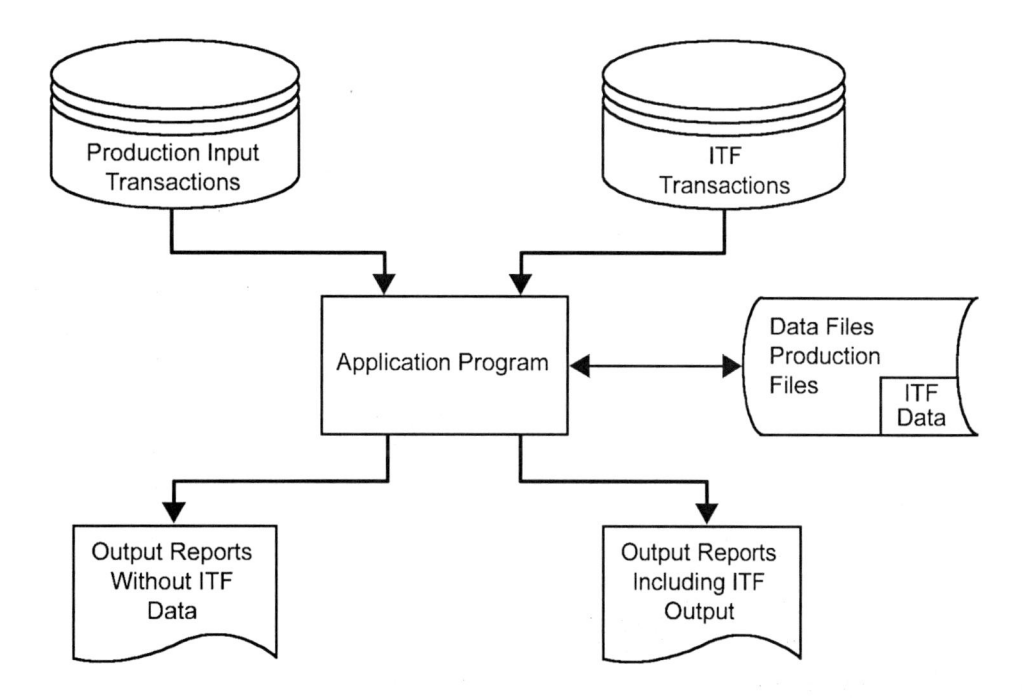

```
  Production Input                         ITF
  Transactions                         Transactions
         |                                  |
         v                                  v
         +----------------+----------------+
                          |
                          v
                 +------------------+         Data Files
                 |                  |<------> Production
                 | Application      |          Files
                 | Program          |         ( ITF Data )
                 +------------------+
                     |           |
                     v           v
             Output Reports   Output Reports
             Without ITF      Including ITF
               Data              Output
```

3232.09 The use of **parallel simulation** requires the CPA to construct a computer simulation that mimics the client's production programs. The CPA processes actual client data through the simulated program and compares the results with the client's processing of the data.

3232.10 Typically, auditing through the computer approaches are used for tests of controls.

3233 Auditing with the Computer

3233.01 Two approaches to *auditing with the computer* are as follows:
1. Specialized audit programs
2. Generalized audit software

3233.02 **Specialized audit programs** are written in a basic computer language to assess a given client file.

3233.03 Specialized programs require the expertise of computer audit specialists and programmers.

3233.04 If the specialized programs are written and developed by the client, the CPA must thoroughly test them for relevance and reliability.

3233.05 Specialized programs are used by the auditor to process client data to:
a. obtain audit information (e.g., select samples, foot files, perform computations) and
b. duplicate client programs to test client program controls.

3233.06 The advantages of specialized audit programs are as follows:
a. Flexibility
b. Efficiency in processing client files

3233.07 The disadvantages of using specialized audit programs include the following:
a. Cost and effort to develop
b. Required technical knowledge
c. The need for constant modification and updating
d. The need for early planning

3233.08 **Generalized audit software (GAS)** is adaptable to various clients and provides access to data stored in computer files for examination and analysis by the CPA. Generalized audit software consists of a series of computer programs that can be used by the CPA to perform various data processing functions. This type of software provides a high-level computer language that allows the auditor to easily perform various functions on a client's computer files and databases.

3233.09 In applying a typical generalized audit software application, the CPA would perform the following steps:
a. Set the objectives of the application (e.g., mathematical computations, confirmations).
b. Design the application (describe data files and desired data analysis).
c. Code the instructions for the application (instructions to the program to tell the GAS what to do with the client files).
d. Process the application (access the client database and perform the required applications).
e. Evaluate the results of the application (analyze the output and apply additional audit procedures as necessary).

3233.10 Generalized audit software programs are typically used to perform the following types of tests and functions:

    a. Cash:

        (1) Testing footings of outstanding checks

        (2) Tracing paid checks to cash disbursement master files

    b. Accounts receivable:

        (1) Preparing and/or checking the aged trial balance

        (2) Testing open balances against authorized credit limits

        (3) Selecting accounts for confirmation and preparing confirmation requests

    c. Inventories:

        (1) Selecting the items from perpetual records to be test counted

        (2) Tracing test counts to perpetual or final inventory summary

        (3) Checking footings and extensions

        (4) Tracing final prices against master price records

    d. Payroll:

        (1) Selecting employees with master file changes (e.g., pay rate increase) for manual verification

        (2) Checking payroll computations

    e. Other:

        (1) Testing depreciation computations

        (2) Listing of fixed asset additions and retirements for detailed testing

3233.11 Generalized audit software programs have the following advantages:

    a. Ease of use

    b. Limited computer or programming expertise required

    c. Time involved to prepare and execute the application is limited

3233.12 The following are disadvantages of generalized audit software programs:

    a. Written for ease of application rather than efficiency

    b. Provide limited ability to verify programming logic

    c. Does not allow for auditing while the data is being processed by the client

3233.13 Parallel simulation illustrates how a GAS system may be used for tests of controls. Typically, GAS systems are used for substantive testing.

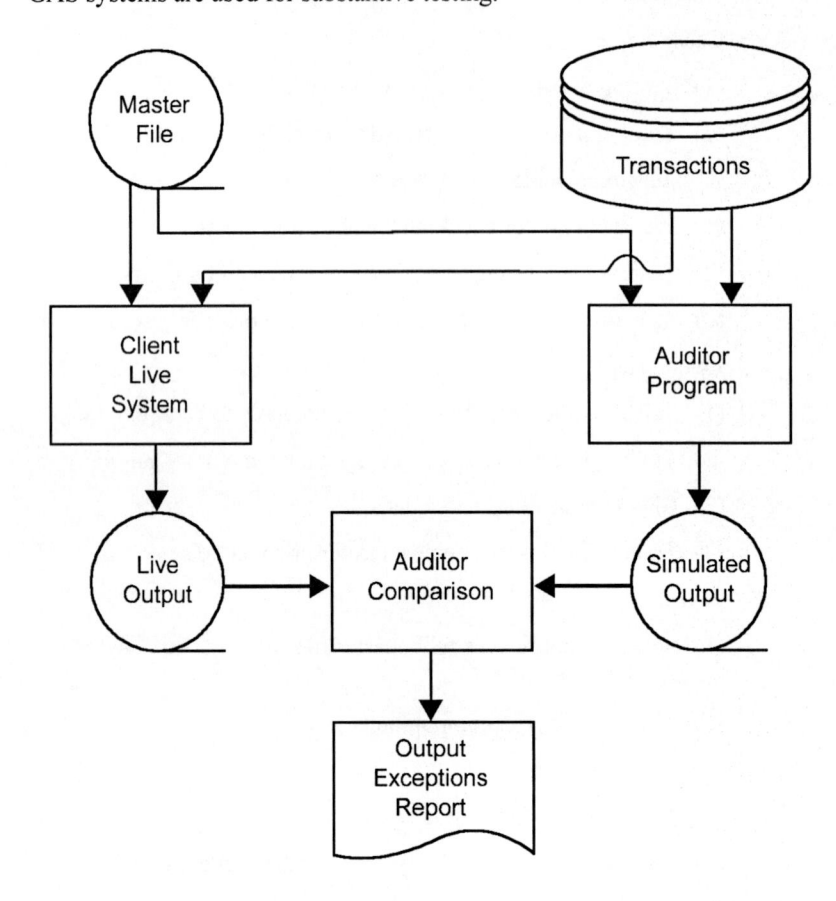

3240 Auditing Advanced Computer Systems

3241 Unique Controls

3241.01 In an on-line remote terminal system, to avoid the expense associated with a printed audit trail, a **history log** is often maintained. The history log is a complete audit trail maintained in the form of a transaction history on a low-cost mechanized medium.

3241.02 Before using a telecommunication operating system (computer with remote terminals), individuals wishing to use the system must identify themselves via a system of *passwords*. Failure to enter the correct password after a set number of tries causes the terminal to be shut down.

3242 Advanced Audit Techniques

3242.01 **Tagging** is a technique of affixing an identifier to a transaction. The tag indicates that this is a special transaction. At predetermined points throughout the computer system's application, an audit trail is provided by the flow that the tagged transaction took during processing.

    a. The tagging technique is useful for compliance testing purposes.

    b. The CPA analyzes the trail provided by the tagged transaction to determine if internal control procedures are being followed.

3242.02 **Real-time notification** permits the CPA to identify unusual transactions shortly after they occur. Traditionally, CPAs will examine a group of transactions and in that examination process look for unusual transactions. This is a hit-or-miss process. Real-time notification enables the CPA to concentrate efforts on known unusual transactions selected according to predefined criteria.

This page intentionally left blank.

Section 3300
Audit Evidence

3310 The Nature of Audit Evidence
- 3311 Concept of Audit Evidence
- 3312 Use of Assertions in Obtaining Audit Evidence
- 3313 Audit Procedures for Obtaining Audit Evidence
- 3314 Audit Documentation

3320 Performing Audit Procedures in Response to Assessed Risks and Evaluating the Audit Evidence Obtained (AU 318)
- 3321 Overall Responses
- 3322 Considering the Nature, Timing and Extent of Further Audit Procedures
- 3323 Tests of Controls
- 3324 Substantive Procedures
- 3325 Evaluating the Sufficiency and Appropriateness of Audit Evidence Obtained

3330 Types of Audit Evidence
- 3331 Internal Control
- 3332 Visual Evidence
- 3333 The Confirmation Process (AU 330)
- 3334 Documentary Evidence
- 3335 Oral Evidence
- 3336 Management Representations (AU 333)
- 3337 Independent Calculations
- 3338 Accounting Records
- 3339 Analytical Procedures (AU 329)

3340 Some Statements on Auditing Standards Related to Audit Evidence
- 3341 Related Parties (AU 334)
- 3342 Using the Work of a Specialist (AU 336)
- 3343 Inquiry of a Client's Lawyer (AU 337)
- 3344 Auditing Accounting Estimates (AU 342)
- 3345 Compliance Auditing Considerations in Audits of Governmental Entities and Recipients of Governmental Financial Assistance (AU 801)
- 3346 Auditing Fair Value Measurements and Disclosures (AU 328)
- 3347 Auditing Derivative Instruments, Hedging Activities, and Investments in Securities (SAS 92)

3350 General Audit Procedures
- 3351 Preliminary Steps
- 3352 General Review of Permanent Files and Records
- 3353 Audit Objectives—Apply as Appropriate
- 3354 Audit Procedures—Apply as Appropriate
- 3355 End of Audit Procedures

3360 Auditing Procedures for Assets and Related Revenue and Expense
  3361 Cash
  3362 Marketable Securities and Investment Revenue
  3363 Accounts Receivable and Revenues
  3364 Notes Receivable and Interest Income
  3365 Inventories and Cost of Goods Sold
  3366 Property, Plant, and Equipment—Depreciation and Depletion
  3367 Long-Term Investments (Items .04–.07 Based on AU 332)

3370 Auditing Procedures for Liabilities and Stockholders' Equity
  3371 Accounts Payable
  3372 Other Current Liabilities—Examples: Accrued Payroll and Payroll Expense
  3373 Interest-Bearing Debt and Related Expense
  3374 Contingent Liabilities
  3375 Stockholders' Equity and Dividends

3310 The Nature of Audit Evidence

3311 Concept of Audit Evidence

3311.01 **Audit evidence** is all the information used by the auditor in arriving at the conclusions on which the audit opinion is based and includes the information contained in the accounting records underlying the financial statements and other information. Auditors are not expected to examine all information that may exist.

3311.02 Accounting records generally include the records of initial entries and supporting records, such as checks and records of electronic fund transfers; invoices; contracts; the general and subsidiary ledgers, journal entries, and other adjustments to the financial statements that are not reflected in formal journal entries; and records such as worksheets and spreadsheets supporting cost allocations, computations, reconciliations, and disclosures.

3311.03 Management is responsible for the preparation of the financial statements based on the accounting records of the entity. The auditor should obtain some audit evidence by testing the accounting records, for example, through analysis and review, reperforming procedures followed in the financial reporting process, and reconciling related types and applications of the same information.

3311.04 The **sufficiency** of audit evidence is measured by the quantity. **Appropriateness** is the measure of the quality of audit evidence, that is, its relevance and its reliability in providing support for, or detecting misstatements in, the classes of transactions, account balances, and disclosures and related assertions.

3311.05 The quantity of audit evidence needed is affected by the risk of misstatement (the greater the risk, the more audit evidence is likely to be required) and also by the quality of such audit evidence (the higher the quality, the less the audit evidence that may be required).

3311.06 The reliability of audit evidence is influenced by its source and by its nature and is dependent on the individual circumstances under which it is obtained. Generalizations about the reliability of various kinds of audit evidence can be made; however, such generalizations are subject to important exceptions. While recognizing that exceptions may exist, the following generalizations about the reliability of audit evidence may be useful:

    a. Audit evidence is more reliable when it is obtained from knowledgeable independent sources outside the entity.

    b. Audit evidence that is generated internally is more reliable when the related controls imposed by the entity are effective.

    c. Audit evidence obtained directly by the auditor (for example, observation of the application of a control) is more reliable than audit evidence obtained indirectly or by inference (for example, inquiry about the application of a control).

    d. Audit evidence is more reliable when it exists in documentary form, whether paper, electronic, or other medium (written records are superior to oral representations).

    e. Audit evidence provided by original documents is more reliable than audit evidence provided by photocopies or facsimiles.

3311.07 The auditor ordinarily obtains more assurance from consistent audit evidence obtained from different sources or of a different nature than from items of audit evidence considered individually.

3311.08 The auditor may consider the relationship between cost or obtaining audit evidence and the usefulness of the information obtained. However, the matter of difficulty or expense involved is not in itself a valid basis for omitting an audit procedure for which there is no alternative.

3312 Use of Assertions in Obtaining Audit Evidence

3312.01 In representing that the financial statements are fairly presented in conformity with generally accepted accounting principles, management implicitly or explicitly makes assertions regarding the recognition, measurement, presentation, and disclosure of information in the financial statements and related disclosures.

3312.02 Assertions used by the auditor fall into the following categories:

    a. Assertions about classes of transactions and events for the period under audit.

        (1) *Occurrence.* Transactions and events that have been recorded have occurred and pertain to the entity.

        (2) *Completeness.* All transactions and events that should have been recorded have been recorded.

        (3) *Accuracy.* Amounts and other data relating to recorded transactions and events have been recorded appropriately.

        (4) *Cutoff.* Transactions and events have been recorded in the correct accounting period.

        (5) *Classification.* Transactions and events have been recorded in the proper accounts.

    b. Assertions about account balances at the period end.

        (1) *Existence.* Assets, liabilities, and equity interests exist.

        (2) *Rights and obligations.* The entity holds or controls the rights to assets, and liabilities are the obligations of the entity.

- (3) *Completeness.* All assets, liabilities, and equity interests that should have been recorded have been recorded.
- (4) *Valuation and allocation.* Assets, liabilities, and equity interests are included in the financial statements at appropriate amounts and any resulting valuation or allocation adjustments are appropriately recorded.

c. Assertions about presentation and disclosure.
- (1) *Occurrence and rights and obligations.* Disclosed events and transactions have occurred and pertain to the entity.
- (2) *Completeness.* All disclosures that should have been included in the financial statements have been included.
- (3) *Classification and understandability.* Financial information is appropriately presented and described and information in disclosures is clearly expressed.
- (4) *Accuracy and valuation.* Financial and other information is disclosed fairly and at appropriate amounts.

3312.03 The auditor may use the relevant assertions as they are described in section **3312.03** or may express them differently provided aspects described have been covered. The auditor should use relevant assertions for classes of transactions, account balances, and presentation and disclosures in sufficient detail to form a basis for the assessment of risks of material misstatement and the design and performance of further audit procedures.

3313 Audit Procedures for Obtaining Audit Evidence

3313.01 The auditor should obtain audit evidence to draw reasonable conclusions on which to base the audit by performing audit procedures to:

a. obtain an understanding of the entity and its environment, including its internal control, to assess the risks of material misstatement at the financial statement and relevant assertion levels (audit procedures performed for this purpose are referred to as **risk assessment procedures**);

b. when necessary or when the auditor has determined to do so, test the operating effectiveness of controls in preventing or detecting material misstatements at the relevant assertion level (audit procedures performed for this purpose are referred to as **tests of controls**); and

c. detect material misstatements at the relevant assertion level (audit procedures performed for this purpose are referred to as **substantive procedures** and include tests of details or classes of transactions, account balances, and disclosures, and substantive analytical procedures).

3313.02 The auditor should perform risk assessment procedures to provide a satisfactory basis for the assessment of risk at the financial statement and relevant assertion levels.

3313.03 Tests of controls are necessary in two circumstances:

1. When the auditor's risk assessment includes an expectation of the operating effectiveness of controls, the auditor should identify and test those controls relevant to assertions associated with substantive procedures to support the risk assessment.

2. When the level of substantive procedures alone does not provide sufficient appropriate audit evidence, the auditor should perform tests of controls to obtain audit evidence about their operating effectiveness.

3313.04 The auditor should plan and should perform substantive procedures to be responsive to the related assessment of the risk of material misstatement, which includes the results of tests of controls, if any. The auditor's risk assessment is judgmental, however, and may not be sufficiently precise to identify all risks of material misstatement.

3313.05 The auditor should use one or more of the types of audit procedures described below. These audit procedures, or combinations thereof, may be used as risk assessment procedures, tests of controls, or substantive procedures, depending on the context in which they are applied by the auditor. When the information is in electronic form, the auditor may carry out certain of these audit procedures through computer-assisted audit techniques (CAATs).

  a. **Inspection of records or documents.** Consists of examining records or documents, whether internal or external, in paper form, electronic form, or other media.

  b. **Inspection of tangible assets.** Consists of physical examination of the assets.

  c. **Observation.** Consists of looking at a process or procedure being performed by others.

  d. **Inquiry.** Consists of seeking information of knowledgeable persons, both financial or nonfinancial, inside or outside the entity.

  e. **Confirmation.** A specific type of inquiry which involves obtaining a representation of information or of an existing condition directly from a third party.

  f. **Recalculation.** Consists of checking the mathematical accuracy of documents or records.

  g. **Reperformance.** Involves the independent execution of procedures or controls that were originally performed as part of the entity's internal control, either manually or through the use of CAATs.

  h. **Analytical procedures.** Consist of evaluations of financial information made by a study of plausible relationships among both financial and nonfinancial data.

3314 Audit Documentation

3314.01 The auditor must prepare audit documentation in connection with each engagement in sufficient detail to provide a clear understanding of the work performed and the audit evidence obtained and its source, and the conclusions reached.

3314.02 Audit documentation provides:

  a. the principal support for the representation in the auditor's report that the auditor performed the audit in accordance with generally accepted auditing standards.

  b. the principal support for the opinion expressed regarding the financial information or the assertion to the effect that an opinion cannot be expressed.

3314.03 An auditor should be aware of and consider the following characteristics of audit documentation:

  a. Audit documentation is an essential element of audit quality.

  b. Audit documentation is the record of audit procedures performed, relevant audit evidence obtained, and conclusions the auditor reached.

  c. Audit documentation (audit working papers) may be recorded on paper or on electronic or other media.

  d. Audit documentation includes, for example, audit programs, analysis, issues memoranda, summaries of significant findings or issues, letters of confirmation and representation, checklists, copies of important documents, correspondence, and schedules of the work the auditor performed.

3314.04 The auditor need **not** retain in audit documentation superseded drafts of working papers or financial statements, notes that reflect incomplete or preliminary thinking, previous copies of documents corrected for typographical or other errors, and duplicates of documents.

3314.05 Additional purposes served by audit documentation include:

a. assisting the audit team to plan and perform the audit.

b. assisting auditors who are new to an engagement and review the prior year's documentation to understand the work performed as an aid in planning and performing the current engagement.

c. assisting members of the audit team responsible for supervision to direct and supervise the audit work, and to review the quality of work performed.

d. demonstrating the accountability of the audit team for its work by documenting the procedures performed, the audit evidence examined, and the conclusions reached.

e. retaining a record of matters of continuing significance to future audits of the same entity.

f. assisting quality control reviewers.

g. enabling an experienced auditor to conduct inspections or peer reviews in accordance with applicable legal, regulatory, or other requirements.

h. assisting a successor auditor who reviews a predecessor auditor's audit documentation.

3314.06 The auditor should prepare audit documentation that enables an experienced auditor having no previous connection to the audit, to understand:

a. the nature, timing, and extent of auditing procedures performed to comply with SASs and applicable legal and regulatory requirements.

b. the results of the audit procedures performed and the audit evidence obtained.

c. the conclusions reached on significant matters.

d. that the accounting records agree or reconcile with the audited financial statements or other audited information.

3314.07 The form, content, and extent of audit documentation depend on the circumstances of the engagement and the audit methodology and tools used. These aspects of audit documentation are a matter of professional judgment on the part of the auditor.

3314.08 Certain matters, such as auditor independence and staff training, that are not engagement specific, may be documented either centrally within a firm or in the audit documentation for an audit engagement.

3314.09 The auditor should document significant findings or issues, actions taken to address them, and the basis for the final conclusion reached. Significant findings or issues include, but are not limited to, the following:

a. Significant matters involving the selection, application, and consistency of accounting principles with regard to the financial statements, including related disclosures

b. Results of audit procedures indicate (1) that financial information or disclosures could be materially misstated or (2) a need to revise the auditor's previous assessment of the risks of material misstatement and the auditor's response to those risks

- c. Circumstances that cause the auditor significant difficulty in applying auditing procedures the auditor considered necessary
- d. Findings that could result in a modification of the auditor's report
- e. Audit adjustments

3314.10 The auditor should document discussions of significant findings or issues with management and others on a timely basis, including responses. The audit documentation should include documentation of the significant findings or issues discussed, and when and with whom the discussion took place.

3314.11 In documenting the nature, timing, and extent of audit procedures performed, the auditor should record (a) who performed the audit work and the date such work was completed, and (b) who reviewed specific audit documentation and the date of the review.

3314.12 As required by paragraph 5 of SAS 95, *Generally Accepted Auditing Standards*, when, in rare circumstances, the auditor departs from a presumptively mandatory requirement, he/she must document in the working papers his/her justification for the departure and how the alternative procedures performed in the circumstances were sufficient to achieve the objectives of the presumptively mandatory requirements.

3314.13 If as a result of consideration of the procedures performed and the evidence obtained, the auditor concludes that procedures considered necessary at the time of the audit in the circumstances then existing were omitted from the audit of the financial information, the auditor should follow the guidance in SAS 46, *Consideration of Omitted Procedures After the Report Date*.

3314.14 If the auditor subsequently becomes aware of information relating to financial information previously reported on by him/her that was not known to him/her at the date of the report, he/she should follow the guidance in SAS 1, AU 561, *Subsequent Discovery of Facts Existing at the Date of the Auditor's Report*.

3314.15 The auditor should complete the assembly of the final audit file on a timely basis, but within 60 days following the report release date (documentation completion date). At any time prior to the documentation completion date, the auditor may make changes to the audit documentation to:

- a. complete the documentation and assembly of audit evidence that the auditor has obtained, discussed, and agreed with relevant members of the audit team prior to the date of the auditor's report.
- b. perform routine file-assembling procedures such as deleting or discarding superseded documentation and sorting, collating, and cross-referencing final working papers.
- c. sign off on file completion checklists prior to completing and archiving the audit file.
- d. add information received after the date of the auditor's report; for example, an original confirmation that was previously faxed.

3314.16 After the documentation completion date, the auditor must not delete or discard audit documentation before the end of the specified retention period (not shorter than five years from the report release date).

3314.17 Audit documentation is the property of the auditor, and some states recognize this right of ownership in their statues. The auditor may make available to the entity at his/her discretion copies of the audit documentation, provided such disclosure does not undermine the independence or the validity of the audit process.

3314.18 The auditor has an ethical and, in some situations, a legal obligation to maintain the confidentiality of client information. Because audit documentation often contains confidential client information, the auditor should adopt reasonable procedures to maintain the confidentiality of that information.

3320 Performing Audit Procedures in Response to Assessed Risks and Evaluating the Audit Evidence Obtained (AU 318)

3321 Overall Responses

3321.01 In order to reduce audit risk to an acceptably low level, the auditor should determine overall responses to address risks of material misstatement at the financial statement level, and should design and perform further audit procedures whose nature, extent, and timing are responsive to the assessed risks of material misstatement at the relevant assertion level.

3321.02 The auditor's overall responses to address the assessed risks of material misstatement at the financial statement level may include emphasizing to the audit team the need to maintain professional skepticism in gathering and evaluating audit evidence, assigning more experienced staff or those with specialized skills such as specialists.

3321.03 The auditor may also make general changes to the audit procedures as an overall response; for example, performing substantive procedures at period end instead of at an interim date.

3321.04 The assessment of the risks of material misstatement at the financial statement level is affected by the auditor's understanding of the control environment. An effective control environment may allow the auditor to have more confidence in internal control and the reliability of audit evidence generated internally within the entity.

3321.05 If there are weaknesses in the control environment, the auditor should conduct more audit procedures as of the period end rather than at an interim date. In such situations, the auditor should also consider seeking more extensive audit evidence from substantive procedures, modify the nature of audit procedures to obtain more persuasive audit evidence, or increase the number of locations to be included in the audit scope.

3321.06 Evaluation of the control environment will also have a significant bearing on the auditor's general approach. The auditor may use a substantive approach which emphasizes substantive procedures or the use of a combined approach which tests controls along with the performance of substantive procedures.

3321.07 The auditor should design and perform further audit procedures that are responsive to the assessed risks of material misstatement at the relevant assertion level. In designing further audit procedures, the auditor should consider such matters as:

   a. the significance of the risk.

   b. the likelihood that a material misstatement will occur.

   c. the characteristics of the class of transactions, account balance, or disclosure involved.

   d. the nature of the specific controls used by the entity and whether they are manual or automated.

   e. whether the auditor expects to obtain audit evidence to determine if the entity's controls are effective in preventing or detecting material misstatements.

3321.08 Regardless of the audit approach selected, the auditor should design and perform substantive procedures for all relevant assertions related to each material class of transactions, account balance, and disclosure.

3321.09 Because effective internal controls generally reduce, but do not eliminate, the risk of material misstatement, test of controls reduce, but do not eliminate, the need for substantive procedures.

3321.10 In the case of very small entities, there may not be many control activities that could be identified by the auditor. For this reason, the auditor's further audit procedures are likely to be primarily substantive procedures.

3322 Considering the Nature, Timing, and Extent of Further Audit Procedures

3322.01 The **nature** of further audit procedures refers to their purpose (tests of controls or substantive procedures) and their type, that is, inspection, observation, inquiry, confirmation, recalculation, reperformance, or analytical procedures.

3322.02 Certain audit procedures may by more appropriate for some assertions than others. For example, in relation to revenue, tests of controls may be more responsive to the assessed risk of misstatement of the completeness assertion, whereas substantive procedures may be more responsive to the assessed risk of misstatement of the occurrence assertion.

3322.03 The higher the auditor's assessment of risk, the more reliable and relevant is the audit evidence sought by the auditor from substantive procedures.

3322.04 **Timing** refers to when audit procedures are performed or the period or date to which the audit evidence applies. The auditor may perform tests of controls or substantive procedures at an interim date or at period end.

3322.05 The higher the risk of material misstatement, the more likely it is that the auditor may decide it is more effective to perform substantive procedures nearer to, or at, the period end rather than at an earlier date, or to perform audit procedures unannounced or at unpredictable times.

3322.06 A contrary argument to that expressed in section **3322.05** is that performing audit procedures before the period end may assist the auditor in identifying significant matters at an early stage of the audit, and consequently resolving them with the assistance of management or developing an effective audit approach to address such matters.

3322.07 In considering when to perform audit procedures, the auditor should also consider such matters as:

　　a. the control environment.

　　b. when relevant information is available.

　　c. the nature of the risk.

　　d. the period or date to which the audit evidence relates.

3322.08 **Extent** refers to the quantity of a specific audit procedure to be performed; for example, a sample size or the number of observations of a control activity.

3322.09 The extent of an audit procedure is determined by the judgment of the auditor after considering the materiality, the assessed risk of material misstatement, and the degree of assurance the auditor plans to obtain. In particular, the auditor ordinarily increases the extent of audit procedures as the risk of material misstatement increases.

3322.10 Valid conclusions may ordinarily be drawn using sampling approaches that are properly applied and evaluated. SAS 111, *Amendment to SAS No. 39, Audit Sampling* (outlined in section **3500**), provides guidance on planning, performing, and evaluating audit samples.

3323 Tests of Controls

3323.01 The auditor should perform tests of controls when the auditor's risk assessment includes expectations of the operating effectiveness of controls or when substantive procedures alone do not provide sufficient appropriate audit evidence at the relevant assertion level.

3323.02 When the auditor has determined that it is not possible or practicable to reduce the risks of material misstatement at the relevant assertion level to an acceptably low level with audit evidence obtained only from substantive procedures, he/she should perform tests of controls to obtain audit evidence about their operating effectiveness.

3323.03 Tests of the operating effectiveness of controls are performed only on those controls that the auditor has determined are suitably designed to prevent or detect a material misstatement in a relevant assertion.

3323.04 When performing tests of controls, the auditor should obtain audit evidence that controls operate effectively. This includes obtaining audit evidence about how controls were applied at relevant times during the period under audit, the consistency with which they were applied, and by whom or by what means they were applied.

3323.05 Tests of the operating effectiveness of controls ordinarily include the same types of audit procedures used to evaluate the design and implementation of controls, and may also include reperformance of the application of the control by the auditor. Since inquiry alone is not sufficient, the auditor should use a combination of audit procedures to obtain sufficient appropriate audit evidence regarding the operating effectiveness of controls.

3323.06 The absence of misstatements detected by a substantive procedure does not provide audit evidence that controls related to the relevant assertion being tested are effective; however, misstatements that the auditor detects by performing substantive procedures should be considered by the auditor when assessing the operating effectiveness of related controls.

3323.07 A material misstatement detected by the auditor's procedures that was not identified by the entity ordinarily is indicative of the existence of a material weakness in internal control and should be communicated to management and those charged with governance.

3323.08 The timing of tests of controls depends on the auditor's objective and determines the period of reliance on those controls. If the auditor tests controls at a particular time, the auditor only obtains audit evidence that the controls operated effectively at that time. However, if the auditor tests controls throughout a period, the auditor should obtain audit evidence of the effectiveness of the operation of the controls during that period.

3323.09 Audit evidence pertaining only to a point in time may be sufficient for the auditor's purpose; for example, when testing controls over the entity's physical inventory counting at the period end. However, if the auditor needs audit evidence of the effectiveness of a control over a period, audit evidence pertaining only to a point in time may be insufficient and the auditor should supplement those tests with other tests of controls that would relate to the entire period.

3323.10 If based on the understanding of the entity and its environment, the auditor plans to rely on controls that have not changed since they were last tested, the auditor should test the operating effectiveness of such controls at least once in every third audit.

3323.11 The auditor may not rely on audit evidence about the operating effectiveness of controls obtained in prior audits for controls that have changed since they were last tested or for controls that mitigate a significant risk.

3323.12 In considering whether it is appropriate to use audit evidence about the operating effectiveness of controls obtained in prior audits and, if so, the length of the time period that may elapse before retesting a control, the auditor should consider:

   a. the effectiveness of other elements of internal control, including the control environment, the entity's monitoring of controls, and the entity's risk assessment process.

   b. the risks arising from the characteristics of the control, including whether controls are manual or automated.

   c. the effectiveness of IT general controls.

   d. the effectiveness of the control and its application by the entity, including the nature and extent of deviations in the application of the control from tests of operating effectiveness in prior audits.

   e. whether the lack of a change in a particular control poses a risk due to changing circumstances.

   f. the risk of material misstatement and the extent of reliance on the control.

3323.13 The auditor should design sufficient tests of controls to obtain reasonable assurance that the controls are operating effectively throughout the period of reliance. Factors that the auditor may consider in determining the extent of tests of controls include the following:

   a. The frequency of the performance of the control by the entity during the period

   b. The length of time during the audit period that the auditor is relying on the operating effectiveness of the control

   c. The relevance and reliability of the audit evidence to be obtained in supporting that the control prevents, or detects and corrects, material misstatements at the relevant assertion level

   d. The extent to which audit evidence is obtained from tests of other controls related to the relevant assertion

   e. The extent to which the auditor plans to rely on the operating effectiveness of the control in assessment of risk (and thereby reduce substantive procedures based on the reliance on such control)

   f. The expected deviation from the control

3323.14 The more the auditor relies on the operating effectiveness of controls in the assessment of risk, the greater is the extent of the auditor's tests of controls. In addition, as the rate of expected deviation from a control increases, the auditor should increase the extent of testing of the control.

3324 Substantive Procedures

3324.01 Substantive procedures are performed to detect material misstatements at the relevant assertion level, and include tests of details of classes of transactions, account balances, and disclosures and substantive analytical procedures. The auditor should plan and perform substantive procedures to be responsive to the related assessment of the risk of material misstatement.

3324.02 Regardless of the assessed risk of material misstatement, the auditor should design and perform substantive procedures for all relevant assertions related to each material class of transactions, account balance, and disclosure.

3324.03 The auditor's substantive procedures should include the following audit procedures related to the financial statement reporting system:

    a. Agreeing the financial statements, including their accompanying notes, to the underlying accounting records

    b. Examining material journal entries and other adjustments made during the course of preparing the financial statements

3324.04 Substantive procedures include tests of details and substantive analytical procedures. Substantive analytical procedures are generally more applicable to large volumes of transactions that tend to be predictable over time. Tests of details are ordinarily more appropriate to obtain audit evidence regarding certain relevant assertions about account balances, including existence and valuation.

3324.05 In designing substantive procedures related to the existence or occurrence assertion, the auditor should select from items contained in a financial statement amount and should obtain the relevant audit evidence. Alternatively, in designing audit procedures related to the completeness assertion, the auditor should select from audit evidence indicating that an item should be included in the relevant financial statement amount and investigates whether that item is so included.

3324.06 In designing substantive analytical procedures, the auditor should consider such matters as:

    a. the suitability of using substantive analytical procedures, given the assertion.

    b. the reliability of the data, whether internal or external, from which the expectation of recorded amounts or ratios is developed.

    c. whether the expectation is sufficiently precise to identify the possibility of a material misstatement at the desired level of assurance.

    d. the amount of any difference in recorded amounts from expected values that is acceptable.

3324.07 The auditor should consider testing the controls, if any, over the entity's preparation of information to be used by the auditor in applying analytical procedures.

3324.08 When substantive procedures are performed at an interim date, the auditor should perform further substantive procedures or substantive procedures combined with tests of controls to cover the remaining period that provide a reasonable basis for extending the audit conclusions from the interim date to the period end.

3324.09 In deciding whether to perform substantive procedures at an interim date, the auditor should consider such factors as:

    a. the control environment and other relevant controls.

    b. the availability of information at a later data that is necessary for the auditor's procedures.

    c. the objective of the substantive procedure.

    d. the assessed risk of material misstatement.

    e. the nature of the class of transactions or account balance and relevant assertions.

    f. the ability of the auditor to reduce the risk that misstatements that exist at the period end are not detected by performing appropriate substantive procedures or substantive procedures combined with tests of controls to cover the remaining period in order to reduce the risk that misstatements that exist at period end are not detected.

3324.10 If misstatements are detected in classes of transactions or account balances at an interim date, the auditor should consider modifying the related assessment of risk and the planned nature, timing, or extent of the substantive procedures covering the remaining period that relate to such classes of transactions, or account balances, or the auditor extends or repeats such audit procedures at the period end.

3324.11 Regarding the extent of substantive procedures performed, the greater the risk of material misstatement, the greater the extent of substantive procedures.

3324.12 In designing tests of details, the extent of testing is ordinarily thought of in terms of the sample size, which is affected by the risk of material misstatement, tolerable misstatement, expected misstatement, and nature of the population. SAS 111, *Audit Sampling*, contains guidance on the use of sampling and other means of selecting items for testing.

3324.13 In designing substantive analytical procedures, the auditor should consider the amount of difference from the expectation that can be accepted without further investigation. This consideration is influenced primarily by materiality and should be consistent with the desired level of assurance.

3325 Evaluating the Sufficiency and Appropriateness of Audit Evidence Obtained

3325.01 An audit of financial statements is a cumulative and iterative process. As the auditor performs planned audit procedures, the audit evidence obtained may cause the auditor to modify the nature, timing, or extent of other planned audit procedures.

3325.02 Based on the audit procedures performed and the audit evidence obtained, the auditor should evaluate whether the assessments of the risks of material misstatement at the relevant assertion level remain appropriate.

3325.03 The auditor should not assume that an instance of fraud or error is an isolated occurrence, and therefore should consider how the detection of such misstatement affects the assessed risks of material misstatement.

3325.04 In developing an opinion, the auditor should consider all relevant audit evidence, regardless of whether it appears to corroborate or to contradict the relevant assertions in the financial statements.

3325.05 The sufficiency and appropriateness of audit evidence to support the auditor's conclusions throughout the audit are a matter of professional judgment. The auditor's judgment as to what constitutes sufficient appropriate audit evidence is influenced by such factors as the:

   a. significance of the potential misstatement in the relevant assertion and the likelihood of its having a material effect, including or aggregating with other potential misstatements, on the financial statements.

   b. effectiveness of management's responses and controls to address the risks.

   c. results of audit procedures performed, including whether such audit procedures identified specific instances of fraud or error.

   d. sources and reliability of available information.

   e. persuasiveness of the audit evidence.

   f. understanding of the entity and its environment, including its internal control.

3325.06 If the auditor has not obtained sufficient appropriate audit evidence as to a material financial statement assertion, the auditor should attempt to obtain further audit evidence. If the auditor is unable to obtain sufficient appropriate audit evidence, the auditor should express a qualified opinion or a disclaimer of opinion.

3325.07 The auditor should document:

   a. the overall responses to address the assessed risk of misstatements at the financial statement level.

   b. the nature, timing, and extent of the further audit procedures.

   c. the linkage of those procedures with the assessed risks at the relevant assertion level.

   d. the results of the audit procedures.

   e. the conclusions reached with regard to the use in the current audit of audit evidence about the operating effectiveness of controls that was obtained in a prior audit.

3330 Types of Audit Evidence

3331 Internal Control

3331.01 The assessment of control risk provides evidence as to the reliability of the accounting system and other internal evidence.

3332 Visual Evidence

3332.01 Visual evidence is obtained by observation of pertinent activity, physical observation, and count. Although visual evidence is very reliable evidence when the auditor is qualified to make the observations, it is limited as to the assertions that it corroborates. For example, it confirms existence and quantities but not necessarily ownership or value.

3333 The Confirmation Process (AU 330)

3333.01 Unusual or complex transactions may be associated with high levels of inherent and control risk. If the entity has entered into an unusual or complex transaction and the combined assessed level of inherent and control risk is high, the auditor should consider confirming the terms of the transaction with the other parties in addition to examining documentation held by the entity.

3333.02 Confirmation requests may address one or more of the five assertions noted in AU 330. However, confirmations do not address all assertions equally well. When obtaining evidence for assertions not adequately addressed by confirmations, auditors should consider other auditing procedures.

3333.03 The auditor should exercise an appropriate level of professional skepticism throughout the confirmation process. Professional skepticism is important in designing the confirmation request, performing the confirmation procedures, and evaluating the results of the confirmation process.

3333.04 Negative confirmation requests should be used to reduce audit risk to an acceptable level only when:

   a. the combined assessed level of inherent and control risk is low,

   b. a large number of small balances is involved, *and*

   c. the auditor has no reason to believe that the recipients of the requests are unlikely to give them consideration.

3333.05 In determining the effectiveness and efficiency of confirmation requests, the auditor may consider information from prior years' audits or audits of similar entities. When designing confirmation requests, the auditor should consider the types of information respondents will be readily able to confirm. The auditor's understanding of the client's arrangements and transactions with third parties is key to determining the information to be confirmed.

3333.06 The auditor should direct the confirmation request to a third party the auditor believes is knowledgeable about the information to be confirmed. During the confirmation process, the auditor should maintain control over the confirmation requests and responses. The need to maintain control does not preclude the use of internal auditors in the confirmation process.

3333.07 When the auditor has not received replies to positive confirmation requests, the auditor should apply alternative procedures (see accompanying flowchart). The omission of alternative procedures may be acceptable:

   a. when the auditor has not identified unusual qualitative factors or systematic characteristics related to the nonresponses or

   b. when testing for overstatement of amounts, the nonresponses in the aggregate, when projected as 100% misstatements to the population and added to the sum of all other unadjusted differences, would not affect the auditor's decision about the reasonableness of the account.

Receivable Confirmation Flowchart

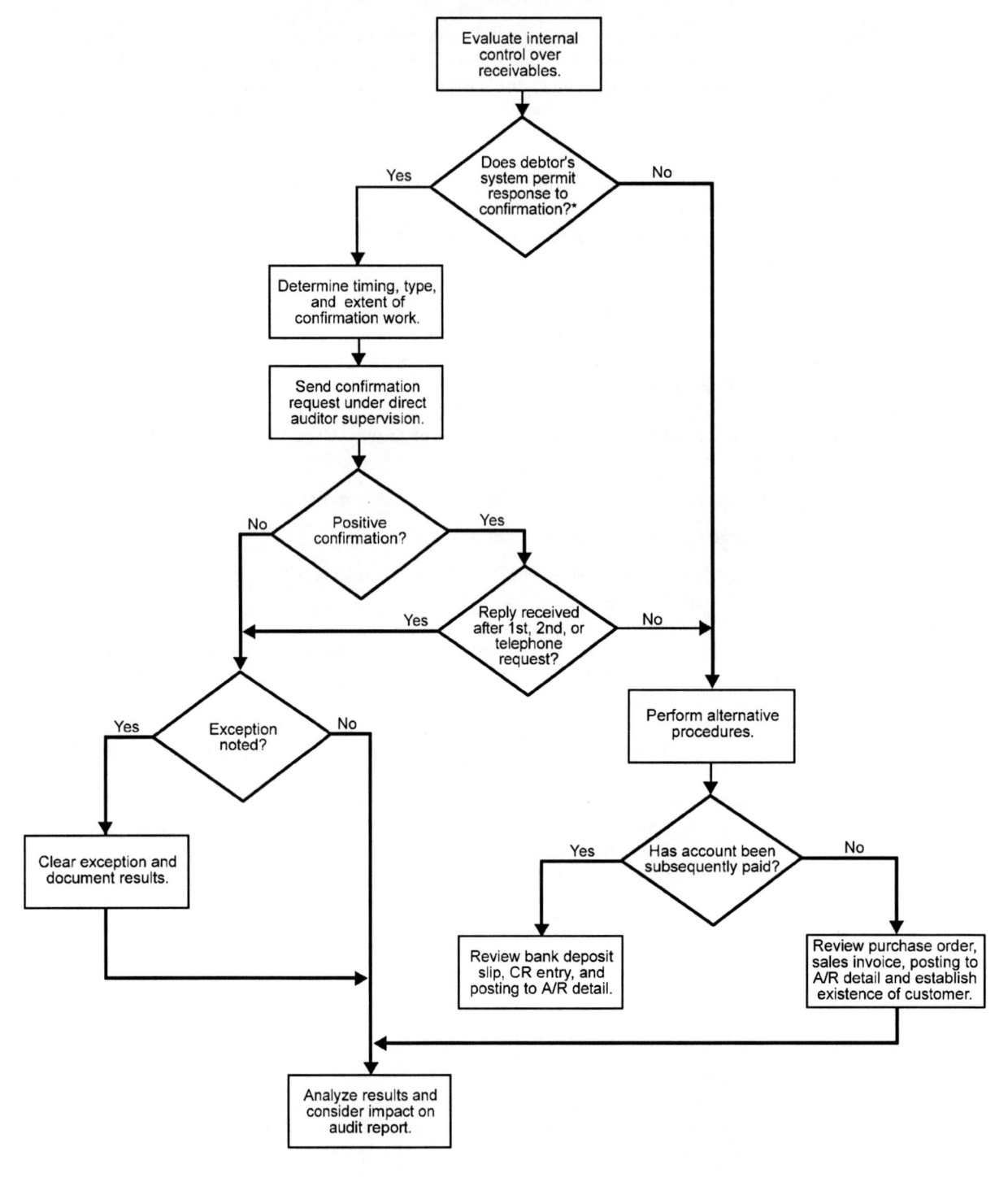

```
                    ┌─────────────────┐
                    │ Evaluate internal│
                    │ control over    │
                    │ receivables.    │
                    └────────┬────────┘
                             │
                    ┌────────▼────────┐
            Yes    ╱  Does debtor's   ╲    No
          ┌───────╱   system permit    ╲───────┐
          │       ╲   response to     ╱        │
          │        ╲  confirmation?* ╱         │
          │         ╲───────────────╱          │
          │                                    │
          ▼                                    │
┌──────────────────┐                           │
│ Determine timing,│                           │
│ type, and extent │                           │
│ of confirmation  │                           │
│ work.            │                           │
└────────┬─────────┘                           │
         │                                     │
┌────────▼─────────┐                           │
│ Send confirmation│                           │
│ request under    │                           │
│ direct auditor   │                           │
│ supervision.     │                           │
└────────┬─────────┘                           │
         │                                     │
    ┌────▼────╲                                │
No ╱ Positive  ╲ Yes                           │
┌─╱confirmation?╲─┐                            │
│ ╲             ╱ │                            │
│  ╲───────────╱  │                            │
│                 ▼                            │
│           ┌─────────────╲   No               │
│    Yes   ╱Reply received ╲──────────┐        │
│   ┌─────╱ after 1st, 2nd,╲          │        │
│   │     ╲ or telephone   ╱          │        │
│   │      ╲  request?    ╱           │        │
│   │       ╲────────────╱            │        │
│   ▼                                 ▼        ▼
│  ┌──────────╲                  ┌──────────────┐
│Yes Exception  No               │ Perform      │
│┌──╱  noted? ╲──┐               │ alternative  │
││  ╲         ╱  │               │ procedures.  │
││   ╲───────╱   │               └──────┬───────┘
│▼               │                      │
│┌─────────────┐ │                 ┌────▼────╲
││Clear        │ │           Yes  ╱Has account╲  No
││exception and│ │         ┌─────╱ been       ╲──┐
││document     │ │         │     ╲subsequently╱  │
││results.     │ │         │      ╲  paid?   ╱   │
│└──────┬──────┘ │         ▼       ╲────────╱    ▼
│       │        │  ┌──────────────┐    ┌──────────────┐
│       │        │  │Review bank   │    │Review purchase│
│       │        │  │deposit slip, │    │order, sales   │
│       │        │  │CR entry, and │    │invoice,posting│
│       │        │  │posting to    │    │to A/R detail  │
│       │        │  │A/R detail.   │    │and establish  │
│       │        │  └──────┬───────┘    │existence of   │
│       │        │         │            │customer.      │
│       │        │         │            └──────┬───────┘
│       └────────┴─────────┴───────────────────┘
│                         │
│                ┌────────▼────────┐
└───────────────►│ Analyze results │
                 │ and consider    │
                 │ impact on audit │
                 │ report.         │
                 └─────────────────┘
```

* If debtor has a voucher system, they may not be able to determine the total amount currently payable to the client.

3333.08 Confirmation of accounts receivable is a generally accepted auditing procedure. Thus, there is a presumption that the auditor will request the confirmation of accounts receivable during an audit unless *one* of the following is true:

   a. Accounts receivable are immaterial.

   b. The use of confirmations would be ineffective.

   c. The auditor's combined assessed level of inherent and control risk is low, and the assessed level, in conjunction with the evidence expected to be provided by analytical procedures or other substantive tests of details, is sufficient to reduce audit risk to an acceptably low level for the applicable financial statement assertions. In many situations, both confirmation of accounts receivable and other substantive tests of details are necessary to reduce audit risk to an acceptably low level for the applicable financial statement assertions (AU 330.34).

   An auditor who has not requested confirmations of accounts receivable should document how this presumption was overcome.

3334 Documentary Evidence

3334.01 Documents underlie or corroborate most transactions. Examples of documents are requisitions, purchase orders, supplier invoices, receiving reports, checks, sales invoices, cash register tapes, deposit slips, and bank statements.

3334.02 The reliability of documentary evidence depends on its source (external, internal, or external/internal), the assessed level of control risk, and the susceptibility of documents to manipulation or forgery.

3335 Oral Evidence

3335.01 CPAs inquire of clients to obtain corroborative evidence, background information underlying judgments, and information about unrecorded transactions or other items not found in the accounting records.

3336 Management Representations (AU 333)

3336.01 During an audit, management makes many representations to the auditor, both oral and written, in response to the specific inquiries or through the financial statements. Such representations from management are part of the audit evidence the independent auditor obtains, but they are not a substitute for the application of those auditing procedures necessary to afford a reasonable basis for an opinion on the financial statements under audit.

3336.02 If management makes a representation that is contradicted by other audit evidence, the auditor should investigate the circumstances and consider the reliability of the representations made. Based on the circumstances, the auditor should consider whether reliance on management's representations relating to other aspects of the financial statements is appropriate and justified.

3336.03 Written representations from management should be obtained for all financial statements and periods covered by the auditor's report.

In connection with an audit of financial statements, presented in accordance with GAAP or other comprehensive basis of accounting, specific representations should be made. These specific representations should be related to the following matters:

a. Financial statements:

   (1) Management's acknowledgment of its responsibility for the fair presentation of financial position, results of operations, and cash flows

   (2) Management's belief that the financial statements are fairly presented in conformity with GAAP

b. Completeness of information:

   (1) Availability of all financial records and related data

   (2) Completeness and availability of all minutes of stockholders, directors, and committees of directors

   (3) Communications from regulatory agencies concerning noncompliance with or deficiencies in financial reporting practices

   (4) Absence of unrecorded transactions

c. Recognition, measurement, and disclosure:

   (1) Management's belief that the effects of any uncorrected financial statement misstatements aggregated by the auditor during the current engagement and pertaining to the latest period presented are immaterial, both individually and in the aggregate, to the financial statements taken as a whole

   (2) Management's acknowledgment of its responsibility for the design and implementation of programs and controls to prevent and detect fraud

   (3) Information concerning fraud involving (a) management, (b) employees who have significant roles in internal control, or (c) others where the fraud could have a material effect on the financial statements

   (4) Knowledge of any allegations of fraud or suspected fraud affecting the entity received in communications from employees, former employees, analysts, regulators, short sellers, or others

   (5) Plans or intentions that may affect the carrying value or classification of assets or liabilities

   (6) Information concerning related party transactions and amounts receivable from or payable to related parties

   (7) Guarantees, whether written or oral, under which the entity is contingently liable

   (8) Significant estimates and material concentrations known to management that are required to be disclosed in accordance with SOP 94-6, *Disclosure of Certain Significant Risks and Uncertainties*

   (9) Violations or possible violations of laws or regulations whose effects should be considered for disclosure in the financial statements or as a basis for recording a loss contingency

   (10) Unasserted claims or assessments that the entity's lawyer has advised are probable of assertion and must be disclosed in accordance with SFAS 5, *Accounting for Contingencies*

   (11) Other liabilities and gain or loss contingencies that are required to be accrued or disclosed by SFAS 5

   (12) Satisfactory title to assets, liens, or encumbrances on assets, and assets pledged as collateral

   (13) Compliance with aspects of contractual agreements that may affect the financial statements

d. Information concerning subsequent events

3336.04 Management's representations may be limited to matters that are considered either individually or collectively material to the financial statements, provided management and the auditor have reached an understanding on materiality for this purpose. Materiality may be different for different representations. If necessary, a discussion of materiality may be included in the representation letter.

3336.05 Materiality considerations would not apply to those representations that are not directly related to amounts included in the financial statements, such as management's acknowledgment of its responsibility for the financial statements and the availability of all financial records.

3336.06 The management representation letter should be addressed to the auditor and should be dated the date of the auditor's report.

3336.07 The letter should be signed by those members of management with overall responsibility for financial and operating matters whom the auditor believes are responsible for and knowledgeable about the matters covered by the representations. Such members of management normally include the chief executive officer and chief financial officer or others with equivalent positions in the entity.

3336.08 If current management was not present during all periods covered by the auditor's report, the auditor should nevertheless obtain written representations from current management on all such periods. The auditor may also want to obtain written representations from other individuals. For example, representations that the board minutes are complete might warrant representation from the person responsible for keeping the minutes.

3336.09 If a predecessor auditor is requested by a former client to reissue the report on prior-period financial statements, and those statements are to be presented on a comparative basis with audited financial statements of a subsequent period, the predecessor auditor should obtain an updating representation letter from the management of the former client. The updating representation letter should state (a) whether any information has come to management's attention that would cause them to believe that any of the previous representations should be modified and (b) whether any events have occurred subsequent to the balance sheet date of the latest financial statements that would require adjustment of or disclosure in those financial statements.

3336.10 If management refuses to furnish a written representation, this is a scope limitation that is sufficient to preclude an unqualified opinion and is ordinarily sufficient to cause an auditor to disclaim an opinion or withdraw from the engagement. However, based on the nature of the representations not obtained or the circumstances of the refusal, the auditor may conclude that a qualified opinion is appropriate. The auditor should consider the effects of the refusal on the ability to rely on other management representations.

3336.11 If the auditor is precluded from performing procedures considered necessary in the circumstances, even though management has given representations concerning the matter, this is a scope limitation and the auditor should issue a qualified opinion or disclaim an opinion on the financial statements.

3337 Independent Calculations

3337.01 The CPA should independently confirm the arithmetic accuracy of the financial statements by footing journals and ledgers, proving account balances, and recalculating depreciation, dividends, interest, accruals, tax liabilities, and other amounts based on formulas.

3338 Accounting Records

3338.01 The CPA should perform tests of the accounting records. These tests may be of balances or of transactions. For example, the CPA will want to verify the beginning and ending inventory and test a sample of debit entries (purchases and purchase returns) and credit entries (shipments and sales).

3338.02 Testing of the accounting records can involve vouching to underlying documents or retracing bookkeeping entries. In making these tests, the direction of the test is important. For example, to vouch from the source document to the entry in the journal tests the objective "all transactions are recorded." To vouch from the journal to the source document tests the objective "all recorded entries have proper documentation."

3338.03 Tests may also be directed primarily toward a particular type of error. For example, tests of receivables are primarily for overstatements, and tests of payables are primarily for understatements.

3339 Analytical Procedures (AU 329)

3339.01 Analytical procedures consist of evaluations of financial information made by a study of plausible relationships among both financial and nonfinancial data. A basic premise underlying the application of analytical procedures is that plausible relationships among data may reasonably be expected to exist and continue in the absence of known conditions to the contrary.

3339.02 Analytical procedures should be applied at two distinct phases in all audits.

1. At the initial planning stages of the audit to assist the auditor in planning the nature, extent, and timing of other auditing procedures

2. As an overall review of the financial information in the final review stage of the audit

3339.03 In some cases, analytical procedures can be more effective or efficient than tests of details for achieving particular substantive testing objectives. For some assertions, analytical procedures are effective in providing the desired level of assurance.

3339.04 Analytical procedures used in planning the audit should focus on the following:

a. Enhancing the auditor's understanding of the client's business and the transactions and events that have occurred since the last audit data

b. Identifying areas that may represent specific risks relevant to the audit

3339.05 Analytical procedures involve comparisons of recorded amounts, or ratios developed from recorded amounts, to expectations developed by the auditor. Examples of sources of information for developing expectations include the following:

a. Financial information for comparable prior period(s) giving consideration to known changes

b. Anticipated results (e.g., budgets or forecasts including extrapolations from interim or annual data)

c. Relationships among elements of financial information within the period

- d. Information regarding the industry in which the client operates (e.g., gross margin information)
- e. Relationships of financial information with relevant nonfinancial information

3339.06 Analytical procedures may be effective and efficient tests for assertions in which potential misstatements would not be apparent from an examination of the detailed evidence or in which detailed evidence is not readily available.

3339.07 The reliability of the data used by the auditor to develop expectations should be appropriate for the desired level of assurance from the analytical procedures. The following factors influence the auditor's consideration of the reliability of data for purposes of achieving audit objectives:

- a. Whether the data was obtained from independent sources outside the entity or from sources within the entity
- b. Whether sources within the entity were independent of those who are responsible for the amount being audited
- c. Whether the data was developed under a reliable system with adequate controls
- d. Whether the data was subjected to audit testing in the current or prior year
- e. Whether the expectations were developed using data from a variety of sources

3339.08 The objective of analytical procedures used in the overall review stage of the audit is to assist the auditor in assessing the conclusions reached and in the evaluation of the overall financial statement presentation. Results of an overall review could indicate that additional evidence may be needed.

3340 Some Statements on Auditing Standards Related to Audit Evidence

3341 Related Parties (AU 334)

3341.01 Related parties of a reporting entity consist of the following:

- a. Its *affiliates*
- b. Its *management* and immediate family
- c. Its *principal owners* and immediate family
- d. Entities for which investments are accounted for under the *equity method*
- e. Any other party with which the reporting entity may deal when one party controls or has the ability to *significantly influence* the management or operating policies of the other

3341.02 Examples of related party transactions include transactions between parent and unconsolidated subsidiaries and transactions between the company and principal shareholders.

3341.03 Sometimes common control—two or more entities under common ownership or management control—should be disclosed even though they do not transact business between or among themselves because mere existence of common control can affect operating results or financial position.

3341.04 In the absence of evidence to the contrary, transactions with related parties should not be assumed to be outside the ordinary course of business.

Related Parties

```
┌─────────────────────────┐         ┌─────────────────────────┐
│ A related party may be  │         │ Entity has the ability  │
│ an affiliate, principal │         │ to significantly        │
│ owner, or management    │- - - - -│ influence management    │
│ and immediate family,   │         │ or operating policies   │
│ investments accounted   │         │ of another entity.      │
│ for by the equity       │         └─────────────────────────┘
│ method.                 │
└───────────┬─────────────┘
            ▼
┌─────────────────────────┐
│ Determine existence of  │
│ related parties.        │
│ See Note 1.             │
└───────────┬─────────────┘
            ▼
┌─────────────────────────┐
│ Identify transactions   │
│ with related parties.   │
│ See Note 2.             │
└───────────┬─────────────┘
            ▼
       ◇ Do related-party ◇
  No ◀── transactions exist? ──▶ Yes
                                  │
                                  ▼
                      ┌─────────────────────┐
                      │ Examine identified  │
                      │ related-party       │
                      │ transactions.       │
                      │ See Note 3.         │
                      └──────────┬──────────┘
                                 ▼
                    Yes ◇ Does auditor fully ◇ No
                     ◀── understand transaction? ──▶
                                                     │
                                                     ▼
                                         ┌───────────────────────┐
                                         │ Apply additional      │
                                         │ procedures.           │
                                         │ See AU 334.10.        │
                                         └───────────┬───────────┘
                      ┌─────────────────────┐        │
                      │ Disclose details of │◀───────┘
                      │ transaction in      │
                      │ financial           │
                      │ statements.         │
                      └──────────┬──────────┘
                                 ▼
                ◇ Do financials contain assertion ◇
         No  ◀── that transaction is equivalent   ──▶ Yes
                    to arms'-length? ◇
                                                       │
                                                       ▼
                              ◇ Is auditor able to determine ◇  Assertion is unsubstantiated
                        Yes ◀── propriety of assertion? ──────▶
                                          │
                                    Auditor is uncertain
```

| If common control exists, disclosure may be necessary for fair presentation. | Issue unqualified opinion. | Add a paragraph describing the uncertainty. | Issue qualified or adverse opinion. |

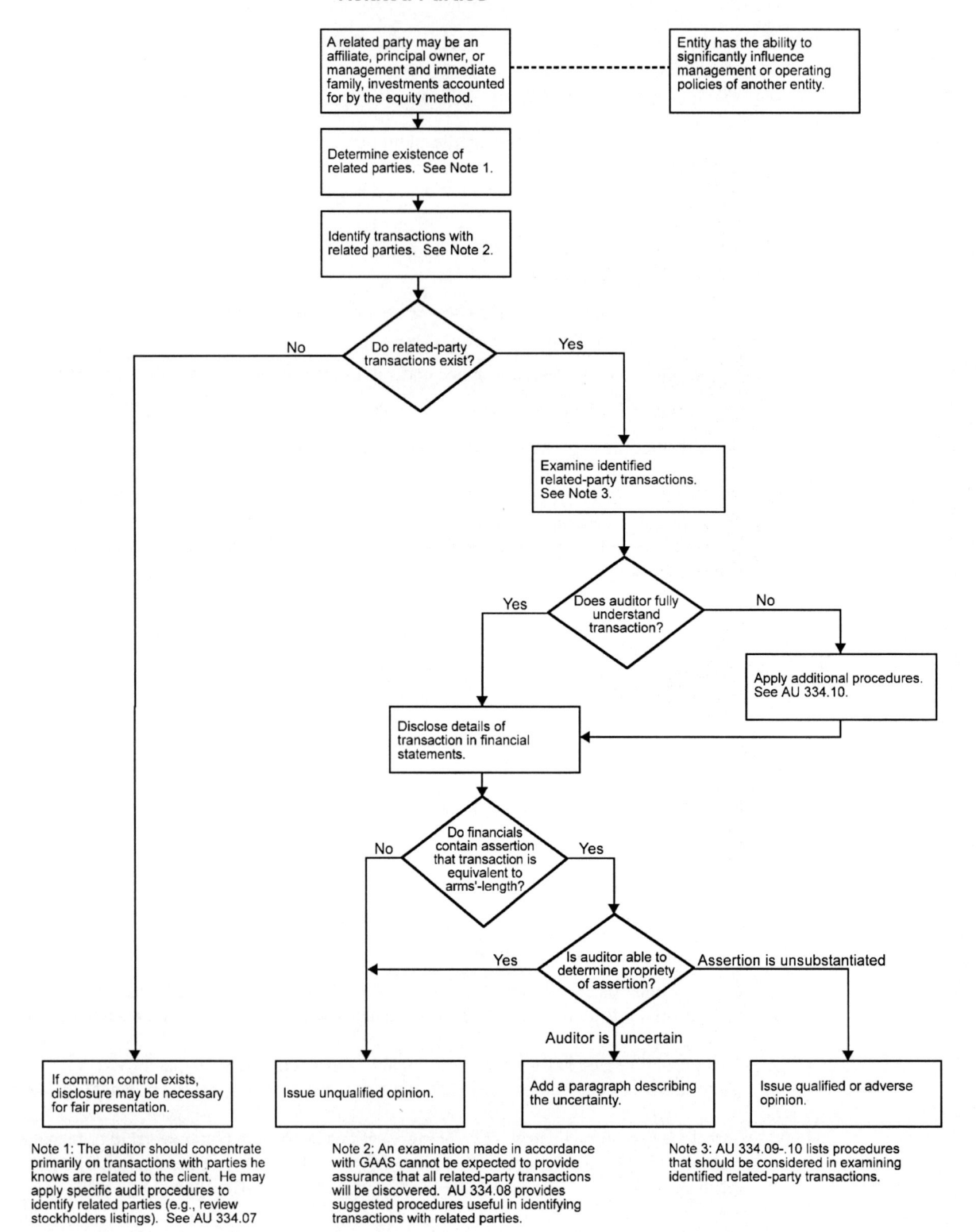

Note 1: The auditor should concentrate primarily on transactions with parties he knows are related to the client. He may apply specific audit procedures to identify related parties (e.g., review stockholders listings). See AU 334.07

Note 2: An examination made in accordance with GAAS cannot be expected to provide assurance that all related-party transactions will be discovered. AU 334.08 provides suggested procedures useful in identifying transactions with related parties.

Note 3: AU 334.09-.10 lists procedures that should be considered in examining identified related-party transactions.

Dan M. Guy and Raymond J. Clay, *The Journal of Accountancy*, July 1977, pp 40-41, updated for SAS 45 issued in August 1983.

3341.05   When the economic substance of a transaction is different from its legal form, the economic substance should be emphasized. Examples of transactions that raise questions as to their substance include the following:

   a. Borrowing or lending on an interest-free basis or at a rate of interest significantly above or below current market rates

   b. Selling real estate at a price that differs significantly from its appraised value

   c. Nonmonetary exchanges

   d. Making loans with no written terms

3341.06   The auditor should be alert to situations, such as the following, that might result in questionable related party transactions:

   a. Lack of sufficient working capital or credit

   b. An urgent desire to improve earnings to bolster the price of stock

   c. An overly optimistic earnings forecast

   d. Dependence on a few products or customers

   e. A declining industry

   f. Excess capacity

   g. Significant litigation

   h. Significant obsolescence in a high technology industry

3341.07   The audit procedure, with regard to related party transactions consists of four steps (see also SFAS 57).

   1. Determine the existence of related parties.

   2. Identify transactions with related parties.

   3. Examine the transactions as to their business purpose, substance, extent, and effect on financial statements.

   4. Be certain the following regarding material related party transactions are disclosed:

      (a) The nature of the relationship(s)

      (b) Description of transactions

      (c) Dollar volume of transactions

      (d) Amounts due from or to related parties and terms, if relevant

3341.08   If the statements contain a representation that is unsubstantiated (e.g., that a related party transaction was equivalent to an arm's-length transaction) with regard to related party transactions, issue a qualified or adverse opinion.

3341.09   Study the flowchart on the preceding page which summarizes the decision steps for related party transactions.

3342 Using the Work of a Specialist (AU 336)

3342.01 A **specialist** is a person or firm possessing special skill or knowledge in a particular field other than accounting or auditing. Guidance applies whether the specialist was engaged by the auditor or by management.

3342.02 The purpose of using a specialist is to obtain sufficient appropriate evidence about items material to the financial statements of which the auditor does not have knowledge. Examples include the following:

a. Valuation—art appraisers, real estate appraisers

b. Physical characteristics relating to quantity on hand or condition—engineers, geologists

c. Amounts derived by special techniques—actuaries

d. Interpretation of technical requirements or documents—attorneys

3342.03 Selecting a specialist. The CPA should consider the specialist's:

a. certification, license, degrees, or other credentials,

b. reputation, and

c. experience.

3342.04 The agreement between the CPA and the specialist should contain the following:

a. Objectives and scope of the work

b. Representations as to relationship, if any, of specialist to the client

c. Methods or assumptions to be used this period

d. Comparison of methods or assumptions to be used with those used in the preceding period

e. Specialist's understanding as to use of results and the appropriateness of using the work for the intended purpose

f. Form and content of specialist's report

3342.05 Use of findings:

a. The CPA should accept the findings of the specialist unless there is evidence to the contrary.

b. If the client and specialist agree, accept results.

c. If the client and specialist disagree, obtain another opinion, if possible. If the difference cannot be resolved, issue a qualified opinion or disclaimer.

d. If an unqualified opinion is issued, do not mention the use of a specialist. In a qualified or adverse opinion, mention the use of a specialist *only* if it will help readers understand the reason of the qualification.

3342.06 Study the following flowchart, which summarizes the decision steps with regard to the use of a specialist.

Using the Work of a Specialist

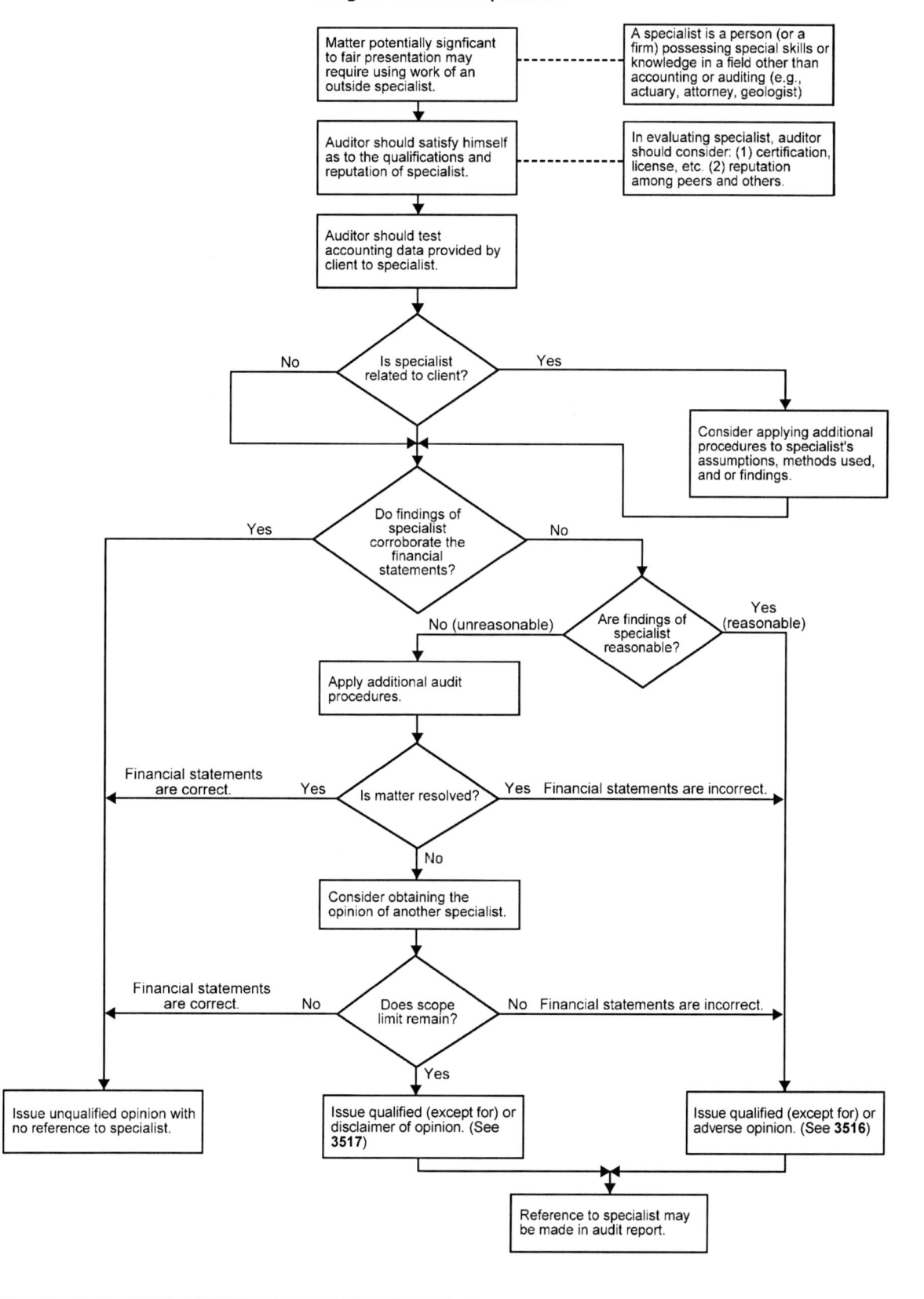

```
┌─────────────────────────────┐         ┌──────────────────────────────┐
│ Matter potentially signficant│ ------- │ A specialist is a person (or │
│ to fair presentation may     │         │ a firm) possessing special   │
│ require using work of an     │         │ skills or knowledge in a     │
│ outside specialist.          │         │ field other than accounting  │
└─────────────┬───────────────┘         │ or auditing (e.g., actuary,  │
              │                          │ attorney, geologist)         │
              ▼                          └──────────────────────────────┘
┌─────────────────────────────┐         ┌──────────────────────────────┐
│ Auditor should satisfy       │ ------- │ In evaluating specialist,    │
│ himself as to the            │         │ auditor should consider:     │
│ qualifications and           │         │ (1) certification, license,  │
│ reputation of specialist.    │         │ etc. (2) reputation among    │
└─────────────┬───────────────┘         │ peers and others.            │
              │                          └──────────────────────────────┘
              ▼
┌─────────────────────────────┐
│ Auditor should test          │
│ accounting data provided by  │
│ client to specialist.        │
└─────────────┬───────────────┘
              ▼
         ◇ Is specialist related to client? ◇
       No ←                              → Yes
                                              ▼
                                  ┌──────────────────────────────┐
                                  │ Consider applying additional │
                                  │ procedures to specialist's   │
                                  │ assumptions, methods used,   │
                                  │ and or findings.             │
                                  └──────────────────────────────┘
         ◇ Do findings of specialist corroborate the financial statements? ◇
  Yes ←                                    → No
                                                ▼
                                    ◇ Are findings of specialist reasonable? ◇
                         No (unreasonable) ←        → Yes (reasonable)
                                    ▼
                         ┌──────────────────────┐
                         │ Apply additional     │
                         │ audit procedures.    │
                         └──────────┬───────────┘
                                    ▼
                         ◇ Is matter resolved? ◇
  Financial statements are correct.  Yes ←    → Yes  Financial statements are incorrect.
                                    ▼ No
                         ┌──────────────────────┐
                         │ Consider obtaining   │
                         │ the opinion of       │
                         │ another specialist.  │
                         └──────────┬───────────┘
                                    ▼
                         ◇ Does scope limit remain? ◇
  Financial statements are correct.  No ←    → No  Financial statements are incorrect.
                                    ▼ Yes
┌──────────────────────┐  ┌────────────────────────┐  ┌──────────────────────┐
│ Issue unqualified    │  │ Issue qualified        │  │ Issue qualified      │
│ opinion with no      │  │ (except for) or        │  │ (except for) or      │
│ reference to         │  │ disclaimer of opinion. │  │ adverse opinion.     │
│ specialist.          │  │ (See 3517)             │  │ (See 3516)           │
└──────────────────────┘  └────────────────────────┘  └──────────────────────┘
                                    │
                         ┌──────────────────────┐
                         │ Reference to         │
                         │ specialist may be    │
                         │ made in audit report.│
                         └──────────────────────┘
```

© 2010 ExamMatrix   Section 3300

3343 Inquiry of a Client's Lawyer (AU 337)

3343.01 Summary of SFAS 5, *Accounting for Contingencies* (AU 337B):

    a. A **contingency** is defined as an existing condition involving uncertainty as to possible gain or loss.

    b. A contingency may be probable, reasonably possible, or remote.

    c. A loss contingency should be accrued if the loss:

        (1) is probable and

        (2) can be reasonably estimated.

    d. Disclosure of contingencies not accrued is required under the following conditions:

        (1) No amount can be reasonably estimated for a probable contingency.

        (2) The contingency is reasonably possible.

        (3) Unasserted claims when assertion is probable and a loss is reasonably possible.

    e. When possible, disclosure should include the range of the estimated loss.

3343.02 Management is responsible for adopting all procedures to identify and account for asserted and unasserted litigation, claims, and assessments (LCA), and management is the primary source of information.

3343.03 With regard to LCA and in accordance with SFAS 5, the auditor must obtain audit evidence relevant to:

    a. its existence,

    b. the accounting period in which its underlying cause occurred,

    c. the degree of probability of an unfavorable outcome, and

    d. the range of potential loss.

3343.04 In addition to normal procedures of inquiry, examining documents, and others, a letter of inquiry must be addressed, with the client's permission, to the client's lawyer as a primary means of obtaining corroborating evidence of LCA.

3343.05 In addition to identifying the company and relevant dates, the letter contains management's list of asserted and unasserted claims. With regard to these items, the lawyer is asked to indicate:

    a. an evaluation of an unfavorable outcome and

    b. an estimated range (if estimable) of potential loss.

3343.06 If any material LCA are omitted from management's list, the lawyer is expected to advise the client of the client's need to disclose any unasserted claims under the provisions of SFAS 5. In some cases, a client's failure to do so may require that the attorney resign.

3343.07 A lawyer may limit a response to matters to which the lawyer has given substantive attention and to matters which individually or collectively are material to the financial statements.

3343.08 A lawyer's refusal to cooperate is a limitation of scope sufficient to preclude an unqualified opinion. Other methods, such as relying on an internal legal department, do not provide evidence of equal quality.

3343.09 If the lawyer is unable to respond in estimating the likelihood of loss and/or the estimated amount, the auditor will ordinarily conclude that he is unable to express an unqualified opinion.

3343.10 The resignation of a client's lawyer should be investigated.

3343.11 Special audit procedures include the following:

   a. Evaluate management policies for identifying and accounting for LCA.

   b. Obtain a listing of LCA through date of report.

   c. Obtain a representation letter from client (see section **3336**).

   d. Examine documents in client's possession, including invoices from lawyers.

   e. Obtain assurance from client regarding unasserted claims for which lawyer has recommended disclosures (it is desirable to confirm with lawyer).

   f. Consider evidence from other standard audit procedures (review of minutes, contracts, etc.) in terms of LCA.

   g. Obtain a letter of audit inquiry:

   (1) List all asserted LCA and unasserted LCA (list prepared by client with lawyer's comment as to completeness or list prepared by lawyer).

   (2) Obtain a description, evaluation of likelihood, and estimation of amount.

   (3) Include a client statement that indicates the client's reliance on the lawyer to advise disclosure with regard to unasserted LCA. Request the lawyer's confirmation.

   h. If lawyer has resigned, then investigate.

3343.12 Study the following flowchart, which summarizes the procedures and decision points with regard to inquiries of client's lawyers.

Inquiry of Client's Lawyer Concerning Litigation, Claims, and Assessments

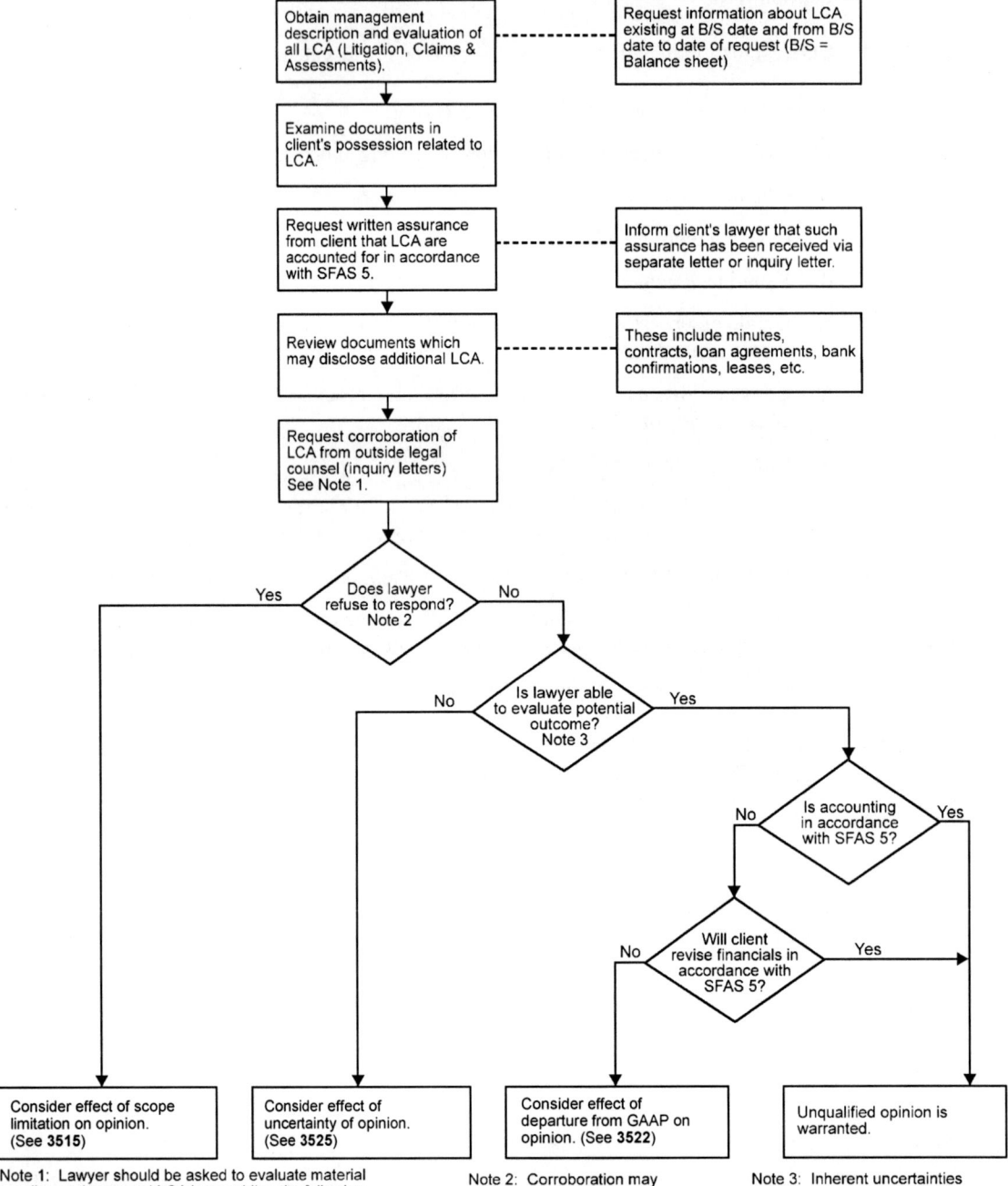

```
┌─────────────────────────┐         ┌─────────────────────────┐
│ Obtain management       │         │ Request information about│
│ description and         │- - - - -│ LCA existing at B/S date │
│ evaluation of all LCA   │         │ and from B/S date to date│
│ (Litigation, Claims &   │         │ of request (B/S =        │
│ Assessments).           │         │ Balance sheet)           │
└───────────┬─────────────┘         └─────────────────────────┘
            ▼
┌─────────────────────────┐
│ Examine documents in    │
│ client's possession     │
│ related to LCA.         │
└───────────┬─────────────┘
            ▼
┌─────────────────────────┐         ┌─────────────────────────┐
│ Request written         │         │ Inform client's lawyer   │
│ assurance from client   │- - - - -│ that such assurance has  │
│ that LCA are accounted  │         │ been received via        │
│ for in accordance with  │         │ separate letter or       │
│ SFAS 5.                 │         │ inquiry letter.          │
└───────────┬─────────────┘         └─────────────────────────┘
            ▼
┌─────────────────────────┐         ┌─────────────────────────┐
│ Review documents which  │         │ These include minutes,   │
│ may disclose additional │- - - - -│ contracts, loan          │
│ LCA.                    │         │ agreements, bank         │
│                         │         │ confirmations, leases,etc│
└───────────┬─────────────┘         └─────────────────────────┘
            ▼
┌─────────────────────────┐
│ Request corroboration of│
│ LCA from outside legal  │
│ counsel (inquiry letters)│
│ See Note 1.             │
└───────────┬─────────────┘
            ▼
       ╱Does lawyer╲
  Yes ╱ refuse to   ╲ No
◄────╱  respond?     ╲────►
     ╲   Note 2     ╱
      ╲           ╱
       ╲         ╱
            │
            ▼
       ╱ Is lawyer  ╲
  No  ╱ able to      ╲ Yes
◄────╱ evaluate       ╲────►
     ╲ potential     ╱
      ╲ outcome?    ╱
       ╲ Note 3   ╱
            │
            ▼
                    ╱ Is accounting╲
                No ╱ in accordance  ╲ Yes
              ◄───╱   with SFAS 5?   ╲───►
                  ╲                 ╱
                            │
                            ▼
                       ╱ Will client ╲
                   No ╱ revise         ╲ Yes
                 ◄───╱ financials in    ╲───►
                     ╲ accordance with ╱
                      ╲    SFAS 5?    ╱
```

| Consider effect of scope limitation on opinion. (See 3515) | Consider effect of uncertainty of opinion. (See 3525) | Consider effect of departure from GAAP on opinion. (See 3522) | Unqualified opinion is warranted. |

Note 1: Lawyer should be asked to evaluate material pending or threatened LCA by providing the following information:
1. Nature and progress of each.
2. Client proposed course of action.
3. Likelihood of unfavorable outcome and amount or range of potential loss.
4. Any LCA omitted by client's representation.
5. Disagreement with client's stated position.
6. Acknowledge that any unasserted claims required to be disclosed according to SFAS 5 will be discussed with client.
7. The reason for any limitation on his response.

Note 2: Corroboration may come from inside counsel but should never be considered a substitute for refusal by outside counsel.

Note 3: Inherent uncertainties sometimes preclude evaluation of potential outcomes by legal counsel.

3344 Auditing Accounting Estimates (AU 342)

3344.01 Management is responsible for making the accounting estimates included in the financial statements. As estimates are based on subjective as well as objective factors, it may be difficult for management to establish controls over them.

3344.02 The auditor is responsible for evaluating the reasonableness of accounting estimates made by management. When planning and performing procedures to evaluate accounting estimates, the auditor should consider, with an attitude of professional skepticism, both the subjective and objective factors.

3344.03 An entity's internal control may reduce the likelihood of material misstatements of accounting estimates.

3344.04 The auditor's objective when evaluating accounting estimates is to obtain sufficient appropriate audit evidence to provide reasonable assurance that:

    a. all accounting estimates that could be material to the financial statements have been developed,

    b. those accounting estimates are reasonable in the circumstances, and

    c. the accounting estimates are presented in conformity with applicable accounting principles and are properly disclosed.

3344.05 In evaluating the reasonableness of an estimate, the auditor normally concentrates on key factors and assumptions that are significant to the accounting estimate. The auditor should consider the historical experience of the entity in making past estimates as well as the auditor's experience in the industry.

3345 Compliance Auditing Considerations in Audits of Governmental Entities and Recipients of Governmental Financial Assistance (AU 801)

3345.01 SAS 74 reduces the level of detail provided at the auditing standards level. The detail being eliminated by superseding SAS 68 with SAS 74 is currently provided in the *Audit Guide, Audits of State and Local Governmental Units,* and in SOP 92-9. The detailed guidance on testing and reporting provided in the audit guide and in the SOP are the same as the guidance provided in SAS 68. There is no change in that guidance.

3345.02 Specifically, SAS 74 provides general guidance to the auditor to do the following:

    a. Apply the guidance of SAS 54, *Illegal Acts by Clients,* relative to detecting misstatements resulting from illegal acts related to laws and regulations that have a direct and material effect on the determination of financial statement amounts in audits of financial statements of governmental entities and recipients of financial assistance.

    b. Perform a financial audit in accordance with Government Auditing Standards (the Yellow Book).

    c. Perform a single or organization-wide audit or a program-specific audit in accordance with federal audit requirements.

    d. Communicate with management when the auditor becomes aware that the entity is subject to an audit requirement that may not be encompassed in the terms of the engagement.

3345.03 To clarify the applicability of SSAE 3, SAS 74 states that SSAE 3 provides guidance for engagements related to management's assertions about an entity's compliance with the requirements of specified laws, regulations, rules, or contracts not involving governmental financial assistance.

3345.04 Management is responsible for ensuring that the entity complies with the laws and regulations applicable to its activities. That responsibility encompasses the identification of applicable laws and regulations and the establishment of internal control policies and procedures designed to provide reasonable assurance that the entity complies with those laws and regulations.

3345.05 The auditor's responsibility for testing and reporting on compliance with laws and regulations varies according to the terms of the engagement. SAS 54 describes the auditor's responsibility, in an audit performed in accordance with GAAS, for considering laws and regulations and how they affect the audit.

3345.06 The auditor should obtain an understanding of the possible effects on financial statements of laws and regulations that are generally recognized by auditors to have a direct and material effect on the determination of amounts in an entity's financial statements. Paragraph 7 of SAS 74 lists procedures the auditor should consider performing in assessing laws and regulations and obtaining an understanding of their possible effects on the financial statements.

3345.07 Government auditing standards, which include designing the audit to provide reasonable assurance of detecting material misstatements resulting from noncompliance with provisions of contracts or grant agreements that have a direct and material effect on the determination of financial statement amounts, are to be followed when required by law, regulation, agreement, contract, or policy.

3345.08 A recipient of federal financial assistance may be subject to a single or organization-wide audit or to a program-specific audit. A number of federal audit regulations permit the recipient to "elect" to have a program-specific audit in certain circumstances.

3345.09 In planning the audit, the auditor should determine and consider the specific federal audit requirements applicable to the engagement, including the issuance of additional reports.

3345.10 Compliance requirements applicable to federal financial assistance programs are usually one of two types—general or specific. General requirements involve national policy and apply to all or most federal financial assistance programs. Specific requirements apply to a particular federal program and generally arise from statutory requirements and regulations. Generally, the auditor is required to determine whether the recipient has complied with the general and specific requirements.

3346 Auditing Fair Value Measurements and Disclosures (AU 328)

3346.01 The guidance in this standard deals with fair value measurements and disclosures contained in financial statements.

3346.02 The auditor should obtain sufficient appropriate audit evidence to provide reasonable assurance that fair value measurements and disclosures are in conformity with GAAP.

3346.03 FASB Statement of Financial Accounting Concepts No. 7, *Using Cash Flow Information and Present Value in Accounting Measurements*, defines the fair value of an asset (liability) as "the amount at which that asset (or liability) could be bought (or incurred) or sold (or settled) in a current transaction between willing parties, that is, other than in a forced or liquidation sale."

3346.04 Although GAAP may not proscribe the method for measuring the fair value of an item, it expresses a preference for the use of observable market prices to make that determination. In the absence of observable market prices, GAAP requires fair value to be based on the best information available in the circumstances.

3346.05 Assumptions used in fair value measurements are similar in nature to those required when developing other accounting estimates. However, if observable market prices are not available, GAAP requires that valuation methods incorporate assumptions that marketplace participants would use in their estimates of fair value whenever that information is available without undue cost and effort.

3346.06 The auditor should obtain an understanding of the entity's process for determining fair value measurements and disclosures and of the relevant controls sufficient to develop an effective audit approach.

3346.07 The auditor should evaluate whether the fair value measurements and disclosures in the financial statements are in conformity with GAAP. The evaluation of the entity's fair value measurements and of the audit evidence depends, in part, on the auditor's knowledge of the nature of the business.

3346.08 When there are no observable market prices and the entity estimates fair value using a valuation method, the auditor should evaluate whether the entity's method of measurement is appropriate in the circumstances. That evaluation requires the use of professional judgment and the auditor should consider whether:

   a. management has sufficiently evaluated and appropriately applied the criteria, if any, provided by GAAP to support the selected method.

   b. the valuation method is appropriate in the circumstances given the nature of the item being valued.

   c. the valuation method is appropriate in relation to the business, industry, and environment.

3346.09 The auditor should consider whether to engage a specialist and use the work of that specialist as audit evidence in performing substantive tests to evaluate material financial statement assertions. The auditor may have the necessary skill and knowledge to plan and perform audit procedures related to fair values or may decide to use the work of a specialist.

3346.10 Because of the wide range of possible fair value measurements, from relatively simple to complex, and the varying levels of risk of material misstatement associated with the process for determining fair values, the auditor's planned audit procedures can vary significantly in nature, timing, and extent.

3346.11 The auditor's understanding of the reliability of the process used by management to determine fair value is an important element in support of the resulting amounts and therefore affects the nature, timing, and extent of audit procedures. When testing the entity's fair value measurements and disclosures, the auditor evaluates whether:

   a. management's assumptions are reasonable and reflect, or are not inconsistent with, market information.

   b. the fair value measurement was determined using an appropriate model, if applicable.

   c. management used relevant information that was reasonably available at the time.

3346.12 The auditor considers the sensitivity of the valuation to changes in significant assumptions, including market conditions that may affect the value. Where applicable, the auditor encourages management to use techniques such as sensitivity analysis to help identify particularly sensitive assumptions.

3346.13 To be reasonable, the assumptions on which the fair value measurements are based individually and taken as a whole, need to be realistic and consistent with:

   a. the general economic environment, the economic environment of the specific industry, and the entity's economic circumstances.

   b. existing market information.

   c. the plans of the entity, including what management expects will be the outcome of specific objectives and strategies.

   d. assumptions made in prior periods, if appropriate.

   e. past experience of, or previous conditions experienced by, the entity to the extent currently applicable.

   f. other matters, relating to the financial statements. For example, assumptions used by management in accounting estimates for financial statement accounts other than those relating to fair value measurements and disclosures.

   g. the risk associated with cash flows, if applicable, including the potential variability in the amount and timing of the cash flows and the related effect on the discount rate.

3346.14 The auditor should evaluate whether the disclosures about fair values made by the entity are in conformity with GAAP. Disclosure of fair value information is an important aspect of financial statements. Often, fair value disclosure is required because of the relevance to users in the evaluation of an entity's performance and financial position.

3346.15 When disclosure of fair value information under GAAP is omitted because it is not practicable to determine fair value with sufficient reliability, the auditor evaluates the adequacy of disclosures required in these circumstances. If the entity has not appropriately disclosed fair value information required by GAAP, the auditor evaluates whether the financial statements are materially misstated.

3346.16 The auditor ordinarily should obtain written representations from management regarding the reasonableness of significant assumptions, including whether they appropriately reflect management's intent and ability to carry out specific courses of action on behalf of the entity where relevant to the use of fair value measurements and disclosures.

3346.17 Depending on the nature, materiality, and complexity of fair values, management representations about fair value measurements and disclosures contained in the financial statements also may include representations about:

    a. the appropriateness of the measurement methods, including related assumptions, used by management in determining fair value and the consistency in application of the methods.

    b. the completeness and adequacy of disclosures related to fair values.

    c. whether subsequent events require adjustment to the fair value measurement and disclosures included in the financial statements.

3346.18 The auditor should determine that the audit committee is informed about the process used by management in formulating particularly sensitive accounting estimates, including fair value estimates, and about the basis for the auditor's conclusions regarding the reasonableness of those estimates.

3347 Auditing Derivative Instruments, Hedging Activities, and Investments in Securities (SAS 92)

3347.01 SAS 92 provides guidance to auditors in planning and performing auditing procedures for assertions about derivative instruments, hedging activities, and investments in securities that are made in an entity's financial statements.

3347.02 The term *derivative* as used in this SAS is defined in SFAS 133, *Accounting for Derivative Instruments and Hedging Activities.* This SAS uses the definitions of debt security and equity security that are in SFAS 115, *Accounting for Certain Investments in Debt and Equity Securities.*

3347.03 The auditor may need special skill or knowledge to plan and perform auditing procedures for certain assertions about derivatives and securities. Such skills would apply to understanding the entity's information system for derivatives and securities, identifying controls, understanding GAAP and fair value techniques, and assessing risk.

3347.04 The inherent risk for an assertion about a derivative or security is its susceptibility to a material misstatement, assuming there are no related controls. Examples of considerations that might affect the auditor's assessment of inherent risk for assertions about a derivative or security include the following:

    a. Management's objectives

    b. The complexity of the features of the derivative or security

    c. Whether the transaction that gave rise to the derivative or security involved the exchange of cash

    d. The entity's experience with the derivative or security

    e. Whether a derivative is freestanding or an embedded feature of an agreement

    f. Whether external factors affect the assertion

    g. The evolving nature of derivatives and the applicable GAAP

    h. Significant reliance on outside parties

    i. GAAP may require developing assumptions about future conditions

3347.05 The extent of the understanding of internal control over derivatives and securities obtained by the auditor depends on how much information the auditor needs to identify the types of potential misstatements, consider factors that affect the risk of material misstatement, design tests of controls where appropriate, and design substantive tests.

3347.06 After obtaining the understanding of internal control over derivatives and security transactions, the auditor should assess control risk for the related assertions.

3347.07 The auditor should use the assessed level of inherent risk and control risk for assertions about derivatives and securities to determine the nature, extent, and timing of the substantive procedures to be performed to detect material misstatements of the financial statement assertions.

3347.08 The consideration of financial statement assertions by the auditor, related to derivatives and securities, should include the following:

    a. **Existence or occurrence:** Address whether the derivatives and securities reported in the financial statements through recognition or disclosure exist at the date of the statement of financial position, and that transactions reported in the financial statements related to derivatives and securities have occurred.

    b. **Completeness:** Address whether all of the entity's derivatives and securities are reported in the financial statements through recognition or disclosure. It also addresses whether all derivatives and securities transactions are reported in the financial statements as a part of earnings, other comprehensive income, cash flows, or through disclosure.

    c. **Rights and obligations:** Address whether the entity has the rights and obligations associated with derivatives and securities, including pledging arrangements, reported in the financial statements.

    d. **Valuation:** Address whether the amounts reported in the financial statements through measurement or disclosure were determined in conformity with GAAP.

    e. **Presentation and disclosure:** Address whether the classification, description, and disclosure of derivatives and securities in the entity's financial statements are in conformity with GAAP.

3347.09 The auditor should gather audit evidence to determine whether management complied with the hedge accounting requirements of GAAP, including designation and documentation requirements.

3347.10 The auditor should gather audit evidence to support management's expectation at the inception of the hedge that the hedging relationship will be highly effective and its periodic assessment of the ongoing effectiveness of the hedging relationship as required by GAAP.

3347.11 The auditor ordinarily should obtain written representations from management confirming aspects of management's intent and ability that affect assertions about derivatives and securities, such as its intent and ability to hold a debt security until its maturity or to enter into a forecasted transaction for which hedge accounting is applied.

3350 General Audit Procedures

3351 Preliminary Steps

    3351.01   Arrange preengagement review and conference.

    3351.02   Take plant and office tour.

    3351.03   Have discussion with predecessor auditor, if applicable.

    3351.04   Decide whether to accept or continue client.

    3351.05   Prepare engagement letter.

    3351.06   Plan and schedule the audit.

3352 General Review of Permanent Files and Records

    3352.01   Review organizational chart.

    3352.02   Review articles of incorporation and bylaws.

    3352.03   Read minutes of board of directors' meetings with regard to the following:

        a. Officer compensation

        b. Union contracts

        c. Fringe benefits

        d. Pension plans

        e. Profit sharing and bonuses

        f. Dividends

        g. Treasury stock transactions

        h. Investment transactions

        i. Bond issues

        j. Purchase contracts

        k. Sales contracts

    3352.04   Review financial statements and audit reports of prior years.

    3352.05   Review registration and other SEC reports.

    3352.06   Review prior years' tax returns.

    3352.07   Review financial records, including the following:

        a. Chart of accounts

        b. Accounting policies

        c. General ledger

    d. Subsidiary ledger

    e. General journal

    f. Special journals

3353 Audit Objectives—Apply as Appropriate

3353.01 Internal control.

3353.02 Existence.

3353.03 Valuation.

3353.04 Authorization.

3353.05 Ownership.

3353.06 Restrictions.

3353.07 Cutoff.

3353.08 Reasonable accuracy.

3353.09 Unrecorded items.

3353.10 Financial statement presentation.

3354 Audit Procedures—Apply as Appropriate

3354.01 Assess control risk.

3354.02 Compare beginning balance with last year's figures.

3354.03 Foot totals.

3354.04 Analyze account transactions.

3354.05 Scan for unusual transactions.

3354.06 Trace bookkeeping entries.

3354.07 Vouch to underlying documents.

3354.08 Agree subsidiary records to general ledger.

3354.09 Review cutoff.

3354.10 Perform analytical review.

3354.11 Inquire of appropriate client management.

3354.12 Count cash, investments, etc.

3354.13 Examine or inspect authoritative documents.

3354.14 Observe pertinent activities.

3354.15 Confirm payables, receivables, cash accounts, and investments.

3354.16 Reconcile related records or accounts.

3354.17 Recalculate client's figures.

3354.18 Determine financial statement presentation.

3355 End of Audit Procedures

3355.01 Obtain letter of representation from management.

3355.02 Apply subsequent event procedures.

3355.03 Obtain lawyer's response to letter of inquiry.

3355.04 Prepare auditor's report.

3360 Auditing Procedures for Assets and Related Revenue and Expense

3361 Cash

3361.01 Assess control risk.

3361.02 Test cash transactions as follows:

    a. Foot cash journals.

    b. Trace postings to ledger accounts.

    c. Agree details of bank deposits to client records.

    d. Reconcile bank activity for one or two months with cash account activity.

    e. Verify cash transactions in one or more expense accounts.

3361.03 Count all cash on hand with custodian present.

3361.04 Verify cutoff of cash receipts and cash disbursements.

3361.05 Confirm amounts on deposit with banks.

3361.06 Prepare four-column bank reconciliation as follows:

    a. Trace checks to cash disbursement.

    b. Account for all checks.

    c. Review deposits.

    d. Review outstanding checks beginning and end.

    e. Investigate NSF checks and other unusual items.

3361.07 Obtain bank cutoff statements 10 to 15 days after year-end.

3361.08 Trace all bank transfers—be alert for kiting.

3361.09 Determine balance sheet presentation (restrictions, cash in foreign or closed banks).

3362 Marketable Securities and Investment Revenue

3362.01 Assess control risk.

3362.02 Analyze marketable securities and investment revenue accounts.

3362.03 Examine securities on hand with custodian present (simultaneously with cash, compare serial numbers with records).

3362.04 Confirm securities in possession of others.

3362.05 Verify purchases and sales of securities during the year.

3362.06 Perform cutoff review.

3362.07 Verify gain or loss on security transactions.

3362.08 Recalculate dividend and interest income.

3362.09 Determine proper accounting methods.

3362.10 Investigate investments in related parties.

3362.11 Determine market value.

3362.12 Determine financial statement presentation (at fair value, pledged).

3363 Accounts Receivable and Revenues

3363.01 Assess control risk.

3363.02 Test revenue and receivables transactions as follows:

    a. Examine a sample of sales transactions.

    b. Compare a sample of sales invoices and shipping documents.

    c. Test a sample of sales invoices for clerical accuracy.

    d. Examine a sample of credit memoranda.

    e. Examine a sample of cash discounts.

    f. Vouch a sample of cash register tapes and sales invoices to the sales journal.

    g. Foot the sales journal.

    h. Trace a sample of postings from the sales journal to the accounts receivable ledger.

3363.03 Prepare aging of accounts receivable.

3363.04 Review adequacy of allowance for bad debts and bad-debt expense.

3363.05 Reconcile subsidiary ledger to control accounts.

3363.06 Confirm accounts receivable—positive and negative (see flowchart at section **3333.07**).

3363.07 Review collections subsequent to year-end.

3363.08 Perform cutoff review—vouch sales transactions before and after year-end and examine sales returns.

3363.09 Review receivables from related parties.

3363.10 Inquire as to restrictions.

3363.11 Review write-offs of accounts receivable.

3363.12 Perform analytical review—gross profit.

3363.13 Obtain client representation letter.

3363.14 Determine financial statement presentation (current, nontrade, pledged, or assigned, repaid loans to insiders, installment).

3364 Notes Receivable and Interest Income

3364.01 Assess control risk.

3364.02 Test a sample of transactions.

3364.03 Perform account analysis.

3364.04 Confirm notes receivable.

3364.05 Inspect notes.

3364.06 Evaluate collectibility.

3364.07 Review subsequent collections.

3364.08 Inquire as to discounted notes and other restrictions leading to contingent liabilities.

3364.09 Recalculate interest income.

3364.10 Obtain client representation letter.

3364.11 Determine financial statement presentation (restrictions, insiders, contingent liabilities).

3365 Inventories and Cost of Goods Sold

3365.01 Assess control risk.

3365.02 Test a sample of transactions as follows:
   a. Compare a sample of purchase requisitions, purchase orders, receiving reports, and vendors' invoices.
   b. Test and evaluate cost accounting system.

3365.03 Participate in planning of physical inventory.

3365.04 Observe the taking of physical inventory as follows:
   a. Make test counts.
   b. Trace test counts to inventory sheets.
   c. Trace test counts to perpetual inventory records.
   d. Verify all inventory tagged.
   e. Test clerical accuracy of inventory sheets and perpetual records.

3365.05 Review cutoff receiving reports and invoices, look for F.O.B. shipping point.

3365.06 Determine quality and condition.

3365.07 Inquire about goods held on consignment.

3365.08 Confirm goods held in public warehouses.

3365.09 Confirm and verify goods shipped on consignment.

3365.10 Review basis and methods for inventory pricing.

3365.11 Test pricing.

3365.12 Apply lower of cost or market.

3365.13 Perform analytical review.

3365.14 Inquire as to pledged inventory and other restrictions.

3365.15 Review analysis of cost of sales.

3365.16 Review and test cost accounting system.

3365.17 Investigate cost variances.

3365.18 Obtain client representation letter.

3365.19 Determine financial statement presentation (classification, pledged).

3366 Property, Plant, and Equipment—Depreciation and Depletion

3366.01 Assess control risk.

3366.02 Test transactions.

3366.03 Perform account analysis.

3366.04 Reconcile subsidiary ledgers to control accounts.

3366.05 Verify legal ownership.

3366.06 Verify additions.

3366.07 Verify disposals.

3366.08 Recalculate gains and losses.

3366.09 Make physical inspections of additions.

3366.10 Perform analysis of repairs and maintenance.

3366.11 Review accounting policies with regard to capitalization.

3366.12 Review accounting policies with regard to depreciation.

3366.13 Recalculate depreciation and depletion.

3366.14 Perform analytical review.

3366.15 Investigate property not used in the business.

3366.16 Review revenue from rentals and disposals.

3366.17 Review lease agreements.

3366.18 Inquire as to restrictions and adequacy of depreciation.

3366.19 Determine financial statement presentation (major classes, depreciation methods, basis of valuation, estimated lines restrictions, leases).

3367 Long-Term Investments (Items .04–.07 Based on AU 332)

3367.01 Assess control risk.

3367.02 Perform account analysis.

3367.03 Verify all transactions by reference to authorization and documentary evidence.

3367.04 Inspect and count securities and records.

3367.05 Confirm securities with independent custodian.

3367.06 Obtain evidence for carrying value and earnings therefrom.

    a. Obtain audited statements, if available.

    b. If audited statements are not available, extend unit tests depending on materiality of investment. May rely on investee's auditor.

    c. Use market quotations when based on broad and active market.

    d. Use personal valuations only if available and reasonable.

    e. If collateral is important with regard to collectibility, ascertain existence, market value, and transferability.

3367.07 When equity method is used, the CPA must be satisfied as to client's methods of accounting.

    a. Verify percentage ownership (20%–50%).

    b. Verify significant influence.

    c. Verify consistency from year to year.

    d. Verify elimination of intercompany transactions.

    e. Determine effect of subsequent statement.

3367.08 Recalculate dividend income.

3367.09 Trace dividends received to cash receipts.

3367.10 Inspect land and other assets not used in business.

3367.11 Review scrap sales for unrecorded disposals.

3367.12 Inquire of management with regard to status of long-term investments.

3367.13 Verify income related to investments.

3367.14 Determine financial statement presentation (cost or equity methods).

3370 Auditing Procedures for Liabilities and Stockholders' Equity

3371 Accounts Payable

3371.01 Assess control risk.

3371.02 Test accounts payable transactions as follows:

a. Vouch to postings a sample of transactions in accounts payable subsidiary ledger.

b. Trace postings from accounts payable control to subsidiary ledger.

c. Verify sample of cash discount and purchase returns.

3371.03 Prepare trial balance of accounts payable at balance sheet date and reconcile to general ledger account.

3371.04 Compare a sample of monthly statements to trial balance.

3371.05 Examine subsequent cash payments to search for unrecorded liabilities.

3371.06 Confirm certain accounts, if appropriate.

3371.07 Review payables to related parties.

3371.08 Investigate debit balances.

3371.09 Vouch selected balances payable to supporting documents.

3371.10 Inquire as to unrecorded liabilities.

3371.11 Obtain client representation letter.

3371.12 Determine financial statement presentation (nontrade, related parties, debit balances, consignments).

3372 Other Current Liabilities—Examples: Accrued Payroll and Payroll Expense

3372.01 Assess control risk.

3372.02 Test payroll transactions as follows:

a. Trace names and wage or salary rates to records in personnel department.

b. Trace time shown on payable timecards.

c. Verify payroll deductions to legal requirements and employee requests.

d. Test extensions and footings of payroll.

  e. Compare totals of payroll to totals of payroll checks.

  f. Examine paid checks for endorsements and compare with payroll.

  g. Review treatment of unclaimed checks.

3372.03 Review authorization for all payrolls.

3372.04 Review control procedures for payment of cash and/or distribution of checks.

3372.05 On a surprise basis, observe a payroll distribution.

3372.06 Observe payroll procedures such as use of time clocks.

3372.07 Conduct analytical review.

3372.08 Recalculate accrued payroll.

3372.09 Recalculate payroll taxes and other withholdings.

3372.10 Test subsequent payment of accrued payroll and payroll taxes and other withholdings.

3372.11 Review officers' salaries and trace to authorizations.

3372.12 Perform audit procedures on piece-rate or commissions, if appropriate.

3372.13 Determine financial statement presentation.

3373 Interest-Bearing Debt and Related Expense

3373.01 Assess control risk.

3373.02 Prepare account analysis of notes payable, bonds payable, and related interest, premium, and discount accounts.

3373.03 Verify additions and retirements during year by vouching to supporting documents.

3373.04 Search for unrecorded liabilities.

3373.05 Recalculate interest expense, interest payable, and amortization.

3373.06 Trace interest to debt for completeness.

3373.07 Examine subsequent payments of notes and interest.

3373.08 Confirm interest-bearing debt.

3373.09 Confirm with trustees of sinking funds or other assets.

3373.10 Examine notes, mortgages, and bond indenture.

3373.11 Verify authorization by reading minutes of meetings.

3373.12 Determine that all provisions of indentures have been met.

3373.13 Determine financial statement presentation (interest rate, maturity, pledged assets, current portion, covenants).

3374 Contingent Liabilities

3374.01 Types:

    a. Pending litigation

    b. Income tax disputes

    c. Notes receivable discounted

    d. Accounts sold at recourse

    e. Accommodation endorsement of rates

    f. Renegotiation of U.S. government contracts

3374.02 Read minutes of meetings of board of directors.

3374.03 Read contracts.

3374.04 Review confirmations (banks and others).

3374.05 Obtain a letter from client's lawyer.

3374.06 Review pertinent correspondence.

3374.07 Inquire of client.

3374.08 Obtain client representation letter.

3374.09 Determine financial statement presentation.

3375 Stockholders' Equity and Dividends

3375.01 Assess control risk.

3375.02 Prepare analysis of capital stock and paid-in capital accounts.

3375.03 Verify all transactions as to computation and authorization.

3375.04 Read minutes of meetings of board of directors and officers.

3375.05 Account for proceeds of stock issues.

3375.06 Confirm shares outstanding with registrar and transfer agent.

3375.07 Reconcile subsidiary stock ledger to control account.

3375.08 Inspect treasury stock or confirm with broker.

3375.09 Verify treasury stock transactions.

3375.10 Examine canceled certificates and account for certificate numbers.

3375.11 Review stock option plans for compliance and disclosure.

3375.12 Analyze retained earnings and appropriations of retained earnings.

3375.13 Examine and verify all retained earnings transactions.

3375.14 Recalculate dividends and verify authorization of dividends transactions.

3375.15 Reconcile bank dividend accounts.

3375.16 Obtain client representation letter.

3375.17 Determine financial statement presentation (capital stock described, stock options, appropriations, retained earnings statement, treasury stock).

Section 3400
Audit Sampling

3410 Statistical and Nonstatistical Sampling (AU 350)
    3411 Audit Sampling Defined
    3412 Uncertainty and Audit Sampling
    3413 Sampling in Substantive Tests of Detail
    3414 Sampling in Assessing Control Risk
    3415 Selecting a Sampling Approach

3420 Statistical Sampling
    3421 Definition of Statistical Sampling
    3422 Types of Statistical Sampling Models
    3423 Advantages of Statistical Sampling
    3424 Disadvantages of Statistical Sampling
    3425 Professional Judgment in Statistical Sampling

3430 Selecting a Representative Sample
    3431 Definitions
    3432 Random Number Tables
    3433 Systematic Selection
    3434 Probability-Proportional-to-Size Sampling (Dollar Unit Sampling)
    3435 Difference and Ratio Estimation
    3436 Stratified Sampling
    3437 Factors Influencing Sample Size

3440 Attribute Sampling
    3441 Attributes Defined
    3442 Setting Reliability Levels and Tolerable Rates
    3443 Attribute Sampling Tables

3450 Discovery Sampling
    3451 Discovery Sampling Defined
    3452 Discovery Sampling Tables

3460 Variable Sampling—Accounting Estimation
    3461 Accounting Estimation Defined
    3462 Selected Statistical Terms Defined
    3463 Accounting Estimation Model

3470 Variable Sampling—Audit Hypothesis Approach
    3471 Risks of Incorrect Rejection and Incorrect Acceptance
    3472 Audit Risk (or Ultimate Risk)
    3473 Audit Hypothesis Model

3410 Statistical and Nonstatistical Sampling (AU 350)

3411 Audit Sampling Defined

3411.01 **Audit sampling:** The application of an audit procedure to less than 100% of the items within an account balance or class of transactions.

3411.02 There are two general approaches to audit sampling.

1. Nonstatistical (AU 350 does not use the term *judgment sampling,* because both statistical and nonstatistical sampling require the use of judgment)

2. Statistical

Either approach, when properly applied, can provide sufficient audit evidence.

3412 Uncertainty and Audit Sampling

3412.01 **Audit risk** (also referred to as ultimate risk): A combination of the risk that material error will occur in the accounting process by which the financial statements are developed, and the risk that any material errors that occur will not be detected by the auditor.

3412.02 Audit risk includes both uncertainties due to sampling and uncertainties due to factors other than sampling. These aspects of audit risk are as follows:

a. Sampling risk

b. Nonsampling risk (human error)

3412.03 **Sampling risk:** Arises from the possibility that when a compliance or a substantive test is restricted to a sample of balances or transactions, the auditor's conclusions about the account balance or class of transactions may be different from the conclusions reached if the test were applied in the same way to all items in the account balance or class of transactions.

3412.04 For a sample of a specific design, sampling risk varies inversely with sample size—the smaller the sample size, the greater the sampling risk.

3412.05 **Nonsampling risk:** Includes all the aspects of audit risk that are not due to sampling.

3412.06 Examples of nonsampling risk include the following:

a. Failure to properly define the audit population

b. Failure to define clearly the nature of an audit exception

c. Failure to recognize an error when one exists in the sample

d. Failure to evaluate sample findings properly

3412.07 Nonsampling risk can be reduced to a negligible level by adequate quality control and review.

3412.08 The auditor should consider sampling risk whether nonstatistical or statistical sampling is used and should apply professional judgment to assess this risk.

3412.09 The auditor is concerned with two aspects of sampling risk in performing substantive tests of details:

1. The risk of incorrect acceptance
2. The risk of incorrect rejection

Audit Evidence Indicates	Client's Book Value is: Fairly Stated	Not Fairly Stated
Accept	Correct decision	Risk of incorrect acceptance
Reject	Risk of incorrect rejection	Correct decision

3412.10 The auditor is also concerned with two aspects of sampling risk in performing tests of controls of internal accounting control:

1. The risk of assessing control risk too low
2. The risk of assessing control risk too high

Tests of Controls Sample	Client's Internal Control Structure is: Reliable	Unreliable
Accept	Correct decision	Risk of assessing control risk too low
Reject	Risk of assessing control risk too high	Correct decision

3412.11 Note: AU 350 (*Audit Sampling*) uses the terms *risk of assessing control risk too low* and *risk of incorrect acceptance* instead of *beta risk*. AU 350 also uses the terms *risk of assessing control risk too high* and *risk of incorrect rejection* instead of *alpha risk*.

3413 Sampling in Substantive Tests of Detail

3413.01 When planning a particular sample for a substantive test of details, the auditor should consider the following:

a. The relationship of the sample to the relevant audit objective

b. Preliminary estimates of materiality levels

c. The auditor's allowable risk of incorrect acceptance

d. Characteristics of items comprising the account balance or class of transactions to be sampled

3413.02 The auditor should determine that the population from which the auditor draws the sample is appropriate for the specific audit objective.

3413.03 The auditor should consider how much monetary error in the related account balance or class of transactions may exist without causing the financial statements to be materially misstated.

a. This maximum monetary error for the balance or class is called **tolerable error** for the sample.

b. Tolerable error is a planning concept and is related to the auditor's preliminary estimates of materiality.

3413.04 When planning a sample for a substantive test of details, the auditor uses judgment to determine which items, if any, in an account balance or transaction class should be individually examined and which items should be subject to sampling. For those items for which, in the auditor's judgment, acceptance of some sampling risk is not justified, the auditor should examine each item.

3413.05 The auditor may be able to reduce the sample size required by separating items subject to sampling into relatively homogeneous groups.

3413.06 To determine the number of items to be selected in a sample for a particular substantive test of details, the auditor should consider the tolerable error, the allowable risk of incorrect acceptance, and the characteristics of the population.

3413.07 Sample items should be selected in such a way that the sample can be expected to be *representative* of the population.

3413.08 Auditing procedures that are appropriate to the particular audit objective should be applied to each sample item.

3413.09 The auditor should *project the error* results of the sample to the items from which the sample was selected and add that amount to the errors discovered in any items examined 100%. This total projected error should be compared with the tolerable error for the account balance or class of transactions and appropriate consideration should be given to possible sampling risk.

3413.10 In addition to the evaluation of the frequency and amounts of monetary misstatements, consideration should be given to the *qualitative aspects of the errors.* These include the following:

    a. The nature and cause of misstatements, such as whether there are differences in principles or in application, whether there are errors or fraud, or whether the misstatements are due to misunderstanding of instructions or to carelessness

    b. The possible relationship of the misstatements to other phases of the audit

3413.11 Projected error results for all audit sampling applications and all known errors from nonsampling applications should be considered in the aggregate by the auditor when they evaluate whether the financial statements taken as whole may be materially misstated.

3414 Sampling in Assessing Control Risk

3414.01 When planning a particular audit sample for assessing control risk, the auditor should consider the following:

    a. The relationship of the sample to the objective of the test

    b. The maximum rate of deviations from prescribed control procedures that would support the planned reliance

    c. The auditor's allowable risk of assessing control risk too low

    d. Characteristics of items comprising the accounting balance or class of transactions to be sampled

3414.02 Sampling generally is not applicable to tests of controls of the internal control when the tests depend primarily on appropriate segregation of duties or otherwise provide no documentary evidence of performance.

3414.03 When designing samples for tests of controls that leave an audit trail of documentary evidence, the auditor should ordinarily plan to evaluate compliance in terms of deviations from or compliance with pertinent control procedures.

3414.04 Pertinent control procedures are ones that, had they not been included in the design of the system, would have affected adversely the auditor's preliminary evaluation of the internal control.

3414.05 The auditor's overall evaluation of controls for a particular purpose involves combining judgments about the prescribed controls, the sample results of tests of controls, and the results of observation and inquiry about controls not leaving an audit trail of documentary evidence.

3414.06 The auditor should assess the maximum rate of deviations from prescribed control procedures that the auditor would be willing to accept without altering the planned reliance on the control. This rate is the **tolerable rate.**

3414.07 Sampling applies when the auditor needs to decide whether the rate of deviation from a prescribed procedure is no greater than a tolerable rate; for example, in testing a matching process or an approval process.

3414.08 However, risk assessment procedures performed to obtain an understanding of internal control do not involve sampling. Sampling concepts also do not apply for some tests of controls. Tests of automated application controls are generally tested only once or a few times when effective (IT) general controls are present, and thus do not rely on the concepts of risk and tolerable deviation as applied in other sampling procedures.

3414.09 Because the test of controls is the primary source of evidence as to whether the procedure is being applied as prescribed, the auditor should allow for a low level of risk of overreliance (e.g., 5% or 10%) whether the auditor is using nonstatistical or statistical sampling.

3414.10 Sample items should be selected in such a way that the sample can be expected to be *representative* of the population.

3414.11 Ideally, the auditor should use a selection method that has the potential for selecting items from the entire period under audit.

3414.12 Auditing procedures that are appropriate to achieve the objective of assessing control risk should be applied to each sample item.

3414.13 Consideration should be given to the qualitative aspects of the deviations.

3415 Selecting a Sampling Approach

3415.01 Statistical sampling helps the auditor to do the following:

    a. Design an efficient sample.

    b. Measure the sufficiency of the audit evidence obtained.

    c. Evaluate the sample results.

3415.02 Statistical sampling involves additional costs of training auditors and designing and selecting individual samples to meet the statistical requirements.

3415.03 Because either nonstatistical or statistical sampling can provide sufficient audit evidence, the auditor chooses between them after considering their relative cost and effectiveness in the circumstances.

3420 Statistical Sampling

3421 Definition of Statistical Sampling

3421.01 **Statistical sampling:** The use of a sampling plan in such a manner that the laws of probability can be used to make statements about a population.

3421.02 **Nonstatistical sampling:** Includes all samples that are not statistical, or any sampling plan that does not meet *all* the rigorous requirements (identified in section **3421.03**) of statistical sampling.

3421.03 For a sampling plan to be *statistical,* the following two requirements must be met:

1. The sample must be statistically selected (e.g., random number table selection).
2. Sample results must be mathematically evaluated.

3422 Types of Statistical Sampling Models

3422.01 There are two broad categories of statistical sampling—attribute (or proportional) and variable (or quantitative) sampling.

3422.02 **Attribute sampling:** A term that is used to refer to two different but related types of proportional sampling.

1. **Attribute sampling:** A sampling plan that is used to estimate the rate (percentage) of occurrence of a specific quality (attribute) in a population. Two common types of attributes for which auditors test are correct account distributions and adequate supporting documentation (see section **3440**).

2. **Discovery sampling:** A sampling plan that is appropriate when the expected occurrence rate is extremely low (near zero). Discovery sampling is used when the auditor desires a specific chance of observing at least one example of an occurrence if the true rate of occurrence is greater than expected (see section **3450**).

3422.03 **Variable or quantitative sampling,** in contrast to attribute sampling, is employed when the auditor wishes to estimate or test a client's book value (see section **3460**).

3422.04 Attribute sampling is used primarily for tests of controls, whereas variable sampling is most useful for substantive testing.

3423 Advantages of Statistical Sampling

3423.01 Statistical sampling allows the auditor to calculate the risk of reliance on the sample for assessing control risk.

3423.02 Statistical sampling enables the auditor to make objective statements about the population on the basis of the sample.

3424 Disadvantages of Statistical Sampling

3424.01 In some cases, the cost of performing statistical sampling may exceed the benefits to be derived—especially variable sampling applications that are not computerized.

3424.02 Whether or not statistical sampling should be used is a question that depends primarily on professional judgment. The AICPA does not require that statistical sampling be used (AU 350.04).

3425 Professional Judgment in Statistical Sampling

3425.01 Statistical sampling does not eliminate professional judgment.

3425.02 The following areas illustrate the kinds of judgmental decisions an auditor must make when using statistical sampling:

a. **Population definition:** The auditor must define the population in terms of its size, the characteristics of significance to the audit, and what constitutes an error.

b. **Sampling method:** The auditor must determine the type of sampling method to be used (e.g., attribute sampling, discovery sampling, variable sampling) and the most efficient means of selecting the sample. In fact, to begin with, the auditor has to decide whether to use nonstatistical or statistical sampling.

c. **Selection technique:** The auditor must decide which sampling selection process is to be used (e.g., random number table selection, systematic selection).

d. **Error analysis:** Statistical sampling findings must be evaluated both *quantitatively* and *qualitatively*. The primary input into the auditor's qualitative evaluation is professional judgment and experience.

3430 Selecting a Representative Sample

3431 Definitions

3431.01 To be **representative,** a sample should be selected from the entire set of data to which the resulting conclusions are to be applied.

3431.02 **Representative sample:** A sample selected in such a way that every element in the population has a known chance of being selected.

3431.03 **Population:** The universe or field about which the auditor wishes to generalize.

3431.04 **Sampling frame:** A listing or other physical representation of the individual items in the population. For example, in testing inventory, the frame might be an inventory listing or the perpetual inventory records.

3431.05 **Sampling with replacement:** A sample selection method that permits a selected sample item to be returned to the population and reselected. In other words, the same item may be included in the sample more than once.

3431.06 **Sampling without replacement:** A technique whereby once an item is selected it is removed from the population and cannot be selected again.

3432 Random Number Tables

3432.01 A random, as opposed to an arbitrary or judgmental, selection offers the best chance that the sample will be representative.

3432.02 A random number table is composed of randomly generated digits 0 through 9. Each digit should appear in the table approximately the same number of times, and the order in which they appear is random. Columns in the tables are purely arbitrary and otherwise meaningless.

3432.03 Selected random numbers should be documented in audit workpapers by identifying each of the following:

    a. **Correspondence:** Relationship between population sampled and random number table.

    b. **Route:** Go up or down the columns—left or right. Any route desired can be selected as long as it is consistently followed until all required numbers are drawn.

    c. **Starting point:** Document row, column, digit starting position, as well as source (book) and page number of starting point.

    d. **Stopping point:** Facilitates adding new sample items, if needed.

3433 Systematic Selection

3433.01 In **systematic selection,** the auditor calculates a sampling interval and then methodically selects the item for the sample based on the size of the interval. For example, if the population size (N) contains 1,000 items and the sample size desired (n) is 100, the sampling interval is 10. A random start between one and 10 is selected as the first sample element. Afterwards, every tenth item is selected.

3433.02 Systematic selection may produce a biased sample. To guard against this, the auditor should be satisfied that the population is in random order and should consider using more than one random start.

3434 Probability-Proportional-to-Size Sampling (Dollar Unit Sampling)

3434.01 In *probability-proportional-to-size* (PPS) sampling, the strategy is to randomly select individual dollars from a population and then audit the balances, transactions, or documents—called logical units—that include the individual dollars selected.

3434.02 PPS sampling gives logical units with larger recorded dollar amounts more opportunity to be selected than logical units with smaller recorded amounts. For example, if an entity has a balance of $1.5 million in its accounts receivable account, the population size is 1.5 million and an individual customer account balance of $90,000 has a 6% chance ($90,000 ÷ $1,500,000) of being selected.

3434.03 You must determine sample size in advance to use PPS. Thus, if the auditor has decided to sample only 100 customer accounts from the accounts receivable balance of $1.5 million described in section **3434.02** and to use systematic selection, the sampling interval is 15,000 ($1,500,000 ÷ 100). With one random start, you would select every fifteen-thousandth dollar in the population. Thus, every customer account with a balance of $15,000 or more will be selected.

3434.04 In projecting the error rate in a PPS sampling plan to the population, the auditor would take the ratio of the sampling interval to the recorded amount of the sampling unit and apply that resulting ratio to the error found to exist in the sample. For example, using the numbers from section **3434.03**, if a sampling unit with a recorded amount of $3,000 was found to have an audited amount of $2,600, the following projection of that error to the population would be made. The sampling unit's recorded amount is $3,000 and the sampling interval is $15,000. Thus, the sampling unit is 1/5 ($3,000 ÷ $15,000) of the sampling interval. In this case the error discovered by the auditor is $400 ($3,000 sampling unit - $2,600 audited amount). This error projected to the population would be $2,000 ($400 × 5).

3434.05 The following advantages are generally associated with PPS sampling:

   a. The use of PPS is not dependent on an estimate of the population standard deviation.

   b. PPS automatically results in a stratified sample because items are selected in proportion to their dollar values.

   c. PPS systematic sample selection automatically identifies any item that is individually significant if its value exceeds the sampling interval.

   d. If the auditor expects no errors, PPS sampling will usually result in a smaller sample size than the sample size that results from the use of classical variable sampling.

   e. Because larger-dollar-value accounts have a higher probability of being selected, overstatements are more likely to be detected than understatements. Thus, PPS sampling is most appropriate when an auditor desires testing for material overstatements.

3435 Difference and Ratio Estimation

3435.01 In many areas of an audit, the auditor is aware of the recorded value and the audit value for each value in a sample. When this is the case, the use of **difference estimation** is appropriate. Difference estimation is an easy sampling method to use and normally results in a smaller sample size than other methods.

3435.02 An example of the application of difference estimation is as follows. Assume that a sample of 50 is drawn from a population of 500 items. Further assume that the mean of the misstatements found in the sample were between $18 and $43 at the 95% confidence level. Thus, the estimate of the error in the population falls between $9,000 and $21,500 (500 × 18 and 500 × 43). The auditor would then compare his/her tolerable error to the range and if the tolerable error were greater than $21,500, the population would be acceptable. However, if the tolerable error were less than $21,500, the auditor would conclude that the population was unacceptable and would most likely expand audit procedures.

3435.03 **Ratio estimation** is similar to difference estimation except that the auditor determines the ratio of misstatements in the audited values to recorded values and estimates the audited balance by multiplying the recorded balance by the computed ratio.

3435.04 As an example of ratio estimation, assume that an auditor samples a population and finds $24,000 of misstatements in the sample that has a recorded value of $320,000. Thus, the ratio of misstatements in the sample is 7.5% ($24,000 ÷ $320,000). If the population from which the sample was drawn totals $2,650,000, the projected misstatement in the population is $198,750 (.075 × $2,650,000). The auditor would then apply a calculation of confidence limits to analyze the sample results and his/her confidence in the recorded dollar amount of the population.

3436 Stratified Sampling

3436.01 When a population is highly variable (large standard deviation), unstratified sampling may produce excessively large variable sample sizes. **Stratification** increases efficiency because each stratum has a relatively small standard deviation, and the weighted sum of standard deviations is less than the standard deviation for the whole population.

3436.02 To stratify a variable sampling application, the following three rules must be followed:

1. Every population element (item) must belong to one and only one stratum.
2. There must be a tangible, specifiable difference that defines and distinguishes the stratum.
3. The exact number of elements in each stratum must be known.

3436.03 In stratifying a population, one rule of thumb is to select stratum boundaries so that each stratum contains approximately the same total dollars.

3437 Factors Influencing Sample Size

3437.01 The following table, included in the appendix to SAS 39, describes certain factors that influence sample sizes.

3437.02 This table is designed to be used in connection with tests of details in sample planning.

Factors Influencing Sample Size for a Substantive Test of Details in Sample Planning

Factor	Smaller Sample Size	Larger Sample Size	Related Factor for Substantive Sample Planning
a. Assessment of inherent risk.	Low assessed level of inherent risk.	High assessed level of inherent risk.	Allowable risk of incorrect acceptance.
b. Assessment of control risk.	Low assessed level control risk.	High assessed level control risk.	Allowable risk of incorrect acceptance.
c. Assessment of risk for other substantive procedures related to the same assertion (including substantive analytical procedures and other relevant substantive procedures).	Low assessment of risk associated with other relevant substantive procedures.	High assessment of risk associated with other relevant substantive procedures.	Allowable risk of incorrect acceptance.
d. Measure of tolerable misstatement for a specific account.	Larger measure of tolerable misstatement.	Smaller measure of tolerable misstatement.	Tolerable misstatement.
e. Expected size and frequency of misstatements.	Smaller misstatements or lower frequency.	Larger misstatements or higher frequency.	Assessment of population characteristics.
f. Number of items in the population.	Virtually no effect on sample size unless population is very small.		
g. Choice between statistical and nonstatistical sampling.	Sample sizes are comparable.		

3440 Attribute Sampling

3441 Attributes Defined

3441.01 **Attribute sampling** relates to the question of "How many?"; *variable sampling* relates to the question, "How much?"

3441.02 Attribute sampling is used primarily by the auditor in testing compliance with the control where the auditor desires to estimate the extent to which prescribed procedures are being followed and/or the degree of clerical accuracy in an internal control.

3441.03 An *attribute* must be carefully defined before an auditor begins attribute sampling execution. Defining an attribute is difficult and is a matter of professional judgment. Considerable care must be exercised. For example, if the sampling unit is a check and the audit test is concerned with whether or not a check is properly supported, one of the attributes reviewed for proper support may be a receiving report. An error may be defined as a check not supported by a properly signed receiving report. Disbursements for services received (such as rent payments) are not typically supported by receiving reports. There are two ways that the auditor may handle this problem. First, the attribute definition may be structured so that checks selected relating to service acquisitions are excluded from the population. A second way to address this problem is to define the attribute broadly as a properly supported check with identification of what constitutes proper support.

3441.04 In an attribute sampling application, the auditor should make certain that the population they are sampling from is homogeneous. **Homogeneity** means that all the items in the population must have similar characteristics.

3442 Setting Reliability Levels and Tolerable Rates

3442.01 AU 350 uses the concept of risk instead of reliability or confidence level. Risk is the complement of reliability or confidence level.

The terms *reliability level* and *confidence level* are used interchangeably. Reliability refers to the probability of being right in placing reliance on an effective internal accounting control system. For example, if an auditor selects a 95% reliability level, the auditor has a 5% risk of placing reliance on internal accounting control when the system is ineffective given a certain tolerable rate. If the auditor decides that a 90% reliability level is acceptable, the auditor has a 10% chance of accepting reliance given a certain tolerable rate when the auditor should not.

3442.02 The complement of reliability (1.0 - reliability) is the risk that the auditor will rely on the control when, in fact, the control should not be relied on. This risk is referred to as the **risk of assessing control risk too low.**

3442.03 According to many CPA firms, the minimum reliability level should be 90%. However, at least 95% reliability should be used if an attribute is critical to the scope of the remainder of the audit. When evaluating internal accounting control attributes to determine the extent to which audit tests can be limited, a high reliability level or low risk of overreliance should generally be used (AU 350.33).

3442.04 The **maximum tolerable rate** (MTR) on compliance deviations represents a critical value established so that the possibility of deviations in excess of that rate would cause the auditor to place less than full reliance (perhaps no reliance) on the control being evaluated. According to many CPA firms, MTR should not exceed 10% if some reliance is being placed on selected internal accounting control procedures. If substantial reliance is to be placed on internal accounting control, an MTR of 5% or possibly lower would be reasonable.

3442.05 In an attribute sampling application, two deviation rates are generated. One, referred to as the MTR, is preset as discussed in section **3442.04**. The second, referred to as the **projected rate,** is determined after the selected sample has been audited.

3442.06 If the projected rate is greater than the maximum tolerable rate (i.e., MTR is less than the projected rate), the statistical evaluation indicates that the control should not be relied upon. However, the auditor's qualitative error analysis may suggest otherwise.

3442.07 If the projected rate is less than or equal to the MTR, the statistical evaluation indicates that the control may be relied on. However, because of the nature of the few errors or deviations that did occur, the auditor's error analysis may suggest no reliance on the control.

3443 Attribute Sampling Tables

3443.01 The first table presented, Table 1, is used to determine sample size. Table 2 is used to evaluate sample findings. These tables should be used if the auditor desires to project statistically the sample findings. The estimated population occurrence rate is determined by dividing the sample occurrences by the sample size.

3443.02 To determine sample size, the following four requirements must be predefined:

1. Establish the reliability level (or risk of overreliance).
2. Determine which table should be used based on reliability level desired. (To illustrate how the tables are used, only one sample size table and one evaluation of results table are presented.)
3. Estimate population occurrence rate in percentage.
4. Define the maximum tolerable rate.

Table 1.
Determination of Sample Size: Reliability, 95%
Tolerable Rate

Expected Population Deviation Rate (%)	2%	3%	4%	5%	6%	7%	8%	9%	10%	15%	20%
0.00	149(0)	99(0)	74(0)	49(0)	59(0)	42(0)	36(0)	32(0)	29(0)	19(0)	14(0)
0.25	236(1)	157(1)	117(1)	93(1)	78(1)	66(1)	58(1)	51(1)	46(1)	30(1)	22(1)
0.50	*	157(1)	117(1)	93(1)	78(1)	66(1)	58(1)	51(1)	46(1)	30(1)	22(1)
0.75	*	208(2)	117(1)	93(1)	78(1)	66(1)	58(1)	51(1)	46(1)	30(1)	22(1)
1.00	*	*	156(2)	93(1)	78(1)	66(1)	58(1)	51(1)	46(1)	30(1)	22(1)
1.25	*	*	156(2)	124(2)	78(1)	66(1)	58(1)	51(1)	46(1)	30(1)	22(1)
1.50	*	*	192(3)	124(2)	103(2)	66(1)	58(1)	51(1)	46(1)	30(1)	22(1)
1.75	*	*	227(4)	153(3)	103(2)	88(2)	77(2)	51(1)	46(1)	30(1)	22(1)
2.00	*	*	*	181(4)	127(3)	88(2)	77(2)	68(2)	46(1)	30(1)	22(1)
2.25	*	*	*	208(5)	127(3)	88(2)	77(2)	68(2)	61(2)	30(1)	22(1)
2.50	*	*	*	*	150(4)	109(3)	77(2)	68(2)	61(2)	30(1)	22(1)
2.75	*	*	*	*	173(5)	109(3)	95(3)	68(2)	61(2)	30(1)	22(1)
3.00	*	*	*	*	195(6)	129(4)	95(3)	84(3)	61(2)	30(1)	22(1)
3.25	*	*	*	*	*	148(5)	112(4)	84(3)	61(2)	30(1)	22(1)
3.50	*	*	*	*	*	167(6)	112(4)	84(3)	76(3)	40(2)	22(1)
3.75	*	*	*	*	*	185(7)	129(5)	100(4)	76(3)	40(2)	22(1)
4.00	*	*	*	*	*	*	146(6)	100(4)	89(4)	40(2)	22(1)
5.00	*	*	*	*	*	*	*	158(8)	116(6)	40(2)	30(2)
6.00	*	*	*	*	*	*	*	*	179(11)	50(3)	30(2)
7.00	*	*	*	*	*	*	*	*	*	68(5)	37(3)

* Sample size is too large to be cost-effective for most audit applications.
Note: This table assumes a large population.
Adapted and used with permission of the American Institute of Certified Public Accountants.

3443.03 To illustrate, assume that an auditor desires to verify the footings of 20,000 sales invoices. The auditor desires a statistical sample that will give 95% confidence that not more than 5% of the sales invoices are in error. The auditor estimates from previous experience that about 1.75% of the invoices are in error.

   a. Estimated error rate = 1.75%

   b. Maximum tolerable rate = 5%

   c. Reliability level = 95%

   d. The required sample (n) size is 153. This is determined by going down the 5% maximum tolerable rate column in Table 1 until the expected error rate 1.75% or the next higher number is located.

3443.04 In situations where the auditor does not know what the estimated error rate is (1.75%), select a sample of 50 to estimate the population occurrence rate. To illustrate, if a sample of 50 is selected and one error is discovered for a given attribute, the estimated population occurrence rate is (1/50), or 2%. Assuming the reliability level desired is 95% and the maximum tolerable rate is 7%, the sample size from Table 1 is equal to 88.

3443.05 To evaluate sample findings, Table 2 is used. (To illustrate, consider the example from section **3443.03** where the sample size was calculated to be 153.) If four occurrences are found in the sample of 153, the projected rate is 6%. This is determined by the intersection of the 150 sample size row with "4" errors.

Table 2
Statistical Sampling Results Evaluation: Reliability, 95%
Table for Compliance Tests
Upper Limits at 5% Risk of Overreliance

Actual Number Of Deviations Found

Sample Size	0	1	2	3	4	5	6	7	8	9	10
25	11.3	17.6	*	*	*	*	*	*	*	*	*
30	9.5	14.9	19.6	*	*	*	*	*	*	*	*
35	8.3	12.9	17.0	*	*	*	*	*	*	*	*
40	7.3	11.4	15.0	18.3	*	*	*	*	*	*	*
45	6.5	10.2	13.4	16.4	19.2	*	*	*	*	*	*
50	5.9	9.2	12.1	14.8	17.4	19.9	*	*	*	*	*
55	5.4	8.4	11.1	13.5	15.9	18.2	*	*	*	*	*
60	4.9	7.7	10.2	12.5	14.7	16.8	18.8	*	*	*	*
65	4.6	7.1	9.4	11.5	13.6	15.5	17.4	19.3	*	*	*
70	4.2	6.6	8.8	10.8	12.6	14.5	16.3	18.0	19.7	*	*
75	4.0	6.2	8.2	10.1	11.8	13.6	15.2	16.9	18.5	20.0	*
80	3.7	5.8	7.7	9.5	11.1	12.7	14.3	15.9	17.4	18.9	*
90	3.3	5.2	6.9	8.4	9.9	11.4	12.8	14.2	15.5	16.8	18.2
100	3.0	4.7	6.2	7.6	9.0	10.3	11.5	12.8	14.0	15.2	16.4
125	2.4	3.8	5.0	6.1	7.2	8.3	9.3	10.3	11.3	12.3	13.2
150	2.0	3.2	4.2	5.1	6.0	6.9	7.8	8.6	9.5	10.3	11.1
200	1.5	2.4	3.2	3.9	4.6	5.2	5.9	6.5	7.2	7.8	8.4

* Over 20%

Note: This table presents upper limits as percentages. This table assumes a large population.
Adapted and used with permission of the American Institute of Certified Public Accountants.

3443.06 Other error findings for the sample size of 150 are evaluated as follows:

Errors Discovered		Projected Rate
0	=	2%
1	=	3.2%
2	=	4.2%
5	=	6.9%
10	=	11.1%

3443.07 Since the maximum tolerable rate was 5%, three or more errors would probably cause the auditor to conclude that this aspect of internal accounting control should not be relied on.

3450 Discovery Sampling

3451 Discovery Sampling Defined

3451.01 **Discovery sampling:** Used when the auditor believes that the population occurrence rate is near zero. In case the occurrence rate is not zero, discovery sampling applications are designed to yield a large enough sample size so that if the auditor is wrong, at least one occurrence will be produced. Discovery sampling is a special case of attribute sampling.

3451.02 The following two conditions must exist before discovery sampling should be used:

1. Discovery sampling is used when the auditor's best judgment of the population occurrence rate is 0% or near 0%.

2. In a discovery sampling application, the auditor is usually looking for a very critical characteristic (e.g., payroll padding), which if discovered might be indicative of more widespread fraud or serious errors in the financial statements.

3451.03 To properly frame a discovery sampling application, the following prerequisites must be defined:

a. Characteristic to be evaluated

b. Reliability desired

c. Maximum tolerable occurrence rate

d. Definition and size of population

3452 Discovery Sampling Tables

3452.01 To determine which table to use in a discovery sampling application, define the population and its size. The population size determines which sample size table is appropriate.

3452.02 **Table 3** is presented to illustrate how discovery sampling tables are used. Note that Table 3 is for population sizes between 2,000 and 5,000.

Table 3
Probability in Percentage of Including at Least One Occurrence in a Sample for Population Between 2,000 and 5,000
Maximum Tolerable Occurrence Rate

Sample Size	.3%	.4%	.5%	.6%	.8%	1%	1.5%	2%
50	14%	18%	22%	26%	33%	40%	53%	64%
60	17	21	26	30	38	45	60	70
70	19	25	30	35	43	51	66	76
80	22	28	33	38	48	56	70	80
90	24	31	37	42	52	60	75	84
100	26	33	40	46	56	64	78	87
120	31	39	46	52	62	70	84	91
140	35	43	51	57	68	76	88	94
160	39	48	56	62	73	80	91	96
200	46	56	64	71	81	87	95	98
240	52	63	71	77	86	92	98	99
300	61	71	79	84	92	96	99	99+
340	65	76	83	88	94	97	99+	99+
400	71	81	88	92	96	98	99+	99+
460	77	86	91	95	98	99	99+	99+
500	79	88	93	96	99	99	99+	99+
600	85	92	96	98	99	99+	99+	99+
700	90	95	98	99	99+	99+	99+	99+
800	93	97	99	99	99+	99+	99+	99+
900	95	98	99	99+	99+	99+	99+	99+
1000	97	99	99+	99+	99+	99+	99+	99+

Adapted and used with permission of the American Institute of Certified Public Accountants.

3452.03 Assume that the auditor is examining a population of 4,500 payroll checks. The auditor desires 95% reliability of seeing an example of payroll padding if 1% or more of the checks are not payable to bona fide employees. To determine sample size, go down the 1% column of Table 3 until the desired reliability (or the next reliability level if the one you are looking for is not in the table) is located. The sample size is 300 (located across from 96% reliability).

3452.04 If *no* errors are discovered in the sample examined, the auditor can immediately state that the sampling plan criteria has been achieved (i.e., the auditor can state that they are 96% certain that the worst likely error rate in the population of payroll checks does not exceed 1%).

3452.05 If one or more errors are located, the statistical statement, "If no errors are discovered in the sample examined, the auditor can immediately state that the sampling plan criteria has been achieved (i.e., the auditor can state that they are 96% certain that the worst likely error rate in the population of payroll checks does not exceed 1%)," cannot be made. No statistical conclusion should be expressed. Expanded audit procedures should be applied. Perhaps client employees under auditor supervision will examine every one of the remaining population items.

3460 Variable Sampling—Accounting Estimation

3461 Accounting Estimation Defined

3461.01 In designing a substantive sampling plan, the auditor must consider whether the audit objective is:

    a. to make an independent estimate of some amount (e.g., LIFO inventory) *or*

    b. to test the reasonableness of a financial statement representation (e.g., the balance in accounts receivable).

3461.02 In the first case, when the client does not state an amount that purports to be correct (such as when improper accounting principles have been used or numerous errors are known to exist in the records), the auditor should use an *accounting estimation* approach to develop an estimate of the correct account balance. In such cases, the auditor generally intends to propose an adjustment to bring the account balance into agreement with the statistical estimate.

3461.03 On the other hand, if the auditor desires to accept the client's representation without adjustment if it is reasonably correct and to propose an adjustment only if it is probable that there might be a material error in the amount as stated by the client, an *audit hypothesis* approach should be used. The audit hypothesis approach statistically discriminates between the hypothesis that the amount as represented is fairly stated and the alternative hypothesis that the amount is materially misstated.

3462 Selected Statistical Terms Defined

3462.01 **Mean:** A measure of central tendency that is obtained by totaling all the values and dividing by the number of items. The mean of a population is expressed symbolically as $\overline{X}$. The mean of a sample is expressed symbolically as $\overline{X}$. To illustrate a sample mean calculation, assume that a sample of 10 items was selected. The numeric values are as follows:

x
$10
18
15
20
24
26
26
17
25
19
$\sum x_i = \$200$

Formula:

$$\overline{x} = \frac{\sum x_i}{n} = \frac{200}{10} = 20$$

3462.02 **Standard deviation:** A widely used statistic that is employed to measure the extent to which the values of the items are spread about the mean. To illustrate the calculation of the standard deviation, the sample items selected to illustrate a sample mean calculation are used.

x	$\bar{x}$(1)	x - $\bar{x}$	(x - $\bar{x}$)²
10	20	-10	100
18	20	-2	4
15	20	-5	25
20	20	0	0
24	20	4	16
26	20	6	36
26	20	6	36
17	20	3	9
25	20	5	25
19	20	-1	1
		$\Sigma(x - \bar{x})^2 =$	__252__

Formula:

$$SD = \sqrt{\frac{\Sigma(x - \bar{x})^2}{n - 2}}$$

$$SD = \sqrt{\frac{252}{8}} = 5.61$$

Where:

SD = Standard deviation

(1) Computed in paragraph .01.

3462.03 **Normal distribution:** The distribution shown following is a normal distribution. An important feature of this distribution is that the relative frequency of any interval be determined by knowing only the mean $\bar{X}$ and the standard deviation (SD). The interval from $\bar{X} \pm$ SD contains 68% of the items; from $\bar{X} \pm$ 1.96 SD contains 95% of the items; and from $\bar{X} \pm$ 3 SD contains 99% of the items.

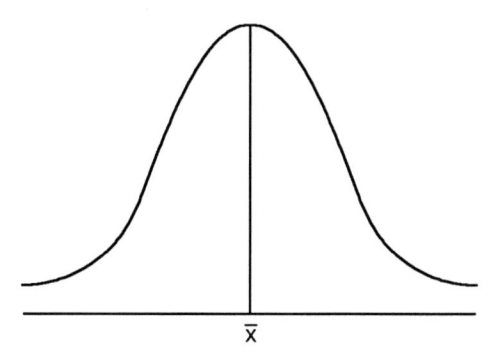

3462.04 **Central limit theorem:** For large sample sizes (typically, 30 is a reasonable *lower* bound), the distribution of sample means tends to be normally distributed, almost independently of the shape of the original population. The fact that sample means from a lopsided accounting population converge to a normal distribution is the reason why normal theory is useful in accounting and auditing.

3462.05 **Distribution of sample means:** A distribution of sample means (means calculated from repeated samples of the same size) has three properties:

1. The shape of the distribution is approximately normal if the sample size is large enough.

2. The distribution is centered at the population mean $\bar{X}$.

3. The standard of error of the mean equals the estimated population standard deviation (SD) divided by the square root of the sample size.

3463 Accounting Estimation Model

3463.01 The simple extension method is used in projecting an estimated value from a sample. This method is also called *mean estimation.* After a sample is selected and an audited value determined for each sample element, the sample mean $\overline{X}$ of audited values is multiplied by the number of elements in the population (N) to produce an estimate of the total dollar value of the population.

3463.02 A 15-step approach to applying *mean estimation* or *unstratified sample extension* is presented as follows:

1. Define reliability level—generally, a high reliability level (95%) should be used.

2. Based on the following table, convert step 1 into a U_R factor (reliability factor).

Reliability		U_R Factor
.99	=	2.58
.95	=	1.96
.90	=	1.65

3. Set tolerable error equal to materiality.

   Tolerable error = A
   Mathematically A = U_R x SE x N
   Where: SE = standard error *or* the mean calculated as the standard deviation ÷ $\sqrt{n}$ and
   N = population size

4. Calculate required sample size with replacement.

$$n = \left(\frac{U_R \times SD \times N}{A}\right)^2$$

   Where: n = sample size with replacement and

   SD = standard deviation

   Note: The sample size formula is very important on the CPA Examination. The impact of changing U_R, dispersion (SD), N, and A on n should be studied for the examination. If the standard deviation (SD) is known from prior sampling work, use that as an estimate. If SD is unknown, an estimate must be made. To estimate SD:

   (a) Select a preliminary random sample of 30 items from the population.

   (b) Calculate SD.

   (c) Substitute (b) into the sample size formula.

5. Randomly select the additional sample items using random number tables or systematic selection if n is greater than 30.

6. Audit the additional sample.

7. Calculate the standard deviation of the total sample.

8. Calculate the standard error using the following formula.

$$SE = \frac{SD}{\sqrt{n}}$$

9. Calculate projected error (A′) based on the following formula. Use SE from *step 8*. (See text.)

10. Is (A′) ≤ A? If *yes,* go to *step 12;* if no, go to *step 11*.

11. Increase the sample size according to the following formula. Afterwards, go back to *step 6*.

$$\text{Adjusted } n = \left(\frac{U_R \times SD \text{ (step 4)} \times N}{A} \right)^2$$

12. Calculate the mean $\overline{X}$ of the total sample.

$$\overline{x} = \frac{\text{Sum of each audited sample}}{n}$$

13. Calculate estimated audited value (EAV).

$$EAV = \overline{x} \times (N)$$

14. Conclude that you are certain at the reliability level specified in *step 1* that the client's book value is within EAV ± A′. Your conclusion should also address the effectiveness of the procedures used to generate the audited amount and whether or not audit personnel applied the procedures correctly.

15. State the client's book value at EAV.

3470 Variable Sampling—Audit Hypothesis Approach

3471 Risks of Incorrect Rejection and Incorrect Acceptance

3471.01 There are two risks in using variable sampling to determine whether or not a client's book value is fairly stated—risk of incorrect rejection and risk of incorrect acceptance. The **risk of incorrect rejection** is the chance that the statistical evidence might fail to support fair statement of a correct book value. This type of error usually results in testing additional sample items. The risk of incorrect rejection is the complement of reliability specified when calculating sample size—U_R factor. The risk of incorrect rejection is controlled by decreasing or increasing reliability. Many practitioners believe the risk of incorrect rejection should be set at 5% or less (U_R = 1.96 at 95% reliability).

3471.02 The **risk of incorrect acceptance** is the chance that the statistical evidence might support fair statement of a materially misstated book value. The risk of incorrect acceptance is controlled by adjusting the ratio of tolerable error (A) to materiality (M).

3472 Audit Risk (or Ultimate Risk)

3472.01 According to AU 350, audit risk is the risk that an auditor incurs if the auditor expresses an unqualified opinion on materially erroneous financial statements.

3472.02 Audit risk is actually a combination of two risks:

1. The client's internal accounting control system does not detect a material error that has occurred.

2. The auditor's examination fails to detect the error.

3472.03 According to the Appendix of AU 350, an appropriate risk of incorrect acceptance for a substantive test of detail is calculated as follows:

$$TD = \frac{UR}{IC \times AR}$$

where:
- UR = Audit risk
- IC = Auditor's assessment of the risk that the client's control system fails to detect material errors
- AR = Auditor's assessment of the risk that analytical review procedures and other relevant substantive tests fail to detect material errors
- TD = Risk of incorrect acceptance

In practice, UR is generally preset at 10% or lower. IC and AR are judgmentally determined.

3472.04 The relationship of the risk of incorrect acceptance to the sample size formula is as follows:

a. The risk of incorrect acceptance is calculated according to the given formula.

b. Tolerable error is set in relation to materiality based on the risk of incorrect acceptance.

c. Tolerable error, as determined in step b, is introduced into the sample size formula.

3472.05 See section 3130 for a summary of SAS 47 (AU 312), which provides another discussion of audit risk and materiality.

3473 Audit Hypothesis Model

3473.01 The audit hypothesis model consists of 19 steps, commencing with a preliminary evaluation of internal accounting control and finishing with an accept or reject decision as to the fairness of an account balance.

3473.02 The audit hypothesis model should be used whenever the auditor is testing a client's book value to determine if the book value is fairly stated or not; otherwise, the accounting estimation approach should be used. The 19-step model is presented as follows:

Evaluating control risk:

1. Make preliminary assessment of control risk.

2. Decide which controls to place reliance on to limit substantive testing.

3. Set desired reliability levels (90% or higher—usually 95% or higher) and tolerable rate (10% or less) for compliance tests.

4. Test control risk. There is no need for a compliance test when internal accounting controls are evaluated as nonexistent or weak.

5. Make final evaluation of internal accounting control risk for each class of transaction and related assets. Concluding that internal accounting controls over a particular transaction cycle are, for example, 10% risky means that there is a 10% risk that error could occur on enough accounts or to such a degree that the cumulative effect would be a material misstatement of the account balance.

Substantive test planning:

6. Define audit risk at 10% or lower (usually 5%), define risk of AR, and calculate the risk of incorrect acceptance.

7. Set the risk of incorrect rejection at 5% or lower. The risk of incorrect rejection is the complement of reliability. Reliability should be set at 95% or higher.

8. Based on the following table, convert *step 7* into a UR factor.

Reliability		U_R Factor
.99	=	2.58
.95	=	1.96
.90	=	1.65

9. Define materiality for the account balance. Materiality is judgmentally determined and is dependent on such factors as net income, total assets, equity, and other considerations.

10. Determine amount of tolerable error to place in the sample size formula. Tolerable error is based on the risk of incorrect rejection specified in *step 7* and materiality in *step 9*. For 95% reliability (risk of incorrect rejection of 5%) and different risk of incorrect acceptance levels, the following table depicts the factor that materiality should be multiplied by to yield tolerable error.

Risk of Incorrect Acceptance %	Multiplication Factor
1	.457
2.5	.500
5	.543
7.5	.576
10	.605
15	.653
20	.700
25	.742
30	.787
35	.834
40	.883
45	.973
50	1.000

11. Calculate required sample size. The following formula is appropriate:

$$n = \left(\frac{U_R \times SD \times N}{A}\right)^2 = \text{Sample size with replacement}$$

Substantive test execution:

12. Randomly select the additional sample items using random number tables or systematic selection.

13. Perform audit procedures on sample items selected for substantive tests.

14. Analyze errors noted in the sample to determine their cause, nature, and whether a systematic pattern exists.

Substantive test evaluation:

15. Calculate projected error (A').

    $A' = U_R \times SE \times N$

16. Calculate estimated audited value (EAV).

17. Calculate a *decision* interval as follows:

    Book value adjusted for any systematic differences plus-or-minus A' or calculate a *precision* interval as follows:

    $EAV \pm A'$

18. Determine whether sample evidence supports fair statement of the client's book value. If EAV from *step 16* (or the client's book value) falls within the decision interval (or precision interval) in *step 17*, conclude that the statistical evidence supports fair statement of the book value and stop. If the EAV (or the client's book value) does not fall within the decision interval (or precision interval) in *step 17*, go to *step 19*.

19. If statistical evidence does not support fair statement of the book value and the differences do not show a systematic pattern, the client should be requested to perform a thorough investigation of the account detail and possibly a complete reevaluation. The client's work, of course, should be tested by the auditor. If the client makes an adjustment after the investigation, book value should fall within the decision interval.

Section 3500
Report on Audited Financial Statements

3510 The Auditor's Standard Report
- 3511 The Fourth Standard of Reporting (AU 508.01–.05)
- 3512 Review of the Auditor's Standard Report
- 3513 Meaning of Present Fairly (AU 411)
- 3514 Explanatory Language Added to the Auditor's Standard Report (AU 508.11–.19)
- 3515 Qualified Opinions (AU 508.20–.57)
- 3516 Adverse Opinions (508.58–.60)
- 3517 Disclaimer of Opinion (AU 508.61–.63)
- 3518 Summary of Audit Report Forms
- 3519 Reports on Comparative Financial Statements (AU 508.65–.74)

3520 Modifications of the Standard Report
- 3521 Reliance on Another Auditor (AU 543)
- 3522 Departures from GAAP
- 3523 Reporting on Consistency (AU 508.16–.18 and AU 420.07–.11)
- 3524 Inadequate Disclosure (AU 431)
- 3525 Uncertainties, Scope Limitations, and Departures from GAAP Involving Risks or Uncertainties (AU 508.29–.32 and .45–.49)
- 3526 Consideration of an Entity's Ability to Continue As a Going Concern (AU 341)
- 3527 Emphasis of a Matter (AU 508.19)

3530 Subsequent Events and Subsequent Discoveries
- 3531 Subsequent Events (AU 560)
- 3532 Subsequent Discoveries (AU 561)
- 3533 Consideration of Omitted Procedures After the Report Date (AU 390)
- 3534 Dating the Report (AU 530)

3540 The Auditor's Communication with Those Charged with Governance (AU 380)
- 3541 The Role of Communication
- 3542 Those Charged with Governance
- 3543 Communication with Management
- 3544 Matters to Be Communicated
- 3545 The Communication Process

3550 Other Information in Documents Containing Audited Financial Statements (AU 550)

3560 Required Supplementary Information (AU 558)
- 3561 General Guidelines on Supplementary Information

3570 Reporting on Information Accompanying the Basic Financial Statements in Auditor-Submitted Documents (AU 551)
- 3571 Applicability
- 3572 Auditor's Reporting Responsibility (AU 551.04–.11)

3580 Other Reporting Issues
- 3581 Reports on Condensed Financial Statements and Selected Financial Data (AU 552)
- 3582 Reports on the Application of Accounting Principles (AU 625)
- 3583 Reporting on Financial Statements Prepared for Use in Other Countries (AU 534)
- 3584 Restricting the Use of an Auditor's Report (AU 532)

3510 The Auditor's Standard Report

3511 The Fourth Standard of Reporting (AU 508.01–.05)

3511.01 **The fourth standard of reporting** requires that the report contain an expression of opinion regarding the financial statements, taken as a whole, or an assertion to the effect that an opinion cannot be expressed (with reasons why it cannot be expressed).

3511.02 It also requires that, whenever an auditor is associated with financial statements, a clear-cut indication be given of the character of the examination and the degree of responsibility the auditor is taking.

3511.03 The objective of the fourth standard is to prevent misunderstanding the degree of responsibility the CPA is assuming when their name is associated with financial statements.

3511.04 The basis of the CPA's opinion lies with:
   a. the conformity of the examination with generally accepted auditing standards and
   b. the audit findings.

3511.05 The CPA's report may be addressed to the following:
   a. The company whose financial statements are being examined
   b. Its board of directors
   c. Its stockholders
   d. A third party who engaged the auditor

3511.06 The fourth standard of reporting applies to all audits of public and nonpublic companies.

3511.07 Reference in the fourth reporting standard to the financial statements "taken as a whole" applies equally to a complete set of financial statements and to an individual financial statement (e.g., to a balance sheet) for one or more periods presented.

3512 Review of the Auditor's Standard Report

3512.01 The auditor's standard report states that the financial statements present fairly, in all material respects, an entity's financial position, results of operations, and cash flows in conformity with generally accepted accounting principles.

3512.02 The auditor's standard report identifies the financial statements audited in an opening (introductory) paragraph, describes the nature of an audit in a scope paragraph, and expresses the auditor's opinion in a separate opinion paragraph. For an unqualified opinion, each item listed must be satisfied:

Title:

The title must include the word *independent.*

Introductory paragraph:

a. Financial statements identified were audited.

b. Financial statements are the responsibility of the company's management.

c. Auditor is responsible for the expression of an opinion on the financial statements.

Scope paragraph:

a. Audit conducted in accordance with GAAS, and an indication of the country of origin of those standards.

b. Audit planned and performed to obtain reasonable assurance that the financial statements are free from material misstatements.

c. Audit includes examining evidence, assessing principles and significant estimates, and evaluating overall statement presentation.

Opinion paragraph:

a. The financial statements are presented fairly,

b. in all material respects,

c. in conformity with GAAP, including an indication of the country of origin of those accounting principles.

3512.03 The following is the wording of the standard auditor's report issued for comparative financial statements:

Independent Auditor's Report

We have audited the accompanying balance sheet of X Company as of December 31, 20X2, and 20X1, and the related statements of income, retained earnings, and cash flows for the years then ended. These financial statements are the responsibility of the Company's management. Our responsibility is to express an opinion on these financial statements based on our audits.

We conducted our audits in accordance with (U.S. or other country of origin) generally accepted auditing standards. Those standards require that we plan and perform the audit to obtain reasonable assurance about whether the financial statements are free of material misstatement. An audit includes examining, on a test basis, evidence supporting the amounts and disclosures in the financial statements. An audit also includes assessing the accounting principles used and significant estimates made by management, as well as evaluating the overall financial statement presentation. We believe our audits provide a reasonable basis for our opinion.

In our opinion, the financial statements referred to above present fairly, in all material respects, the financial position of X Company as of December 31, 20X2, and 20X1, and the results of its operations and its cash flows for the years then ended in conformity with (U.S. or other country of origin) generally accepted accounting principles.

(Signature)
(Date)

3512.04 The CPA may express an unqualified opinion on one of the financial statements and express a qualified or adverse opinion or disclaim an opinion on another if the circumstances call for this treatment.

3512.05 When the CPA expresses an unqualified opinion on comparative financial statements, the opinion applies to the current year's statements and to all other years presented, each of which should be identified.

3513 Meaning of Present Fairly (AU 411)

3513.01 The CPA's opinion that financial statements "present fairly" should be based on their judgment as to whether:

    a. the accounting principles selected have general acceptance,

    b. the accounting principles are appropriate in the circumstances,

    c. the financial statements, including the related notes, are informative of matters that may affect their use, understanding, and interpretation,

    d. the information is classified and summarized in a reasonable manner, and

    e. the financial statements reflect underlying events within a reasonable range of limits.

3513.02 No single source of reference exists for all established accounting principles. The sources of established accounting principles that are generally accepted in the United States are as follows:

    a. Accounting principles promulgated by a body designated by AICPA Council to establish such principles, pursuant to Rule 203 of the AICPA Code of Professional Conduct

    b. Pronouncements of bodies, composed of expert accountants, that deliberate accounting issues in public forums for the purpose of establishing accounting principles or describing existing accounting practices that are generally accepted, provided those pronouncements have been exposed for public comment and have been cleared by a body referred to in *item a.*

    c. Pronouncements of bodies organized by a body referred to in *item a.* and composed of expert accountants that deliberate accounting issues in public forums for the purpose of interpreting or establishing accounting principles

    d. Practices or pronouncements that are widely recognized as being generally accepted because they represent prevalent practice in a particular industry

3513.03 SAS 69 (AU 411) establishes three separate but parallel GAAP hierarchies: one for nongovernmental entities, one for state and local governmental entities, and one for federal governmental entities. Each hierarchy has five levels of authoritative pronouncements as noted in the following paragraphs.

3513.04 The hierarchy for nongovernmental entities is as follows:

    1. FASB Statements and Interpretations, APB Opinions, and AICPA Accounting Research Bulletins

    2. FASB Technical Bulletins, AICPA Industry Audit and Accounting Guides, and AICPA Statements of Position

    3. Consensus positions of the FASB Emerging Issues Task Force (EITF) and AICPA Practice Bulletins

    4. AICPA Accounting Interpretations, "Qs and As" published by the FASB staff, as well as industry practice widely recognized and prevalent

    5. Other accounting literature

3513.05 The hierarchy for state and local governments is as follows:

    1. GASB Statements and Interpretations

2. GASB Technical Bulletins, and the following pronouncements if specifically made applicable to state and local governments by the AICPA—AICPA Industry Audit Guides and AICPA Statements of Position

3. Consensus positions of the GASB EITF and AICPA Practice Bulletins, if specifically made applicable to state and local governments by the AICPA

4. "Qs and As" published by the GASB staff, as well as industry practices widely recognized and prevalent

5. Other accounting literature

3513.06 The Federal Accounting Standards Advisory Board (FASAB) is the body designated to establish generally accepted accounting principles (GAAP) for federal governmental entities under Rule 203.

3513.07 The hierarchy for federal governmental entities is as follows:

1. FASAB Statements and Interpretations and AICPA and FASB pronouncements specifically made applicable to federal governmental entities by FASAB Statements or Interpretations

2. FASAB Technical Bulletins and, if specifically made applicable to federal governmental entities by the AICPA and cleared by the FASAB, AICPA Industry Audit and Accounting Guides and AICPA Statements of Position

3. AICPA AcSEC Practice Bulletins, if specifically made applicable to federal governmental entities and cleared by the FASAB, and Technical Releases of the Accounting and Auditing Policy Committee of the FASAB

4. Implementation guides published by the FASAB staff and practices that are widely recognized and prevalent in the federal government

5. Other accounting literature

3514 Explanatory Language Added to the Auditor's Standard Report (AU 508.11–.19)

3514.01 The auditor may add explanatory language to the report for a variety of circumstances and not alter the fact that an unqualified opinion is issued on the financial statements. These circumstances include the following:

a. The auditor's opinion is based in part on the report of another auditor (section **3521**).

b. The financial statements contain a departure from GAAP with which the auditor concurs to prevent the financial statements from being misleading because of unusual circumstances (section **3522.04**).

c. There is substantial doubt about the entity's ability to continue as a going concern (section **3526**).

d. There has been a material change between periods in accounting principles or in the method of their application (section **3523**).

e. Certain circumstances relating to reports on comparative financial statements exist (section **3519**).

f. Selected quarterly financial data required by SEC Regulation S-K has been omitted or has not been reviewed.

g. Supplementary information required by the FASB or GASB has been omitted, or departs from presentation guidelines, or the auditor is unable to apply prescribed procedures to remove doubt about conformity with FASB or GASB guidelines (section **3560**).

h. Other information in documents containing audited financial statements is materially inconsistent with information appearing in the financial statements (section **3550**).

i. The auditor believes there is a need to emphasize a matter regarding the financial statements (section **3527**).

3515 Qualified Opinions (AU 508.20–.57)

3515.01 A qualified opinion states that, *except for* the effects of the matter to which the qualification relates, the financial statements present fairly, in all material respects, financial position, results of operations, and cash flows in conformity with GAAP.

3515.02 A qualified opinion is necessary when a matter is material enough to mention but not sufficiently material to require an adverse opinion or a disclaimer of opinion. A material scope limitation or a material departure from GAAP will cause the CPA to issue a qualified opinion.

3515.03 When the auditor expresses a qualified opinion, the auditor should disclose all of the substantive reasons in one or more separate explanatory paragraph(s) preceding the opinion paragraph of the report. The auditor should also include, in the opinion paragraph, the appropriate qualifying language and a reference to the explanatory paragraph.

3515.04 When the qualified opinion results from a scope limitation, the auditor should mention the scope limitation in *both* the scope and opinion paragraphs and should only refer to an explanatory paragraph; the scope limitation should *not* be explained in a note to the financial statements.

3515.05 An example of a qualified opinion due to a scope limitation concerning an investment in a foreign subsidiary is shown as follows (AU 508.26):

Independent Auditor's Report

(Same first paragraph as the standard report)

Except as discussed in the following paragraph, we conducted our audits in accordance with generally accepted auditing standards. Those standards require that we plan and perform the audit to obtain reasonable assurance about whether the financial statements are free of material misstatement. An audit includes examining, on a test basis, evidence supporting the amounts and disclosures in the financial statements. An audit also includes assessing the accounting principles used and significant estimates made by management, as well as evaluating the overall financial statement presentation. We believe that our audits provide a reasonable basis for our opinion.

We were unable to obtain audited financial statements supporting the Company's investment in a foreign affiliate stated at $_____ and $_____ at December 31, 20X2, and 20X1, respectively, or its equity in earnings of that affiliate of $_____ and $_____, which is included in net income for the years then ended as described in Note X to the financial statements; nor were we able to satisfy ourselves as to the carrying value of the investment in the foreign affiliate or the equity in its earnings by other auditing procedures.

In our opinion, except for the effects of such adjustments, if any, as might have been determined to be necessary had we been able to examine evidence regarding the foreign affiliate investment and earnings, the financial statements referred to in the first paragraph above present fairly, in all material respects, the financial position of X Company as of December 31, 20X2, and 20X1, and the results of its operations and its cash flows for the years then ended in conformity with generally accepted accounting principles.

3515.06 When the qualified opinion results from a material departure from GAAP, the explanatory paragraph should disclose the principal effects of the qualification, if reasonably determinable, or refer to a footnote in the financial statements disclosing the effect.

3515.07 An example of a qualified opinion due to the use of an accounting principle at variance with GAAP is shown as follows (AU 508.39):

Independent Auditor's Report

(Same first and second paragraphs as the standard report)

The Company has excluded from property and debt in the accompanying balance sheets certain lease obligations that, in our opinion, should be capitalized in order to conform with generally accepted accounting principles. If these lease obligations were capitalized, property would be increased by $_____ and $_____, long-term debt by $_____ and $_____, and retained earnings by $_____ and $_____ as of December 31, 20X2, and 20X1, respectively. Additionally, net income would be increased (decreased) by $_____ and $_____ and earnings per share would be increased (decreased) by $_____ and $_____, respectively, for the years then ended.

In our opinion, except for the effects of not capitalizing certain lease obligations as discussed in the preceding paragraph, the financial statements referred to above present fairly, in all material respects, the financial position of X Company as of December 31, 20X2, and 20X1, and the results of its operations and its cash flows for the years then ended in conformity with generally accepted accounting principles.

3515.08 An example of a qualified opinion as a result of inadequate disclosure (AU 508.42):

Independent Auditor's Report

(Same first and second paragraphs as the standard report)

The Company's financial statements do not disclose (give the nature of the omitted disclosures). In our opinion, disclosure of this information is required by generally accepted accounting principles.

In our opinion, except for the omission of the information discussed in the preceding paragraph,...

3515.09 The auditor is not required to prepare a basic financial statement (such as the statement of cash flow) and include it in the report if the company's management declines to present the statement. Accordingly, in these cases, the auditor should ordinarily qualify the report (AU 508.44).

3515.10 The auditor should evaluate a change in accounting principle by management. If a newly adopted accounting principle is not GAAP, the method of accounting for the effect of the change is not in conformity with GAAP, or management has not provided reasonable justification for the change, the auditor should express a qualified opinion or an adverse opinion depending on the materiality of the item (AU 508.51).

3516 Adverse Opinions (508.58–.60)

3516.01 An adverse opinion states that the financial statements do not present fairly the financial position or the results of operations or cash flow in conformity with GAAP.

3516.02 When the auditor expresses an adverse opinion, the auditor should disclose in a separate explanatory paragraph(s) preceding the opinion paragraph of the report (a) all the substantive reasons for the adverse opinion and (b) the principal effects of the subject matter of the adverse opinion on the financial statements, if possible.

3516.03 An example of an adverse opinion is shown as follows (AU 508.60):

Independent Auditor's Report

(Same first and second paragraphs as the standard report)

As discussed in Note X to the financial statements, the Company carries its property, plant, and equipment accounts at appraisal values and provides depreciation on the basis of such values. Further, the Company does not provide for income taxes with respect to differences between financial income and taxable income arising because of the use, for income tax purposes, of the installment method of reporting gross profit from certain types of sales. Generally accepted accounting principles require that property, plant, and equipment be stated at an amount not in excess of cost, reduced by depreciation based on such amount, and that deferred income taxes be provided.

Because of the departures from generally accepted accounting principles identified above, as of December 31, 20X2, and 20X1, inventories have been increased $ _____ and $ _____ by inclusion in manufacturing overhead of depreciation in excess of that based on cost; property, plant, and equipment, less accumulated depreciation, is carried at $ _____ and $ _____ in excess of an amount based on the cost to the Company; and deferred income taxes of $ _____ and $ _____ have not been recorded, resulting in an increase of $ _____ and $ _____ in retained earnings and in appraisal surplus of $ _____ and $ _____, respectively. For the years ended December 31, 20X2, and 20X1, cost of goods sold has been increased $ _____ and $ _____, respectively, because of the effects of the depreciation accounting referred to above, and deferred income taxes of $ _____ and $ _____ have not been provided, resulting in an increase in net income of $ _____ and $ _____, respectively.

In our opinion, because of the effects of the matters discussed in the preceding paragraphs, the financial statements referred to above do not present fairly, in conformity with generally accepted accounting principles, the financial position of X Company as of December 31, 20X2, and 20X1, or the results of its operations or its cash flows for the years then ended.

3517 Disclaimer of Opinion (AU 508.61–.63)

3517.01 A disclaimer of opinion states that the auditor does not express an opinion on the financial statements. A disclaimer is normally issued when the auditor has not performed an audit sufficient in scope to enable the auditor to form an opinion on the financial statements.

3517.02 When disclaiming an opinion because of a scope limitation, the auditor should not identify the procedures that were performed nor include the scope paragraph of the auditor's standard report.

3517.03 If the auditor has made an examination sufficient to reveal material departures from GAAP, a disclaimer should not be issued. A disclaimer of opinion is not a substitute for an adverse opinion.

3517.04 Typically, the test for an adverse opinion is whether or not the CPA can provide a correcting entry or a note to the financial statements that would provide a fair representation. If the CPA cannot do this, a disclaimer may be appropriate.

3517.05 An example of a report disclaiming an opinion resulting from an inability to obtain sufficient appropriate audit evidence because of the scope limitation is shown as follows (AU 508.63):

Independent Auditor's Report

We were engaged to audit the accompanying balance sheets of X Company as of December 31, 20X2, and 20X1, and the related statements of income, retained earnings, and cash flows for the years then ended. These financial statements are the responsibility of the Company's management.

(Second paragraph of standard report should be omitted)

The Company did not make a count of its physical inventory in 20X2 or 20X1, stated in the accompanying financial statements at $ _____ as of December 31, 20X2, and at $ _____ as of December 31, 20X1. Further, evidence supporting the cost of property and equipment acquired prior to December 31, 20X1, is no longer available. The Company's records do not permit the application of other auditing procedures to inventories or property and equipment.

Since the Company did not take physical inventories and we were not able to apply other auditing procedures to satisfy ourselves as to inventory quantities and the cost of property and equipment, the scope of our work was not sufficient to enable us to express, and we do not express, an opinion on these financial statements.

3518 Summary of Audit Report Forms

3518.01 The summary chart as follows reflects the alternative forms of audit reports and the circumstances under which they should be issued:

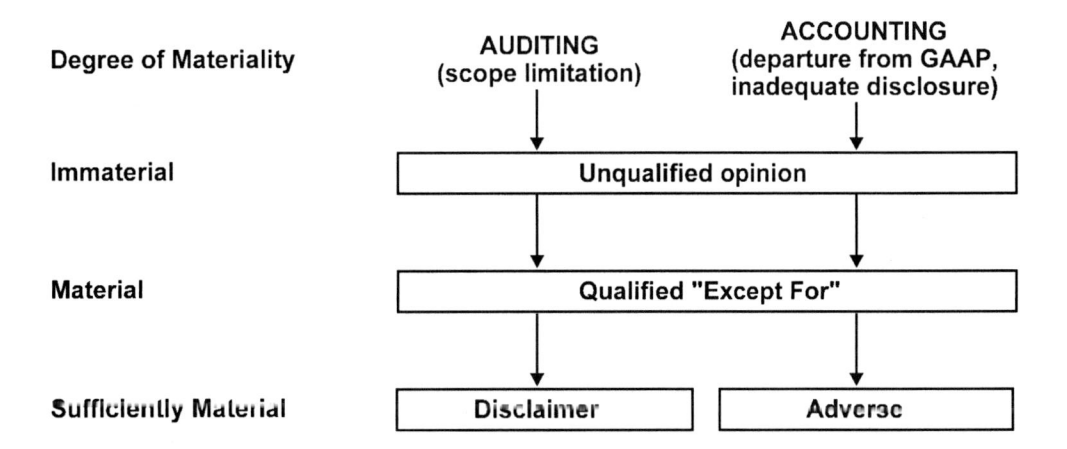

Degree of Materiality	AUDITING (scope limitation)	ACCOUNTING (departure from GAAP, inadequate disclosure)
Immaterial	Unqualified opinion	Unqualified opinion
Material	Qualified "Except For"	Qualified "Except For"
Sufficiently Material	Disclaimer	Adverse

3519 Reports on Comparative Financial Statements (AU 508.65–.74)

3519.01 A continuing auditor should update the report on the individual financial statements of the one or more prior periods presented on a comparative basis with those of the current period.

3519.02 An auditor may express a qualified or adverse opinion, disclaim an opinion, or include an explanatory paragraph with respect to one or more financial statements for one or more periods, while issuing a different report on the other financial statements presented.

3519.03 Examples of reports on comparative financial statements with different reports on one or more financial statements are presented as follows (AU 508.67):

    a. Standard report on the prior-year financial statements and a qualified opinion on the current-year financial statements:

Independent Auditor's Report

(Same first and second paragraphs as the standard report)

The Company has excluded, from property and debt in the accompanying 20X2 balance sheet, certain lease obligations that were entered into in 20X2 which, in our opinion, should be capitalized in order to conform with generally accepted accounting principles. If these lease obligations were capitalized, property would be increased by $ _____, long-term debt by $ _____, and retained earnings by $ _____ as of December 31, 20X2, and net income and earnings per share would be increased (decreased) by $ _____ and $ _____, respectively, for the year then ended.

In our opinion, except for the effects on the 20X2 financial statements of not capitalizing certain lease obligations as described in the preceding paragraph, the financial statements referred to above present fairly, in all material respects, the financial position of ABC Company as of December 31, 20X2, and 20X1, and the results of its operations and its cash flows for the years then ended in conformity with generally accepted accounting principles.

    b. Standard report on the current-year financial statements with a disclaimer of opinion on the prior-year statements of income, retained earnings, and cash flows:

Independent Auditor's Report

(Same first paragraph as the standard report)

Except as explained in the following paragraph, we conducted our audits in accordance with generally accepted auditing standards. Those standards require that we plan and perform our audit to obtain reasonable assurance about whether the financial statements are free of material misstatement. An audit includes examining, on a test basis, evidence supporting the amounts and disclosures in the financial statements. An audit also includes assessing the accounting principles used and significant estimates made by management, as well as evaluating the overall financial statement presentation. We believe that our audits provide a reasonable basis for our opinion.

We did not observe the taking of the physical inventory as of December 31, 20X0, since that date was prior to our appointment as auditors for the Company, and we were unable to satisfy ourselves regarding inventory quantities by means of other auditing procedures. Inventory amounts as of December 31, 20X0, enter into the determination of net income and cash flows for the year ended December 31, 20X1.

Because of the matter discussed in the preceding paragraph, the scope of our work was not sufficient to enable us to express, and we do not express, an opinion of the results of operations and cash flows for the year ended December 31, 20X1.

In our opinion, the balance sheets of ABC Company as of December 31, 20X2, and 20X1, and the related statements of income, retained earnings, and cash flows for the year ended December 31, 20X2, present fairly, in all material respects, the financial position of ABC Company as of December 31, 20X2, and 20X1, and the results of its operations and its cash flows for the year ended December 31, 20X2, in conformity with generally accepted accounting principles.

3519.04 If, during the current audit, an auditor becomes aware of circumstances or events that affect the financial statements of a prior period, the auditor should consider such matters when updating the report on the financial statements of the prior period.

3519.05 If, in an updated report, the opinion is different from the opinion previously expressed, the auditor should disclose all the substantive reasons for the different opinion in a separate explanatory paragraph(s) preceding the opinion paragraph of the report.

3519.06 An example of an explanatory paragraph in an updated report on the financial statements of a prior period that contains an opinion different from the one previously expressed is shown as follows (AU 508.69):

Independent Auditor's Report

(Same first and second paragraphs as the standard report)

In our report dated March 1, 20X2, we expressed an opinion that the 20X1 financial statements did not fairly present financial position, results of operations, and cash flows in conformity with generally accepted accounting principles because of two departures from such principles: (1) the Company carried its property, plant, and equipment at appraisal values and provided for depreciation on the basis of such values; and (2) the Company did not provide for deferred income taxes with respect to differences between income for financial reporting purposes and taxable income. As described in Note X, the Company has changed its method of accounting for these items and restated its 20X1 financial statements to conform with generally accepted accounting principles. Accordingly, our present opinion on the 20X1 financial statements, as presented herein, is different from that expressed in our previous report.

In our opinion, the financial statements referred to above present fairly, in all material respects, the financial position of X Company as of December 31, 20X2, and 20X1, and the results of its operations and its cash flows for the years then ended in conformity with generally accepted accounting principles.

3519.07 Before reissuing (or consenting to the reuse of) a report previously issued on the financial statements of a prior period, a *predecessor auditor* should consider whether the previous report on those financial statements is still appropriate.

3519.08 In determining the appropriateness of the previous report, a predecessor auditor should do the following:

   a. Read the financial statements of the current period.

   b. Compare the prior-period financial statements reported on with the financial statements to be presented for comparative purposes.

   c. Obtain a letter of representation from the successor auditor indicating any matters that might have a material effect on the financial statements reported on by the predecessor.

3519.09 If the prior-period financials have been audited by a predecessor whose report is not presented, the successor auditor should indicate the following in the introductory paragraph of the report:

   a. That the financial statements of the prior period were audited by another auditor

   b. The date of the report

   c. The type of report issued by the predecessor

   d. If the report was other than a standard report, the substantive reasons therefore (AU 508.74)

3520 Modifications of the Standard Report

3521 Reliance on Another Auditor (AU 543)

3521.01 Reference to the report of another CPA reflects *division of responsibility* and is *not* a qualification of opinion. It is disclosed in the introductory paragraph and referred to in both the scope and opinion paragraphs. An example of the wording to be added at the end of the scope paragraph is as follows:

> ... We did not audit the financial statements of B Company, a consolidated subsidiary, whose statements reflect total assets and revenues constituting 20% and 22%, respectively, of the related consolidated totals. These statements were audited by other auditors whose report has been furnished to us, and our opinion, insofar as it relates to the amounts included for B Company, is based solely on the report of the other auditors.

> ... We believe that our audit and the report of the other auditors provide a reasonable basis for our opinion.

> ... In our opinion, based on our examination and the report of other auditors, balance sheet and consolidated statements of income and retained earnings and cash flows present fairly...

3521.02 A CPA may rely on the work and reports of other CPAs who have examined one or more subsidiaries, divisions, branches, or investments that are part of the financial statements being audited.

3521.03 The CPA must decide whether the CPA's participation is sufficient to be the *principal auditor*. In making this decision, consideration of the following must be given:

a. Materiality of their portion of the overall examination

b. Extent of their knowledge of the overall financial statements

c. Importance of the components audited by the auditor to the company taken as a whole

3521.04 The principal auditor must decide whether to accept responsibility for the work of the other CPA.

a. If so, no mention of the other CPA is made in the opinion.

b. If not, the work of the other CPA is mentioned and responsibility is divided.

3521.05 If no reference is to be made of the other CPA, the principal auditor must be satisfied as to the other CPA's:

a. independence,

b. professional reputation, and

c. audit examination.

3521.06 No reference would usually be made when:

a. the other CPA is a correspondent CPA,

b. the other CPA is retained by the principal CPA,

c. the principal auditor is satisfied as to the other CPA's work, and

d. the portion of the financial statements examined by the other CPA is immaterial.

3521.07 When reference is made to the work of the other CPA, the report must clearly indicate the division of responsibility by stating in the scope paragraph the magnitude of the other CPA's examination in dollar amounts or percentages of total assets, revenues, or other measures. The division of responsibility should also be referred to in the opinion paragraph.

3521.08 In either case (reference or no reference to other auditor), the following procedures should be followed:

    a. Inquire of professional organizations, other CPAs, banks, and creditors as to the reputation of the other auditor.

    b. Obtain a letter of representation from the other CPA stating their independence.

    c. Ascertain that the other CPA:

        (1) knows component financial statements and the reports will be used by the principal CPA,

        (2) is familiar with GAAP and GAAS,

        (3) is familiar with SEC rules, if applicable, and

        (4) knows a review of intercompany transactions will be made by the principal auditor.

3521.09 After deciding to rely on the work of the other CPA, the following should be done:

    a. Discuss with the other CPA the appropriate audit procedures to be carried out.

    b. Review the other CPA's workpapers.

3521.10 If the principal auditor determines that they cannot rely on the work of the other CPA, a disclaimer is appropriate.

3521.11 A CPA is the principal auditor when they use financial statements of an investee under the equity method.

3521.12 If the other CPA's report is qualified, the principal auditor must assess its materiality to the financial statements under examination.

3521.13 When one CPA succeeds another, the successor should not refer to the other CPA even though there may be some reliance on the work of the predecessor.

3521.14 When a pooling of interest occurs, the principal auditor must have audited one of the companies pooled to express an opinion on the restated statements of prior periods; otherwise, the opinion can relate only to the compilation of the statements (math accuracy, etc.).

3521.15 Study the following flowchart, which summarizes the procedures and decision points in this section.

Using the Work and Reports of Other Auditors (AU543)

```
                    ┌─────────────────────────┐
                    │ CPA "X" utilizes work and│
                    │ reports of other auditor │
                    │ "C."                     │
                    └────────────┬─────────────┘
                                 ▼
                         ◇ Is portion of
                No   ◇ financials examined ◇  Yes
           ┌────────◇   by X material to   ◇────────┐
           │        ◇  portion examined    ◇        │
           │        ◇       by C?          ◇        │
           │                                        ▼
           │                              ◇ Does X have ◇
           │                          No  ◇   adequate  ◇  Yes
           │◄────────────────────────────◇ knowledge of ◇────┐
           │                              ◇ the overall ◇    │
           │                              ◇  financial  ◇    │
           │                              ◇ statements? ◇    │
           │                                                 ▼
           │                                       ◇ Is portion audited ◇
           │                                   No  ◇    by X important  ◇  Yes
           │◄─────────────────────────────────────◇    to the enterprise◇───┐
           │                                       ◇    as a whole?      ◇   │
           │                                                                 ▼
           ▼                                              ┌──────────────────────────┐
  ┌──────────────────┐                                    │ X should investigate C   │
  │ X should not     │                                    │ for (1) Reputation, and  │
  │ report as        │                                    │ (2) Independence.        │
  │ principal        │                                    └────────────┬─────────────┘
  │ auditor.         │                                                 ▼
  └──────────────────┘                                     ◇  Is X able to   ◇
                                                   Yes    ◇  satisfy himself ◇   No
                                                 ┌───────◇ as to reputation  ◇───────┐
                                                 │       ◇ and independence  ◇       │
                                                 │       ◇      of C?        ◇       │
                                                 ▼                                   ▼
                                   ┌──────────────────────┐              ┌──────────────────────┐
                                   │ X should communicate │              │ Issue qualified or   │
                                   │ with C concerning    │              │ disclaimer of opinion│
                                   │ divided              │              │ of financial         │
                                   │ responsibilities.    │              │ statements.          │
                                   │ (Note 1)             │              └──────────────────────┘
                                   └──────────┬───────────┘
                                              ▼
                                     ◇  Is X going to  ◇
                          Yes (Note 2)◇    assume      ◇ No (Note 3)
                         ┌───────────◇ responsibility  ◇────────┐
                         │           ◇ for the work    ◇        │
                         │           ◇     of C?       ◇        │
                         ▼                                      ▼
             ┌──────────────────────┐              ┌──────────────────────┐
             │ Consider performing  │              │ Modify report to show│
             │ one or more of the   │              │ divided responsibility│
             │ following:           │              │ (scope and opinion). │
             └──────────┬───────────┘              └──────────┬───────────┘
                        ▼                                     ▼
             ┌──────────────────────┐              ┌──────────────────────┐
             │ Visit C to discuss   │              │ Disclose in audit    │
             │ audit procedures and │              │ report percentage    │
             │ results of audit.    │              │ (total assets and/or │
             └──────────┬───────────┘              │ total revenue) of    │
                        ▼                          │ work done by C.      │
             ┌──────────────────────┐              └──────────────────────┘
             │ Review audit program │
             │ of C.                │
             └──────────┬───────────┘
                        ▼
             ┌──────────────────────┐
             │ Review the workpapers│
             │ of C.                │
             └──────────┬───────────┘
                        ▼
             ┌──────────────────────┐
             │ Perform supplemental │
             │ audit test.          │
             └──────────┬───────────┘
                        ▼
             ┌──────────────────────┐
             │ No change in audit   │
             │ report required--no  │
             │ mention of C.        │
             └──────────────────────┘
```

Note 1: X should ensure that C understands (1) that the financial statements examined by him will be included in financial statements reported on by X, (2) United States GAAP and auditing standards, (3) the relevant reporting requirements of the SEC (if appropriate), and (4) a review will be made of (a) matters affecting intercompany eliminations and, if appropriate, (b) uniformity of accounting practices employed in component statements.

Note 2: Ordinarily, this alternative is adopted when C (other auditor) is a correspondent firm, an agent of X, or the portion of financial statements examined by C is not material.

Note 3: This alternative is usually adopted when (1) it is impracticable for X to review C's work or apply other procedures to gain satisfaction, and (2) financial statements examined by C are material in relation to overall financial statements.

(Dan M. Guy, "SAP Flowcharts," *The Journal of Accountancy,* March 1974, p. 84)

3522 Departures from GAAP

3522.01 The **first standard of reporting** is: "The report shall state whether the financial statements are presented in accordance with GAAP" (AU 410).

3522.02 When there is a departure from GAAP, the reporting options are as follows:

    a. Unqualified opinion—if not material

    b. Qualified opinion—if material

    c. Adverse opinion—if sufficiently material (AU 508.58)

3522.03 In evaluating the materiality of a departure from GAAP, the CPA should consider the following:

    a. Dollar magnitude

    b. Qualitative factors:

        (1) Significance of an item to a company (e.g., inventories to a manufacturing company)

        (2) Pervasiveness of the misstatement

        (3) The impact of the item on the statements taken as a whole

    c. Lack of disclosure of essential data (AU 508.54)

3522.04 GAAP is defined as ARBs, APB Opinions, or FASB Statements and Interpretations unless, due to unusual circumstances, the financial statement is caused to be misleading using these principles. When such circumstances exist, an unqualified opinion may be issued, but the circumstances should be explained in a separate paragraph in the report (AU 508.14–.15).

3522.05 GAAP also applies to companies whose accounting practices are dictated by governmental regulatory bodies or commissions, and the reporting requirements in sections **3522.01** and **3522.04** should be followed (AU 544).

3523 Reporting on Consistency (AU 508.16–.18 and AU 420.07–.11)

3523.01 The auditor's standard report does not include an expression related to the consistent application of generally accepted accounting principles if (a) no change in accounting principles has occurred or (b) there has been a change in accounting principles or the method of their application, but the effect of the change is not material.

3523.02 The following is an example of an appropriate explanatory paragraph when a change in an accounting principle has occurred:

As discussed in Note X to the financial statements, the company changed its method of computing depreciation in 20X1.

3523.03 The addition of this explanatory paragraph in the auditor's report is required in reports on financial statements of subsequent years as long as the year of the change is presented and reported on.

3523.04 AU 420.07–.11, *Reporting on Consistency,* conforms the list of changes that constitute a change in the reporting entity to the guidance in paragraph 12 of APB Opinion 20, *Accounting Changes.* It further clarifies that the auditor need **not** add a consistency explanatory paragraph to the auditor's report when a change in the reporting entity results from a transaction or event.

3523.05 The requirement for a consistency explanatory paragraph in the auditor's report if a pooling of interests is not accounted for retroactively in comparative financial statements is eliminated. However, in these circumstances, the auditor would still be required to express a qualified or adverse opinion because of the departure from GAAP.

3523.06 A change in the reporting entity is a special type of change in accounting principle which results in financial statements that, in effect, are those of a different reporting entity. This type of change is limited to the following:

    a. Presenting consolidated or combined statements in place of statements on individual companies

    b. Changing specific subsidiaries comprising the group of companies for which consolidated statements are presented

    c. Changing the companies included in combined financial statements

    d. A business combination accounted for by the pooling of interests method

3523.07 A change in the reporting entity resulting from a transaction or event (such as a pooling of interests, or the creation, cessation, or complete or partial purchase or disposition of a subsidiary or other business unit) does not require that an explanatory paragraph about consistency be included in the auditor's report.

3523.08 A change in the reporting entity that does **not** result from a transaction or event requires recognition in the auditor's report through inclusion of an explanatory paragraph.

3523.09 If prior-years' financial statements, presented in comparison with current-year financial statements, are not restated to give appropriate recognition to a pooling of interests, a departure from GAAP has occurred which necessitates that the auditor express a qualified or adverse opinion.

3524 Inadequate Disclosure (AU 431)

3524.01 The **third standard of reporting** is "informative disclosures in the financial statements are to be regarded as adequate unless otherwise stated in the report."

3524.02 Examples of disclosure issues include the following:

    a. Form, content, and arrangement of statements

    b. Terminology

    c. Detail given

    d. Classification

3524.03 Verbosity is not a substitute for adequate disclosure.

3524.04 Lack of adequate disclosure or omission of information required by GAAP requires a qualified opinion or an adverse opinion (AU 508.41).

    a. Disclosure of the omitted information in a paragraph of the report is required if the omission is not recognized in a specific SAS and if it is practical to provide the omitted data.

    b. Disclosure of the omitted information is not required if the omission is allowed by a specific SAS (see section **3524.07**) or if it is not practical to provide the omitted data.

    c. It is practical to provide the information if it is reasonably obtainable and if the providing of the information does not require the auditor to assume the position of a preparer of the information (AU 545 and AU 431).

3524.05 Confidential client information not associated with fairness of presentation should not be disclosed.

3524.06 Misstatement of segment information or omission of required segment information requires a qualified opinion because of departure from GAAP.

3524.07 If the statement of cash flows is omitted, qualify the opinion but do not place the omitted statement in the middle paragraph (AU 508.43).

3525 Uncertainties, Scope Limitations, and Departures from GAAP Involving Risks or Uncertainties (AU 508.29–.32 and .45–.49)

3525.01 A matter involving an uncertainty is one that is expected to be resolved at a future date, at which time conclusive audit evidence concerning its outcome would be expected to become available.

3525.02 Conclusive audit evidence concerning the ultimate outcome of uncertainties cannot be expected to exist at the time of the audit because the outcome and related audit evidence are prospective. Management is responsible for appropriate estimates or required disclosures in accordance with GAAP.

3525.03 If the auditor is unable to obtain sufficient audit evidence to support management's assertions about the nature of a matter involving an uncertainty and its presentation or disclosure in the financial statements, the auditor should consider the need to express a qualified opinion or to disclaim an opinion because of a scope limitation.

3525.04 If the auditor concludes that a matter involving a risk or an uncertainty is not adequately disclosed in the financial statements in conformity with GAAP, the auditor should express a qualified or an adverse opinion.

3525.05 In preparing financial statements, management estimates the outcome of certain types of future events. In some cases, the inability to make a reasonable estimate may raise questions about the appropriateness of the accounting principles used. If the auditor concludes that the accounting principles used cause the financial statements to be materially misstated, the auditor should express a qualified or adverse opinion.

3525.06 Usually, the auditor is able to be satisfied regarding the reasonableness of management's estimate of the effects of future events by considering various types of audit evidence, including the historical experience of the entity. If the auditor concludes that management's estimate is unreasonable and that its effect is to cause the financial statements to be materially misstated, the auditor should express a qualified or an adverse opinion.

3526 Consideration of an Entity's Ability to Continue As a Going Concern (AU 341)

3526.01 The auditor has a responsibility to evaluate whether there is substantial doubt about the entity's ability to continue as a going concern for a reasonable period of time, not to exceed one year beyond the date of the financial statements being audited.

3526.02 Information about conditions or events that raise a question about an entity's ability to continue as a going concern is obtained from the application of auditing procedures planned and performed to achieve objectives in the financial statements being audited.

3526.03 The auditor is not responsible for predicting future conditions or events. The fact that the entity may cease to exist as a going concern subsequent to receiving a report from the auditor that does not refer to substantial doubt, even within one year following the date of the financial statements, does not (in itself) indicate inadequate performance by the auditor.

3526.04 The results of auditing procedures designed and performed to achieve other audit objectives are normally sufficient to identify circumstances indicating doubt about an entity's continued existence.

3526.05 Examples of conditions or events that might alert an auditor to the identification of substantial doubt include the following:

   a. Negative trends (e.g., recurring operating losses)

   b. Other indications of possible financial difficulties (e.g., default on loan or similar agreements)

   c. Internal matters (e.g., work stoppages or other labor difficulties)

   d. External matters that have occurred (e.g., legal proceedings, legislation, or similar matters that might jeopardize an entity's ability to operate)

3526.06 Once substantial doubt about an entity's ability to continue as a going concern surfaces, the auditor should discuss the matter with management and consider management's plans for dealing with the conditions and events identified. A primary concern of the auditor in assessing management's plans is an evaluation of management's ability to accomplish the plans for alleviating the adverse conditions identified.

3526.07 The auditor's consideration relating to management's plans may include the following:

   a. Plans to dispose of assets

   b. Plans to borrow money or restructure debt

   c. Plans to reduce or delay expenditures

   d. Plans to increase ownership equity

3526.08 If, after considering identified conditions and events and management's plans, the auditor concludes that substantial doubt remains, the audit report should include an explanatory paragraph that reflects that conclusion. Adequate disclosure of the circumstances relating to the conditions surrounding the substantial doubt should be provided in the financial statements. If such disclosure is not provided or is considered inadequate by the auditor, either a qualified or adverse opinion may be issued as a result of the inadequate disclosure.

3526.09 The addition of a going concern explanatory paragraph does not result in a qualified opinion. The explanatory paragraph should follow the opinion paragraph in the auditor's report.

3526.10 An example of a going concern explanatory paragraph is shown as follows (AU 341.13):

> The accompanying financial statements have been prepared assuming that the Company Y will continue as a going concern. As discussed in Note X to the financial statements, the Company has suffered recurring losses from operations and has a net capital deficiency that raises substantial doubt about its ability to continue as a going concern. Management's plans in regard to these matters are also described in Note X. The financial statements do not include any adjustments that might result from the outcome of this uncertainty.

3526.11 The auditor is precluded from using conditional language in the report regarding a conclusion about the entity's ability to continue as a going concern in a going concern explanatory paragraph. Conditional terminology such as the following is not appropriate: "If the company is unable to obtain refinancing, there may be substantial doubt about the company's ability to continue as a going concern."

3527 Emphasis of a Matter (AU 508.19)

3527.01 In some circumstances, an auditor may wish to emphasize a matter regarding the financial statements, but nevertheless intends to express an unqualified opinion. Such explanatory information should be presented in a separate paragraph of the auditor's report, normally after the opinion paragraph.

3527.02 Examples of matters that might be emphasized in an auditor's report include the following:

   a. Client is a component of a larger entity

   b. Significant related party transactions

   c. An important subsequent event

   d. Matters affecting comparability

   e. Omission of supplementary information required by the FASB

3530 Subsequent Events and Subsequent Discoveries

3531 Subsequent Events (AU 560)

3531.01 A **subsequent event** is an event or transaction that occurs after the balance sheet date, but before the date of the auditor's report, that has a material effect on the financial statements.

3531.02 The CPA must review subsequent events—of which there are two types—up to the date of the report.

3531.03 **Adjustment type** (the first type), which requires adjustment of the financial statements, consists of those events that provide additional evidence as to conditions that existed at the date of the balance sheet and affect the estimates inherent in the process of preparing financial statements. Examples of this type of event include the following:

   a. Losses on receivables resulting from the bankruptcy of a major customer that was in a weak financial position

   b. Settlement of litigation or other uncertainty

   c. Final determination of an amount that was estimated at the balance sheet date

   In these cases, the financial statements should be adjusted (e.g., a journal entry should be booked).

3531.04 **Disclosure type** (the second type), which requires disclosure only, consists of those events that provide evidence with respect to conditions that did not exist at the date the balance sheet was reported on but arose after that date. Examples include the following:

   a. Sale of a bond or capital stock issue

   b. Purchase of a business

   c. Settlement of litigation when the event giving rise to the claim took place subsequent to the balance sheet date

   d. Fire or flood loss

   e. Loss on receivable due to a post-balance sheet date (customer's major casualty)

   In these cases, disclose in a note to the financial statements or, in extreme cases, provide pro forma financial statements.

3531.05 The following are examples of events that would not normally be considered subsequent events requiring disclosure:

   a. Product changes

   b. Changes in management

   c. Loss of customer

   d. Strikes

   e. Proxy fights

   Notice that none of these examples would normally result in a journal entry when the event occurred.

3531.06 The CPA is required to do some detailed audit procedures after the balance date. Such procedures may reveal subsequent events. Examples of these procedures include the following:

   a. Cutoff procedures

   b. Evaluation of assets and liabilities at the balance sheet dates (e.g., subsequent collection of receivables)

3531.07 In addition, the CPA is required to do the following procedures related to subsequent events:

   a. Read and review interim financial statements.

   b. Inquire of officers.

   c. Read minutes of stockholders', directors', and officers' meetings.

   d. Inquire of legal counsel.

   e. Observe events in subsequent period.

   f. Scan records for unusual transactions.

   g. Obtain letter of representation on subsequent events.

3532 Subsequent Discoveries (AU 561)

3532.01 A **subsequent discovery** is the discovery of facts that existed at the date of the audit report but that were not known at that time. It is *not* an event that occurs after the report date *or* the resolution of a contingency that existed at that date.

3532.02 The CPA has *no* obligation to perform any further audit procedures after the report date, but new information may come to the CPA's attention. If this happens, the CPA should (1) consult with an attorney and (2) determine if the subsequently discovered information:

   a. is reliable,

   b. existed at the date of the report,

   c. is material to report (would or might change opinion), and

   d. is applicable to the report that is still being relied on.

3532.03 If the four conditions in section **3532.02** exist, the CPA should do the following:

   a. Advise the client to revise and reissue the statements and auditor's report.

   b. Make disclosure in financial statements of a subsequent period if the date of issue is imminent.

   c. Notify persons relying on statements of the facts that are known to the auditor, if the effect cannot be promptly determined and it appears the financial statements will be revised after investigation.

   d. Discuss with the SEC or other regulatory body, if appropriate.

3532.04 If the client refuses to cooperate in disclosing the facts, the CPA should notify the following:

   a. Client (management and board of directors) that the auditor's report cannot be associated with statements

   b. Regulatory bodies

   c. Each person known by the auditor to be relying on the statements

3532.05 When the CPA makes a satisfactory investigation, disclosure should consist of precise and factual statements of:

   a. facts as known by the CPA and

   b. effects on financial statements and the CPA's report.

3532.06 If the client refuses to cooperate, disclosure by the CPA cannot be as precise and should contain a statement that the client has not cooperated.

3532.07 Study the flowchart on the following page, which summarizes the requirements of this reaction.

Subsequent Discovery of Facts Existing at the Date of the Auditor's Report (AU561)

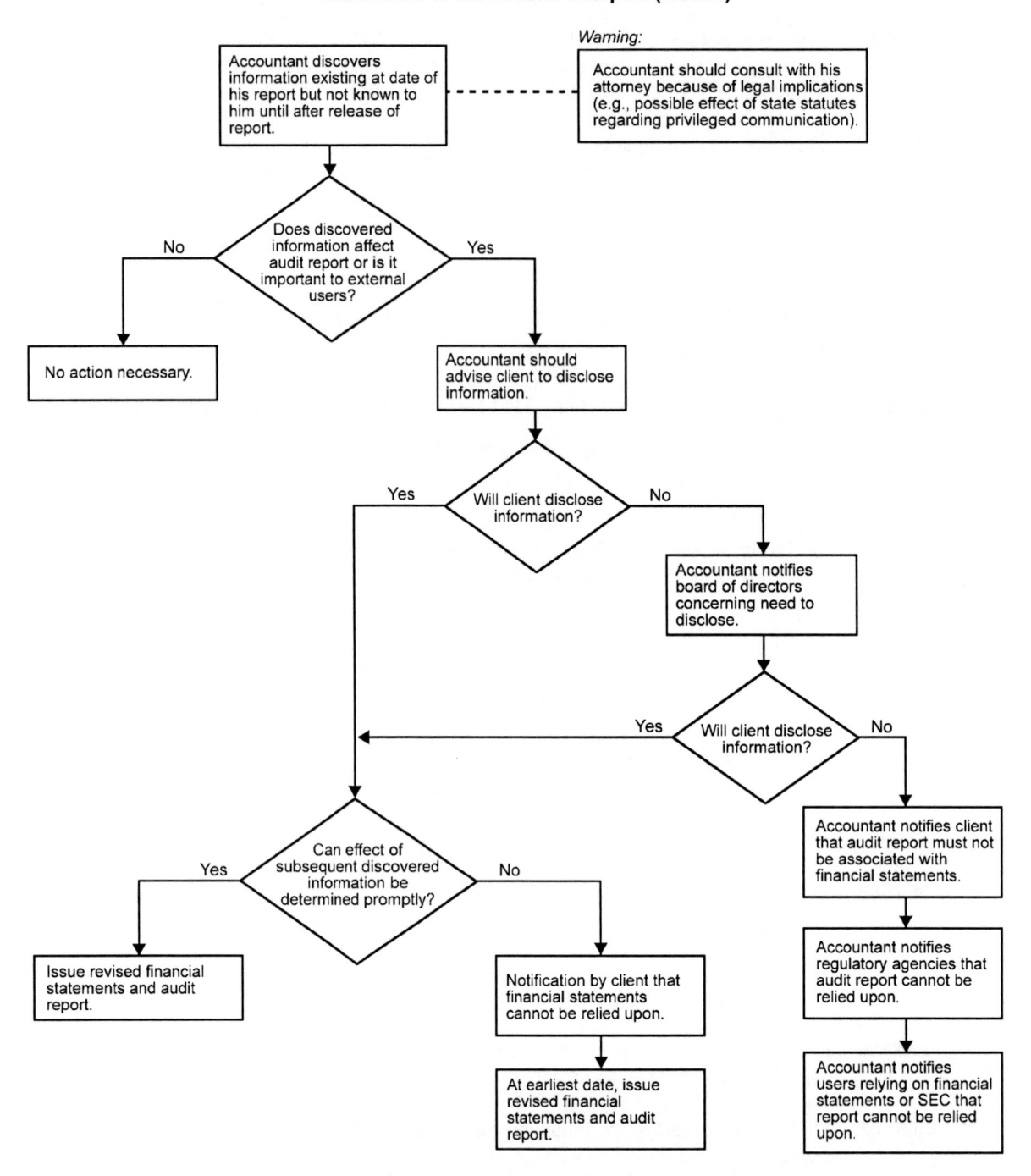

Warning: Accountant should consult with his attorney because of legal implications (e.g., possible effect of state statutes regarding privileged communication).

- Accountant discovers information existing at date of his report but not known to him until after release of report.

- **Does discovered information affect audit report or is it important to external users?**
  - **No** → No action necessary.
  - **Yes** → Accountant should advise client to disclose information.

- **Will client disclose information?**
  - **Yes** → (proceed to "Can effect..." decision)
  - **No** → Accountant notifies board of directors concerning need to disclose.

- **Will client disclose information?** (after board notification)
  - **Yes** → (proceed to "Can effect..." decision)
  - **No** →
    - Accountant notifies client that audit report must not be associated with financial statements.
    - Accountant notifies regulatory agencies that audit report cannot be relied upon.
    - Accountant notifies users relying on financial statements or SEC that report cannot be relied upon.

- **Can effect of subsequent discovered information be determined promptly?**
  - **Yes** → Issue revised financial statements and audit report.
  - **No** → Notification by client that financial statements cannot be relied upon. At earliest date, issue revised financial statements and audit report.

(Dan M. Guy, "SAP Flowcharts," *The Journal of Accountancy*, March 1974, p. 82)

3533 Consideration of Omitted Procedures After the Report Date (AU 390)

3533.01 The CPA concludes that one or more auditing procedures considered necessary at the time of the audit in the circumstances then existing were not performed.

3533.02 See section **3532** if the CPA, subsequent to the date of the report, becomes aware of facts pertaining to the financial statements that were overlooked that might have affected the audit report.

3533.03 The CPA has no obligation to carry out a retrospective review of their work. However, an omitted procedure may come to the CPA's attention from a:

  a. peer review or

  b. postissuance review in connection with firm's internal inspection program.

3533.04 This SAS does not apply to an engagement involving threatened or pending legal proceedings or a regulatory investigation.

3533.05 The CPA should consult with an attorney when an important audit procedure has been omitted.

3533.06 When the CPA concludes that an important audit procedure was omitted, the CPA should determine if the audit opinion can be supported by other procedures that were performed. Subsequent audits may provide audit evidence supporting the previously expressed opinion.

3533.07 If the omitted procedure impairs the CPA's present ability to support the previously expressed opinion and the opinion is being relied on, the CPA should promptly undertake to apply the omitted audit procedure or alternative procedures.

3533.08 If the CPA is unable to comply with section **3533.07** the CPA should consult an attorney to determine a course of action concerning responsibilities to the client, regulatory authorities, and others.

3534 Dating the Report (AU 530)

General Rules

3534.01 An auditor's report should be dated as of the date that substantially all fieldwork is completed. In the case of reports on comparative financial statements, the auditor's report should be dated as of the date of completion of fieldwork for the most recent audit.

3534.02 The auditor is primarily responsible for subsequent events up to this date.

3534.03 There is no responsibility after this date, except in SEC filings and for disclosure-type subsequent events that occur between the audit report date and before release date and that come to the CPA's attention.

Subsequent Events

3534.04 Adjustment type—make adjustment and date last date of fieldwork.

3534.05 Disclosure type—either of the following:

    a. Dual date—date report as of end of fieldwork and date note of the financial statements in which disclosure is made later.

    Example: March 15, 20XX, except for Note—as to which April 9, 20XX.

    b. Date report at date of subsequent event. This procedure extends auditor responsibility.

Reissuance of the Report

3534.06 Use of original report date implies no further examination.

3534.07 Dual dating may be used for subsequent events that need to be disclosed.

3540 The Auditor's Communication with Those Charged with Governance (AU 380)

3541 The Role of Communication

3541.01 The principal purposes of communication with those charged with governance are to:

    a. communicate clearly with those charged with governance the responsibilities of the auditor in relation to the financial statement audit, and an overview of the scope and timing of the audit.

    b. obtain from those charged with governance information relevant to the audit.

    c. provide those charged with governance with timely observations arising from the audit that are relevant to their responsibilities in overseeing the financial reporting process.

3541.02 Although the auditor is responsible for communicating specific matters in accordance with this Statement, management also has a responsibility to communicate matters of governance interest to those charged with governance. Communication by the auditor does not relieve management of the responsibility.

3542 Those Charged with Governance

3542.01 The auditor should determine the appropriate person(s) within the entity's governance structure with whom to communicate. The appropriate persons may vary depending on the matter to be communicated.

3542.02 In most entities, governance is the collective responsibility of a governing body, such as a board of directors, a supervisory board, partners, proprietors, a committee of management, trustees, or equivalent persons. In some smaller entities, however, one person may be charged with governance, such as the owner-manager where there are no other owners, or a sole trustee.

3542.03 When governance is a collective responsibility, a subgroup, such as an audit committee or even an individual, may be charged with specific tasks to assist the governing body in meeting its responsibilities.

3542.04 Such diversity means that it is not possible for AU 380 to specify for all audits the person(s) with whom the auditor is to communicate particular matters. The auditor's understanding of the entity's governance structure and process obtained in accordance with SAS 109, *Understanding the Entity and Its Environment and Assessing the Risks of Material Misstatement*, is relevant in deciding with whom to communicate matters.

3542.05 When the appropriate person(s) with whom to communicate are not clearly identifiable, the auditor and the engaging party should agree on the relevant person(s) within the entity's governance structure with whom the auditor will communicate.

3542.06 Audit committees (or similar subgroups with different names) exist in many entities. Although their specific authority and functions may differ, communication with the audit committee, where one exists, is a key element in the auditor's communication with those charged with governance. Good governance principles suggest that:

    a. the auditor has access to the audit committee as necessary.

    b. the chair of the audit committee and, when relevant, the other members of the audit committee meet with the auditor periodically.

    c. the audit committee meets with the auditor without management present at least annually.

3542.07 When considering communicating with a subgroup of those charged with governance, the auditor may take into account such matters as:

    a. the respective responsibilities of the subgroup and the governing body.

    b. the nature of the matter to be communicated.

    c. whether the subgroup (a) has the authority to take action in relation to the information communicated and (b) can provide further information and explanations the auditor may need.

    d. whether there is also a need to communicate the information, in full or in summary form, to the governing body.

3543 Communication with Management

3543.01 Many matters may be discussed with management in the ordinary course of an audit, including matters to be communicated with those charged with governance. Before communicating matters with those charged with governance, the auditor may discuss them with management unless that is inappropriate. Similarly, when an entity has an internal audit function, the auditor may discuss matters with the internal auditor before communicating with those charged with governance.

3543.02 In some cases, all of those charged with governance are involved in managing the entity. In these cases, if matters required by AU 380 are communicated with person(s) also having governance responsibilities, the matters need not be communicated again with those same person(s) in their governance role.

3544 Matters to Be Communicated

3544.01 The auditor should communicate with those charged with governance:

    a. the auditor's responsibilities under generally accepted auditing standards.

    b. an overview of the planned scope and timing of the audit.

    c. significant findings from the audit.

3544.02 When the auditor communicates his/her responsibilities under generally accepted auditing standards with those charged with governance, the auditor should indicate that:

    a. he/she is responsible for forming and expressing an opinion about whether the financial statements that have been prepared by management with the oversight of those charged with governance are presented fairly, in all material respects, in conformity with GAAP.

    b. the audit of the financial statements does not relieve management or those charged with governance of their responsibilities.

3544.03 Communication regarding the planned scope and timing of the audit should not result in compromising the effectiveness of the audit, particularly where some or all of those charged with governance are involved in managing the entity.

3544.04 Matters communicated concerning the scope and timing of the audit may include:

    a. how the auditor proposes to address the significant risks of material misstatement, whether due to error or fraud.

    b. the auditor's approach to internal control relevant to the audit, including, when applicable, whether the auditor will express an opinion on the effectiveness of internal control over financial reporting.

    c. the concept of materiality in planning and executing the audit, focusing on the factors considered rather than on specific thresholds or amounts.

    d. where the entity has an internal audit function, the extent to which the auditor will use the work of internal audit, and how the external and internal auditor can best work together.

3544.05 While communicating with those charged with governance may assist the auditor in planning the scope and timing of the audit, it does not change the auditor's sole responsibility to determine the overall audit strategy and the audit plan, including the nature, extent, and timing of procedures necessary to obtain sufficient appropriate audit evidence.

3544.06 Regarding significant findings from the audit, the auditor should communicate with those charged with governance the following matters:

    a. The auditor's views about qualitative aspects of the entity's significant accounting practices, including accounting policies, accounting estimates, and financial statement disclosures

    b. Significant difficulties, if any, encountered during the audit

    c. Uncorrected misstatements, other than those the auditor believes are trivial, if any

    d. Disagreements with management, if any

    e. Other findings or issues, if any, arising from the audit that are, in the auditor's professional judgment, significant and relevant to those charged with governance regarding their oversight of the financial reporting process

3544.07 Unless all of those charged with governance are involved in managing the entity, the auditor also should communicate:

  a. material, corrected misstatements that were brought to the attention of management as a result of audit procedures.

  b. representations the auditor is requesting from management.

  c. management's consultations with other accountants.

  d. significant issues, if any, arising from the audit that were discussed, or the subject of correspondence, with management.

3544.08 The auditor should inform those charged with governance of any significant difficulties encountered in dealing with management related to the performance of the audit. Significant difficulties encountered during the audit may include such matters as:

  a. significant delays in management providing required information.

  b. an unnecessarily brief time within which to complete the audit.

  c. extensive unexpected effort required to obtain sufficient appropriate audit evidence.

  d. the unavailability of expected information.

  e. restrictions imposed on the auditors by management.

  f. management's unwillingness to provide information about management's plans for dealing with the adverse effects of the conditions or events that lead the auditor to believe there is substantial doubt about the entity's ability to continue as a going concern.

3544.09 In some circumstances, the matters noted in section **3544.08** may constitute a scope limitation that leads to a modification of the auditor's opinion.

3545 The Communication Process

3545.01 The auditor should communicate in writing with those charged with governance significant findings from the audit when, in the auditor's professional judgment, oral communication would not be adequate. Other communications may be oral or in writing.

3545.02 Effective communication may involve formal presentations and written reports as well as less formal communications, including discussions.

3545.03 The auditor should indicate in the communication that it is intended solely for the information and use of those charged with governance and, if appropriate, management and that it is not intended to be and should not be used by anyone other than those specified parties.

3545.04 The appropriate timing for communications will vary with the circumstances of the engagement. However, the auditor should communicate with those charged with governance on a sufficiently timely basis to enable those charged with governance to take appropriate action.

3545.05 When matters required to be communicated by section **3545.04** have been communicated orally, the auditor should document them. When matters have been communicated in writing, the auditor should retain a copy of the communication.

3550 Other Information in Documents Containing Audited Financial Statements (AU 550)

3550.01 The CPA should read *other information* (such as the president's letter, etc.) presented in conjunction with the audited financial statements and consider the following questions:

   a. Is the information or the manner of its presentation materially inconsistent with the information presented in the financial statements?

   b. Does the information contain a material misstatement of fact?

3550.02 If either of the questions in section **3550.01** is answered yes, the CPA should discuss the inconsistency or misstatement with the client. If the situation is not satisfactorily resolved or corrected, the CPA will have to revise the report, withdraw the report, or withdraw from the engagement.

3550.03 If certain other information has been subjected to auditing procedures applied in the audit of the basic financial statements, the auditor may express an opinion on whether the information is fairly stated in all material respects in relation to those financial statements taken as a whole. In those circumstances, the auditor's report on the information should describe clearly the character of the auditor's work and the degree of responsibility the auditor is taking.

3550.04 Other information does not include supplemental information required by the FASB or additional information accompanying the basic financial statements.

3550.05 Study the flowchart on the next page, which summarizes the CPA's decision processes with regard to this section.

Other Information in Documents Containing Audited Financial Statements (AU 550)

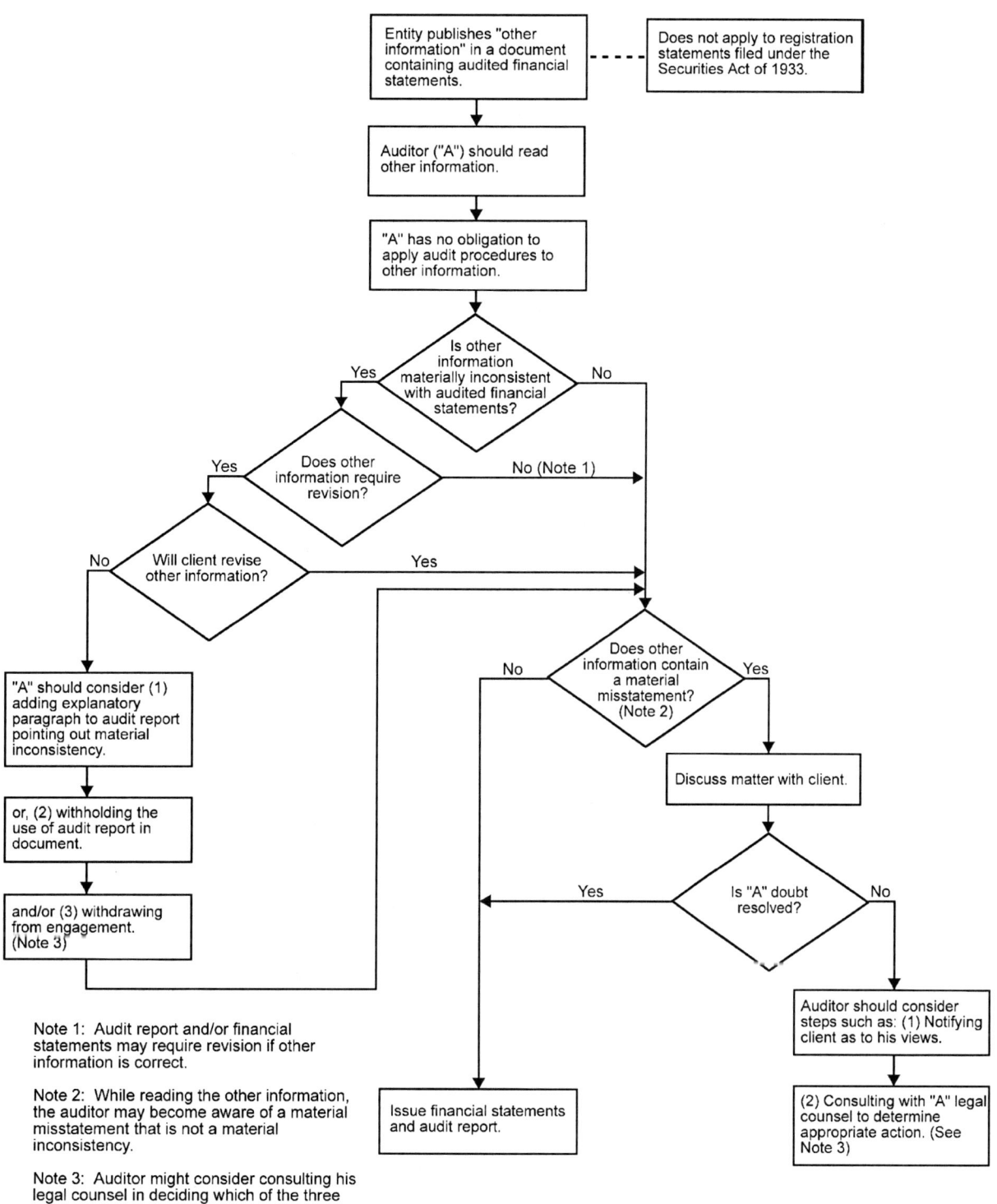

```
                    ┌─────────────────────┐       ┌─────────────────────┐
                    │ Entity publishes    │       │ Does not apply to   │
                    │ "other information" │- - - -│ registration        │
                    │ in a document       │       │ statements filed    │
                    │ containing audited  │       │ under the           │
                    │ financial           │       │ Securities Act of   │
                    │ statements.         │       │ 1933.               │
                    └──────────┬──────────┘       └─────────────────────┘
                               ▼
                    ┌─────────────────────┐
                    │ Auditor ("A") should│
                    │ read other          │
                    │ information.        │
                    └──────────┬──────────┘
                               ▼
                    ┌─────────────────────┐
                    │ "A" has no          │
                    │ obligation to apply │
                    │ audit procedures to │
                    │ other information.  │
                    └──────────┬──────────┘
                               ▼
                         ╱ Is other  ╲
                   Yes  ╱ information ╲  No
             ◄────────╱ materially    ╲─────────►
                      ╲ inconsistent  ╱
                       ╲ with audited╱
                        ╲ financial ╱
                         ╲stmts?   ╱
```

Left branch (Yes — materially inconsistent):

- Does other information require revision?
  - Yes → Will client revise other information?
    - Yes → Issue financial statements and audit report.
    - No → "A" should consider (1) adding explanatory paragraph to audit report pointing out material inconsistency.
      - or, (2) withholding the use of audit report in document.
      - and/or (3) withdrawing from engagement. (Note 3)
  - No (Note 1) → (proceeds to right branch)

Right branch (No — not materially inconsistent):

- Does other information contain a material misstatement? (Note 2)
  - No → Issue financial statements and audit report.
  - Yes → Discuss matter with client.
    - Is "A" doubt resolved?
      - Yes → Issue financial statements and audit report.
      - No → Auditor should consider steps such as: (1) Notifying client as to his views.
        - (2) Consulting with "A" legal counsel to determine appropriate action. (See Note 3)

Note 1: Audit report and/or financial statements may require revision if other information is correct.

Note 2: While reading the other information, the auditor may become aware of a material misstatement that is not a material inconsistency.

Note 3: Auditor might consider consulting his legal counsel in deciding which of the three desirable alternatives will be selected.

(Dan M. Guy and Raymond J. Clay, "SAS No. 8 flowchart," *The Journal of Accountancy,* July 1978, p. 53)

3560 Required Supplementary Information (AU 558)

3561 General Guidelines on Supplementary Information

3561.01 **Supplementary information required by the FASB or GASB** differs from other types of information outside the financial statements because the information is considered by the FASB or GASB to be an essential part of the financial reporting of the entities required to supply the information.

3561.02 The CPA has an obligation to apply limited procedures to such supplemental information and to report deficiencies in, or the omission of, such information.

3561.03 The limited procedures must be applied to companies that must report the supplemental information and to companies that voluntarily report the information.

3561.04 If the CPA has determined that supplemental information is required, the CPA should apply the following procedures to the information:

    a. Inquire of management regarding methods of preparing the information.

       (1) Is it measured and presented within the guidelines prescribed by the FASB or GASB?

       (2) Have the methods of measurement or presentation been changed from those used in a prior period (and reasons given for change)?

       (3) What are any significant assumptions or interpretations underlying the measurement or presentation?

    b. Compare the information for lack of consistency with the following:

       (1) Management's responses to the foregoing inquiries

       (2) The audited financial statements

       (3) Other information obtained during the examination

    c. Consider whether representations regarding required supplementary information should be included in the client representation letter.

    d. Apply additional procedures, if any, specified in other SASs for specific types of supplementary information.

    e. Make additional inquiries if the results of the foregoing procedures cause the CPA to believe information may not be measured or presented properly.

3561.05 Ordinarily, the supplementary information should be:

    a. distinct from the audited financial statements,

    b. separately identifiable from other information outside the financial statements that is not required by the FASB or GASB, and

    c. clearly marked as unaudited.

3561.06 The auditor should expand (*not qualify*) the standard report by adding an explanatory paragraph to call attention to the following:

   a. Omission of supplementary information required by the FASB or GASB

   b. Material departures from FASB or GASB guidelines on the measurement or presentation of such information

   c. The inability to complete the procedures in section **3561.04**

3561.07 Study the following flowchart, which summarizes the information in this section.

Required Supplementary Information (AU558)

(Section **3561** establishes general standards for the auditor's involvement with supplementary information (SI) required by the FASB or GASB. Section **3561** is not applicable if the auditor has been engaged to audit the SI.)

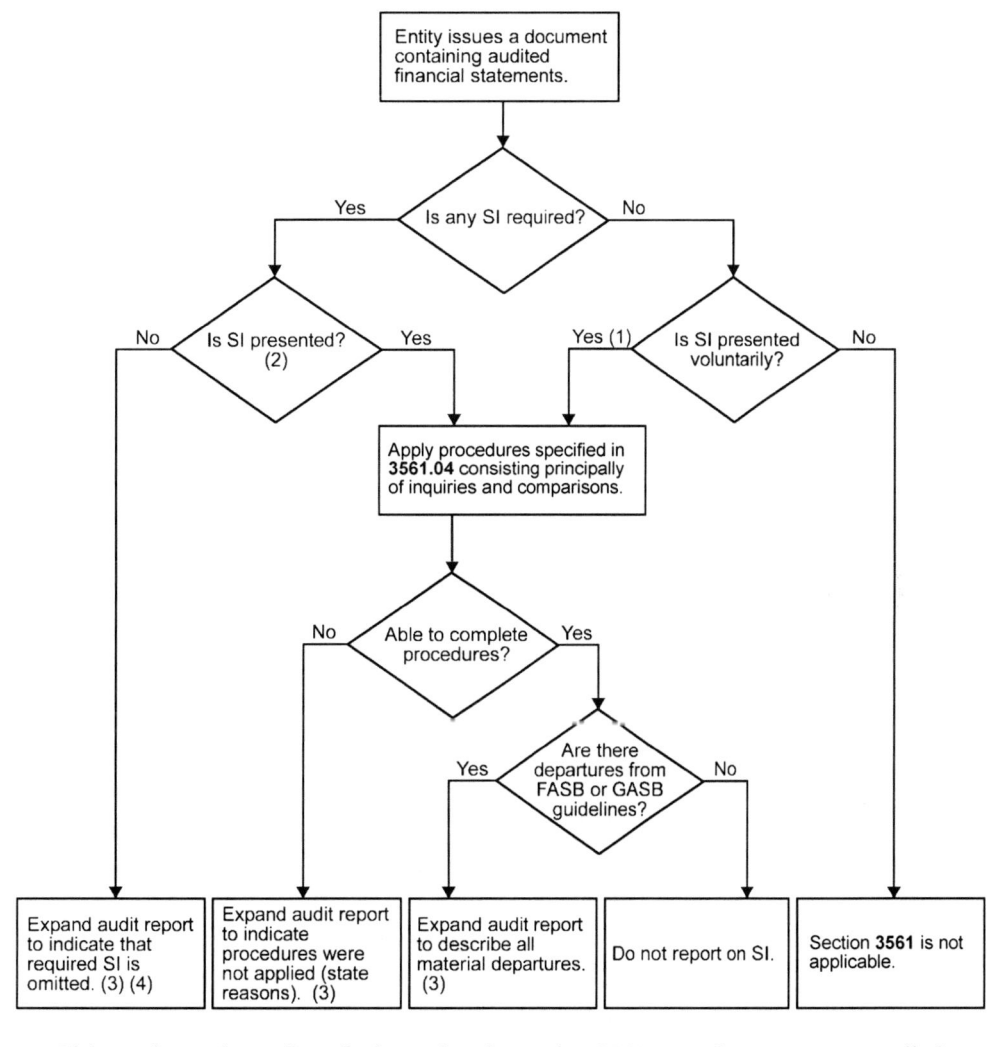

```
Entity issues a document containing audited financial statements.
         |
         v
   Is any SI required?
    Yes /        \ No
       v          v
  Is SI presented? (2)     Is SI presented voluntarily?
   No /   \ Yes           Yes (1) /        \ No
     |     |                |              |
     |     v                v              |
     | Apply procedures specified in       |
     | 3561.04 consisting principally      |
     | of inquiries and comparisons.       |
     |         |                           |
     |         v                           |
     |   Able to complete procedures?      |
     |    No /        \ Yes                |
     |      |          v                   |
     |      |   Are there departures from  |
     |      |   FASB or GASB guidelines?   |
     |      |    Yes /        \ No         |
     v      v       v          v           v
  Expand  Expand  Expand     Do not    Section 3561
  audit   audit   audit      report    is not
  report  report  report     on SI.    applicable.
  to      to      to
  indicate indicate describe
  that    procedures all
  required were    material
  SI is   not      departures.
  omitted. applied (3)
  (3)(4)  (state
          reasons).
          (3)
```

(1) If the entity or the auditor discloses that the section **3561** procedures were not applied, section **3550**, *Other Information in Documents Containing Audited Financial Statements*, would then apply, not section **3561**.

(2) If SI is presented in a note to the financial statements, the note should be marked "unaudited."

(3) The auditor's opinion on the financial statements is not affected.

(4) The auditor need not present the SI if it is omitted by the entity.

3570 Reporting on Information Accompanying the Basic Financial Statements in Auditor-Submitted Documents (AU 551)

3571 Applicability

3571.01 This section applies when the auditor submits a document that contains *information accompanying the client's basic financial statements and the auditor's standard report thereon.*

3571.02 Examples of information not considered part of the basic financial statements are details or explanations of items in, or related to, the basic financial statements, consolidating information, historical summaries of items extracted from the basic financial statements, statistical data, and other material, some of which may be from sources outside the accounting system or outside the entity.

3572 Auditor's Reporting Responsibility (AU 551.04–.11)

3572.01 **Reporting alternatives:**

a. **Auditor-submitted documents:** Responsibility to report on all information included (i.e., to describe clearly the character of the examination and the degree of responsibility, if any, taken)

b. **Client-reported documents** (which include the auditor's standard report): Responsibility to apply (1) *Other Information in Documents Containing Audited Financial Statements* (AU 550), section **3550** (*Other Information...*) and (2) section **3560**, *Required Supplementary Information* (AU 558)

3572.02 In reporting on accompanying information, the CPA should do the following:

a. State that the examination is made for purposes of forming an opinion on the basic financial statements taken as a whole.

b. Identify the accompanying information (by title or page number).

c. State that the accompanying information is presented for purposes of analysis and is not a required part of the basic financial statements.

d. State an opinion based on examination (auditor may give opinion on part of accompanying information and disclaim on rest).

e. Report on accompanying information either by adding it to a standard report or presenting it separately.

3572.03 Although the auditor has no obligation to apply auditing procedures to information outside the basic financial statements, the auditor may do so to express an opinion on that information in the manner described in section **3572.02**. When doing so, the same materiality guidelines apply as to the statements as a whole; thus, procedures do not need to be as extensive as when expressing an opinion on the information taken by itself.

3572.04 If accompanying information is materially misstated:

    a. discuss with client and propose modification.

    b. if not satisfied:

        (1) modify report and describe misstatement *or*

        (2) refuse to include the information in the document.

    c. consider effects of misstatements on standard report.

3572.05 If an adverse opinion or disclaimer is made in the standard report, no opinion should be expressed on the accompanying information.

3572.06 The auditor will usually not subject nonaccounting information in the accompanying information to auditing procedures and will disclaim an opinion on it. Exception: When the nonaccounting data comes from the accounting records (e.g., number of employees).

3572.07 An example of reporting on information accompanying the basic financial statements in an auditor-submitted document follows (AU 551.12):

> Our audit was conducted for the purpose of forming an opinion on the basic financial statements taken as a whole. The (identify accompanying information) is presented for purposes of additional analysis and is not a required part of the basic financial statements. Such information has been subjected to the auditing procedures applied in the examination of the basic financial statements and, in our opinion, is fairly stated in all material respects in relation to the basic financial statements taken as a whole.

3572.08 If some or all of the accompanying information is subject to a disclaimer, the information should be marked "unaudited" or should include a reference to the auditor's disclaimer, an example of which follows (AU 551.13):

> Our audit was conducted for the purpose of forming an opinion on the basic financial statements taken as a whole. The (identify the accompanying information) is presented for purposes of additional analysis and is not a required part of the basic financial statements. Such information has not been subjected to the auditing procedures applied in the examination of the basic financial statements and, accordingly, we express no opinion on it.

3572.09 When supplementary information required by the FASB is presented in an auditor-submitted document, the auditor should disclaim on the information unless the auditor has been engaged to examine and express an opinion on it. Apply provisions of section **3560**.

3572.10 The provisions of this section apply to consolidating information presented with the basic financial statements.

3572.11 Additional comments by the auditor describing procedures applied to specific items should not contradict or detract from the scope description in the standard report and should be set forth separately from the accompanying information.

3572.12 The basic financial statements should be complete within themselves apart from the accompanying information so that future use of them by the client will not be misleading.

3572.13 Study the flowchart, which summarizes the information in this section.

Reporting on Information Accompanying the Basic Financial Statements in Auditor-Submitted Documents (AU 551)

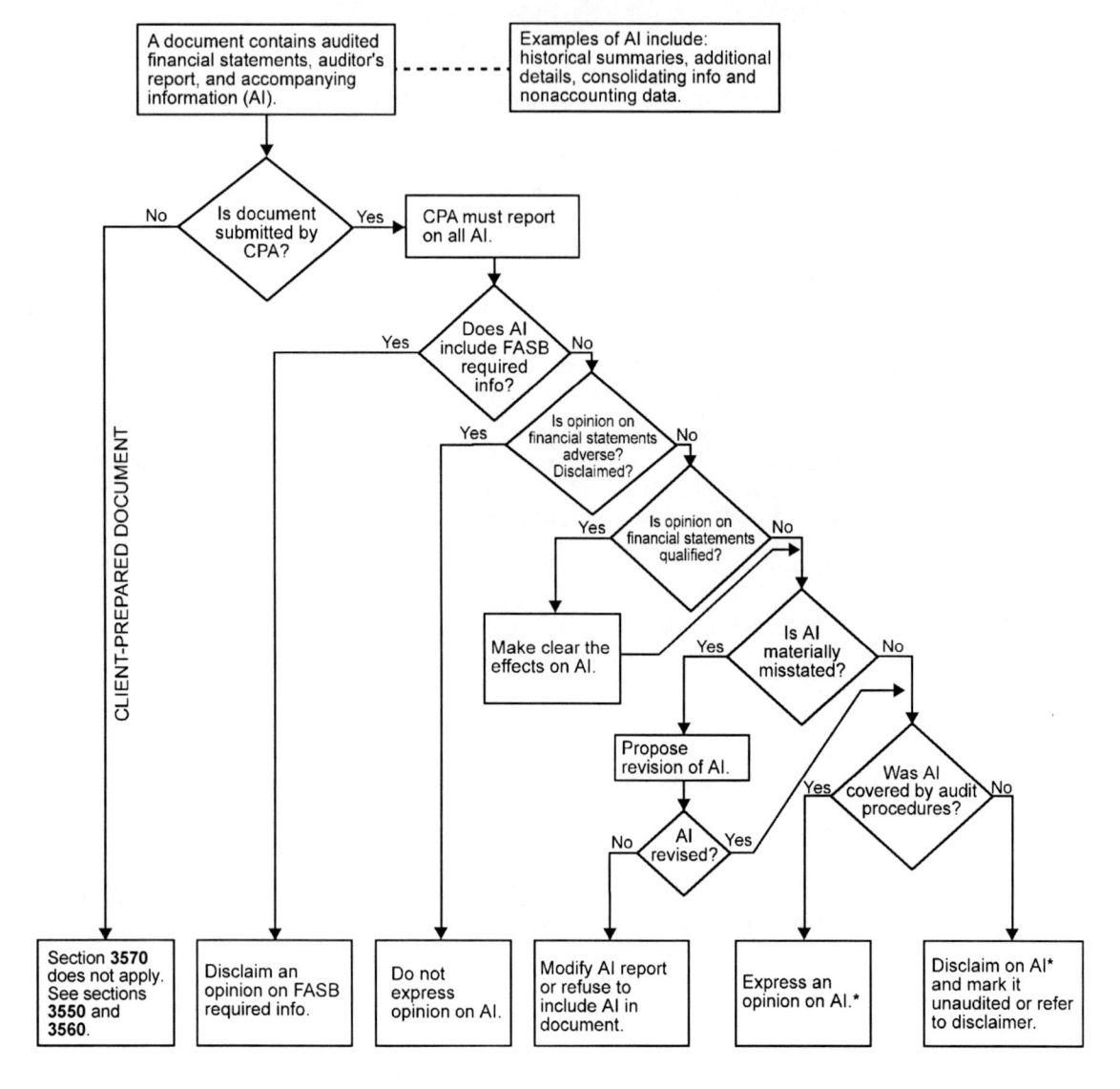

```
                    ┌─────────────────────────┐         ┌──────────────────────────┐
                    │ A document contains      │         │ Examples of AI include:   │
                    │ audited financial        │---------│ historical summaries,     │
                    │ statements, auditor's    │         │ additional details,       │
                    │ report, and accompanying │         │ consolidating info and    │
                    │ information (AI).        │         │ nonaccounting data.       │
                    └───────────┬─────────────┘         └──────────────────────────┘
                                │
                    ┌───────────▼─────────────┐
            No      │   Is document            │   Yes   ┌─────────────────────┐
         ◄──────────│   submitted by CPA?      ├────────►│ CPA must report     │
         │          └─────────────────────────┘         │ on all AI.          │
         │                                               └──────────┬──────────┘
         │                                                           │
         │                                       ┌───────────────────▼──────────┐
         │                              Yes      │  Does AI include FASB         │  No
         │                         ◄─────────────│  required info?               ├────────►
         │                         │             └──────────────────────────────┘         │
  CLIENT-PREPARED                  │                                                       │
    DOCUMENT                       │                        ┌──────────────────────┐      │
         │                         │              Yes       │ Is opinion on        │ No   │
         │                         │             ◄──────────│ financial statements ├──────►
         │                         │             │          │ adverse? Disclaimed? │      │
         │                         │             │          └──────────────────────┘      │
         │                         │             │                                         │
         │                         │             │                ┌───────────────────┐   │
         │                         │             │         Yes    │ Is opinion on      │ No│
         │                         │             │         ◄──────│ financial          ├──►│
         │                         │             │         │      │ statements         │   │
         │                         │             │         │      │ qualified?         │   │
         │                         │             │         │      └───────────────────┘   │
         │                         │             │         │                               │
         │                         │             ▼         ▼               ┌──────────────┐│
         │                         │        ┌────────────────┐      Yes    │ Is AI         │ No
         │                         │        │ Make clear the │     ◄───────│ materially    ├───►
         │                         │        │ effects on AI. │     │       │ misstated?    │   │
         │                         │        └────────────────┘     │       └──────────────┘   │
         │                         │                                │                          │
         │                         │                          ┌─────▼─────┐                   │
         │                         │                          │ Propose    │                   │
         │                         │                          │ revision   │                   │
         │                         │                          │ of AI.     │                   │
         │                         │                          └────┬──────┘                    │
         │                         │                               │                           │
         │                         │                      ┌────────▼─────┐                    │
         │                         │                 No   │  AI           │ Yes               │
         │                         │                 ◄────│  revised?     ├────►               │
         │                         │                 │    └──────────────┘    │                │
         │                         │                 │                        │   ┌──────────────────┐
         │                         │                 │                        │   │ Was AI covered    │
         │                         │                 │                        │   │ by audit          │
         │                         │                 │                        │   │ procedures?       │
         │                         │                 │                        │   └─Yes────────No───┘
         │                         │                 │                        │     │           │
         ▼                         ▼                 ▼                        ▼     ▼           ▼
 ┌─────────────┐  ┌──────────────┐ ┌─────────────┐ ┌──────────────┐  ┌─────────────┐ ┌──────────────────┐
 │ Section 3570 │ │ Disclaim an   │ │ Do not       │ │ Modify AI     │ │ Express an   │ │ Disclaim on AI*   │
 │ does not    │ │ opinion on    │ │ express      │ │ report or     │ │ opinion on   │ │ and mark it       │
 │ apply. See  │ │ FASB          │ │ opinion      │ │ refuse to     │ │ AI.*         │ │ unaudited or      │
 │ sections    │ │ required info.│ │ on AI.       │ │ include AI in │ │              │ │ refer to          │
 │ 3550 and    │ │               │ │              │ │ document.     │ │              │ │ disclaimer.       │
 │ 3560.       │ │               │ │              │ │               │ │              │ │                   │
 └─────────────┘  └──────────────┘ └─────────────┘ └──────────────┘  └─────────────┘ └──────────────────┘
```

*The report expressing an opinion on AI should:

   a. state that the examination was made for purposes of forming an opinion on the basic financial statements,

   b. identify the accompanying information,

   c. state that accompanying information is presented for purposes of additional analysis and is not a required part of the financial statements, and

   d. be added to the auditor's standard report or presented as a separate report.

3580 Other Reporting Issues

3581 Reports on Condensed Financial Statements and Selected Financial Data (AU 552)

3581.01 Condensed financial statements are abbreviated and thus should be read in conjunction with the most recent complete financial statements.

3581.02 If a CPA has expressed an unqualified opinion on the complete financial statements from which the condensed statements are derived, the report on the condensed financial statements should be as follows (AU 552.06):

> We have audited, in accordance with generally accepted auditing standards, the consolidated balance sheet of X company and subsidiaries as of December 31, 20X0, and the related consolidated statements of income, retained earnings, and cash flows for the year then ended (not presented herein), and in our report dated February 15, 20X1, we expressed an unqualified opinion on those consolidated financial statements.
>
> In our opinion, the information set forth in the accompanying condensed consolidated financial statements is fairly stated in all material respects to the consolidated financial statements from which it has been derived.

3581.03 Selected financial data is not a required part of the basic financial statements, and management determines the specific selected financial data to be presented.

3581.04 A CPA may report on selected financial data derived from audited financial statements that the CPA has audited.

3581.05 The audited financial statements must be included in the same document containing the selected financial data.

3581.06 The following paragraph might be included in the auditor's report after the opinion paragraph in a client-prepared document that includes audited financial statements (AU 552.10):

> We have also previously audited, in accordance with generally accepted auditing standards, the consolidated balance sheets as of December 31, 20X3, 20X2, and 20X1, and the related consolidated statements of income, retained earnings, and cash flows for the years ended December 31, 20X3, and 20X2 (none of which are presented herein); and we expressed an unqualified opinion on those consolidated financial statements. In our opinion, the information set forth in the selected financial data for each of the five years in the period ended December 31, 20X3, appearing on page xx, is fairly stated in all material respects in relation to the consolidated financial statements from which it was derived.

3582 Reports on the Application of Accounting Principles (AU 625)

3582.01 There may be situations where differing interpretations as to whether and, if so, how existing accounting principles apply to new transactions and financial products. Management and others often consult with accountants on the application of accounting principles to those transactions and products.

3582.02 As used in SASs 50 and 97, a **reporting accountant** refers to an accountant in public practice who prepares a written report or provides oral advice on the application of accounting principles to specified transactions involving facts and circumstances of a specific entity, or the type of opinion that may be rendered on a specific entity's financial statements. A **continuing accountant** refers to an accountant who has been engaged to report on the financial statements of a specific entity.

3582.03 Because of the nature of a transaction not involving facts or circumstances of a specific entity (hypothetical transaction), a reporting accountant cannot know whether the continuing accountant has reached a different conclusion on the application of accounting principles for the same or a similar transaction. Therefore, an accountant should not undertake an engagement to provide a written report on the application of accounting principles to a hypothetical transaction.

3582.04 The reporting accountant should exercise due professional care in performing the engagement and should have adequate technical training and proficiency. The reporting accountant should also plan the engagement adequately, supervise the work of assistants, if any, and accumulate sufficient information to provide a reasonable basis for the professional judgment described in the report.

3582.05 To aid in forming a judgment, the reporting accountant should perform the following procedures:

    a. Obtain an understanding of the form and substance of the transaction.

    b. Review applicable generally accepted accounting principles.

    c. If appropriate, consult with other professionals or experts.

    d. If appropriate, perform research or other procedures to ascertain and consider the existence of creditable precedents or analogies.

3582.06 When evaluating accounting principles that relate to a specific transaction or determining the type of opinion that may be rendered on a specific entity's financial statements, the reporting accountant should consult with the continuing accountant of the entity to ascertain all the available facts relevant to forming a professional judgment.

3582.07 The responsibilities of an entity's continuing accountant to respond to inquiries by the reporting accountant are the same as the responsibilities of a predecessor auditor to respond to inquiries by a successor auditor as described in SAS 84, *Communications Between Predecessor and Successor Auditors.*

3582.08 The accountant's written report should be addressed to the requesting entity and should ordinarily include the following:

    a. A brief description of the nature of the engagement and a statement that the engagement was performed in accordance with applicable AICPA standards

    b. Identification of the specific entity, description of the transaction(s), a statement of the relevant facts, circumstances, and assumptions, and a statement about the source of the information

    c. A statement describing the appropriate accounting principle(s) (including the country of origin) to be applied or type of opinion that may be rendered on the entity's financial statements, and, if appropriate, a description of the reasons for the reporting accountant's conclusion

    d. A statement that the responsibility for the proper accounting treatment rests with the preparers of the financial statements, who should consult with their continuing accountants

e. A statement that any difference in the facts, circumstances, or assumptions presented may change the report

f. A separate paragraph at the end of the report that includes the following elements:

— A statement indicating that the report is intended solely for the information and use of the specified parties

— An identification of the specified parties to whom use is restricted

— A statement that the report is not intended to be and should not be used by anyone other than the specified parties

3583 Reporting on Financial Statements Prepared for Use in Other Countries (AU 534)

3583.01 U.S. entities may wish to prepare financial statements in conformity with accounting principles generally accepted in another country.

3583.02 When involved with such statements, the auditor should obtain written representation on the purpose and use of the statements. The auditor should comply with the general and fieldwork standards of U.S. GAAS, even if auditing standards of another country are being followed in conducting the engagement.

3583.03 If the accounting principles of the other country are not established with sufficient authority, the auditor may report on the financial statements if those principles are appropriate in the circumstances and disclosed in a clear and comprehensive manner.

3583.04 If the financial statements are prepared for use outside the United States, or have only limited distribution in the United States, the auditor may use either:

a. a U.S.-style report modified to report on the accounting principles of another country *or*

b. the standard report form of the other country.

3583.05 If the financial statements will have more than limited distribution in the United States, the auditor should use a U.S. report modified for departures from U.S. GAAP and may add a separate opinion paragraph on conformity with accounting principles of the other country.

3583.06 The auditor should comply with the reporting standards of the other country when using the standard report of that country and should consider consulting with persons having expertise in the audit reporting practices of the other country.

3584 Restricting the Use of an Auditor's Report (AU 532)

3584.01 The term *general use* applies to auditor's reports that are not restricted to specified parties. The term *restricted use* applies to auditor's reports intended only for specified parties.

3584.02 An auditor should restrict the use of a report in the following circumstances:

  a. The subject matter of the auditor's report or the presentation being reported on is based on measurement or disclosure criteria contained in contractual agreements or regulatory provisions that are not in conformity with generally accepted accounting principles (GAAP) or an other comprehensive basis of accounting (OCBOA).

  b. The accountant's report is based on procedures that are specifically designed and performed to satisfy the needs of specified parties who accept responsibility for the sufficiency of the procedures.

  c. The auditor's report is issued as a byproduct of a financial statement audit and is based on the results of procedures designed to enable the auditor to express an opinion on the financial statements taken as a whole, not to provide assurance on the specific subject matter of the report.

3584.03 From time to time, an auditor is required to issue "byproduct" reports based on matters that arise during an audit engagement. These reports result from *Communication of Internal Control Related Matters Notes in an Audit* (SAS 60), and *Communication with Audit Committees* (SAS 61), to name a couple of instances. Reports that result from such circumstances are based on the results of procedures designed to enable an auditor to express an opinion on the financial statements taken as a whole, not to provide assurance on the specific subject matter of the report.

3584.04 Because the issuance of the byproduct report is not the primary objective of the engagement, an audit generally includes only limited procedures directed toward the subject matter of the byproduct report.

3584.05 Accordingly, because of the potential for misunderstanding or misinterpretation of the limited degree of assurance associated with a byproduct report, the use of such reports should be restricted.

3584.06 If an auditor issues a single combined report covering both (a) subject matter or presentations that require a restriction on use to specified parties and (b) subject matter or presentations that ordinarily do not require such a restriction, the use of such a single combined report should be restricted to the specified parties.

3584.07 In some instances, a separate restricted-use report may be included in a document that also contains a general-use report. In such circumstances, the restricted-use report remains restricted as to use, and the general-use report continues to be for general use.

3584.08 Subsequent to the completion of an engagement resulting in a restricted-use report, or in the course of such an engagement, an auditor may be asked to consider adding other parties as specified users. In the case of presentations based on measurement or disclosure criteria contained in contractual agreements or regulatory provisions, the auditor may agree to add other parties.

3584.09 In such situations, the auditor should consider factors such as the identity of the other parties and the intended use of the report. When an auditor agrees to add other parties as specified users, the auditor should obtain, ordinarily in writing, affirmative acknowledgment from the other parties of their understanding of the engagement, the criteria used in the engagement, and the related report.

3584.10 Auditors should inform their clients that restricted-use reports should not be distributed to nonspecified parties. However, an auditor is not responsible for controlling a client's distribution of restricted-use reports.

3584.11 An auditor's report that is restricted as to use should contain a separate paragraph at the end of the report that includes the following elements:

   a. A statement that the report is intended solely for the information and use of the specified parties

   b. An identification of the specified parties to whom use is restricted

   c. A statement that the report is not intended to be and should not be used by anyone other than the specified parties

This page intentionally left blank.

Section 3600
Other Reporting Standards

3610 Interim Financial Information
- 3611 Applicability of Interim Reviews (AU 722)
- 3612 Objectives and Scope of a Review of Interim Financial Information
- 3613 Accountant's Knowledge of the Entity's Business and Its Internal Control
- 3614 Performing Review Procedures
- 3615 Evaluation of Results and Communications to Management
- 3616 Reporting on a Review of Interim Financial Information

3620 Special Reports (AU 623)
- 3621 Types of Special Reports
- 3622 Reports on OCBOA Financial Statements
- 3623 Opinions on Specified Elements, Accounts, or Items
- 3624 Compliance with Aspects of Contractual Agreements or Regulatory Requirements Related to Audited Financial Statements
- 3625 Special-Purpose Financial Presentations to Comply with Contractual Agreements or Regulatory Provisions
- 3626 Financial Information Presented in Prescribed Forms or Schedules

3630 Unaudited Financial Statements of Public Companies (AU 504)
- 3631 Unaudited Disclaimer (Applies Only to Public Companies)
- 3632 Nonindependence Disclaimer (for Public Companies Only)
- 3633 Types of Association

3640 Statements on Standards for Accounting and Review Services (AR)
- 3641 Standards for Accounting and Review Services (AR 50)
- 3642 Compilation and Review of Financial Statements (AR 100)
- 3643 A Compilation Engagement (AR 100.06 to 100.23)
- 3644 A Review Engagement (AR 100.24 to 100.45)
- 3645 Comparison of Compilation, Review, and Audit Engagements
- 3646 Reporting on Comparative Financial Statements (AR 200)
- 3647 Compilation Reports on Financial Statements Included in Certain Prescribed Forms (AR 300)
- 3648 Communications Between Predecessor and Successor Accountants (AR 400)
- 3649 Reporting on Personal Financial Statements Included in Written Personal Financial Plans (AR 600)

3650 Additional SSARS Guidance
- 3651 Additional Compilation Performance Requirements
- 3652 Compilation of Specified Elements, Accounts, or Items of a Financial Statement
- 3653 Compilation of Pro Forma Financial Information
- 3654 Defining Professional Requirements in Statements on Standards for Accounting and Review Services (SSARSs)

- **3660 SEC Reporting**
  - 3661 Summary of Securities Act of 1933
  - 3662 Letters for Underwriters and Certain Other Requesting Parties (AU 634)
  - 3663 Accountant's Responsibility (AU 711)
  - 3664 Summary of Securities Exchange Act of 1934

- **3670 Government Auditing Standards (Issued by Government Accountability Office)**
  - 3671 Broad Scope Audits
  - 3672 General Standards
  - 3673 Examination and Evaluation Standards
  - 3674 Reporting Standards

- **3680 Statements on Standards for Attestation Engagements**
  - 3681 Attestation Standards: Revision and Recodification
  - 3682 Attest Engagements (AT 101)
  - 3683 Agreed-Upon Procedures Engagements (AT 201)
  - 3684 Financial Forecasts and Projections
  - 3685 Reporting on Pro Forma Financial Information (AT 401)
  - 3686 Compliance Attestation (AT 601)
  - 3687 Management's Discussion and Analysis (AT 701)

- **3690 Reporting on an Entity's Internal Control over Financial Reporting (AT 501)**
  - 3691 Applicability
  - 3692 Conditions for Engagement Performance
  - 3693 Performing an Examination Engagement
  - 3694 Deficiencies in an Entity's Internal Control
  - 3695 Reporting Standards
  - 3696 Service Organizations (AU 324)
  - 3697 Communication of Internal Control Related Matters Identified in an Audit (AU 325)

3610 Interim Financial Information

3611 Applicability of Interim Reviews (AU 722)

3611.01 This Statement establishes standards and provides guidance on the nature, extent, and timing of the procedures to be performed by an independent accountant when conducting a review of interim financial information.

3611.02 The term *interim financial information* refers to financial information or statements covering a period less than a full year or for a 12-month period ending on a date other than the entity's fiscal year end.

3611.03 The three general standards discussed in SAS 95, *Generally Accepted Auditing Standards*, are applicable to a review of interim financial information conducted in accordance with SAS 100. This Statement discusses the extent to which the fieldwork and reporting standards are relevant to an engagement to review interim financial information.

3611.04 Although this Statement does *not* require an accountant to issue a written report on a review of interim financial information, the SEC requires that an accountant's review report be filed with the interim financial information if, in any filing, the entity states that the interim financial information has been reviewed by an independent public accountant.

3611.05 An accountant may conduct, in accordance with this Statement, a review of the interim financial information of an SEC registrant or of a non-SEC registrant that makes a filing with a regulatory agency in preparation for a public offering or listing, if the entity's latest annual financial statements have been or are being audited.

3612 Objectives and Scope of a Review of Interim Financial Information

3612.01 The objective of a review of interim financial information pursuant to this Statement is to provide the accountant with a basis for communicating whether he/she is aware of any material modification that should be made to the interim financial information for it to conform with generally accepted accounting principles (GAAP).

3612.02 A review of interim financial information does not provide a basis for expressing an opinion about whether the financial information is presented fairly, in all material respects, with GAAP.

3612.03 A review consists principally of performing analytical procedures and making inquiries of persons responsible for financial and accounting matters, and does not contemplate:

   a. tests of accounting records through inspection, observation, or confirmation;

   b. tests of control to evaluate their effectiveness;

   c. obtaining corroborating evidence in response to inquiries; or

   d. performing certain other procedures ordinarily performed in an audit.

3612.04 The accountant should establish an understanding with the client regarding the services to be performed in an engagement to review interim financial information.

3613 Accountant's Knowledge of the Entity's Business and Its Internal Control

3613.01 To perform a review of interim financial information, the accountant should have sufficient knowledge of the entity's business and its internal control related to the preparation of interim financial information.

3613.02 This knowledge should allow the accountant the ability to:

   a. identify the types of potential material misstatements in the interim financial information and consider the likelihood of their occurrence.

   b. select the inquiries and analytical procedures that will provide the accountant with the basis for communicating whether he/she is aware of any material modifications that should be made to the interim financial information for it to be in conformity with GAAP.

3613.03 In planning a review of interim financial information, the accountant should perform procedures to update his/her knowledge of the entity's business and its internal control. Such procedures should include:

    a. reading documentation of the preceding year's audit and of reviews of prior interim period(s) of the current year and corresponding quarterly and year-to-date interim period(s) of the prior year.

    b. reading the most recent annual and comparable prior interim period financial information.

    c. considering the results of any audit procedures performed with respect to the current year's financial statements.

    d. inquiry of management about changes in the entity's business activities.

    e. inquiry of management about whether significant changes in internal control, related to the preparation of interim financial information, have been made.

3613.04 The accountant who has audited the entity's financial statements for one or more annual periods would have acquired sufficient knowledge of an entity's internal control as it relates to the preparation of annual financial information and may have acquired such knowledge with respect to interim financial information.

3613.05 If the accountant has not audited the most recent annual financial statements, the accountant should perform procedures to obtain such knowledge.

3613.06 A restriction on the scope of the review may be imposed if the entity's internal control appears to contain deficiencies so significant that it would be impracticable for the accountant, based on his/her judgment, to effectively perform review procedures.

3614 Performing Review Procedures

3614.01 Procedures for conducting a review of interim financial information generally are limited to analytical procedures, inquiries, and other procedures that address significant accounting and disclosure matters relating to the interim financial information to be reported.

3614.02 The accountant performs these procedures to obtain a basis for communicating whether he/she is aware of any material modifications that should be made to the interim financial information for it to be in conformity with GAAP.

3614.03 The accountant should apply analytical procedures to the interim financial information to identify and provide a basis for inquiry about the relationships and individual items that appear to be unusual and that may indicate a material misstatement.

3614.04 Expectations developed by the accountant in performing analytical procedures in connection with a review of interim financial information ordinarily are less precise than those developed in an audit.

3614.05 In a review the accountant is not ordinarily required to corroborate management's responses with other evidence. However, the accountant should consider the reasonableness and consistency of management's responses in light of the results of other review procedures and the accountant's knowledge of the entity's business and its internal control.

3614.06 Review procedures can normally be performed before or simultaneously with the entity's preparation of the interim financial information. Performing some of the review procedures early in the interim period also permits early identification and consideration of significant accounting matters affecting the interim financial information.

3614.07 A review of interim financial information does not require sending a lawyer's letter concerning litigation, claims, and assessments. Also, this review is not designed to identify conditions or events that may indicate substantial doubt about an entity's ability to continue as a going concern.

3614.08 However, if the accountant becomes aware of information that leads him/her to believe that the interim financial information may not be in conformity with GAAP, he/she should expand the review procedures to address the concern.

3614.09 Written representations from management should be obtained for all interim financial information presented and for all periods covered by the review. Specific representations related to the following five broad categories are identified in SAS 100:

1. Financial Statements
2. Internal Control
3. Completeness of Information
4. Recognition, Measurement, and Disclosure
5. Subsequent Events

3615 Evaluation of Results and Communications to Management

3615.01 A review of interim financial information is not designed to obtain reasonable assurance that the interim financial information is free of material misstatements. However, based on the review procedures performed, the accountant may become aware of *likely misstatements*.

3615.02 In the context of an interim review, a likely misstatement is the accountant's best estimate of the total misstatement in the account balances or classes of transactions on which he/she has performed review procedures.

3615.03 Misstatements identified by the accountant or brought to the accountant's attention, including inadequate disclosure, should be evaluated individually and in the aggregate to determine whether material modifications should be made to the interim financial information for it to conform with GAAP.

3615.04 The accountant should use his/her professional judgment in evaluating the materiality of any likely misstatements that the entity has not corrected.

3615.05 When an accountant is unable to perform the procedures he/she considers necessary to achieve the objectives of a review of interim financial information, or the client does not provide the accountant with the written representations the accountant believes are necessary, the review will be incomplete.

3615.06 An incomplete review, or a review where the accountant believes material modifications should be made to the interim financial information for it to conform with GAAP, is not an adequate basis for issuing a review report. In such circumstances, the accountant should communicate the matter(s) to the appropriate level of management as soon as practicable.

3615.07 If, in the accountant's judgment, management does not respond appropriately to the accountant's communication within a reasonable period of time, the accountant should inform the audit committee or others with equivalent authority and responsibility of the matters as soon as practicable.

3615.08 If, in the accountant's judgment, the audit committee does not respond appropriately to the accountant's communication within a reasonable period of time, the accountant should evaluate whether to resign from the review engagement and as the entity's auditor.

3615.09 The accountant may become aware of fraud or illegal acts in connection with the review engagement. If the matter involves fraud, it should be brought to the attention of the appropriate level of management. If the fraud involves senior management or results in a material misstatement in the financial statements, the accountant should communicate the matter directly to the audit committee.

3615.10 If the matter involves possible illegal acts, the accountant should assure him/herself that the audit committee is adequately informed, unless the matter is clearly inconsequential.

3615.11 The communication of significant deficiencies, as well as the matters covered in SAS 61, *Communications with Audit Committees*, are applicable in an engagement to review interim financial information.

3616 Reporting on a Review of Interim Financial Information

3616.01 The accountant's review report should include the following:

    a. A title that includes the word *independent*

    b. A statement that the interim financial information identified in the report was reviewed

    c. A statement that the interim financial information is the responsibility of management

    d. A statement that the review was conducted in accordance with standards established by the AICPA

    e. A description of the procedures for a review

    f. A statement that a review is substantially less in scope than an audit conducted in accordance with GAAS

    g. A statement about whether the accountant is aware of any material modifications that should be made to the interim financial information for it to conform with GAAP

    h. The manual or printed signature of the accountant's firm

    i. The date of the review report (generally when procedures are complete)

3616.02 The accountant's review report should be modified for departures from GAAP, which include inadequate disclosure.

3616.03 The existence of substantial doubt about the entity's ability to continue as a going concern or lack of consistent application of GAAP, would not require mention in the accountant's report, provided that the interim financial information appropriately discloses such matters.

3616.04 If a client represents in a document filed with a regulatory agency or issued to stockholders or third parties, that the accountant has reviewed the interim financial information included in the document, the accountant should advise the entity that his/her review report must be included in the document.

3616.05 If the client refuses to include the accountant's review report the accountant should perform the following procedures:

    a. Request that the accountant's name be neither associated with the interim financial information nor referred to in the document.

    b. If the client will not comply with the request, advise the client that the accountant will not consent either to the use of his/her name or to reference to him/her.

    c. When appropriate, recommend that the client consult with its legal counsel about the application of relevant laws and regulations to the circumstances.

    d. Consider what other actions might be appropriate.

3616.06 Interim financial information may be presented as supplementary information outside audited financial statements. In such circumstances, each page of the interim financial information should be clearly marked as unaudited.

3616.07 The accountant should prepare documentation in connection with a review of interim financial information, the form and content of which should be designed to meet the circumstances of the particular engagement.

3616.08 In addition to documentation of the review procedures performed and the conclusions reached, the documentation should include any findings or issues that in the accountant's judgment are significant.

3620 Special Reports (AU 623)

3621 Types of Special Reports

3621.01 Financial statements prepared on a comprehensive basis of accounting (OCBOA) other than GAAP.

3621.02 Specified elements, accounts, or items of a financial statement.

3621.03 Compliance with aspects of contractual agreements or regulatory requirements related to audited financial statements.

3621.04 Financial presentations to comply with contractual agreements or regulatory provisions.

3621.05 Financial information presented in prescribed forms or schedules that require a prescribed form of auditor's report.

3621.06 Results of applying agreed-upon procedures.

3622 Reports on OCBOA Financial Statements

3622.01 A comprehensive basis of accounting other than GAAP is one of the following:

    a. A basis of accounting that the reporting entity uses to comply with the requirements of financial reporting provisions of a governmental regulatory agency

    b. A basis of accounting that the reporting entity uses or expects to use to file its income tax return for the period covered by the financial statements

c. The cash receipts and disbursement basis of accounting and modifications of the cash basis that have substantial support, such as recording depreciation on fixed assets or accruing income taxes

d. A definite set of criteria having substantial support that is applied to all material items appearing in financial statements, such as the price-level basis of accounting

3622.02 Unless the financial statements meet the conditions for presentation in conformity with an OCBOA as defined, the auditor should use the standard form of report (SAS 58) modified as appropriate because of the departure from GAAP.

3622.03 Do not use statement names that can be confused with statements prepared in accordance with GAAP. For example, use statement of cash receipts and disbursements instead of income statement.

3622.04 Special reports on statements prepared under provision of a government regulatory agency should be restricted to individuals within the agency.

3622.05 When reporting on OCBOA financial statements, all disclosures appropriate for the basis should be disclosed. This includes a disclosure that discusses the basis of presentation and describes how the basis differs from GAAP. If GAAP disclosures are relevant to the financial statements, they should be included.

3622.06 An example of an unqualified audit report on financial statements prepared on an entity's income tax basis is shown as follows:

Independent Auditor's Report

We have audited the accompanying statements of assets, liabilities, and capital income tax basis of ABC Partnership as of December 31, 20X2, and 20X1, and the related statements of revenue and expenses income tax basis and of changes in partners' capital accounts income tax basis for the years then ended. These financial statements are the responsibility of the Partnership's management. Our responsibility is to express an opinion on these financial statements based on our audits.

We conducted our audits in accordance with generally accepted auditing standards. Those standards require that we plan and perform the audit to obtain reasonable assurance about whether the financial statements are free of material misstatement. An audit includes examining, on a test basis, evidence supporting the amounts and disclosures in the financial statements. An audit also includes assessing the accounting principles used and significant estimates made by management, as well as evaluating the overall financial statement presentation. We believe that our audits provide a reasonable basis for our opinion.

As described in Note X, these financial statements were prepared on the basis of accounting the Partnership uses for income tax purposes, which is a comprehensive basis of accounting other than generally accepted accounting principles.

In our opinion, the financial statements referred to above present fairly, in all material respects, the assets, liabilities, and capital of ABC Partnership as of (at) December 31, 20X2, and 20X1, and its revenue and expenses and changes in partners' capital accounts for the years then ended, on the basis of accounting described in Note X.

3623 Opinions on Specified Elements, Accounts, or Items

3623.01 These engagements include reports on rentals, royalties, a profit sharing plan, or a provision for income taxes.

3623.02 With the exception of the first standard of reporting, the 10 GAAS are applicable to any engagement to express an opinion on one or more specified elements, accounts, or items.

3623.03 An audit of specified elements, accounts, or items is usually more extensive than if the same information was being considered in conjunction with an audit of financial statements taken as a whole.

3623.04 A special report should not be a piecemeal opinion (i.e., it should not be issued on an element of financial statements that carries an adverse or disclaimer opinion).

3623.05 If, based on a contract or agreement, the element, account, or item results in a presentation that is not in conformity with GAAP or OCBOA, the report should be restricted to those within the entity and parties to the contract or agreement.

3623.06 An opinion on a report relating to accounts receivable is illustrated as follows:

Independent Auditor's Report

We have audited the accompanying schedule of accounts receivable of ABC Company as of December 31, 20X1. This schedule is the responsibility of the Company's management. Our responsibility is to express an opinion on this schedule based on our audit.

We conducted our audit in accordance with generally accepted auditing standards. Those standards require that we plan and perform the audit to obtain reasonable assurance about whether the schedule of accounts receivable is free of material misstatements. An audit includes examining, on a test basis, evidence supporting the amounts and disclosures in the schedule of accounts receivable. An audit also includes assessing the accounting principles used and significant estimates made by management, as well as evaluating the overall schedule presentation. We believe that our audit provides a reasonable basis for our opinion.

In our opinion, the schedule of accounts receivable referred to above presents fairly, in all material respects, the accounts receivable of ABC Company as of December 31, 20X1, in conformity with generally accepted accounting principles.

3624 Compliance with Aspects of Contractual Agreements or Regulatory Requirements Related to Audited Financial Statements

3624.01 Entities may be required by contractual agreements, such as certain bond indentures and loan agreements, or by regulatory agencies to furnish compliance reports by independent auditors. The independent auditor may satisfy this request by giving negative assurance relative to the applicable covenants based on the audit of the financial statements.

3624.02 Such assurance should not be given unless the auditor has audited the financial statements to which the contractual agreements or regulatory requirements relate.

3624.03 An example report on compliance with contractual provisions given in a separate report is illustrated as follows:

Independent Auditor's Report

We have audited, in accordance with generally accepted auditing standards, the balance sheet of XYZ Company as of December 31, 20X2, and the related statement of income, retained earnings, and cash flows for the year then ended, and have issued our report thereon dated February 16, 20X3.

In connection with our audits, nothing came to our attention that caused us to believe that the Company failed to comply with the terms, covenants, provisions, or conditions of sections XX to YY, inclusive, of the Indenture dated July 21, 20X0, with ABC Bank insofar as they relate to accounting matters. However, our audit was not directed primarily toward obtaining knowledge of such noncompliance.

This report is intended solely for the information and use of the boards of directors and managements of XYZ Company and ABC Bank and should not be used for any other purpose.

3625 Special-Purpose Financial Presentations to Comply with Contractual Agreements or Regulatory Provisions

3625.01 An auditor may sometimes be asked to report on special-purpose statements prepared to comply with contractual agreements or regulatory provisions. In most circumstances, these types of presentations are intended solely for the use of the parties to the agreement or regulatory bodies.

3625.02 There are two types of contractual special reports:

1. A special-purpose financial presentation prepared in compliance with a contractual agreement or regulatory provision that does not constitute a complete presentation of the entity's assets, liabilities, revenues, and expenses, but is otherwise prepared in conformity with GAAP or OCBOA

2. A special-purpose financial presentation (may be a complete set of financial statements or a single financial statement) prepared on a basis of accounting prescribed in an agreement that does not result in a presentation in conformity with GAAP or OCBOA

3626 Financial Information Presented in Prescribed Forms or Schedules

3626.01 When a prescribed form or schedule has wording for the auditor's report that is not acceptable because assertions in the statement are not compatible with the auditor's function, the auditor should revise or rewrite the report.

3630 Unaudited Financial Statements of Public Companies (AU 504)

3631 Unaudited Disclaimer (Applies Only to Public Companies)

3631.01 Even though a CPA may assist in the preparation of financial statements for a client, the statements are management's representations, and management has responsibility for their fair presentation.

3631.02 Statements of a public company are unaudited if the CPA:

    a. has not performed any audit procedures,

    b. has not performed sufficient procedures to form an audit opinion, and

    c. has not reviewed the statements in accordance with interim review standards.

3631.03 A CPA is associated with unaudited financial statements if:

    a. the CPA is named in a document containing financial statements and

    b. the CPA prepares or assists in preparing statements, even if the statements are on plain paper.

3631.04 If the CPA is associated with unaudited financial statements of a public entity, a disclaimer of opinion is required, and each page of the statements should be clearly and conspicuously marked "unaudited." The disclaimer to be issued is as follows (AU 504.05):

> The accompanying balance sheet of X Company as of December 31, 20X1, and the related statements of income and retained earnings and cash flows for the year then ended were not audited by us, and accordingly, we do not express an opinion on them.

3631.05 If the auditor knows unaudited statements are not in accordance with GAAP (or another comprehensive basis of accounting), the auditor should insist on change or disclosure in the disclaimer. If the auditor knows statements to be false and misleading, the auditor should refuse to be associated and, if necessary, withdraw from the engagement.

3631.06 If the financial statements do not include a statement of cash flows, the auditor may be associated but does not have to include the statement in the disclaimer. The auditor should simply say that statements do not conform to GAAP because the statement of cash flows is not presented.

3631.07 Any auditing procedures performed should not be mentioned in a disclaimer except in the case of:

    a. letters to underwriters or

    b. reports in connection with a proposed acquisition.

3631.08 The CPA's name should not appear in client-prepared reports. If it does, insist on:

    a. deletion of the CPA's name *or*

    b. the marking of statements as unaudited and the inclusion of a statement that the CPA expresses no opinion.

3632 Nonindependence Disclaimer (for Public Companies Only)

3632.01 When the CPA is not independent, the CPA should disclaim an opinion indicating that they are not independent but not give the reasons for lack of independence or list any procedures performed.

3632.02 Other rules in the case of nonindependence are the same as for unaudited financial statement (see sections **3631.05** and **3631.06**).

3632.03 An illustrative nonindependence disclaimer follows (AU 504.10):

> We are not independent with respect to XYZ Company, and the accompanying balance sheet as of December 31, 20X1, and the related statements of income and retained earnings and cash flows for the year then ended were not audited by us, and accordingly, we do not express an opinion on them.

3633 Types of Association

3633.01 Financial statements of a *public* entity with which a CPA is associated may be:

    a. audited,

    b. reviewed according to SAS 36 (AU 722) (see section **3610**), or

    c. unaudited according to SAS 26 (AU 504).

3633.02 If the entity is *nonpublic,* the financial statements with which a CPA is associated may be:

    a. audited,

    b. reviewed according to AR 100 (see section **3644**), or

    c. compiled according to AR 100 (see section **3643**).

3633.03 If the CPA is not *independent,* the following are the only reporting alternatives available when the CPA is associated with a client's financial statements:

    a. A nonindependence disclaimer if the company is public (see section **3632**)

    b. A compilation report if the company is nonpublic (see section **3643**)

3640 Statements on Standards for Accounting and Review Services (AR)

3641 Standards for Accounting and Review Services (AR 50)

3641.01 The **Accounting and Review Services Committee** is the senior technical committee of the American Institute of CPAs authorized to develop, on a continuing basis, standards concerning the accounting and review services a CPA may render in connection with unaudited financial statements or other unaudited financial information of an entity that is not required to file financial statements with a regulatory agency in connection with the sale or trading of its securities in a public market (*nonpublic entity*).

3641.02 The standards issued by the Accounting and Review Services Committee are referred to as Statements on Standards for Accounting and Review Services (SSARS). Interpretations of the standards are issued to provide guidance on the application of the SSARS. Interpretations are not as authoritative as a SSARS, but members should be aware that they may have to justify a departure from an Interpretation if the quality of their work is questioned.

3641.03 An accountant must perform a compilation or review of a nonpublic entity in accordance with SSARS issued by the AICPA. SSARS provide a measure of quality and the objectives to be achieved in both a compilation and review.

3641.04 The accountant should be aware of and consider interpretative publications applicable to his or her compilation or review. Interpretative publications consist of compilation and review interpretations of the SSARS, appendices to the SSARS, compilation and review guidance included in AICPA Audit and Accounting Guides, and the AICPA's Statements of Position to the extent that those Statements are applicable to compilation and review engagements.

3641.05 The AICPA's annual Compilation and Review Alert, compilation and review articles appearing in the Journal of Accountancy and other professional journals, compilation and review articles in the AICPA The CPA Letter, continuing professional education courses and other related instructional and professional material are commonly referred to as other compilation and review publications. Such publications have no authoritative status; however, they may assist the accountant in his/her understanding and application of the SSARS. If another compilation and review publication has been published by the AICPA and subsequently reviewed by the AICPA Audit and Attest Standards staff, it is presumed to be appropriate.

3642 Compilation and Review of Financial Statements (AR 100)

3642.01 SSARS 1 defines a compilation engagement and a review engagement, including their respective objectives, as follows:

a. **Compilation of financial statements:** A service, the objective of which is to present in the form of financial statements, information that is the representation of management (owners) without undertaking to express any assurance on the financial statements.

b. **Review of financial statements:** A service, the objective of which is to express limited assurance that there are no material modifications that should be made to the financial statements in order for the statements to be in conformity with GAAP.

3642.02 The accountant should not issue any report on unaudited financial statements of a nonpublic entity or submit such financial statements to the client or others unless the accountant complies with SSARS 1 or AR 100.

3642.03 SASs provide guidance to the accountant who performs services in connection with unaudited financial statements of a *public* entity.

3642.04 When the accountant performs more than one service (e.g., a compilation and an audit), the accountant should issue the report that is appropriate for the highest level of service rendered.

3642.05 An accountant should not consent to the use of their name in a document or written communication containing unaudited financial statements of a nonpublic entity unless:

a. the accountant has compiled or reviewed the financial statements and the report accompanies them *or*

b. the financial statements are accompanied by an indication that the accountant has not compiled or reviewed the financial statements and that the accountant assumes no responsibility for them.

3642.06 If an accountant becomes aware that his/her name has been used improperly in any client-prepared document containing unaudited financial statements, the accountant should advise the client that the use of his/her name is inappropriate and should consider what other actions might be appropriate, including consultation with his/her attorney.

3642.07 SSARS 1 describes the limitations of a compilation engagement and a review engagement as follows:

    a. Limitations of a Compilation Engagement: A compilation differs from a review or an audit of financial statements. A compilation does not contemplate performing inquiry, analytical procedures, or other procedures performed in a review. Additionally, a compilation does not contemplate obtaining an understanding of the entity's internal control; assessing fraud risk; tests of accounting records by obtaining sufficient appropriate audit evidence through inspection, observation, confirmation, or the examination of source documents; or other procedures ordinarily performed in an audit. Therefore, a compilation does not provide a basis for expressing any level of assurance on the financial statements being compiled.

    b. Limitations of a Review Engagement: A review differs from an audit of financial statements, in which the auditor provides reasonable assurance that the financial statements, taken as a whole, are free from material misstatement. A review does not contemplate obtaining an understanding of the entity's internal control; assessing fraud risk; tests of accounting records by obtaining sufficient appropriate audit evidence through inspection, observation, confirmation, or the examination of source documents; or other procedures normally performed in an audit. Accordingly, a review does not provide assurance that the accountant will become aware of all significant matters that would be disclosed in an audit. Therefore, a review provides only limited assurance that there are no material modifications that should be made to the financial statements in order for the statements to be in conformity with GAAP.

3642.08 The accountant should establish an understanding with the entity, preferably in writing, regarding the services to be performed. However, if the engagement is to compile financial statements not expected to be used by a third party, a written communication is required. In addition to the description of the nature and limitations of the services to be performed, the understanding should also provide:

    a. that the engagement cannot be relied upon to disclose errors, fraud, or illegal acts and

    b. that the accountant will inform the appropriate level of management of any material errors and of any evidence or information that comes to the accountant's attention during the performance of compilation or review procedures that fraud or an illegal act may have occurred. The accountant need not report any matters regarding illegal acts that may have occurred that are clearly inconsequential and may reach agreement in advance with the entity on the nature of any such matters to be communicated.

3642.09 When evidence or information comes to the accountant's attention during the performance of compilation or review procedures that fraud or an illegal act may have occurred, that matter should be brought to the attention of the appropriate level of management. When matters involving fraud or an illegal act involve senior management, the accountant should report the matter to an individual or group at a higher level within the entity, such as the manager (owner) or the board of directors.

3642.10 The disclosure of any evidence or information that comes to the accountant's attention during the performance of compilation or review procedures that fraud or an illegal act may have occurred to parties other than senior management ordinarily is not part of the accountant's responsibility and ordinarily would be precluded by the accountant's ethical or legal obligations or confidentiality. However, the accountant should recognize that in the following circumstances a duty to disclose to parties outside of the entity may exist:

    a. To comply with certain legal and regulatory requirements

    b. To a successor accountant when the successor decides to communicate with the predecessor in accordance with SSARS 4 or AR 400

c. In response to a subpoena

3642.11 The following definitions apply to compilations and reviews:

a. **Submission of financial statements.** Presenting to a client or third parties financial statements that the accountant has prepared either manually or through the use of computer software.

b. **Third party.** All parties except for members of management who are knowledgeable about the nature of the procedures applied, the basis of accounting, and the assumptions used in the preparation of the financial statements.

c. **Nonpublic entity.** Any entity other than (1) one whose securities trade in a public market either on a stock exchange or in the over-the-counter market, including securities quoted only locally or regionally; (2) one that makes a filing with a regulatory agency in preparation for the sale of any class of its securities in a public market; or (3) a subsidiary, corporate joint venture, or other entity controlled by an entity covered by (1) or (2).

3642.12 The accountant can type or reproduce financial statements as an accommodation to the client without complying with section **3642.05**.

3642.13 The General Standards (Rule 201 of the Code of Professional Conduct) apply to both compilation and review engagements.

3642.14 The following form of standard report is used for a compilation (AR 100.14):

I (we) have compiled the accompanying balance sheet of XYZ Company as of December 31, 20XX, and the related statements of income, retained earnings, and cash flows for the year then ended, in accordance with Statements on Standards for Accounting and Review Services issued by the American Institute of Certified Public Accountants.

A compilation is limited to presenting, in the form of financial statements, information that is the representation of management (owners). I (we) have not audited or reviewed the accompanying financial statements and, accordingly, do not express an opinion or any other form of assurance on them.

3642.15 The following form of standard report is used for a review (AR 100.42):

I (we) have reviewed the accompanying balance sheet of XYZ Company as of December 31, 20XX, and the related statements of income, retained earnings, and cash flows for the year then ended, in accordance with Statements on Standards for Accounting and Review Services issued by the American Institute of Certified Public Accountants. All information included in these financial statements is the representation of the management (owners) of XYZ Company.

A review consists principally of inquiries of company personnel and analytical procedures applied to financial data. It is substantially less in scope than an examination in accordance with generally accepted auditing standards, the objective of which is the expression of an opinion regarding the financial statements taken as a whole. Accordingly, I (we) do not express such an opinion.

Based on my (our) review, I am (we are) not aware of any material modifications that should be made to the accompanying financial statements for them to be in conformity with generally accepted accounting principles.

3642.16 The term *general use* applies to accountant's reports that are not restricted to specified parties. Accountant's reports on financial statements prepared in conformity with generally accepted accounting principles or a comprehensive basis of accounting other than GAAP ordinarily are not restricted regarding use.

3642.17 The term *restricted use* applies to accountant's reports intended only for one or more specified third parties. The need for restriction on the use of a report may result from a number of circumstances, including, but not limited to, the purpose of the report and the potential for the report to be misunderstood when taken out of the context in which it was intended to be used.

3642.18 An accountant should restrict the use of a report when the subject matter of the accountant's report or the presentation being reported on is based on measurement or disclosure criteria contained in contractual agreements or regulatory provisions that are not in conformity with generally accepted accounting principles or a comprehensive basis of accounting other than GAAP. If an accountant issues a single combined report covering both (a) subject matter or presentations that require a restriction on use to specified parties and (b) subject matter or presentations that ordinarily do not require such a restriction, the use of such a single combined report should be restricted to the specified parties.

3642.19 An accountant's report that is restricted as to use should contain a separate paragraph at the end of the report as follows:

> This report is intended solely for the information and use of (the specified parties) and is not intended to be and should not be used by anyone other than these specified parties.

3642.20 An accountant may compile or review a set of financial statements presented on an *other comprehensive basis of accounting* (OCBOA). (See section **3622.01** for an explanation of OCBOA financial statements.)

3642.21 OCBOA financial statements are generally defined as financial statements prepared on a definite set of criteria, other than GAAP, having substantial support underlying the preparation of the financial statements prepared pursuant to that basis.

3642.22 Examples of OCBOA financial statements include (a) a basis of accounting that the reporting entity uses to comply with the requirements or financial reporting provisions of a governmental regulatory agency; (b) a basis of accounting that the reporting entity uses or expects to use to file its income tax return for the period covered by the financial statements; or (c) the cash basis of accounting and modifications of the cash basis having substantial support.

3642.23 An accountant may emphasize, in any report on financial statements, a matter disclosed in the financial statements. Such explanatory information should be presented in a separate paragraph of the accountant's report. Emphasis paragraphs are never required; they may be added solely at the accountant's discretion.

3642.24 Because an emphasis of matter paragraph should not be used in lieu of management disclosures, an accountant should not include an emphasis of matter paragraph in a compilation report on financial statements that omit substantially all disclosures unless the matter is disclosed in the financial statements.

3642.25 After the date of the accountant's compilation or review report, the accountant has no obligation to perform other compilation or review procedures with respect to the financial statements, unless new information has come to his/her attention.

3642.26 However, when the accountant becomes aware of information which relates to financial statements previously reported on by him/her, but which was not known to the accountant at the date of the report, and which is of such a nature and from such a source that the accountant would have investigated it had it come to his/her attention during the course of the compilation or review, the accountant should, as soon as practicable, undertake to determine whether the fact existed at the date of the report.

3642.27 If the nature and effect of the matter are such that (1) the accountant's report or the financial statements would have been affected if the information had been known to the accountant at the accountant's compilation or review report date and had not been reflected in the financial statements and (2) the accountant believes that there are persons currently using or likely to use the financial statements who would attach importance to the information, the accountant should:

   a. in a compilation engagement, obtain additional or revised information.

   b. in a review engagement, perform the additional procedures deemed necessary to achieve limited assurance that there are no material modifications that should be made to the financial statements in order for the statements to be in conformity with GAAP.

3643 A Compilation Engagement (AR 100.06 to 100.23)

3643.01 The steps a CPA should take when retained to compile financial statements of a nonpublic entity are presented in this section. See section **3647** if the alternative form of compilation reports for certain prescribed forms is used.

A Compilation Engagement

Action/Decision:

1. Establish an understanding with the entity regarding the compilation service.

2. Acquire the necessary knowledge of the client's industry, accounting principles, and practices.

3. Acquire a general understanding of the nature of the client's business transactions, the form of the accounting records, the stated qualifications of the accounting personnel, the accounting basis used, and the form and content of the financial statements. It is not necessary to make inquiries or perform other procedures unless the information supplied is incorrect, incomplete, or otherwise unsatisfactory. However, if any evidence or information comes to the accountant's attention regarding fraud or an illegal act that may have occurred, the accountant should consider the effect of the matter on his/her compilation report.

4. Read the financial statements and determine if they are appropriate in form and free from obvious material error.

5. Consider whether all disclosures required by GAAP or an acceptable comprehensive basis of accounting are provided. If they are not, go to *step 6*. If they are, go to *step 7*.

6. If substantially all disclosures required by GAAP or other comprehensive basis of accounting are omitted, indicate this in a separate paragraph in your report. If a comprehensive basis of accounting other than GAAP is used, disclose this basis either in the financial statement or in your report. If the statement of cash flows is also omitted, modify the scope paragraph and disclosure deficiency paragraph accordingly. If most, but not all, disclosures are omitted, notes to the financial statements should be labeled "Selected Information—Substantially All Disclosures Required by Generally Accepted Accounting Principles Are Not Included".

7. Consider whether the financial statements contain measurement departures from GAAP or another comprehensive basis of accounting. If they do, go to *step 8*. If they do not, go to *step 9*.

8. Get the client to revise the financial statements. Failing that, consider modifying your report by adding a separate paragraph or paragraphs. If the impact of the departure has been determined by management or is known by you, disclose the dollar effects in your report. (However, uncertainties and inconsistencies are not measurement departures if

they are properly disclosed—see *step 5.*) Withdraw from the engagement if the modified report is not adequate to communicate the deficiencies.

9. Are the resulting compiled financial statements expected to be used by a third party? If the resulting compiled financial statements are *not* expected to be used by a third party, the accountant may issue a compilation report in accordance with the reporting requirements of SSARS 1, or follow the guidance presented in section **3651** of this manual concerning SSARS 8.

10. Determine whether you are independent. If you are not, go to *step 11*. If you are, go to *step 12*.

11. If you are not independent, add a separate paragraph to your report: "I am (we are) not independent with respect to XYZ Company."

12. If the financial statements are accompanied by information presented for supplementary analysis purposes, indicate in the report the degree of responsibility taken. If you have also compiled this supplementary information, include such other data in the compilation report.

13. Mark each page of the financial statements, including any supplemental data, "See Accountant's Compilation Report".

14. Date your report using the date the compilation was complete.

15. Issue the financial statements and related compilation report.

16. If, subsequent to the date of the report, facts that could possibly cause the financial statements to be misleading are discovered (and were in existence at the report date), consult AU 561 (see section **3632**) and your attorney.

3644   A Review Engagement (AR 100.24 to 100.45)

3644.01   The steps a CPA should take when retained to review financial statements of a nonpublic entity are presented in this section.

A Review Engagement

Action/Decision:

1. Establish an understanding with the entity regarding the review service.

2. Determine whether you are independent. If you are not, go to *step 3*. If you are, go to *step 4*.

3. Stop. Do not issue a review report (however, it may be possible to issue a compilation report).

4. Acquire the necessary knowledge of the client's industry accounting principles and practices.

5. Acquire a general understanding of the nature of the client's business, including (a) its operating characteristics and (b) the nature of its assets, liabilities, revenues, and expenses. These include a general knowledge of the client's production, distribution, and compensation methods, types of products and services, operating locations, and material transactions with related parties.

6. The accountant should apply appropriate inquiry and analytical procedures to obtain a basis for communicating whether he/she is aware of any material modifications that should be made to the financial statements for them to be in conformity with generally accepted accounting principles. The specific inquiries made and the analytical and other procedures performed should be tailored to the engagement based on the accountant's knowledge of the entity's business. The accountant's understanding of the entity's

business should include a general understanding of the entity's organization, its operating characteristics, and the nature of its assets, liabilities, revenues, and expenses.

A review does not contemplate obtaining an understanding of internal control or assessing control risk, assessing fraud risks, tests of accounting records and of responses to inquiries by obtaining corroborating audit evidence, and certain other procedures ordinarily performed during an audit. Thus, a review does not provide assurance that the accountant will become aware of all significant matters that would be disclosed in an audit.

The accountant should apply analytical procedures to the financial statements to identify and provide a basis for inquiry about the relationships and individual items that appear to be unusual and that may indicate a material misstatement. Analytical procedures include:

a. developing expectations by identifying and using plausible relationships that are reasonably expected to exist based on the accountant's understanding of the entity and the industry in which the entity operates.

b. comparing recorded amounts, or ratios developed from recorded amounts, to expectations developed by the accountant.

The accountant should consider making the following inquiries in a review engagement:

a. Inquiries of members of management about whether financial statements have been prepared in accordance with GAAP

b. The methods used by the entity in performing the accounting function and how significant, unusual, or complex transactions are handled

c. The status of uncorrected misstatements identified during previous engagements, subsequent events, and any knowledge of fraud or suspected fraud

d. Inquiries concerning actions taken at meetings of stockholders, board of directors, or other meetings that may have an effect on the financial statements

e. Inquire about reports, if any, from other accountants related to work on the entity's financial data or financial statements.

7. Read the financial statements to determine whether, based on the information presented, they appear to conform to GAAP or other comprehensive basis of accounting. Obtain reports of other accountants, if any, and indicate degree of responsibility taken if reference is made to other accountants.

8. If any evidence or information comes to the accountant's attention regarding fraud or an illegal act that may have occurred, the accountant should request that management consider the effect of the matter on the financial statements. Additionally, the accountant should consider the effect of the matter on his/her review report.

9. Document in your workpapers matters covered in *steps 6 and 7*. Describe unusual matters that were considered and how they were resolved.

10. Determine whether the inquiry and analytical procedures (considered necessary to achieve limited assurance) are incomplete or restricted in any way. If they are, go to *step 11*. If they are not, go to *step 12*.

11. Consider whether a compilation report should be issued rather than a review report (a review that is incomplete or restricted is not an adequate basis for issuing a review report).

12. Consider whether the financial statements contain known departures from GAAP or other comprehensive basis of accounting, including disclosure departures. If they do, go to *step 13*. If they do not, go to *step 14*.

13. Get client to revise the financial statements. Failing that, consider modifying your report by adding a separate paragraph or paragraphs. If the impact of the departure has been determined by management or is known by you, disclose the dollar effects in your report. (However, uncertainties and inconsistencies should not cause the report to be modified if they are properly disclosed.) Withdraw from the engagement if the modified report is not adequate to communicate the deficiencies.

14. Obtain a representation letter from the client (required).

15. Determine whether the basic financial statements are accompanied by information presented for supplementary analysis purposes. If they are, go to *step 16*. If they are not, go to *step 17*.

16. Indicate the degree of responsibility assumed for the supplementary information in your review report or in a separate report. The report should disclose whether (a) the supplemental information has been reviewed (as part of the basic financial statement review) and you are not aware of any needed material modification, or (b) the supplementary information has not been reviewed, but only compiled.

17. Mark each page of the financial statements, including any supplemental data, "See Accountant's Review Report".

18. Date your report using the date the inquiry and analytical procedures were complete.

19. Issue the financial statements and related review report.

20. If subsequent to the date of the report, facts that could possibly cause the financial statements to be misleading are discovered (and were in existence at the report date), consult AU 561 (see section **3632**) and your attorney.

3645 Comparison of Compilation, Review, and Audit Engagements

3645.01 In your study program, you should concentrate on being able to distinguish among compilations, reviews, and audit engagements. The following chart summarizes the important distinctions.

Comparison of Compilation, Review, and Audit Engagements[a]

Nonpublic Company

	Compilation Engagement	Review Engagement	Audit Engagement
1. Level of assurance	No assurance as to GAAP	Limited assurance as to GAAP	Statements are fairly presented in accordance with GAAP
2. Entities covered	Nonpublic only	Nonpublic only	Public or nonpublic
3. Knowledge of client's industry	Knowledge of the accounting principles and practices of the industry and a general understanding of the business	Knowledge same as compilation *plus* an increased understanding of the client's business	Extensive knowledge of the economy, the client's business, and the relevant industry (SAS 22, *Planning and Supervision*)
4. Inquiry procedures required	Inquiries not required unless information supplied by the client is questionable	Inquiry and analytical procedures required plus additional procedures if the information appears questionable	Inquiry, analytical (SAS 23, *Analytical Review Procedures*)
5. GAAP disclosures omitted	Substantially all disclosures required by GAAP may be omitted, without restriction on use	All disclosures required by GAAP must be included or report must be modified	Inadequate disclosure requires qualified ("except for") or adverse opinion
6. Known departures from GAAP measurement	Disclosure required in compilation report	Disclosure required in review report	Departure from GAAP requires qualified ("except for") or adverse opinion
7. Accountant's independence	Accountant does not have to be independent	Lack of independence precludes issuing review report	Lack of independence requires disclaimer (SAS 26, *Association with Financial Statements*)
8. Engagement letter	Recommended	Recommended	Not addressed in SASs
9. Representation letter	No mention	Must obtain	Must obtain (SAS 85, *Client Representations*)

[a] *Adapted from Dan M. Guy, "Disclosure Needs in Financial Reporting for Closely Held Businesses," University of Alabama, 1978, Accounting Research Convocation.*

3646 Reporting on Comparative Financial Statements (AR 200)

3646.01 Client-prepared financial statements of 20X1 are not comparable to compiled or reviewed financial statements of 20X2. However, they may be included in the same document if they are:

   a. presented on separate pages of the document containing the 20X2 financial statements and

   b. accompanied by an indication by the client that the accountant has not *audited, reviewed,* or *compiled* the 20X1 financial statements.

3646.02 Compiled financial statements that omit substantially all disclosures required by GAAP are not comparable to financial statements that include such disclosures.

3646.03 When comparative statements are presented (20X1 and 20X2), the accountant should select the appropriate reporting option. The following alternatives are available:

   a. Reissue the previous report on the 20X1 statements.

   b. Make reference (by adding an additional paragraph to the 20X2 report) to the previously issued 20X1 report and describe the degree of responsibility assumed for the 20X1 statements in the 20X2 report.

   c. Update the 20X1 report.

   d. Compile or review the 20X1 financial statements.

3646.04 For a *continuing* accountant, the alternative to reissue a previous report (section **3646.03a**) is appropriate only when the level of service for 20X2 is lower than the prior period (i.e., 20X1 reviewed/20X2 compiled or 20X1 audited/20X2 reviewed). The continuing accountant may make references in the 20X2 report to the 20X1 report in these situations (section **3646.03b**) instead of reissuing the report.

3646.05 If a *preceding* accountant reissues the report on 20X1 financial statements (another accountant audited, reviewed, or compiled the 20X2 financial statements), they should do the following:

   a. Read the 20X2 financial statements and the successor's report thereon.

   b. Compare 20X1 and 20X2 financial statements.

   c. Obtain a letter from the successor pertaining to knowledge of any matters having an effect on the 20X1 financial statements.

3646.06 If the predecessor accountant elects not to reissue the 20X1 report, the successor accountant should add to the 20X2 report an additional paragraph explaining that the 20X1 financial statements were compiled or reviewed by other accountants.

3646.07 Updating the 20X1 report alternative, (section **3646.03c**), is required when the level of service is the *same* (i.e., 20X1 compiled/20X2 compiled) or *higher* for 20X2. A predecessor cannot update a report.

3646.08 If the 20X2 financial statements are audited and the 20X1 financial statements are compiled or reviewed, SASs govern.

3646.09 If the 20X2 financial statements are compiled or reviewed and the 20X1 financial statements are audited, SSARSs govern.

3646.10 The current status of the entity determines whether SASs or SSARSs apply.

    a. If the entity's current status is a nonpublic entity, SSARSs apply.

    b. If the entity's current status is a public entity, SASs apply.

3646.11 A previously issued report that is not appropriate for the current status of the entity should not be reissued or referred to in the report of the financial statements of the current period.

3646.12 The following table summarizes sections **3646.03** and **3646.07**.

Report Alternatives	Continuing Accountant*	Preceding Accountant**
Reissue report	Yes, if current level of service is lower.	Yes, if they elect to do so.
Make reference (additional paragraph) in report	Yes, if current level of service is lower and if predecessor accountant elects *not* to reissue report.	N/A
Update report	Yes, is required if current level of service is same or higher.	Not permitted
Compile or review prior financial statements	Yes, if predecessor accountant elects *not* to reissue report.	N/A

* "Continuing accountant" is an accountant who has been engaged to audit, review, or compile and report on the financial statements of the current period and one or more consecutive periods immediately prior to the current period.

** "Preceding accountant" is the accountant who has resigned or has been notified that their services have been terminated.

3646.13 When prior-period financial statements have been restated, the predecessor accountant would normally reissue his/her report. If the predecessor decides not to reissue his/her report, the successor accountant may be engaged to report on the financial statements for the prior year.

3646.14 If the predecessor accountant does not reissue his/her report and the successor accountant is not engaged to report on the prior-year financial statements, the successor accountant should indicate in the introductory paragraph of his/her compilation or review report that a predecessor accountant reported on the financial statements of the prior period before restatement. In addition, if the successor accountant is engaged to compile or review the restatement adjustment(s), he/she may also indicate in the accountant's report that he/she compiled or reviewed the adjustment(s) that was (were) applied to restate prior-year financial statements.

3647 Compilation Reports on Financial Statements Included in Certain Prescribed Forms (AR 300)

3647.01 SSARS 3 amends SSARS 1 and 2 to provide for an alternative form of standard compilation report when a prescribed form calls for departures from GAAP.

3647.02 A prescribed form is any standard preprinted form designed or adopted by the body to which it is to be submitted.

3647.03 Before the alternative report in section **3647.05** can be used, the prescribed form has to call for GAAP measurement or GAAP disclosure departures. Otherwise, the SSARS 1 report, at section **3642.15** appropriately modified, is used.

3647.04 SSARS 3 does not provide for an alternate form of review report on financial statements included in prescribed form.

3647.05 Example of the alternative form of prescribed form compilation report:

XYZ Company

I (we) have compiled the (identification of financial statements, including period covered and name of entity) included in the accompanying prescribed form in accordance with Statements on Standards in Accounting and Review Services issued by the American Institute of Certified Public Accountants.

My (our) compilation was limited to presenting in the form prescribed by (name of body) information that is the representation of management (owners). I (we) have not audited or reviewed the financial statements referred to above and, accordingly, do not express an opinion or any other form of assurance on them.

These financial statements (including related disclosures) are presented in accordance with requirements of (name of body) which differ from generally accepted accounting principles. Accordingly, these financial statements are not designed for those who are not informed about such differences.

3648 Communications Between Predecessor and Successor Accountants (AR 400)

3648.01 This section provides guidance on communications between a predecessor and successor accountant when the successor accountant decides to communicate with the predecessor accountant regarding acceptance of an engagement to compile or review the financial statements of a non-public entity.

3648.02 This section also requires a successor accountant who becomes aware of information that leads him/her to believe the financial statements reported on by the predecessor accountant may require revision to request that the client communicate this information to the predecessor accountant.

3648.03 The following definitions are relevant to this section:

a. **Successor accountant.** An accountant who has been invited to make a proposal for an engagement to compile or review financial statements and is considering accepting the engagement or an accountant who has accepted such an engagement.

b. **Predecessor accountant.** An accountant who (1) has reported on the most recent compiled or reviewed financial statements or was engaged to perform but did not complete a compilation or review of the financial statements, and (2) has resigned, declined to stand for reappointment, or been notified that his/her services have been or may be terminated.

3648.04 The successor accountant is not required to communicate with the predecessor. However, if the successor accountant chooses to communicate with the predecessor, the predecessor must respond promptly and fully to reasonable inquiries.

3648.05 Reasonable inquiries on the part of the successor accountant would include:

    a. information that might bear on the integrity of management (owners).

    b. disagreements with management (owners) about accounting principles or the necessity for the performance of certain procedures or similarly significant matters.

    c. the cooperation of management (owners) in providing additional or revised information, if necessary.

    d. the predecessor's knowledge of any fraud or illegal acts perpetrated within the client.

    e. the predecessor's understanding of the reason for the change of accountants.

3649 Reporting on Personal Financial Statements Included in Written Personal Financial Plans (AR 600)

3649.01 SSARS 6 provides an exemption from compliance with SSARS 1 for personal financial statements included in written personal financial plans prepared by an accountant and specifies the form of the written report required under the exemption.

3649.02 This exemption was issued because the purpose of such personal financial statements is solely to assist in developing the client's personal financial plan, and thus they frequently omit disclosures required by GAAP.

3649.03 Note that stand-alone personal financial statements must follow the guidance contained in AICPA Statement of Position 82-1.

3650 Additional SSARS Guidance

3651 Additional Compilation Performance Requirements

3651.01 An accountant who performs a compilation engagement must adhere to the compilation performance requirements of SSARS 1, regardless of whether the accountant is engaged to report on the financial statements or if the financial statements will be used by a third party.

3651.02 Under SSARS 8, if an accountant submits unaudited financial statements to a client that are not expected to be used by a third party, a communication to management is required. The type of communication depends on the following.

    a. If an accountant is engaged to report on compiled financial statements or submits financial statements to a client that are, or reasonably might be expected to be, used by a third party, the accountant must issue a normal compilation report.

    b. If an accountant submits financial statements to a client that are not expected to be used by a third party, the accountant should either:

        (1) issue a compilation report in accordance with the reporting requirements of SSARS 1 or

        (2) document an understanding with the client through the use of an engagement letter, preferably signed by management, regarding the services to be performed and the limitations on the use of those financial statements.

3651.03 The documentation of the understanding in the engagement letter, referred to earlier, should include the following matters:

    a. Nature and limitations of the services to be performed

    b. A compilation is limited to presenting in the form of financial statements information that is the representation of management.

    c. The financial statements will not be audited or reviewed.

    d. No opinion or any other form of assurance on the financial statements will be provided.

    e. Management has knowledge about the nature of the procedures applied and the basis of accounting and assumptions used in the preparation of the financial statements.

    f. Acknowledgment of management's representation and agreement that the financial statements are not to be used by third parties

    g. The engagement cannot be relied on to disclose errors, fraud, or illegal acts.

3651.04 The information included in the engagement letter should also address the following additional matters if applicable:

    a. Material departures from GAAP or other comprehensive basis of accounting (OCBOA) may exist and the effects of those departures, if any, on the financial statements may not be disclosed.

    b. Substantially all disclosures (and statement of cash flow, if applicable) required by GAAP or OCBOA may be omitted.

    c. Lack of independence

    d. Refer to supplementary information

3651.05 The accountant is required to include a notation on each page of the financial statements, such as, "Restricted for Management's Use Only," or "Solely for the information and use by the management of (name of entity) and not intended to be and should not be used by anyone other than the specified party."

3651.06 If the accountant becomes aware that the financial statements have been distributed to third parties, the accountant should discuss the situation with the client and request that the client have the statements returned.

3651.07 If the client does not comply with the request within a reasonable period of time, the accountant should notify known third parties that the financial statements are not intended for third-party use, preferably in consultation with the accountant's attorney.

3652 Compilation of Specified Elements, Accounts, or Items of a Financial Statement

3652.01 Compilation of one or more specified elements, accounts, or items of a financial statement is limited to presenting financial information that is the representation of management without undertaking to express any assurance on that information. Examples of specified elements, accounts, or items of a financial statement that an accountant may compile include schedules or rentals, royalties, profit participation, or provision for income taxes.

3652.02 An engagement to compile one or more specified elements, accounts, or items of a financial statement may be undertaken as a separate engagement or in conjunction with a compilation of financial statements.

3652.03 When the accountant is engaged to compile or issues a compilation report on one or more specified elements, accounts, or items of a financial statement, he/she must adhere to the compilation performance requirements contained in SSARS 1, including the requirement to establish an understanding with the entity regarding the engagement.

3652.04 Before issuing a compilation report on one or more specified elements, accounts, or items of a financial statement, the accountant should read such compiled specified elements, accounts, or items and consider whether the information appears to be appropriate in form and free from obvious material errors.

3652.05 The following is an example of a compilation report on a schedule of accounts receivable:

I (we) have compiled the accompanying schedule of accounts receivable of XYZ Company as of December 31, 20XX, in accordance with Statements on Standards for Accounting and Review Services issued by the American Institute of Certified Public Accountants.

A compilation is limited to presenting financial information that is the representation of management (owners). I (we) have not audited or reviewed the accompanying schedule of accounts receivable and, accordingly, do not express an opinion or any other form of assurance on it.

3652.06 An accountant is not precluded from issuing a compilation report on one or more specified elements, accounts, or items of a financial statement for an entity with respect to which the accountant is not independent. When the accountant is not independent, the following should be included as the last paragraph of the report: "I am (we are) not independent with respect to XYZ Company."

3653 Compilation of Pro Forma Financial Information

3653.01 A compilation of pro forma financial information is limited to presenting financial information that is the representation of management without undertaking to express any assurance on that information.

3653.02 The objective of pro forma financial information is to show what the significant effects on historical financial information might have been had a consummated or proposed transaction (or event) occurred at an earlier date. Pro forma financial information is commonly used to show the effects of transactions such as the following:

a. Business combinations

b. Change in capitalization

c. Disposition of a significant portion of the business

d. Change in the form of business organization or status as an autonomous entity

e. Proposed sale of securities and the application of the proceeds

3653.03 Pro forma financial information should be labeled as such to distinguish it from historical financial information. This presentation should describe the transaction (or event) that is reflected in the pro forma financial information, the source of the historical financial information on which it is based, the significant assumptions used in developing the pro forma adjustments, and any significant uncertainties about those assumptions.

3653.04 Nothing in SSARS 14 is intended to preclude an accountant from preparing or assisting in the preparation of pro forma financial information and submitting such pro forma financial information to the client without the issuance of a compilation report, unless the accountant has been engaged to compile such pro forma financial information. If the accountant believes that he/she will be associated with the information, the accountant should consider issuing a compilation report so a user will not infer a level of assurance that does not exist.

3653.05 An engagement to compile pro forma financial information may be undertaken as a separate engagement or in conjunction with a compilation of financial statements. Additionally, the historical financial statements of the entity on which the pro forma financial information is based must have been compiled, reviewed, or audited. The accountant's compilation or review report or the auditor's report on the historical financial statements should be included in the document containing the pro forma financial information.

3653.06 When an accountant is engaged to compile pro forma financial information, the accountant should establish an understanding with the entity, preferably in writing, regarding the services to be performed. In addition to a description of the nature and limitations of the service and a description of the report, the understanding should also provide:

    a. that the engagement cannot be relied upon to disclose errors, fraud, or illegal acts and

    b. that the accountant will inform the appropriate level of management of any material errors and of any evidence or information that comes to the accountant's attention during the engagement that fraud or an illegal act may have occurred.

3653.07 When the accountant is engaged to compile or issues a compilation report on pro forma financial information, he/she must adhere to the compilation performance requirements contained in SSARS 1.

3653.08 Before issuance of a compilation report on pro forma financial information, the accountant should read such compiled pro forma financial information, including the summary of significant assumptions, and consider whether the information appears to be appropriate in form and free from obvious material errors.

3653.09 The following is an illustration of an accountant's compilation report on pro forma financial information.

    I (we) have compiled the accompanying pro forma financial information as of and for the year ended December 31, 20XX, reflecting the business combination of the Company and ABC Company in accordance with Statements on Standards for Accounting and Review Services issued by the American Institute of Certified Public Accountants. The historical condensed financial statements are derived from the historical unaudited financial statements of XYZ Company, which were compiled by me (us), and of ABC Company, which were compiled by another (other) accountant(s).

    A compilation is limited to presenting pro forma financial information that is the representation of management (owners). I (we) have not audited or reviewed the accompanying pro forma financial information and, accordingly, do not express an opinion or any form of assurance on it.

    The objective of this pro forma financial information is to show what the significant effects on the historical financial information might have been had the transaction (or event) occurred at an earlier date. However, the pro forma financial information is not necessarily indicative of the results of operations or related effects on financial position that would have been attained had the above mentioned transaction (or event) actually occurred earlier.

3653.10 Failure to include applicable disclosures or a lack of independence on the part of the accountant performing the compilation of the pro forma information should be handled in the same manner as they would in a compilation of financial statements under SSARS 1.

3654 Defining Professional Requirements in Statements on Standards for Accounting and Review Services (SSARSs)

3654.01 Statements on Standards for Accounting and Review Services (SSARSs) contain professional requirements, together with related guidance, in the form of explanatory material. Accountants performing a compilation or review engagement have a responsibility to consider the entire text of a SSARS in carrying out their work on an engagement and in understanding and applying the professional requirements of the relevant SSARSs.

3654.02 Not every paragraph of a Statement on Standards for Accounting and Review Services (SSARS) carries a professional requirement that the accountant is expected to fulfill. Rather, the professional requirements are communicated by the language and the meaning of the words used in the SSARS.

3654.03 Statements on Standards for Accounting and Review Services (SSARSs) use two categories of professional requirements identified by specific terms to describe the degree of responsibility they impose on accountants:

1. **Unconditional requirements.** The accountant is required to comply with an unconditional requirement in all cases in which the circumstances exist to which the unconditional requirement applies. SSARSs use the words *must* or *is required* to indicate an unconditional requirement.

2. **Presumptively mandatory requirements.** The accountant is also required to comply with a presumptively mandatory requirement in all cases in which the circumstances exist to which the presumptively mandatory requirement applies. However, in rare circumstances, the accountant may depart from a presumptively mandatory requirement provided that the accountant documents his/her justification for the departure and how the alternative procedures performed in the circumstances were sufficient to achieve the objectives of the presumptively mandatory requirement. SSARSs use the word *should* to indicate a presumptively mandatory requirement.

3654.04 Explanatory material is defined as the text within a Statement on Standards for Accounting and Review Services (SSARS) that may:

a. provide further explanation and guidance on the professional requirements or

b. identify and describe other procedures or actions relating to the activities of the accountant.

3654.05 Explanatory material that provides further explanation and guidance on the professional requirements is intended to be descriptive rather than imperative.

3654.06 Explanatory material that identifies and describes other procedures or actions relating to the activities of the accountant is not intended to impose a professional requirement for the accountant to perform the suggested procedures or actions. How and whether the accountant carries out such procedures or actions in the engagement depends on the exercise of professional judgment.

3654.07 Statements on Standards for Accounting and Review Services (SSARSs) use the words *may, might,* and *could* to describe these actions and procedures.

3660 SEC Reporting

3661 Summary of Securities Act of 1933

3661.01 The objectives of the 1933 Act are as follows:

a. To provide information on securities offered for public sale

b. To prohibit misrepresentation or fraud in sales of securities generally

3661.02 The SEC is interested in full and fair disclosure so that the investor has an informed choice and that those associated with the registration statement take responsibility for its accuracy.

3661.03 Firms offering securities for public sale, except those specifically exempted, must file a registration statement with the SEC and provide the investor with a prospectus. The financial statements in the registration statement must be audited by a CPA, who is referred to in the registration statement as the expert in accounting and auditing.

3661.04 Exemptions include the following:

a. Private offerings to a limited number of persons or institutions who have access to the kind of information registration would disclose and who do not propose to redistribute the securities (sometimes called *letter stock*)

b. Offerings restricted to the residents of the state in which the issuing company is organized and doing business

c. Securities of municipal, state, federal, and other governments; charitable institutions; banks; and interstate commerce carriers

d. Offerings not in excess of a certain amount (currently $1.5 million)

e. Offerings of small business investment companies

3662 Letters for Underwriters and Certain Other Requesting Parties (AU 634)

3662.01 Accountants may provide a comfort letter to underwriters, or to other parties with a statutory due diligence defense under Section 11 of the Securities Act of 1933, in connection with financial statements and financial statement schedules included in registration statements filed with the SEC under the Act.

3662.02 The services of independent accountants include audits of financial statements and financial statement schedules included in registration statements filed with the SEC.

3662.03 Much of the uncertainty and consequent risk of misunderstanding with regard to the nature and scope of comfort letters has arisen from a lack of recognition of the necessarily limited nature of the comments that accountants can properly make with respect to financial information in a registration statement or other offering document that has not been audited in accordance with generally accepted auditing standards and, accordingly, is not covered by their opinion.

3662.04 Comfort letters are not required under the act, and copies are not filed with the SEC. It is nonetheless a common condition of an underwriting agreement that accountants are to furnish a comfort letter in connection with the offering for sale of securities registered with the SEC under the act.

3662.05 Because the underwriter will expect the accountants to furnish a comfort letter of a scope to be specified in the underwriting agreement, a draft of that agreement should be furnished to the accountants so that they can indicate whether they will be able to furnish a letter in acceptable form.

3662.06 The purpose of comfort letters is to provide the underwriter with evidence that a "reasonable investigation" of the financial data in the prospectus has been made. The assurance provided by the accountant is limited by the fact that the procedures performed do not constitute an audit. Thus, the extent of assurance that accountants can provide by way of a comfort letter is limited to negative assurance.

3663 Accountant's Responsibility (AU 711)

3663.01 The Securities Act of 1933 imposes responsibility on accountants for false and misleading statements if the CPA has consented to have their name associated with statements in the registration documents.

3663.02 The CPA is protected if, after a reasonable (prudent-person test) investigation, the CPA had grounds to believe that statements were true and not misleading.

3663.03 Subsequent events procedures extend the investigation of financial statements to the effective date of registration by:

    a. reading prospectus,

    b. inquiry of management, and

    c. written representation by management.

3663.04 Under SEC rules, an independent accountant's report based on a review of interim financial statements is not governed by Section 11 of the Securities Act of 1933. Thus, the accountant does not have a statutory responsibility to the effective date of the registration statement.

3663.05 The predecessor CPA also has responsibility for subsequent events. The CPA should read the prospectus and registration statement and obtain a representation letter from the successor CPA.

3663.06 Further discussion of the CPA's responsibilities may be found in section **4101** of the *Regulation CPA Review* textbook.

3664 Summary of Securities Exchange Act of 1934

3664.01 The objective of this Act is the regulation of securities registered on national exchanges plus over-the-counter stocks of companies with more than $10 million in assets and 500 or more shareholders.

3664.02 Registration under this Act is separate from the 1933 Act. The major periodic reports required are the following:

    a. 10-K annual report

    b. 10-Q quarterly report

    c. 8-K current report

    d. Proxy statement

3664.03 The 10-K must be accompanied by an auditor's report. The 10-Q may be subject to a limited review (see section **3610**). The 8-K is not audited, but must be filed in writing 15 days after a significant event such as a change in control, sale or purchase of division, start or termination of material litigation, material default or debt, and/or write-down or abandonment of assets. A change in certifying CPA or the resignation of a director must be reported within five business days. Proxy statements are not audited, but require full disclosure with regard to the proxy solicitation. Proxy statements may, however, contain audited financial statements.

3664.04 Regulation S-X is a compilation of reporting regulations required by the SEC.

3664.05 The 1933 Act also regulates exchanges and brokers, protects investors against certain stock manipulations, requires disclosure of tender offers, and provides for regulation of margin requirements by the Federal Reserve Board.

3670 Government Auditing Standards (Issued by Government Accountability Office)

3671 Broad Scope Audits

3671.01 **Financial and compliance audits** determine whether:

a. financial operations are properly conducted,

b. the financial reports of an audited entity are presented fairly, and

c. the entity has complied with applicable laws and regulations.

3671.02 **Economy and efficiency audits** determine whether the entity is managing or utilizing its resources (personnel, property, space, and so forth) in an economical and efficient manner and the causes of any inefficiencies or uneconomical practices, including inadequacies in management information systems, administrative procedures, or organizational structure.

3671.03 **Program results audits** determine whether:

a. the desired results or benefits are being achieved,

b. the objectives established by the legislature or other authorizing body are being met, and

c. the agency has considered alternatives that might yield desired results at a lower cost.

3672 General Standards

3672.01 The auditors assigned to perform the audit must collectively possess *adequate professional proficiency* for the tasks required.

3672.02 In all matters related to the audit work, the audit organization and the individual auditors shall maintain an *independent attitude*.

3672.03 *Due professional care* is to be used in conducting the audit and in preparing the related reports.

3672.04 The auditor should attempt to remove *scope limitations* or, failing that, should report the limitations.

3673 Examination and Evaluation Standards

3673.01 Work is to be *adequately planned* and assistants properly *supervised.*

3673.02 *Workpapers* are to be prepared and retained.

3673.03 A *review* is to be made in *compliance* with legal and regulatory requirements.

3673.04 An *evaluation* is to be made of the *system of internal control* to assess the extent it can be relied on to ensure accurate information, to ensure compliance with laws and regulations, and to provide for efficient and effective operations.

3673.05 *Sufficient, appropriate,* and *relevant evidence* is to be obtained to afford a reasonable basis for the auditor's opinions, judgments, conclusions, and recommendations.

3673.06 Auditors should be alert for situations of fraud and abuse, and if situations are identified, procedures should be extended to identify their effect on financial statements.

3674 Reporting Standards

3674.01 Written audit reports are to be submitted to the appropriate officials of the organizations requiring or arranging for the audits. Copies of the reports should be sent to other officials who may be responsible for taking action on audit findings and recommendations. Copies should also be made available for public inspection.

3674.02 Reports are to be issued on or before the dates specified by law, regulation, or other arrangement and, in any event, as promptly as possible.

3674.03 Reports should state that the examination was made in accordance with generally accepted auditing standards and in accordance with generally accepted government auditing standards for financial and compliance audits.

3674.04 Reports should include any material deficiency findings identified during the audit or indication of fraud, abuse, or illegal acts.

3674.05 Reports should state the nature of any information omitted by prohibition, because of its confidential nature, or on any other basis that makes the omission necessary.

3674.06 Reports for *financial and compliance audits* shall do the following:

   a. Contain either the auditor's report on the entity's financial statements or on those items of compliance that were tested and negative assurance on those items that were not tested.

   b. Include a report on the auditor's study and evaluation of internal accounting controls made as a part of the financial and compliance audit.

3674.07 Reports for *economy and efficiency audits* shall do the following:

   a. Include a description of the scope and objective of the audit.

   b. Describe material weaknesses found in the internal control system.

   c. Recommend actions to improve such problem areas in operations as may be noted in the audit.

   d. Include views of responsible management officials concerning the auditor's findings, conclusions, and recommendations.

- e. Describe noteworthy accomplishments, particularly when management improvements in one area may be applicable elsewhere.
- f. List any issues and questions needing further study and consideration.
- g. Present factual data accurately and fairly in an objective, convincing manner.
- h. Be as concise as possible, but at the same time, clear and complete enough to be understood by the users.
- i. Place primary emphasis on improvement rather than on criticism of the past.

3680 Statements on Standards for Attestation Engagements

3681 Attestation Standards: Revision and Recodification

3681.01 In Statement on Standards for Attestation Engagements 10, the attestation standards are divided into General Standards, Standards of Fieldwork, and Standards of Reporting. These standards apply only to attest services rendered by a certified public accountant in the practice of public accounting. The General Standards are as follows:

- a. The engagement shall be performed by a practitioner having adequate technical training and proficiency in the attest function.
- b. The engagement shall be performed by a practitioner having adequate knowledge of the subject matter.
- c. The practitioner shall perform the engagement only if the practitioner has reason to believe that the subject matter is capable of evaluation against criteria that are suitable and available to users.
- d. In all matters relating to the engagement, an independence in mental attitude shall be maintained by the practitioner.
- e. Due professional care shall be exercised in the planning and performance of the engagement.

3681.02 The Standards of Fieldwork for attestation engagements are as follows:

- a. The work shall be adequately planned and assistants, if any, shall be properly supervised.
- b. Sufficient evidence shall be obtained to provide a reasonable basis for the conclusion that is expressed in the report.

3681.03 The Standards of Reporting for attestation engagements are as follows:

- a. The report shall identify the subject matter or the assertion being reported on and state the character of the engagement.
- b. The report shall state the practitioner's conclusion about the subject matter or the assertion in relation to the criteria against which the subject matter was evaluated.
- c. The report shall state all of the practitioner's significant reservations about the engagement, the subject matter, and, if applicable, the assertion related thereto.
- d. The report shall state that the use of the report is restricted to specified parties under the following circumstances:
    - (1) When the criteria used to evaluate the subject matter are determined by the practitioner to be appropriate only for a limited number of parties who either participated in their establishment or can be presumed to have an adequate understanding of the criteria

(2) When the criteria used to evaluate the subject matter are available only to specified parties

(3) When reporting on subject matter and a written assertion has not been provided by the responsible party

(4) When the report is on an attest engagement to apply agreed-upon procedures to the subject matter

3681.04 **Unconditional requirements:** The practitioner is required to comply with an unconditional requirement in all cases in which the circumstances exist to which the unconditional requirement applies. An unconditional requirement is indicated by the words *must* or *is required*.

3681.05 **Presumptively mandatory requirements**: The practitioner is also required to comply with a presumptively mandatory requirement in all cases in which the circumstances exist to which the presumptively mandatory requirement applies; however, in rare circumstances the practitioner may depart from a presumptively mandatory requirement provided he/she documents the justification for departure and how alternative procedures performed in the circumstances were sufficient to achieve the objectives of the presumptively mandatory requirement. The word *should* indicates a presumptively mandatory requirement.

3682 Attest Engagements (AT 101)

3682.01 An attest engagement is defined as an engagement where a practitioner is engaged to issue or does issue an examination, review, or agreed-upon procedures report on subject matter, or an assertion about the subject matter that is the responsibility of another party.

3682.02 The subject matter of an attest engagement may take many forms, including the following:

a. Historical or prospective performance or condition (e.g., historical or prospective financial information, performance measurements, and backlog data)

b. Physical characteristics (e.g., narrative descriptions, square footage of facilities)

c. Historical events (e.g., the price of a market basket of goods on a certain date)

d. Analysis (e.g., breakeven analysis)

e. Systems and processes (e.g., internal control)

f. Behavior (e.g., corporate governance, compliance with laws and regulations, and human resource practices)

3682.03 An assertion is any declaration or set of declarations about whether the subject matter is based on or in conformity with the criteria selected. A practitioner may report on a written assertion or may report directly on the subject matter. In either case, the practitioner should ordinarily obtain a written assertion in an examination or review engagement.

3682.04 When a written assertion has not been obtained, a practitioner may still report on the subject matter. However, the form of the report will vary depending on the circumstances and its use should be restricted.

3682.05 The responsible party is defined as the person or persons, either as individuals or representatives of the entity, responsible for the subject matter. If the nature of the subject matter is such that no such party exists, a party (identified by the party wishing to engage the practitioner) who has a reasonable basis for making a written assertion about the subject matter may provide such an assertion.

3682.06 Because the practitioner's role in an attest engagement is that of an *attester,* the practitioner should not take on the role of the responsible party in an attest engagement. Therefore, the need to clearly identify a responsible party is a prerequisite for an attest engagement.

3682.07 The practitioner should obtain written acknowledgment or other evidence of the responsible party's responsibility for the subject matter, or the written assertion, as it relates to the objective of the engagement. The responsible party can acknowledge that responsibility in a number of ways (e.g., in an engagement letter, a representation letter, the presentation of the subject matter, or the written assertion).

3682.08 A CPA firm has a responsibility to adopt a system of quality control in the conduct of a firm's attest practice. Thus, a firm should establish quality control policies and procedures to provide it with reasonable assurance that its personnel comply with the attestation standards in its attestation engagements.

3682.09 Written representations from the responsible party ordinarily confirm representations explicitly or implicitly given to the practitioner, indicate and document the continuing appropriateness of such representations, and reduce the possibility of misunderstanding concerning the matters that are the subject of the representation. Accordingly, in an examination or a review engagement, a practitioner should consider obtaining a representation letter from the responsible party.

3682.10 A practitioner's examination report on subject matter or an assertion should include the following:

  a. A title that includes the word *independent*
  b. An identification of the subject matter or assertion and the responsible party
  c. A statement that the subject matter or assertion is the responsibility of the responsible party
  d. A statement that the practitioner's responsibility is to express an opinion on the subject matter or assertion based on the practitioner's examination
  e. A statement that the examination was conducted in accordance with attestation standards established by the AICPA, and, accordingly, included procedures that the practitioner considered necessary in the circumstances
  f. A statement that the practitioner believes the examination provides a reasonable basis for an opinion
  g. The practitioner's opinion on whether the subject matter or assertion is based on (or in conformity with) the criteria in all material respects
  h. A statement restricting the use of the report to specified parties under the following circumstances:
     (1) When the criteria used to evaluate the subject matter or assertion are determined by the practitioner to be appropriate only for a limited number of parties who either participated in their establishment or can be presumed to have an adequate understanding of the criteria
     (2) When the criteria used to evaluate the subject matter are available only to the specified parties
     (3) When a written assertion has not been provided by the responsible party (only applies in an examination of subject matter)
  i. The manual or printed signature of the practitioner's firm
  j. The date of the examination report

3682.11 A practitioner's review report on subject matter or an assertion should include the following:

    a. A title that includes the word *independent*

    b. An identification of the subject matter or assertion and the responsible party

    c. A statement that the subject matter or assertion is the responsibility of the responsible party

    d. A statement that the review was conducted in accordance with standards established by the AICPA

    e. A statement that a review is substantially less in scope than an examination, the objective of which is an expression of opinion on the subject matter or assertion, and accordingly, no such opinion is expressed

    f. A statement about whether the practitioner is aware of any material modifications that should be made to the subject matter or assertion for it to be based on (or in conformity with), in all material respects, the criteria, other than those modifications, if any, indicated in the report

    g. A statement restricting the use of the report to specified parties under the following circumstances:

        (1) When the criteria used to evaluate the subject matter or assertion are determined by the practitioner to be appropriate only for a limited number of parties who either participated in their establishment or can be presumed to have an adequate understanding of the criteria

        (2) When the criteria used to evaluate the subject matter or assertion are available only to the specified users

        (3) When a written assertion has not been provided by the responsible party and the responsible party is not the client (only applies to review reports on subject matter)

    h. The manual or printed signature of the practitioner's firm

    i. The date of the review report

3682.12 The practitioner should prepare and maintain attest documentation, the form and content of which should be designed to meet the circumstances of the particular attest engagement. The quantity, type, and content of attest documentation are matters of the practitioner's professional judgment.

3682.13 Attest documentation serves mainly to:

    a. provide the principal support for the practitioner's report, including the representation regarding observance of the standards of fieldwork, which is implicit in the reference in the report to attestation standards.

    b. aid the practitioner in the conduct and supervision of the attest engagement.

3683 Agreed-Upon Procedures Engagements (AT 201)

3683.01 An agreed-upon procedures engagement is one in which a practitioner is engaged by a client to issue a report of findings based on specific procedures performed on subject matter. The specified parties and the practitioner agree upon the procedures to be performed by the practitioner that the specified parties believe are appropriate.

3683.02 Because the needs of the specified parties may vary widely, the nature, extent, and timing of the agreed-upon procedures may vary as well. Consequently, the specified parties assume responsibility for the sufficiency of the procedures since they best understand their own needs.

3683.03 The general, fieldwork, and reporting standards for attestation engagements should be followed by the practitioner in performing and reporting on agreed-upon procedures engagements.

3683.04 The practitioner may perform an agreed-upon procedures engagement provided that:

a. the practitioner is independent.

b. one of the following conditions is met:

(1) The party wishing to engage the practitioner is responsible for the subject matter, or has a reasonable basis for providing a written assertion about the subject matter when the nature of the subject matter is such that a responsible party does not otherwise exist.

(2) The party wishing to engage the practitioner is not responsible for the subject matter but is able to provide the practitioner, or have a third party who is responsible for the subject matter, provide the practitioner with evidence of the third party's responsibility for the subject matter.

c. the practitioner and the specified parties agree on the procedures performed or to be performed by the practitioner.

d. the specified parties take responsibility for the sufficiency of the agreed-upon procedures for their purposes.

e. the specific subject matter to which the procedures are to be applied is subject to reasonably consistent measurement.

f. criteria to be used in the determination of findings are agreed on between the practitioner and the specified parties.

g. the procedures to be applied to the specific subject matter are expected to result in reasonably consistent findings using the criteria.

h. audit evidence related to the specific subject matter to which the procedures are applied is expected to exist to provide a reasonable basis for expressing the findings in the practitioner's report.

i. where applicable, the practitioner and the specified parties agree on any materiality limits for reporting purposes.

j. use of the report is restricted to the specified parties.

k. for agreed-upon procedures engagements on prospective financial information, the prospective financial statements include a summary of significant assumptions.

3683.05 To satisfy the requirements that the practitioner and the specified parties agree on the procedures performed or to be performed and that the specified parties take responsibility for the sufficiency of the procedures for their purposes, ordinarily the practitioner should communicate directly with and obtain affirmative acknowledgment from each of the specified parties.

3683.06 The practitioner should establish an understanding with the client regarding the services to be performed. When the practitioner documents the understanding through a written communication with the client, such communication should be addressed to the client, and in some circumstances also to all specified parties.

3683.07 The procedures that the practitioner and specified parties agree on may be as limited or as extensive as the specified parties desire. However, mere reading of an assertion or specified information about the subject matter does not constitute sufficient procedures to permit a practitioner to report on the results of applying agreed-upon procedures.

3683.08 The practitioner should not agree to perform procedures that are overly subjective and thus possibly open to varying interpretations. Terms of uncertain meaning (such as general review, limited review, check, or test) should not be used in describing the procedures unless such terms are defined within the agreed-upon procedures.

3683.09 A practitioner should present the results of applying agreed-upon procedures to specific subject matter in the form of findings. The practitioner should not provide negative assurance about whether the subject matter or the assertion is fairly stated based on the criteria.

3683.10 The practitioner should prepare and maintain workpapers in connection with an agreed-upon procedures engagement under the attestation standards. Such workpapers should be appropriate to the circumstances and the practitioner's needs on the engagement to which they apply.

3683.11 The practitioner's report on agreed-upon procedures should be in the form of procedures and findings. The report should contain the following elements:

    a. A title that includes the word *independent*

    b. Identification of the specified parties

    c. Identification of the subject matter or assertion and the character of the engagement

    d. Identification of the responsible party

    e. A statement that the subject matter is the responsibility of the responsible party

    f. A statement that the procedures performed were those agreed to by the specified parties identified in the report

    g. A statement that the agreed-upon procedures engagement was conducted in accordance with attestation standards established by the AICPA

    h. A statement that the sufficiency of the procedures is solely the responsibility of the specified parties and a disclaimer of responsibility for the sufficiency of those procedures

    i. A list of the procedures performed and related findings

    j. Where applicable, a description of any agreed-upon materiality limits

    k. A statement that the practitioner was not engaged to and did not conduct an examination of the subject matter, the objective of which would be the expression of an opinion, a disclaimer of opinion on the subject matter, and a statement that if the practitioner had performed additional procedures, other matters might have come to the practitioner's attention that would have been reported

l. A statement of restriction on the use of the report because it is intended to be used solely by the specified parties

m. Where applicable, reservations or restrictions concerning procedures or findings

n. Where applicable, a description of the nature of the assistance provided by a specialist

o. The manual or printed signature of the practitioner's firm

p. The date of the report

3683.12 A practitioner may find a representation letter to be a useful and practical means of obtaining representation from the responsible party. The need for such a letter may depend on the nature of the engagement and the specified parties.

3683.13 Before a practitioner who was engaged to perform another form of engagement agrees to change the engagement to an agreed-upon procedures engagement, the practitioner should consider the following:

a. The possibility that certain procedures performed as part of another type of engagement are not appropriate for inclusion in an agreed-upon procedures engagement

b. The reason given for the request, particularly the implications of a restriction on the scope of the original engagement or the matters to be reported

c. The additional effort required to complete the original engagement

d. If applicable, the reasons for changing from a general-use report to a restricted-use report

3683.14 If the specified parties acknowledge agreement to the procedures performed or to be performed and assume responsibility for the sufficiency of the procedures to be included in the agreed-upon procedures engagement, either of the following would be considered a reasonable basis for requesting a change in the engagement:

a. A change in circumstances that requires another form of engagement

b. A misunderstanding concerning the nature of the original engagement or the available alternative

3684 Financial Forecasts and Projections

3684.01 The information in this section applies to the guidance practitioners should use when engaged to issue examination, compilation, or agreed-upon procedures reports on prospective financial statements. This section also provides standards for a practitioner who is engaged to examine, compile, or apply agreed-upon procedures to partial presentations.

3684.02 The following definitions are relevant to the guidance on prospective financial statements.

a. **Prospective financial statements:** Either financial forecasts or financial projections including the summaries of significant assumptions and accounting policies.

b. **Partial presentation:** A presentation of prospective financial information that excludes one or more of the items required for prospective financial statements. Partial presentations are not ordinarily appropriate for general use.

c. **Financial forecast:** Prospective financial statements that present, to the best of the responsible party's knowledge and belief, an entity's expected financial position, results of operations, and cash flows. A financial forecast is based on the responsible party's assumptions reflecting the conditions it expects to exist and the course of action it expects to take.

d. **Financial projection:** Prospective financial statements that present, to the best of the responsible party's knowledge and belief, given one or more hypothetical assumptions, an entity's expected financial position, results of operations, and cash flows.

e. **Hypothetical assumption:** An assumption used in a financial projection to present a condition or course of action that is not necessarily expected to occur but is consistent with the purpose of the projection.

3684.03 Prospective financial statements are for either *general use* or *limited use.*

a. *General use* of prospective financial statements refers to the use of the statements by persons with whom the responsible party is not negotiating directly (e.g., in an offering statement of an entity's debt or equity securities). Only a financial forecast is appropriate for general use.

b. *Limited use* of prospective financial statements refers to the use of prospective financial statements by the responsible party alone or by the responsible party and third parties with whom the responsible party is negotiating directly. Either financial forecasts or financial projections are appropriate for limited use.

3684.04 A compilation of prospective financial statements is a professional service that involves the following:

a. Assembling, to the extent necessary, the prospective financial statements based on the responsible party's assumptions

b. Performing the required compilation procedures, including reading the prospective financial statements with their summaries of significant assumptions and accounting policies and considering whether they appear to be presented in conformity with AICPA presentation guidelines and are not obviously inappropriate

c. Issuing a compilation report

3684.05 A practitioner should not compile prospective financial statements that exclude disclosure of the summary of significant assumptions. A practitioner should not compile a financial projection that excludes either (1) an identification of the hypothetical assumptions or (2) a description of the limitations on the usefulness of the presentation.

3684.06 The following standards apply to a compilation of prospective financial statements and the resulting report:

a. The compilation should be performed by a person or persons having adequate technical training and proficiency to compile prospective financial statements.

b. Due professional care should be exercised in the performance of the compilation and the preparation of the report.

c. The work should be adequately planned and assistants, if any, should be properly supervised.

d. Applicable compilation procedures should be performed as a basis for reporting on compiled prospective financial statements.

e. The report based on the practitioner's compilation of prospective financial statements should conform to the applicable guidance, noted in section **3684.07**.

3684.07 The practitioner's standard report on a compilation of prospective financial statements should include the following elements:

    a. An identification of the prospective financial statements presented by the responsible party

    b. A statement that the practitioner has compiled the prospective financial statements in accordance with attestation standards established by the AICPA

    c. A statement that a compilation is limited in scope and does not enable the practitioner to express an opinion or any other form of assurance on the prospective financial statements or the assumptions

    d. A caveat that the prospective results may not be achieved

    e. A statement that the practitioner assumes no responsibility to update the report for events and circumstances occurring after the date of the report

    f. The manual or printed signature of the practitioner's firm

    g. The date of the compilation report

3684.08 An examination of prospective financial statements is a professional service that involves the following:

    a. Evaluating the preparation of the prospective financial statements

    b. Evaluating the support underlying the assumptions

    c. Evaluating the presentation of the prospective financial statements for conformity with AICPA presentation guidelines

    d. Issuing an examination report

3684.09 The practitioner should follow the general, fieldwork, and reporting standards for attestation engagements in performing an examination of prospective financial statements and reporting thereon.

3684.10 The practitioner's standard report on an examination of prospective financial statements should include the following:

    a. A title that includes the word *independent*

    b. An identification of the prospective financial statements presented

    c. An identification of the responsible party and a statement that the prospective financial statements are the responsibility of the responsible party

    d. A statement that the practitioner's responsibility is to express an opinion on the prospective financial statements based on the examination

    e. A statement that the examination of the prospective financial statements was conducted in accordance with attestation standards established by the AICPA and, accordingly, included such procedures as the practitioner considered necessary

    f. A statement that the practitioner believes that the examination provides a reasonable basis for an opinion

    g. The practitioner's opinion that the prospective financial statements are presented in conformity with AICPA presentation guidelines and that the underlying assumptions provide a reasonable basis for the forecast or a reasonable basis for the projection given the hypothetical assumptions

    h. A caveat that the prospective results may not be achieved

      i. A statement that the practitioner assumes no responsibility to update the report for events and circumstances occurring after the date of the report

      j. The manual or printed signature of the practitioner's firm

      k. The date of the examination report

3684.11 A practitioner who accepts an engagement to apply agreed-upon procedures to prospective financial statements should follow the general, fieldwork, and reporting standards for attest engagements. They should also consult the guidance presented in AT 201 (section **3683** in this manual).

3684.12 A practitioner may perform an agreed-upon procedure attest engagement on prospective financial statements provided the following conditions are met:

      a. The practitioner is independent.

      b. The practitioner and the specified parties agree on the procedures performed by the practitioner.

      c. The specified parties take responsibility for the sufficiency of the agreed-upon procedures for their purposes.

      d. The prospective financial statements include a summary of significant assumptions.

      e. The prospective financial statements to which the procedures are to be applied are subject to reasonably consistent evaluation against criteria that are suitable and available to the specified parties.

      f. Criteria to be used in the determination of findings are agreed on between the practitioner and the specified parties.

      g. The procedures to be applied to the prospective financial statements are expected to result in reasonably consistent findings using the criteria.

      h. Audit evidence related to the prospective financial statements to which the procedures are applied is expected to exist to provide a reasonable basis for expressing the findings in the practitioner's report.

      i. Where applicable, the practitioner and the specified users agree on any agreed-upon materiality limits for reporting purposes.

      j. Use of the report is to be restricted to the specified parties.

3685 Reporting on Pro Forma Financial Information (AT 401)

3685.01 The objective of pro forma financial information is to show what the significant effects on historical financial information might have been had a consummated or proposed transaction (or event) occurred at an earlier date.

3685.02 Pro forma financial information is commonly used to show the effects of transactions such as (1) business combinations, (2) changes in capitalization, (3) disposition of a significant portion of the business, (4) changes in the form of business organization or status as an autonomous entity, and (5) proposed sale of securities and the application of the proceeds.

3685.03 The objective of pro forma financial information is achieved primarily by applying pro forma adjustments to historical financial information. Pro forma adjustments should be based on management's assumptions and give effect to all significant effects directly attributable to the transaction.

3685.04 Pro forma financial information should be labeled as such to distinguish it from historical financial information.

3685.05 The presentation of pro forma information should describe the transaction that is reflected in the pro forma data, the source of the historical financial information on which it is based, the significant assumptions used in developing the pro forma adjustments, and any significant uncertainties about those assumptions.

3685.06 The objective of the practitioner's examination procedures applied to pro forma financial information is to provide reasonable assurance as to whether:

   a. management's assumptions provide a reasonable basis for presenting the significant effects directly attributable to the underlying transaction,

   b. the related pro forma adjustments give appropriate effect to those assumptions, and

   c. the pro forma column reflects the proper application of those adjustments to the historical financial statements.

3685.07 The objective of the practitioner's review procedures applied to pro forma financial information is to provide negative assurance as to whether any information came to the practitioner's attention to cause the practitioner to believe that:

   a. management's assumptions do not provide a reasonable basis for presenting the significant effects directly attributed to the underlying transaction,

   b. the related pro forma adjustments do not give appropriate effect to those assumptions, or

   c. the pro forma column does not reflect the proper application of those adjustments to the historical financial statements.

3686 Compliance Attestation (AT 601)

3686.01 Compliance engagements are either used to determine (1) an entity's compliance with requirements of specified laws, regulations, rules, contracts, or grants or (2) the effectiveness of an entity's internal control over compliance with specified requirements.

3686.02 Compliance requirements may be either financial or nonfinancial in nature. Compliance engagements should be conducted in accordance with the general, fieldwork, and reporting attestation standards.

3686.03 A practitioner may be engaged to perform an agreed-upon procedures engagement or an examination engagement in the area of compliance attestation.

3686.04 A practitioner may be engaged to perform agreed-upon procedures to assist users in evaluating the following subject matter:

   a. The entity's compliance with specified requirements

   b. The effectiveness of the entity's internal control over compliance

   c. Both the entity's compliance with specified requirements and the effectiveness of the entity's internal control over compliance

3686.05 An important consideration in determining the type of engagement to be performed is expectations by users of the practitioner's report.

3686.06 A practitioner may perform an agreed-upon procedures engagement related to an entity's compliance with specified requirements or the effectiveness of internal control over compliance if the following conditions are met:

    a. The responsible party accepts responsibility for the entity's compliance with specified requirements and the effectiveness of the entity's internal control over compliance.

    b. The responsible party evaluates the entity's compliance with specified requirements or the effectiveness of the entity's internal control over compliance.

3686.07 A practitioner may perform an examination engagement related to an entity's compliance with specified requirements if the following conditions are met:

    a. The responsible party accepts responsibility for the entity's compliance with specified requirements and the effectiveness of the entity's internal control over compliance.

    b. The responsible party evaluates the entity's compliance with specified requirements.

    c. Sufficient audit evidence exists or could be developed to support management's evaluation.

3686.08 As a part of engagement performance, the practitioner should obtain from the responsible party a written assertion about compliance with specified requirements or internal control over compliance.

3686.09 The objective of the practitioner's agreed-upon procedures engagement is to present specific findings to assist users in evaluating an entity's compliance with specified requirements or the effectiveness of internal control over compliance based on procedures agreed-upon by the users of the report.

3686.10 In an engagement to perform agreed-upon procedures on an entity's compliance with specified requirements or about the effectiveness of an entity's internal control over compliance, the practitioner is required to perform only the procedures that have been agreed to by the users.

3686.11 The objective of a practitioner's examination procedures applied to an entity's compliance with specified requirements is to express an opinion on the entity's compliance based on the specified criteria.

3686.12 In a compliance examination engagement, attestation risk is defined as the risk that the practitioner may unknowingly fail to modify appropriately the opinion. It is composed of inherent risk, control risk, and detection risk. For the purposes of a compliance examination, these components are defined as follows:

    a. *Inherent risk*: The risk that material noncompliance with specified requirements could occur, assuming there are no related controls.

    b. *Control risk*: The risk that material noncompliance that could occur will not be prevented or detected on a timely basis by the entity's controls.

    c. *Detection risk*: The risk that the practitioner's procedures will lead the practitioner to conclude that material noncompliance does not exist when, in fact, such noncompliance does exist.

3686.13 In an examination of the entity's compliance with specified requirements, the practitioner should do the following:

    a. Obtain an understanding of the specified compliance requirements.

    b. Plan the engagement.

c. Consider relevant portions of the entity's internal control over compliance.

d. Obtain sufficient evidence including testing compliance with specified requirements.

e. Consider subsequent events.

f. Form an opinion about whether the entity complied, in all material respects, with specified requirements (or whether the responsible party's assertion about such compliance is fairly stated in all material respects) based on the specified criteria.

3686.14 In an examination engagement or an agreed-upon procedures engagement, the practitioner should obtain a written representation letter from the responsible party.

3687 Management's Discussion and Analysis (AT 701)

3687.01 The information in this section is applicable to the following levels of service when a practitioner is engaged by (1) a public entity that prepares management's discussion and analysis (MD&A) in accordance with the rules and regulations adopted by the SEC, or (2) a nonpublic entity that prepares an MD&A presentation and whose management provides a written assertion that the presentation has been prepared using the rules and regulations adopted by the SEC:

a. An examination of an MD&A presentation

b. A review of an MD&A presentation for an annual period, an interim period, or a combined annual and interim period

3687.02 A practitioner engaged to examine or review MD&A and report thereon should comply with the general, fieldwork, and reporting standards for attestation engagements.

3687.03 The practitioner's objective in an engagement to examine MD&A is to express an opinion on the MD&A presentation taken as a whole by reporting whether:

a. the presentation includes, in all material respects, the required elements of the rules and regulations adopted by the SEC,

b. the historical financial amounts have been accurately derived, in all material respects, from the entity's financial statements, and

c. the underlying information, determinations, estimates, and assumptions of the entity provide a reasonable basis for the disclosures contained therein.

3687.04 A practitioner may accept an engagement to examine MD&A of a public or nonpublic entity, provided the practitioner audits, in accordance with GAAS, the financial statements for at least the latest period to which the MD&A presentation relates and the financial statements for the other periods covered by the MD&A presentation have been audited by the practitioner or a predecessor auditor.

3687.05 The objective of a review of MD&A is to report whether any information came to the practitioner's attention to cause the practitioner to believe that:

a. the MD&A presentation does not include, in all material respects, the required elements of the rules and regulations adopted by the SEC.

b. the historical financial amounts included therein have not been accurately derived, in all material respects, from the entity's financial statements.

c. the underlying information, determinations, estimates, and assumptions of the entity do not provide a reasonable basis for the disclosures contained therein.

3687.06 A practitioner may accept an engagement to review the MD&A presentation of a public entity for an annual period provided the practitioner has audited, in accordance with GAAS, the financial statements for at least the latest annual period to which the MD&A presentation relates and the financial statements for the other periods covered by the MD&A presentation have been audited by the practitioner or a predecessor auditor.

3687.07 A practitioner may accept an engagement to review the MD&A presentation of a nonpublic entity for an interim period provided that all of the following conditions are met:

    a. The practitioner performs one of the following:

        (1) A review of the historical financial statements for the related interim period under the guidance provided by SSARS and issues a review report

        (2) A review of the condensed interim financial information for the related interim periods and issues a review report thereon, and such interim financial information is accompanied by complete annual financial statements for the most recent fiscal year that have been audited

        (3) An audit of the interim financial statements

    b. The MD&A presentation for the most recent fiscal year has been or will be examined or reviewed.

    c. Management will provide a written assertion stating that the presentation has been prepared using the rules and regulations adopted by the SEC as the criteria.

3687.08 Management is responsible for the preparation of the entity's MD&A pursuant to the rules and regulations adopted by the SEC.

3687.09 Factors to be considered by the practitioner in planning an examination of MD&A include (1) the anticipated level of attestation risk related to assertions embodied in the MD&A presentation, (2) preliminary judgments about materiality for attest purposes, (3) the items within the MD&A presentation that are likely to require revision or adjustment, and (4) conditions that may require extension or modification of attest procedures.

3687.10 In an examination of MD&A, the practitioner should perform the following:

    a. Obtain an understanding of the rules and regulations adopted by the SEC for MD&A and management's method of preparing MD&A.

    b. Plan the engagement.

    c. Consider relevant portions of the entity's internal control applicable to the preparation of MD&A.

    d. Obtain sufficient evidence, including testing completeness.

    e. Consider the effect of events subsequent to the balance-sheet date.

    f. Obtain written representation from management concerning its responsibility for MD&A, completeness of minutes, events subsequent to the balance-sheet date, and other matters about which the practitioner believes written representations are appropriate.

    g. Form an opinion about whether the MD&A presentation includes, in all material respects, the required elements of the rules and regulations adopted by the SEC, whether the historical financial amounts included therein have been accurately derived, in all material respects, from the entity's financial statements, and whether the underlying information, determinations, estimates, and assumptions of the entity provide a reasonable basis for the disclosures contained in the MD&A.

3687.11 In a review engagement of MD&A, the practitioner should do the following:

a. Obtain an understanding of the rules and regulations adopted by the SEC for MD&A and management's method of preparing MD&A.

b. Plan the engagement.

c. Consider relevant portions of the entity's internal control applicable to the preparation of the MD&A.

d. Apply analytical procedures and make inquiries of management and others.

e. Consider the effect of events subsequent to the balance sheet date.

f. Obtain written representations from management concerning its responsibility for MD&A, completeness of minutes, events subsequent to the balance sheet date, and other matters about which the practitioner believes written representations are appropriate.

g. Form a conclusion as to whether any information came to the practitioner's attention that causes the practitioner to believe any of the following:

(1) The MD&A presentation does not include, in all material respects, the required elements of the rules and regulations of the SEC.

(2) The historical financial amounts included therein have not been accurately derived, in all material respects, from the entity's financial statements.

(3) The underlying information, determinations, estimates, and assumptions of the entity do not provide a reasonable basis for the disclosures contained therein.

3687.12 If a practitioner concludes that the MD&A presentation contains material inconsistencies with other information included in the document containing the MD&A presentation or with the historical financial statements, material omissions, or material misstatements of fact and management refuses to take corrective action, the practitioner should inform the audit committee or others with equivalent authority and responsibility.

3690 Reporting on an Entity's Internal Control over Financial Reporting (AT 501)

3691 Applicability

3691.01 This standard for reporting on internal control provides guidance to the practitioner who is engaged to issue or does issue an examination report on the effectiveness of an entity's internal control over financial reporting as of a point in time (or on an assertion thereon).

3691.02 An entity's internal control over financial reporting includes those policies and procedures that pertain to an entity's ability to record, process, summarize, and report financial data consistent with the assertions embodied in either annual financial statements or interim financial statements, or both.

3691.03 A practitioner engaged to examine the effectiveness of an entity's internal control should comply with the general, fieldwork, and reporting standards for attest engagements (see section 3681) as well as the specific performance and reporting standards noted in this section.

3692 Conditions for Engagement Performance

3692.01 A practitioner may examine the effectiveness of an entity's internal control if the following conditions are met:

    a. Management of the entity accepts responsibility for the effectiveness of the entity's internal control (the term *responsible party* is used in this section to refer to the management personnel who accept responsibility for the entity's internal control).

    b. The responsible party evaluates the effectiveness of the entity's internal control using suitable criteria (such criteria are referred to as *control criteria* in the standard).

    c. Sufficient audit evidence exists or could be developed to support the responsible party's evaluation.

3692.02 As part of the engagement performance, the practitioner should obtain from the responsible party a written assertion about the effectiveness of the entity's internal control. The responsible party may present its written assertion in either of the following:

    a. A separate report that will accompany the practitioner's report

    b. A representation letter to the practitioner

3692.03 Regardless of whether the practitioner's client is the responsible party, the responsible party's refusal to furnish a written assertion as part of an examination engagement should cause the practitioner to withdraw from the engagement.

3692.04 A practitioner may perform an examination engagement or an agreed-upon procedures engagement relating to the effectiveness of the entity's internal control. However, a practitioner should *not* accept an engagement to review such subject matter or a written assertion about such subject matter.

3693 Performing an Examination Engagement

3693.01 The practitioner's objective in an engagement to examine the effectiveness of the entity's internal control is to express an opinion on:

    a. the effectiveness of the entity's internal control, in all material respects, based on the control criteria and

    b. whether the responsible party's written assertion about the effectiveness of internal control is fairly stated, in all material respects, based on the control criteria.

3693.02 The practitioner's opinion relates to the effectiveness of the entity's internal control taken as a whole and not to the effectiveness of each individual component of the entity's internal control.

3693.03 Performing an examination of the effectiveness of an entity's internal control involves the following:

    a. Planning the engagement

    b. Obtaining an understanding of internal control

    c. Evaluating the design effectiveness of the controls

    d. Testing and evaluating the operating effectiveness of the controls

    e. Forming an opinion on the effectiveness of the entity's internal control, or the responsible party's assertion thereon, based on the control criteria

3693.04 Planning an engagement to examine the effectiveness of the entity's internal control involves developing an overall strategy for the scope and performance of the engagement. When developing the overall strategy, the practitioner should consider factors such as the following:

   a. Matters affecting the industry in which the entity operates, such as financial reporting practices, economic considerations, laws and regulations, and technology changes

   b. Knowledge of the entity's internal control obtained during other professional engagements

   c. Matters relating to the entity's business, including its organization, operating characteristics, capital structure, and distribution methods

   d. The extent of recent changes, if any, in the entity, its operations, or its internal control

   e. The responsible party's method of evaluating the effectiveness of the entity's internal control based on control criteria

   f. Preliminary judgments about materiality, inherent risk, and other factors relating to the determination of material weaknesses

   g. The type and extent of audit evidence pertaining to the effectiveness of the entity's internal control

   h. The nature of specific controls designed to achieve the objectives of the control criteria and their significance to internal control taken as a whole

   i. Preliminary judgments about the effectiveness of internal control

3693.05 A practitioner generally obtains an understanding of the design of specific controls by making inquiries of appropriate management, supervisory, and staff personnel, by inspecting entity documents, and by observing entity activities and operations.

3693.06 The audit evidence that is sufficient to support a practitioner's opinion is a matter of professional judgment. However, the practitioner should consider matters such as the following:

   a. The nature of the control

   b. The significance of the control in achieving the objectives of the control criteria

   c. The nature and extent of tests of the operating effectiveness of the controls performed by the entity, if any

   d. The risk of noncompliance with the control, which might be assessed by considering the following:

      (1) Whether there have been changes in the volume or nature of transactions that might adversely affect control design or operating effectiveness

      (2) Whether there have been changes in controls

      (3) The degree to which the control relies on the effectiveness of other controls

      (4) Whether there have been changes in key personnel who perform the control or monitor its performance

      (5) Whether the control relies on performance by an individual or by electronic equipment

      (6) The complexity of the control

      (7) Whether more than one control achieves a specific objective

3693.07 The practitioner should obtain written representations from the responsible party. Such representations should include the following:

- a. Acknowledgment of the responsible party's responsibility for establishing and maintaining effective internal control
- b. A statement that the responsible party has performed an evaluation of the effectiveness of the entity's internal control and specifying the control criteria
- c. An indication of the responsible party's assertion about the effectiveness of the entity's internal control based on the control criteria as of a specified date
- d. A statement that the responsible party has disclosed to the practitioner all significant deficiencies in the design or operation of internal control which could adversely affect the entity's ability to record, process, summarize, and report financial data consistent with the assertions of management in the financial statements and has identified those that it believes to be material weaknesses in internal control
- e. A description of any material fraud and any other fraud that, although not material, involve management or other employees who have a significant role in the entity's internal control
- f. A statement indicating whether there were, subsequent to the date being reported on, any changes in internal control or other factors that might significantly affect internal control, including any corrective actions taken by the responsible party with regard to significant deficiencies and material weaknesses

3694 Deficiencies in an Entity's Internal Control

3694.01 A significant deficiency is defined by SAS 115 as a deficiency, or combination of deficiencies, in internal control that is less severe than a material weakness, yet important enough to merit attention by those charged with governance.

3694.02 Evaluating whether a significant deficiency is also a material weakness is a subjective process that depends on factors such as the nature of the accounting system and any financial statement amounts exposed to the significant deficiency.

3694.03 A practitioner engaged to examine the effectiveness of the entity's internal control should communicate significant deficiencies to the client's audit committee and identify the significant deficiencies that are also considered to be material weaknesses.

3694.04 When significant deficiencies are found, the AICPA recommends that the following paragraphs be included in a report on internal controls:

"A material weakness is a significant deficiency in which the design or operation of one or more of the internal control components does not reduce to a relatively low level the risk that misstatements caused by error or fraud in amounts that would be material in relation to the financial statements being audited may occur and not be detected within a timely period by employees in the normal course of performing their assigned functions."

"Our consideration of internal controls would not necessarily disclose all matters in internal control that might be significant deficiencies and, accordingly, would not necessarily disclose all significant deficiencies that are also considered to be material weaknesses as defined above. However, none of the significant deficiencies described above is believed to be a material weakness."

3695 Reporting Standards

3695.01 The practitioner may examine and report directly on an entity's effectiveness of internal control or the practitioner may examine and report on the responsible party's written assertion.

3695.02 The practitioner's examination report on the effectiveness of an entity's internal control over financial reporting should include the following:

a. A title that includes the word *independent*

b. An identification of the subject matter and the responsible party

c. A statement that the responsible party is responsible for maintaining effective internal control over financial reporting

d. A statement that the practitioner's responsibility is to express an opinion on the effectiveness of an entity's internal control based on the examination

e. A statement that the examination was conducted in accordance with attestation standards established by the AICPA and, accordingly, included obtaining an understanding of internal control over financial reporting, testing and evaluating the design and operating effectiveness of internal control, and performing such other procedures as the practitioner considered necessary in the circumstances

f. A statement that the practitioner believes the examination provides a reasonable basis for the opinion

g. A paragraph stating that, because of inherent limitations of any internal control, misstatements due to error or fraud may occur and may not be detected

h. The practitioner's opinion on whether the entity has maintained, in all material respects, effective internal control over financial reporting as of the specified date based on the control criteria

i. A statement restricting the use of the report to the specified parties under the following circumstances:

  (1) When the criteria used to evaluate internal control over financial reporting are determined by the practitioner to be appropriate only for a limited number of parties who either participated in their establishment or can be presumed to have an adequate understanding of the criteria

  (2) When the criteria used to evaluate internal control over financial reporting are available only to specified parties

j. The manual or printed signature of the practitioner's firm

k. The date of the examination report

3696 Service Organizations (AU 324)

3696.01 This section provides guidance on the factors an independent auditor should consider when auditing the financial statements of an entity that uses a service organization to process certain transactions.

3696.02 For the purposes of this section, the following definitions apply:

    a. *User Organization*—the entity that has engaged a service organization and whose financial statements are being audited.

    b. *User Auditor*—the auditor who reports on the financial statements of the user organization.

    c. *Service Organization*—the entity that provides services to a user organization that are part of the user organization's information system.

    d. *Service Auditor*—the auditor who reports on controls of a service organization that may be relevant to a user organization's internal control as it relates to an audit of financial statements.

3696.03 A service organization's services are part of an entity's information system if they affect *any* of the following:

    a. How an entity's transactions are initiated

    b. The accounting records, supporting information, and specific accounts in the financial statements involved in the processing and reporting of the entity's transactions

    c. The accounting processing involved from the initiation of the transactions to their inclusion in the financial statements, including electronic means used to transmit, process, maintain, and access information

    d. The financial reporting process used to prepare the entity's financial statements, including significant accounting estimates and disclosures

3696.04 When a user organization uses a service organization, transactions that affect the user organization's financial statements are subjected to controls that are, at least in part, physically and operationally separate from the user organization.

3696.05 When the user organization initiates transactions and the service organization executes and does the accounting processing of those transactions, there is a high degree of interaction between the activities at the user organization and those at the service organization. In these circumstances, it may be feasible for the user organization to implement effective controls for those transactions.

3696.06 When the service organization initiates, executes, and does the accounting processing of the user organization's transactions, there is a lower degree of interaction and it may not be practicable for the user organization to implement effective controls for those transactions.

3696.07 Auditing standards require the auditor to obtain an understanding of each of the five components of an entity's internal control sufficient to plan the audit. This understanding may encompass controls placed in operation by the entity and by service organizations whose services are part of the entity's information system.

3696.08 In planning the audit, such knowledge should be used to do the following:

    a. Identify types of potential misstatements.

    b. Consider factors that affect the risk of material misstatement.

    c. Design substantive tests.

3696.09 Information about the nature of the services provided by a service organization that are part of the user organization's information system and the service organization's controls over those services may be available from a variety of sources. Some of those sources would include the following:

    a. User manuals

    b. System overviews

    c. Technical manuals

    d. The contract between the user organization and the service organization

    e. Reports by service auditors, internal auditors, or regulatory authorities on the service organization's controls

3696.10 If the user auditor concludes that information is not available to obtain a sufficient understanding to plan the audit, the user auditor may consider contacting the service organization, through the user organization, to obtain specific information or request that a service auditor be engaged to perform procedures that will supply the necessary information. The user auditor may also visit the service organization and perform such procedures.

3696.11 If the user auditor is unable to obtain sufficient evidence to achieve the audit objectives, the user auditor should qualify the opinion or disclaim an opinion on the financial statements because of a scope limitation.

3696.12 Although a service auditor has no responsibility to detect subsequent events, the service auditor should inquire of management as to whether it is aware of any subsequent events through the date of the service auditor's report that would have a significant effect on user organizations. In addition, a service auditor should obtain a representation letter from management regarding subsequent events.

3697 Communication of Internal Control Related Matters Identified in an Audit (AU 325)

3697.01 This section establishes standards and provided guidance on communicating matters related to an entity's internal control over financial reporting identified in an audit of financial statements. It is applicable whenever an auditor expresses an opinion on financial statements (including a disclaimer of opinion).

3697.02 Internal control is a process—effected by those charged with governance, management, and other personnel—designed to provide reasonable assurance about the achievement of the entity's objectives with regard to reliability of financial reporting, effectiveness and efficiency of operations, and compliance with applicable laws and regulations.

3697.03 A **control deficiency** exists when the design or operation of a control does not allow management or employees, in the normal course of performing their assigned functions, to prevent or detect misstatements on a timely basis. A deficiency in **design** exists when:

   a. a control necessary to meet the control objective is missing or

   b. an existing control is not properly designed so that even if the control operates as designed, the control objective is not always met.

3697.04 A deficiency in **operation** exists when a properly designed control does not operate as designed or when the person performing the control does not possess the necessary authority or qualifications to perform the control effectively. Control deficiencies may involve one or more of the five interrelated components of internal control.

3697.05 A **significant deficiency** is a control deficiency, or a combination of control deficiencies, that adversely affects the entity's ability to initiate, authorize, record, process, or report financial data reliably in accordance with generally accepted accounting principles such that there is more than a remote likelihood that a misstatement of the entity's financial statements that is more than inconsequential will not be prevented or detected.

3697.06 A **material weakness** is a significant deficiency, or combination of significant deficiencies, that results in more than a remote likelihood that a material misstatement of the financial statements will not be prevented or detected.

3697.07 The phrase "more than inconsequential" as used in the definition of significant deficiencies describes the magnitude of potential misstatement that could occur as a result of a significant deficiency and serves as a threshold for evaluating whether a control deficiency or combination of control deficiencies is a significant deficiency.

3697.08 The auditor must evaluate identified control deficiencies and determine whether these deficiencies, individually or in combination, are significant deficiencies or material weaknesses. The significance of a control deficiency depends on the potential for a misstatement, not on whether a misstatement actually has occurred.

3697.09 When evaluating whether control deficiencies, individually or in combination, are significant deficiencies or material weaknesses, the auditor should consider the likelihood and magnitude of misstatement. The following are examples of factors that may affect the likelihood that a control, or combination of controls, could fail to prevent or detect a misstatement:

   a. The nature of the financial statement accounts, disclosures, and assertions

   b. The susceptibility of the related assets or liabilities to loss or fraud

   c. The subjectivity or complexity of the amount involved, and the extent of judgment needed to determine that amount

   d. The cause and frequency of any known or detected exceptions related to the operating effectiveness of a control

   e. The interaction or relationship of the control with other controls

   f. The possible future consequences of the deficiency

3697.10 Several factors affect the magnitude of a misstatement that could result from a deficiency or deficiencies in controls. The factors include, but are not limited to, the following:

    a. The financial statement amounts or total of transactions exposed to the deficiency

    b. The volume of activity in the account balance or class of transactions exposed to the deficiency in the current period or expected in future periods

3697.11 Control deficiencies identified during the audit that upon evaluation are considered significant deficiencies or material weaknesses must be communicated in writing to management and those charged with governance as a part of each audit, including significant deficiencies and material weaknesses that were communicated to management and those charged with governance in previous audits and have not yet been remediated.

3697.12 The written communication referred to in section **3697.11** is best made by the report release date, which is the date the auditor grants the entity permission to use the auditor's report in connection with the financial statements, but should be made no later than 60 days following the report release date.

3697.13 For some matters, early communication to management or those charged with governance may be important. Accordingly, the auditor may decide to communicate certain identified significant deficiencies and material weaknesses during the audit.

3697.14 Nothing precludes the auditor from communicating to management and those charged with governance other matters that the auditor:

    a. Believes to be of potential benefit to the entity, such as recommendations for operational or administrative efficiency, or for improving internal control.

    b. Has been requested to communicate; for example, control deficiencies that are not significant deficiencies or material weaknesses.

3697.15 The written communication regarding significant deficiencies and material weaknesses identified during an audit of financial statements should:

    a. state that the purpose of the audit was to express an opinion on the financial statements, but not to express an opinion on the effectiveness of the entity's internal control over financial reporting.

    b. state that the auditor is not expressing an opinion on the effectiveness of internal control.

    c. include the definition of the terms *significant deficiency* and, where relevant, *material weakness*.

    d. identify the matters that are considered to be significant deficiencies and, if applicable, those that are considered to be material weaknesses.

    e. state that the communication is intended solely for the information and use of management, those charged with governance, and others within the organization and is not intended to be and should not be used by anyone other than these specified parties. If an entity is required to furnish such auditor communications to a governmental authority, specific reference to such governmental authorities may be made.

3697.16 If the auditor wishes, he/she may include additional statements in the communication regarding the general inherent limitations of internal control, including the possibility of management override of controls, or the specific nature and extent of the auditor's consideration of internal control during the audit.

3697.17 The auditor should not issue a written communication stating that no significant deficiencies were identified during the audit because of the potential for misinterpretation of the limited degree of assurance provided by such a communication.

This page intentionally left blank.

Section 3700
Standards of the Public Company Accounting Oversight Board (PCAOB)

3710 Public Company Accounting Oversight Board: Background, Organization, and Authority and PCAOB Auditing Standard No. 1, *Reference in Auditor's Reports to the Standards of the Public Company Accounting Oversight Board*

    3711 Purpose and Duties of the PCAOB
    3712 Currently Applicable Standards
    3713 Interpretation of Terms Used in Professional Standards
    3714 PCAOB Auditing Standard No. 1

3720 PCAOB Auditing Standard No. 3, *Audit Documentation*

    3721 Objective of Audit Documentation
    3722 Audit Documentation Requirements
    3723 Documentation of Specific Audit Issues
    3724 Retention of and Alterations to Audit Documentation

3730 PCAOB Auditing Standard No. 4, *Reporting on Whether a Previously Reported Material Weakness Continues to Exist*

    3731 Applicability of Standard
    3732 Auditor's Objective in and Engagement to Report on Whether a Previously Reported Material Weakness Continues to Exist
    3733 Conditions for Engagement Performance
    3734 Framework and Definitions for Evaluation
    3735 Performing an Engagement to Report on Whether a Previously Reported Material Weakness Continues to Exist
    3736 Requirement for Written Representations
    3737 Documentation Requirements
    3738 Reporting on Whether a Previously Reported Material Weakness Continues to Exist

3740 PCAOB Auditing Standard No. 5, *An Audit of Internal Control Over Financial Reporting That Is Integrated with an Audit of Financial Statements*

    3741 Introduction
    3742 Planning the Audit
    3743 Using a Top-Down Approach
    3744 Testing Controls
    3745 Evaluating Identified Deficiencies
    3746 Wrapping Up
    3747 Reporting on Internal Control

3750 PCAOB Auditing Standard No. 6, *Evaluating Consistency of Financial Statements*

    3751 Consistency and the Auditor's Report on Financial Statements
    3752 Change in Accounting Principle
    3753 Correction of a Material Misstatement in Previously Issued Financial Statements
    3754 Changes in Classification

3710 Public Company Accounting Oversight Board: Background, Organization, and Authority and PCAOB Auditing Standard No. 1, *Reference in Auditor's Reports to the Standards of the Public Company Accounting Oversight Board*

3711 Purpose and Duties of the PCAOB

3711.01 The Public Company Accounting Oversight Board (PCAOB) was established by the Sarbanes-Oxley Act of 2002. The purpose of the PCAOB is to oversee the audit of public companies that are subject to the securities laws in order to protect the interests of investors and further the public interest in the preparation of informative, accurate, and independent audit reports. The PCAOB is not an agency or establishment of the United States government.

3711.02 The duties of the PCAOB (Board) include the following:

a. Register public accounting firms that prepare audit reports for public companies.

b. Establish or adopt, or both, by rule, auditing, quality control, ethics, independence, and other standards relating to the preparation of audit reports for public companies.

c. Conduct inspections of registered public accounting firms.

d. Conduct investigations and disciplinary proceedings concerning, and impose appropriate sanctions where justified upon, registered public accounting firms and associated persons of such firms.

e. Perform such other duties or functions as necessary or appropriate to promote high professional standards among, and improve the quality of audit services offered by, registered public accounting firms and associated persons thereof, in order to protect investors or to further the public interest.

f. Enforce compliance with the Sarbanes-Oxley Act, the rules of the Board, professional standards, and the securities laws relating to the preparation and issuance of audit reports and the obligations and liabilities of accountants with respect thereto, by registered public accounting firms and associated persons thereof.

g. Set the budget and manage the operations of the Board and the staff of the Board.

3711.03 The PCAOB is composed of five members, with high integrity, who have a demonstrated commitment to the interests of investors and the public. These members should have an understanding of the financial reporting process as it exists under the securities laws as well as the responsibilities of accountants regarding the preparation and issuance of audit reports.

3711.04 Only two members of the Board shall have been or may be certified public accountants (CPA). If one of the CPAs on the Board is the Chairperson, he/she must not have been a practicing CPA for at least five years prior to his/her appointment to the Board. Board membership constitutes full-time employment. A Board member shall not be employed by any other person or engage in any other profession or business activity while serving on the Board.

3711.05 All public accounting firms that issue, or participate in the issuance of, any audit report of a public company must register with the Board. In addition to the registration requirement, the public accounting firm must indicate in a consent statement that the firm understands its responsibility to cooperate with the Board and comply with any request for testimony or the production of documents made by the Board in the furtherance of its authority and responsibility.

3712 Currently Applicable Standards

3712.01 A registered public accounting firm and its associated persons shall comply with all applicable auditing and related professional practice standards. Due to the short tenure of the PCAOB, it has not been possible to draft a complete set of auditing and related professional standards for the audits of public companies.

3712.02 Regarding interim auditing standards, a registered public accounting firm and its associated persons shall comply with generally accepted auditing standards (GAAS) as described in the AICPA Auditing Standards Board's Statement on Auditing Standards No. 95, *Generally Accepted Auditing Standards*. A registered public accounting firm is required to follow these standards in the performance of audits of public companies until they are formally superseded by standards issued by the PCAOB.

3712.03 In addition to the interim auditing standards adopted by the PCAOB, they have also adopted, on an interim basis, the AICPA's attestation standards (see sections **3682** to **3687**), quality control standards (see sections **3145** to **3146**), ethics standards (AICPA Code of Professional Conduct Rule 102), and independence standards (AICPA Code of Professional Conduct Rule 101).

3713 Interpretation of Terms Used in Professional Practice Standards

3713.01 When reading professional standards, it is sometimes difficult to assess the degree of responsibility that the standard imposes on the practitioner. In an effort to provide auditors with clear guidance on the extent of their responsibility in applying professional standards, the PCAOB issued Rule 3101.

3713.02 Rule 3101 indicates the words used in a professional standard that would indicate (1) unconditional responsibility on the part of the auditor, (2) presumptively mandatory responsibility on the part of the auditor, and (3) responsibility to consider on the part of the auditor. Rule 3101 explains the words that indicate these responsibilities as follows:

a. **Unconditional Responsibility**: If guidance included in a professional standard is prefaced by the words "must," "shall," or "required," this indicates an unconditional responsibility that must be performed by the auditor.

b. **Presumptively Mandatory Responsibility**: The use of the word "should" indicates responsibilities that are presumptively mandatory. If a standard indicates that the auditor "should" perform in a certain manner that performance is required unless the auditor can demonstrate that alternative actions he/she followed were sufficient to accomplish the performance required by the standard. Rule 3101 further explains that when a standard indicates that the auditor "should consider" an action or procedure, consideration of the action or procedure is presumptively mandatory, while the procedure is not.

    c. **Responsibility to Consider**: The use of words such as "may," "might," "could," and similar terms or phrases describe actions and procedures that auditors have a responsibility to consider. Auditors should be attentive to and understand matters described in this manner. However, the extent of the attention given to such matters is based on the auditor's professional judgment.

3714 PCAOB Auditing Standard No. 1

3714.01 PCAOB Auditing Standard No. 1, *References in Auditors' Reports to the Standards of the Public Company Accounting Oversight Board*, was issued on May 14, 2004. PCAOB Rule 3100, *Compliance with Auditing and Related Professional Practice Standards*, requires the auditor to comply with all applicable auditing and related professional practice standards of the PCAOB.

3714.02 As noted earlier, the PCAOB has adopted the generally accepted auditing standards (GAAS) issued by the AICPA's Auditing Standards Board as interim auditing standards. Thus, those standards are considered to be a part of the auditing and related professional practice standards of the PCAOB.

3714.03 Accordingly, in connection with any engagement performed in accordance with the auditing and related professional practice standards of the PCAOB, whenever the auditor is required by the interim standards to make reference in a report to generally accepted auditing standards, U.S. GAAS, auditing standards generally accepted in the United States of America, or standards established by the AICPA, the auditor must instead refer to "the standards of the Public Company Accounting Oversight Board (United States)."

3720 PCAOB Auditing Standard No. 3, *Audit Documentation*

3721 Objective of Audit Documentation

3721.01 PCAOB Auditing Standard No. 3 (AS3), *Audit Documentation*, establishes general requirements related to documentation that should be prepared by an auditor in connection with engagements performed under the standards of the PCAOB. These engagements include audits of a public company's financial statements, audits of internal control over financial reporting, and a review of interim financial information. This standard does not eliminate the documentation requirements found in the auditing standards adopted by the PCAOB on an interim basis.

3721.02 The objective of documentation (also referred to as work papers or working papers) prepared by an auditor during the course of an audit engagement is to provide a written record of the basis for the auditor's conclusions and representations.

3721.03 The existing audit standards require the auditor to conduct an audit in a systematic manner adhering to an approach that includes an audit plan, performance of evidence gathering techniques, and supervision of audit staff personnel. Without proper documentation, it would be difficult for the auditor to substantiate his/her adherence to applicable audit standards.

3721.04 An audit opinion is a matter of professional judgment on the part of the auditor and is based on the evidence gathered and evaluated by the auditor. Without documentation of the evidence upon which the opinion is based, the auditor would be helpless in defending his/her report on the financial statements.

3721.05 The information included in audit documentation has numerous potential uses in addition to its support for the auditor's opinion. As noted in AS3, the review of audit documentation can serve a variety of uses such as the following:

    a. Auditors who are new to an engagement can review the prior year's documentation to understand the work performed as an aid in planning and performing the current engagement.

    b. Supervisory personnel who review documentation prepared by assistants on the engagement

    c. Engagement supervisors and engagement quality reviewers who review documentation to understand how the engagement team reached significant conclusions and whether there is adequate evidential support for those conclusions

    d. A successor auditor who reviews a predecessor auditor's audit documentation

    e. Internal and external inspection teams that review documentation to assess audit quality and compliance with auditing and related professional practice standards; applicable laws, rules, and regulations; and the auditor's own quality control policies

    f. Others, including advisors engaged by the audit committee or representatives of a party to an acquisition

3722 Audit Documentation Requirements

3722.01 An auditor is required to prepare audit documentation in connection with every engagement he/she performs that involves adherence to PCAOB standards. The documentation should include a sufficient amount of detail so a reader would clearly understand its purpose, source, and the conclusions reached.

3722.02 AS3 cites the following examples of audit documentation: (a) memoranda, (b) confirmations, (c) correspondence, (d) schedules, (e) audit programs, and (f) letters of representation. The form in which audit documentation may be maintained includes paper, electronic files, or other media.

3722.03 Audit documentation should be designed to provide support for the representations included in the auditor's report. More specifically, it should:

    a. document that the engagement complied with the standards of the PCAOB.

    b. support the basis for the auditor's conclusions concerning every relevant financial statement assertion.

    c. demonstrate that the underlying accounting records agreed or reconciled with the financial statements.

3722.04 A most important aspect of an audit engagement is the auditor's documentation of the auditing procedures performed, the evidence obtained and analyzed, and the conclusions reached with respect to relevant financial statement assertions.

3722.05 The performance of an audit engagement includes the efforts of numerous professional staff members. The efforts of each staff member, as well as the work of any specialists used by the auditor, should be clearly documented in the audit working papers. The auditor in charge of the engagement should be certain that the documentation clearly demonstrates that the work was in fact performed.

3722.06 Audit documentation must contain sufficient information that is clearly presented. AS3 indicates that audit documentation would be considered sufficient if an experienced auditor, having no previous connection with the engagement could read the documentation and:

   a. understand the nature, extent, and timing, and results of the procedures performed, evidence obtained, and conclusions reached, and

   b. determine who performed the work and the date such work was completed as well as the person who reviewed the work and the date of such review.

3722.07 It should be noted that an experienced auditor is defined in AS3 as one having a reasonable understanding of audit activities and who has studied the company's industry as well as the accounting and auditing issues relevant to the industry.

3722.08 In performing an audit engagement, the auditor spends the majority of his/her time obtaining and evaluating audit evidence concerning assertions related to financial statement components. When determining the nature and extent of the documentation related to auditing a particular financial statement assertion, AS3 requires the auditor to consider the following factors:

   a. Nature of the auditing procedure

   b. Risk of material misstatement associated with the assertion

   c. Extent of judgment required in performing the work and evaluating the results, for example, accounting estimates require greater judgment and commensurately more extensive documentation

   d. Significance of the evidence obtained to the assertion being tested

   e. Responsibility to document a conclusion not readily determinable from the documentation of the procedures performed or evidence obtained

3722.09 Along with audit documentation that supports the conclusions reached by the auditor, information that the auditor encountered that is contrary to his/her final conclusions must also be documented. When such contrary information is a part of the audit documentation, the auditor must document the procedures performed in response to the contrary information, and any other information or considerations that served to resolve the impact of the contrary information.

3722.10 Subsequent to the completion of the audit and after the audit documentation completion date (see section **3724.03**), the auditor may have reason to believe that appropriate conclusions regarding financial statement assertions may not have been reached. In such circumstances the auditor must determine, and if so demonstrate, that sufficient evidence was obtained and appropriate conclusions were reached.

3723 Documentation of Specific Audit Issues

3723.01 An auditor is required to document, in his/her working papers, information related to the performance of auditing procedures. Such procedures normally involve substantive tests (tests of details) and/or compliance tests (tests of the operating effectiveness of internal controls).

3723.02 When such tests involve the inspection of documents or confirmation, the auditor's documentation should include identification of the items inspected. Also, audit procedures that involve an inspection of significant contracts or agreements should include copies or abstracts of such documents in the audit documentation.

3723.03 AS3 does provide for some latitude with respect to the documentation of items inspected by the auditor during an audit engagement. According to AS3, the identification of the items inspected may be satisfied by indicating the source from which the items were selected and the specific selection criteria used. The following examples are found in AS3:

   a. If an audit sample is selected from a population of documents, the documentation should include identifying characteristics (for example, the specific check numbers of the items included in the sample).

   b. If all items over a specific dollar amount are selected from a population of documents, the documentation need describe only the scope and the identification of the population (for example, all checks over $10,000 from the October disbursements journal).

   c. If a systematic sample is selected from a population of documents, the documentation need only provide an identification of the source of the documents and an indication of the starting point and the sampling interval (for example, a systematic sample of sales invoices was selected from the sales journal for the period from October 1 to December 31, starting with invoice number 452 and selecting every 40th invoice).

3723.04 The public accounting firm performing an audit engagement has certain responsibilities beyond the gathering of audit evidence that serves as a basis for the auditor's opinion. The independence of the firm and the engagement team performing the audit is an important consideration as is the training and proficiency of audit staff personnel. In addition, quality control standards require the public accounting firm to adhere to certain policies and procedures in performing professional services.

3723.05 Documentation of such matters may be kept in a central repository for the firm or in the specific office performing the engagement. When the documentation of such matters is kept in a central repository, the working papers of the audit engagement should include a reference to the central repository.

3723.06 Significant findings or issues related to an audit are substantive matters that are important to the audit procedures performed, the evidence gathered, and the conclusions reached by the auditor. The auditor is required to document significant findings or issues along with the actions taken to address them, and the basis for the conclusions reached regarding such findings or issues.

3723.07 AS3 includes the following examples of *significant findings or issues*. These examples are not considered an all-inclusive list.

   a. Significant matters involving the selection, application, and consistency of accounting principles, including related disclosures. Significant matters include, but are not limited to, accounting for complex or unusual transactions, accounting estimates, and uncertainties as well as related management assumptions.

   b. Results of auditing procedures that indicate a need for significant modification of planned auditing procedures, the existence of material misstatements, omissions in the financial statements, the existence of significant deficiencies, or material weaknesses in internal control over financial reporting

   c. Audit adjustments. For purposes of this standard, an *audit adjustment* is a correction of a misstatement of the financial statements that was or should have been proposed by the auditor, whether or not recorded by management, that could, either individually or when aggregated with other misstatements, have a material effect on the company's financial statements.

    d. Disagreements among members of the engagement team or with others consulted on the engagement about final conclusions reached on significant accounting or auditing matters

    e. Circumstances that cause significant difficulty in applying auditing procedures

    f. Significant changes in the assessed level of audit risk for particular audit areas and the auditor's response to those changes

    g. Any matters that could result in modification of the auditor's report

3723.08 When significant findings or issues are identified in an audit engagement, they must be recorded in an *engagement completion document*. The information about significant findings and issues included in an engagement completion document should be sufficient to provide a reviewer with a thorough understanding of the significant findings or issues. If pertinent information related to the significant findings or issues is included in other audit documentation, the auditor can merely refer to such documentation in the engagement completion document.

3724 Retention of and Alterations to Audit Documentation

3724.01 The *report release date* is the date an auditor gives the audit client permission to use his/her audit report in association with the financial statements. Audit documentation must be maintained by the auditor for seven years from the report release date, unless relevant law requires a longer period.

3724.02 If the auditor completes substantially all the fieldwork but does not issue an audit report, he/she must retain the audit documentation for seven years from the completion of the fieldwork. If the auditor was unable to complete the engagement, he/she must retain the audit documentation for seven years from the date the engagement was terminated.

3724.03 AS3 requires the auditor to assemble a complete and final set of audit documentation (working papers) within 45 days after the report release date. This is referred to as the *documentation completion date*.

3724.04 If an auditor completes substantially all the fieldwork but does not issue an audit report, the documentation completion date is 45 days from the date of completion of fieldwork. Likewise, if the auditor was unable to complete the engagement, the document completion date is 45 days from the date the engagement was terminated.

3724.05 Circumstances may require additions to audit documentation after the report release date; however, audit documentation must not be deleted or discarded after the documentation completion date. Information may be added to audit documentation after the documentation completion date as long as the auditor indicates the date the information was added, the name of the person who prepared the information, and the reasons for its addition. If an auditor performs any procedures subsequent to the report release date, audit documentation should be adjusted as appropriate following the guidelines outlined above.

3724.06 The office of the public accounting firm responsible for all of the requirements related audit documentation is the office of the firm that issued the auditor's report. Any audit documentation related to the work performed by auditors in other firm offices, in affiliated firms, or in non-affiliated firms must be retained by or be accessible to the office that issued the audit report.

3724.07 When work on an audit is performed by auditors in other offices of the firm, by affiliated firms, or by non-affiliated firms, AS3 requires the office issuing the audit report to obtain, review, and retain the following documentation related to the work of these auditors:

    a. An engagement completion document

b. A list of significant fraud risk factors, the auditor's response, and the results of the auditor's related procedures

c. Sufficient information relating to any significant findings or issues that are inconsistent with or contradict the final conclusions

d. Any findings affecting the consolidating or combining of accounts in the consolidated financial statements

e. Sufficient information to enable the office issuing the auditor's report to agree or to reconcile the financial statement accounts audited by the other auditor to the information underlying the consolidated financial statements

f. A schedule of audit adjustments, including a description of the nature and cause of each misstatement

g. All significant deficiencies and material weaknesses in internal control over financial reporting, including a clear distinction between those two categories

h. Letters of representations from management

i. All matters to be communicated to the audit committee

3724.08 If the auditor responsible for issuing the auditor's report decides to make reference to the work of the other auditor's in the audit report, he/she should refer to AU 543, *Part of Audit Performed by Other Independent Auditors.*

3730 PCAOB Auditing Standard No. 4, *Reporting on Whether a Previously Reported Material Weakness Continues to Exist*

3731 Applicability of Standard

3731.01 PCAOB Auditing Standard No. 4 (AS4), *Reporting on Whether a Previously Reported Material Weakness Continues to Exist,* provides guidance in determining whether a previously reported material weakness in internal control over financial reporting still exists at a later date, as specified by management.

3731.02 An auditor may only be engaged to report on whether a previously reported material weakness continues to exist if:

a. the auditor has audited the company's financial statements and internal control over financial reporting as of the most recent annual assessment or

b. the auditor has been engaged to perform the audit of the financial statements and internal controls over financial reporting for the current year and has sufficient basis for performing the engagement.

3731.03 As part of the engagement, the auditor may report on more than one previously reported material weakness.

3731.04 The engagement to report on whether a previously issued material weakness continues to exist is voluntary. Auditors are not required to undertake such engagement and may audit the company's internal control over financial reporting in accordance with PCAOB Standard No. 5 without performing an engagement under this standard.

3732 Auditor's Objective in and Engagement to Report on Whether a Previously Reported Material Weakness Continues to Exist

3732.01 The auditor's objective is to obtain reasonable evidence whether a previously reported material weakness continues to exist as of the date specified by management and to express an opinion regarding this matter. The opinion relates only to the specifically identified material weakness as of the specified date, not the overall effectiveness of the internal controls over financial reporting.

3732.02 The auditor should obtain and evaluate whether specified controls were in place and operating effectively as of the date set forth by management. Reasonable assurance should be obtained to determine if these controls meet the company's control objectives related to the specified controls.

3733 Conditions for Engagement Performance

3733.01 In order for an auditor to report on whether a previously reported material weakness continues to exist, the following conditions must be met:

    a. Management accepts full responsibility for the effectiveness of internal controls over financial reporting.

    b. Management performs its own evaluation of the effectiveness of the specific controls using the same control criteria used in its most recent annual assessment.

    c. Management makes an assertion that the specified controls identified are effective.

    d. Management supports and documents the assertion with sufficient evidence.

    e. Management provides a written report to accompany the auditor's report. This report must meet the elements contained in section **3738.01**.

3733.02 Unless all conditions specified in section **3733.01** are met, the auditor is prohibited from completing the engagement.

3734 Framework and Definitions for Evaluation

3734.01 Terms and definitions with respect to internal control over financial reporting, control deficiency, and material weakness are defined in Appendix A of PCAOB Standard No. 5.

3734.02 Management must base its annual assessment on the effectiveness of internal controls over financial reporting on suitable, recognized control criteria. In performing an engagement to report whether a previously reported material weakness continues to exist, both management and the auditor must use the same control criteria and control objectives as used in the company's most recent annual assessment of internal controls over financial reporting.

3734.03 Control objectives provide specific criteria to evaluate the effectiveness of controls. They should relate to a specific financial statement assertion and state a criterion to determine whether the company's controls will prevent or detect material misstatements relevant to that assertion in a timely manner.

3734.04 Management should establish control objectives specific to its specific company so that they can be applied in a reasonable and appropriate manner.

3734.05 Auditors are required to identify the controls within each control objective in order to evaluate that the internal controls over financial reporting are designed effectively.

3734.06 If a material weakness has been previously reported, the control objectives were not achieved.

3734.07 In the context of an engagement to report on whether a previously reported material weakness continues to exist, a stated control objective is an objective identified by management that, if met, would result in the elimination of the material weakness.

3734.08 Both management and the auditor must be in agreement that the stated control objective will eliminate the material weakness.

3735 Performing an Engagement to Report on Whether a Previously Reported Material Weakness Continues to Exist

3735.01 In performing this engagement, an auditor must obtain competent evidence regarding the specified controls that the company's stated control objectives are achieved in context of the control criteria.

3735.02 The auditor must abide by the standards of the PCAOB. These include:

    a. planning the engagement,

    b. obtaining an understanding of the controls over financial reporting,

    c. testing and evaluating whether a material weakness exists, and

    d. forming an opinion.

3735.03 The requirements of this process involve gathering, updating, and analyzing information. These procedures and evaluations may be performed concurrently.

3735.04 The engagement must be performed by persons having adequate technical training and proficiency as an auditor. They should be independent and exercise due professional care in all aspects of performing the engagement and preparing the report. Standards of fieldwork and reporting must also be adhered to.

3735.05 Materiality, as defined by PCAOB Standard No. 5 (see section **3742.12**), dictates the application of the general and fieldwork standards. Therefore, an auditor should use materiality at the financial statement level in determining if a material weakness exists. Materiality should be assessed as of the date of management's assertion.

3735.06 The auditor should properly plan and perform the engagement, and supervise any assistants involved in the engagement. Auditors should considered and evaluate matters described in PCAOB Standard No. 5 (see section **3742.01**).

3735.07 In order to perform the engagement, the auditor must obtain a sufficient understanding of the company and its controls over financial reporting. An auditor that has previously audited the company's internal control over financial reporting is presumed to already have a sufficient understanding of the company.

3735.08 Should the engagement be performed by a successor auditor that has not yet performed an audit of the company's internal control over financial reporting, specific procedures must be applied to obtain sufficient knowledge of the company. These procedures include:

    a. comply with standards as set forth by PCAOB Standard No. 5 regarding obtaining an understanding of the internal control over financial reporting (see sections **3743.02–3743.07**);

    b. perform a walkthrough as set forth by PCAOB Standard No. 5 (see sections **3743.14–3743.18**); and

      c. make specific inquiries of the predecessor auditors as described by AU 315. These inquiries should address the basis for determining whether a material weakness existed and any information pertaining to the company's ability to address the material weakness.

3735.09 A successor auditor may determine that procedures, in addition to those described, need to be performed in order for the auditor to gain a sufficient understanding of the client's business and related internal controls over financial reporting. The auditor may also determine that a sufficient understanding may not be obtained without performing a complete audit of internal control over financial reporting.

3735.10 The auditor must obtain an understanding of and evaluate evidence supporting management's assertion that the specified controls are designed and operating effectively, that these controls achieve the company's stated control objectives consistent with the control criteria, and that the previously identified material weakness no longer exists.

3735.11 When evaluating management's evidence, the auditor should determine that management selected an appropriate date for the assertion. The auditor should consider the following:

      a. The date should allow management sufficient time to obtain evidence that the material weakness no longer exists.

      b. Depending on the material weakness, stated control objectives, and specified controls, the date may need to be after one or more period-end financial reporting processes.

      c. Controls involved in daily processes that operate continuously, or nearly continuously, may be evaluated as of almost any date.

      d. Controls over the period-end reporting processes typically can only be tested in conjunction with a period-end.

3735.12 The auditor should gather sufficient evidence regarding the effectiveness of all controls specifically identified in management's assertions. The nature, timing, and extent of the testing will depend on the nature of the specific controls identified by management as meeting the control objectives and the date of the assertion.

3735.13 All controls necessary to meet the stated control objectives should be identified and tested. These include controls that have been modified or newly implemented, as well as controls that were previously determined effective over specified control objectives.

3735.14 The auditor should determine if the control is operating effectively by evaluating if the control is operating as designed and whether the person performing the control is of sufficient authority and qualifications to perform the control effectively.

3735.15 An adequate period of time must exist to determine whether a control is operating effectively. This period of time will vary with how often the control is used within the company.

3735.16 Depending on the nature of the material weakness, the auditor may also determine substantive procedures are needed to support the operating effectiveness of the internal controls over recorded financial statements amounts or disclosures.

3735.17 When specified controls, stated control objectives, and material weaknesses affect multiple locations or business units, care should be given in determining which locations or units to perform procedures.

3735.18 The auditor can use work performed by others in their evaluation. To determine the extent that the work of others can be used, the auditor should apply PCAOB Standard No. 5 (see sections **3742.08–3742.11**).

3735.19 An auditor may use work performed by others to alter the nature, timing, and extent of the procedures they would have normally applied. Work by others that can be considered includes relevant work conducted by internal auditors, company personnel, and third parties working under the direction of the company or audit committee. To be relevant, the work should provide information about the effectiveness of internal control over financial reporting.

3735.20 PCAOB Standard No. 5 should be applied in the context of an engagement to report on whether a previously reported material weakness continues to exist (see sections **3742.10** and **3742.11**). Certain procedures, such as walkthroughs, should only be performed by the auditor due to the degree of judgment required in performing the procedures.

3735.21 In an engagement to report on whether a previously reported material weakness continues to exist, auditors should comply with the relevant concepts of AU 543 with the following exception: auditors may not divide the responsibility for the engagement with other auditors and therefore may not make reference to other auditors in their report.

3735.22 In forming their opinion, auditors should consider and evaluate evidence from all sources, including evidence obtained by management and the results of the auditor's evaluation of specific controls.

3735.23 In forming its assertion, management may conclude that a previously reported material weakness no longer exists, as it has been reduced to a significant deficiency. If management does not plan to correct the significant deficiency within a reasonable period of time, the auditor should determine whether the significant deficiency is indicative of a material weakness. A significant deficiency not corrected after a reasonable period of time is an indicator of a material weakness. As auditors are not required to provide an opinion under this type of engagement, they may decline to provide an opinion under these circumstances.

3735.24 The auditor may only issue an opinion when no scope limitations are present. Should a scope limitation exist, the auditor should issue either a disclaimer or withdrawal from the engagement. A qualified opinion is not permitted under AS4 (see section **3738.04**).

3736 Requirement for Written Representations

3736.01 In an engagement to report on whether a previously reported material weakness continues to exist, the auditor should obtain written representations from management. These representations include the following:

   a. Acknowledging management's responsibility for establishing and maintaining effective internal controls over financial reporting

   b. Stating management has evaluated the effectiveness of the specified controls using specified control criteria and stated control objectives

   c. Stating the assertion that the specified controls are effective in achieving stated control objectives as of a specified date

   d. Stating that the identified material weakness no longer exists as of the same specified date

   e. Stating that the assertions are supported by sufficient evidence

   f. Describing any material fraud, or any fraud that involves senior management or other employees that have a significant role in the company's internal control over financial reporting, that has come to management's attention and occurred since the most recent annual assessment

  g. Stating whether any changes in internal control over financial reporting or other factors that may impact internal control over financial reporting have occurred as of, or subsequent to, the date specified in management's assertion

3736.02 The representations should be signed by members of management with responsibility for the company's internal control over financial reporting. Typically, this would include the chief executive officer and chief financial officer or equivalent positions within the company.

3736.03 The failure to obtain written representations is considered a scope limitation. As discussed in section **3735.24**, if there is a scope limitation, the auditor must either disclaim an opinion or withdraw from the engagement.

3737 Documentation Requirements

3737.01 Documentation requirements are set forth by PCAOB Standard No. 3 (see section **3720**) and are modified with respect to the report release date. For the purposes of an engagement to report on whether a previously reported material weakness continues to exist, the release date for applying PCAOB Standard No. 3 is the date the auditor grants permission to use the auditor's report on whether a previously reported material weakness continues to exist.

3738 Reporting on Whether a Previously Reported Material Weakness Continues to Exist

3738.01 As a condition of the engagement, management is required to prepare a written report that will accompany the auditor's report. Management's report should include the following:

  a. A statement of management's responsibility for maintaining and evaluating internal control over financial reporting

  b. A statement identifying the control criteria used to conduct the required annual assessment of the company's internal control over financial reporting

  c. Identification of the material weakness that was identified as part of management's annual assessment

  d. Identification of the control objectives addressed by the specified controls and a statement that the specified controls achieve the control objectives as of a specified date

  e. A statement that the identified material weakness no longer exists as of the same specified date as the specified controls correct the material weakness

3738.02 The auditor should evaluate management's report with respect to the following matters:

  a. Whether management has properly stated its responsibility for establishing and maintaining effective internal control over financial reporting

  b. Whether the control criteria used by management are suitable

  c. Whether the material weakness, stated control objectives, and specified controls are properly identified

  d. Whether management's assertions are free from material misstatement as of the date specified in the report

3738.03 Based on the auditor's evaluations, should the auditor determine that management's report does not meet the requirements described in section **3738.01**, the conditions for engagement performance have not been met.

3738.04 The auditor's report on whether a previously reported material weakness continues to exist must include the following items:

    a. A title that contains the word *independent*

    b. A statement that the auditor previously audited and reported on management's annual assessment of internal control as of a specified date based on the control criteria, as well as a statement that the auditor's report identified a material weakness

    c. A description of the material weakness identified

    d. Identification of management's assertion that the material weakness no longer exists

    e. Identification of management's report that includes management's assertion

    f. A statement that management is responsible for their assertion

    g. Identification of the specific controls identified by management to correct the material weakness

    h. Identification of the stated control objectives achieved by these controls

    i. A statement as to the auditor's responsibility to express an opinion, based on the audit procedures, on whether the material weakness continues to exist as of the date specified by management in its assertion

    j. A statement that the engagement was conducted in accordance with standards of the PCAOB

    k. A statement that the standards of the PCAOB require the engagement be planned and performed by the auditor to obtain reasonable assurance about whether a previously reported material weakness continues to exist

    l. A statement the engagement requires examining evidence supporting management's assertion, as well as performing other procedures determined necessary. The statement should also note that the auditor obtained an understanding of the internal control as part of the annual assessment, and has updated that understanding. In instances where the engagement is performed by a successor auditor, the auditor should include a statement that the engagement includes obtaining an understanding of the internal control over financial reporting.

    m. A statement that the auditor believes the auditing procedures provide a reasonable basis for their opinion

    n. An opinion on whether the identified material weakness continues to exist, or no longer exists, as of the date specified in management's assertion

    o. A paragraph that includes statements that the auditor was not engaged to conduct an audit of the internal control over financial reporting and that the auditor has not applied auditing procedures to reach a conclusion about the effectiveness of the internal controls other than those specifically identified in the auditor's report

    p. A paragraph stating that due to the inherent limitations of internal controls, internal control over financial reporting may not prevent or detect misstatements

    q. The manual or printed signature of the accounting firm

    r. The city and state, or state and country, from which the report is being issued

    s. The date of the auditor's report

3738.05 Appendix A of PCAOB Standard No. 4 contains examples of auditor's reports.

3738.06 As noted in section **3731.03**, an auditor may report on more than one previously reported material weakness. In such circumstances, the auditor's report should be modified accordingly.

3738.07 Should any of the following conditions exist, the auditor should modify the standard report:

    a. Other material weaknesses identified as part of the annual assessment are not addressed by the auditor's opinion.

    b. A significant subsequent event has occurred since the date specified in management's assertion (see sections **3738.10** and **3738.11**).

    c. Management's report includes additional information (see sections **3738.12** and **3738.13**).

3738.08 As noted in section **3735.24**, the auditor may issue an opinion on whether a material weakness continues to exist or they may issue a disclaimer of opinion. A qualified report is not allowed. Any scope limitations will result in either a disclaimer of opinion or the auditor withdrawing from the engagement.

3738.09 When more than one material weakness has been reported by the company in the annual assessment, but the auditor is not engaged to report on all material weaknesses, the auditor should state in the report that the auditor is not reporting on all material weaknesses.

3738.10 Changes in internal control over financial reporting or other factors that may significantly affect the effectiveness of the identified controls or the stated control objectives could occur after the date of management's assertion but prior to the date of the auditor's report. Therefore, the auditor should inquire about such changes or factors. In addition to obtaining written representations from management regarding such matters (see section **3736.01**), the auditor should inquire and examine the following items for the subsequent period:

    a. Internal audit reports relevant to the stated control objectives or identified controls

    b. Independent auditor reports (if other than the current auditor's) of significant deficiencies or material weaknesses relevant to the current engagement

    c. Regulatory agency reports relevant to the stated control objectives or identified controls

    d. Any information regarding the effectiveness of the internal control over financial reporting obtained from other engagements

3738.11 Should the auditor become aware of subsequent events that could adversely affect the effectiveness of the identified controls or the stated control objectives as of the date specified in management's assertion, the auditor should follow the requirements regarding special considerations when a material weakness continues to exist (see section **3738.14**). If the auditor is unable to determine the effect of the subsequent event, the auditor should disclaim an opinion.

3738.12 If management's report includes information in addition to that set forth in section **3738.01**, the auditor should disclaim an opinion on the additional information.

3738.13 If management's additional information contains a material misstatement of fact, the auditor should discuss this information with management. If, after discussing the matter with management, the misstatement of fact still exists, the auditor should notify both management and the audit committee in writing concerning the auditor's views on the information.

3738.14 If the auditor determines that the previously reported material weakness continues to exist, the auditor must express an opinion that the material weakness continues to exist as of the date specified in management's assertion.

3738.15 As addressed in section **3738.08**, the auditor is not required to issue a report as a result of the engagement. However, if they do not issue a report after determining a material weakness continues to exist, they must communicate their conclusion, in writing, to the audit committee. The auditor must also communicate any other material weaknesses identified if they have not been previously reported.

3738.16 Should the auditor determine a material weakness continues to exist, the auditor must consider that conclusion as part of their evaluation of management's quarterly disclosures about internal control over financial reporting.

3740 PCAOB Auditing Standard No. 5, *An Audit of Internal Control Over Financial Reporting That Is Integrated with an Audit of Financial Statements*

3741 Introduction

3741.01 PCAOB Auditing Standard No. 5 (AS5), *An Audit of Internal Control Over Financial Reporting That Is Integrated with an Audit of Financial Statements,* provides the requirements and establishes guidance when an auditor performs an audit of management's assessment of the effectiveness of internal control over financial reporting that is integrated with the audit of financial statements. This standard supersedes and replaces PCAOB Standard No. 2.

3741.02 When effective, internal control over financial reporting can provide reasonable assurance with respect to the reliability of financial reporting and the preparation of the financial statements. Should one or more material weaknesses exist, the company's internal control over financial reporting is not considered effective.

3741.03 The objective in an audit of internal control is to express an opinion on the effectiveness of the internal controls over financial reporting. Since the company's internal control cannot be considered effective if a material weakness exists, the auditor's objective is to plan and perform the audit to obtain evidence to provide reasonable assurance about whether a material weakness exists as of the date of management's assessment. The financial statements may not be materially misstated even when there is a material weakness in the internal control over financial reporting.

3741.04 The general standards that require technical training and proficiency, independence, and due professional care and skepticism apply to audits of internal control over financial reporting. This standard (PCAOB Standard No. 5) establishes standards of fieldwork and reporting for audits of internal control over financial reporting.

3741.05 In performing the audit of internal control over financial reporting, the auditor is to use the same suitable recognized control framework that management uses in its annual evaluation of the effectiveness of internal control over financial reporting.

3741.06 The audit of internal control should be integrated with the audit of the financial statements. While the objectives of the audits are not identical, work must be planned and performed to achieve the objectives of both audits.

3741.07 In the audit of internal control over financial reporting and the audit of the financial statements, the auditor must design their test of controls to meet the objectives of both audits simultaneously. Those objectives are to obtain sufficient evidence to support the auditor's opinion on internal control over financial reporting at year-end and to support the auditor's control risk assessments for the purposes of the financial statement audit.

3741.08 In obtaining sufficient evidence to support reducing control risk assessments, the auditor is able to reduce the amount of evidence that would have otherwise been considered necessary to support their audit opinion of the financial statements.

3742 Planning the Audit

3742.01 The audit should be properly planned and any assistants should be properly supervised. When planning an integrated audit, the auditor should evaluate the following matters:

    a. Knowledge of the company's internal control over financial reporting obtained in the course of other engagements

    b. Matters affecting the company's industry such as financial reporting practices, economic conditions, laws and regulations, and technological changes

    c. Matters affecting the company's business such as its organization, operating characteristics, and capital structure

    d. Recent changes in the company, its operations, or its internal control over financial reporting

    e. Preliminary judgments relating to materiality risk and other factors relating to evaluation of material weaknesses

    f. Previously communicated control deficiencies

    g. Legal or regulatory matters that have come to the attention of the company

    h. Type and extent of available evidence

    i. Preliminary judgments about the effectiveness of internal control

    j. Any public information relevant to the likelihood of material financial statement misstatements and the effectiveness of internal control

    k. Risks related to the company that have arisen as part of the auditor's client acceptance and retention evaluation

    l. The complexity of the company's operations

3742.02 Risk assessment is an integral aspect of this process and should include the determination of significant accounts and disclosures, relevant assertions, the selection of controls to test, and the evidence necessary for a given control.

3742.03 There is a direct relationship between the amount of risk that a material weakness may exist and the amount of evidence needed in a particular area. Therefore, the auditor should focus on areas that have the highest risk present. If a control would not present a risk of material misstatement to the financial statements, even if the control were deficient, it is not necessary to test that control.

3742.04 Factors such as the complexity of the organization, business unit, or process should be considered in the auditor's risk assessment and determination of necessary procedures.

3742.05 The way a company achieves its control objectives may be affected by the size and complexity of the company, its business processes, and its business units. These factors may also affect the risks of misstatement and the controls necessary to mitigate these risks.

3742.06 The auditor should consider the results of their fraud risk assessment when planning and performing the audit of internal control over financial reporting. Controls addressing risks of material misstatement due to fraud and controls identified to address management override should be evaluated. Controls that may address these risks include:

    a. controls over significant and unusual transactions,

    b. controls over journal entries and adjustments made at period-end,

    c. controls over related party transactions,

    d. controls related to significant management estimates, and

    e. controls that address management incentives and pressures to falsify or inappropriately manage financial results.

3742.07 Any deficiencies identified in the controls to prevent or detect fraud during the audit of internal control over financial control should also be taken into consideration when addressing the risks of material misstatement due to fraud during the financial statement audit.

3742.08 The auditor should evaluate the extent to which they will use the work of others to reduce work they would otherwise perform themselves. AU 322 provides guidance that applies to an integrated audit of the financial statements and internal control over financial reporting.

3742.09 The auditor may use the work of internal auditors, company personnel, and third parties working under the direction of management or audit committees to gather evidence in support of the audit of internal control over financial reporting and the audit of financial statements.

3742.10 When relying on the work of others, the auditor should evaluate their competence and objectivity to determine the extent to which they may use their work. The higher the competence and objectivity, the greater the reliance the auditor may place on the work of others.

3742.11 The extent to which the auditor may rely on the work of others also relates to the risk associated with the control being tested. As the risk increases, the auditor should place less emphasis on the work of others and perform more work themselves.

3742.12 The auditor should use the same materiality considerations in the audit of internal control over financial reporting that they use in the audit of a company's financial statements

3743 Using a Top-Down Approach

3743.01 When engaged to perform an audit of internal control over financial reporting, the auditor should employ a top-down approach in selecting controls to test. This begins at the financial statement level and with the understanding of the overall risks to internal control over financial reporting. After focusing on entity-level controls, the auditor migrates down to significant accounts and disclosures and their relevant assertions. This approach focuses on accounts, disclosures, and assertions that present a reasonable possibility of material misstatement to the financial statements and related disclosures. The auditor then selects internal controls for testing that address the assessed risk of misstatement for each relevant assertion.

3743.02 The auditor is required to test entity-level controls that address their conclusion about whether a company has effective internal control over financial reporting. The assessment of the entity-level controls can result in adjusting the testing the auditor performs on other internal controls.

3743.03 Entity-level controls vary in nature and precision as follows:

    a. Some entity-level controls have an important, but indirect, effect on the likelihood that a misstatement will be detected or prevented on a timely basis.

    b. Some entity-level controls monitor the effectiveness of other controls.

    c. Some entity-level controls are designed to adequately prevent or detect misstatements to one or more relevant assertions on a timely basis.

3743.04 Entity-level controls include:

    a. controls related to the control environment,

    b. controls over management override,

    c. controls dictating the company's risk assessment process,

    d. controls over the company's centralized processing and shared service environments,

    e. controls that monitor results of operations,

    f. controls that monitor other controls,

    g. controls over the period-end financial reporting process, and

    h. significant business controls and risk management practices.

3743.05 As part of the internal control over financial reporting, the auditor should address the control environment. This includes:

    a. whether management's philosophy and operating style promote effective internal control,

    b. whether sound integrity and ethical values are developed and understood, and

    c. whether the board of directors or audit committee understands and exercises the appropriate oversight over financial reporting and internal control over financial reporting.

3743.06 The auditor must evaluate the period-end financial reporting process due to its importance in the auditor's opinions on internal control over financial reporting and the financial statements. This process includes:

    a. procedures used to enter transaction totals into the general ledger,

    b. procedures related to the selection and application of accounting policies,

    c. procedures used to initiate, authorize, record, and process journal entries into the general ledger,

    d. procedures used to record recurring and nonrecurring adjustments to the annual and quarterly financial statements, and

    e. procedures used for preparing annual and quarterly financial statements and related disclosures.

3743.07 As part of evaluating the period-end financial report process, the auditor should assess:

    a. inputs, procedures performed, and outputs of the processes used by the company to produce its annual and quarterly statements,

    b. the extent of information technology involvement in the period-end financial reporting process,

    c. who from management participates in the process,

    d. locations within the company that are involved in the period-end financial reporting process,

    e. The types of adjusting and consolidating entries, and

    f. The nature and extent of oversight provided by management, the board of directors, and the audit committee.

3743.08 The auditor should identify significant accounts and disclosures, and the relevant assertions associated with them. The assertions include:

    a. existence or occurrence,

    b. completeness,

    c. valuation or allocation,

    d. rights and obligations, and

    e. presentation and disclosure.

3743.09 To identify significant accounts and disclosures, the auditor should evaluate both qualitative and quantitative risk factors related to financial statement line items and disclosures. Risk factors that should be considered include the following:

    a. The size and composition of the accounts

    b. Susceptibility of accounts to misstatement due to errors or fraud

    c. Volume of activity, complexity, and homogeneity of the transactions processed

    d. The nature of the account or disclosure

    e. Complexities associated with the account or disclosure

    f. Potential exposure to losses in the account

    g. The possibility of significant contingent liabilities arising from activities related to the account or disclosure

    h. Related party transactions in the account

    i. Changes since the prior period in account or disclosure characteristics

3743.10 In addition to identifying significant accounts and disclosures and the related assertions, the auditor should determine the likely sources of potential misstatements that could cause the financial statements to be materially misstated.

3743.11 The risk factors and the related significant accounts and disclosures are the same in both an audit of internal controls over financial reporting and an audit of financial statements.

3743.12 The components of a potential significant account or disclosure may have varying risks. If so, different internal controls may be necessary to address the different components and their related risks.

3743.13 When a company has multiple locations or business units, significant accounts and disclosures and their related assertions should be based on the consolidated financial statements.

3743.14 As part of selecting the controls to test, an auditor should understand the likely sources of potential misstatement. This can be done as follows:

    a. Understanding the flow of transactions related to relevant assertions

    b. Verifying the auditor has identified areas within the company's processes in which misstatements could occur

    c. Identifying the controls that management has implemented to address potential misstatements

    d. Identifying the controls that management has implemented over the prevention or timely detection of unauthorized acquisition, use, or disposition of company assets

3743.15 Because of the high level of judgment required to perform the procedures in section **3743.14**, the auditor should perform the work themselves or supervise the work of others that provided direct assistance.

3743.16 The auditor should also address how information technology affects the company's flow of transactions. AU 319 provides specific guidance on the effect of information technology on internal control over financial reporting and related risks.

3743.17 The most effective way of achieving the objectives in section **3743.14** is typically by performing walkthroughs. Walkthroughs follow a transaction from origination through the company's processes until it is recorded in the financial records. Walkthroughs include a combination of inquiry, observation, inspection, and reperformance.

3743.18 When performing a walkthrough, company personnel are questioned about their understanding of the company's procedures and controls. These questions, combined with procedures already described, allow the auditor to gain a sufficient understanding of the process to identify points where a control is either missing or not designed effectively. This also allows the auditor to gain an understanding of significant transactions handled by the process.

3743.19 Controls that are important to the auditor's conclusion about whether the company's controls sufficiently address the assessed risk of misstatement to each relevant assertion should be tested.

3743.20 There might be more than one control that addresses the risk of misstatement for an assertion. One control may also address the risk of misstatement for more than one assertion. As such, it is not necessary to test all controls related to a particular assertion should the others address the risk of misstatement adequately.

3743.21 The decision as to which controls should be tested depends on which controls sufficiently address the risk of misstatement for a particular assertion.

3744 Testing Controls

3744.01 The auditor should test the design effectiveness of controls by determining if they satisfy the company's control objectives and can effectively prevent or detect errors or fraud that would lead to material misstatements in the financial statements.

3744.02 The auditor should perform a variety of procedures including inquiry of appropriate personnel, observation of the company's operations, and inspection of relevant documentation. Walkthroughs that include these procedures may be sufficient to evaluate design effectiveness.

3744.03 To test operating effectiveness, the auditor should determine whether the control is operating as designed and whether the person performing the control possesses the necessary authority and competence to perform the control as specified.

3744.04 Procedures to test operating effectiveness include those mentioned in section **3744.02** (inquiry, observation, and inspection) as well as reperformance of controls.

3744.05 The evidence needed for each control tested depends on the risk associated with that control. As the risk associated with a control increases, so does the amount of evidence the auditor should obtain.

3744.06 Factors influencing the risk associated with a control include the following:

a. The nature and materiality of misstatements that the control is designed to prevent or detect

b. The inherent risk associated with the account or assertion

c. Changes in the volume or nature of transactions that could adversely affect the control design or effectiveness

d. Previous errors within the account

e. The effectiveness of entity-level controls

f. The nature and frequency of the control

g. The extent to which the control relies on the effectiveness of other controls

h. The competence of personnel implementing the control and whether there have been changes in these personnel

i. Whether the control is subject to human error or if it has been automated

j. The complexity of the control and the significance of judgments that must be made for it to operate effectively

3744.07 When deviations are detected in the company's controls, the auditor should determine the effect of the deviation on the risk assessments and operating effectiveness of the control.

3744.08 The nature, timing, and extent of evidence provided when testing a control will vary based on the auditor's assessment of the effectiveness of the control and the amount of evidence necessary in relation to the risk associated with the control.

3744.09 Some types of tests produce more reliable evidence than others. The following tests, in order of least to most reliable, are tests the auditor might ordinarily perform: inquiry, observation, inspection, and reperformance.

3744.10 The nature of the control to be tested will dictate the nature of the tests of effectiveness that will provide competent evidence.

3744.11 When testing controls, tests conducted over a greater period of time provide more evidence of the effectiveness of the control than testing over a shorter period of time. Also, tests conducted closer to the date of management's assessment provide more evidence than tests performed earlier in the year.

3744.12 Prior to the date specified in management's assessment, management may make changes in the company's controls to make them more effective or to address control deficiencies. Should a sufficient timeframe exist so that the auditor can assess the newly implemented controls, the auditor will not need to test the superseded controls for the purpose of expressing an opinion on the internal control over financial reporting.

3744.13 The more a control is tested, the greater the evidence obtained from that test.

3744.14 If an auditor reports on the effectiveness of controls as of a specific date, but obtains evidence as of an interim date, the auditor should determine what additional evidence is necessary for the remaining period of time.

3744.15 The following factors dictate the additional evidence needed to update the results of interim testing to a company's year-end:

    a. The specific control tested, the risks associated with the control, the nature of the control, and the results of interim testing

    b. The sufficiency of the evidence obtained during interim testing

    c. The length of the period between interim testing and year-end

    d. The possibility of any changes in internal control between the interim date and year-end

3744.16 In subsequent audits, the auditor should incorporate knowledge obtained from past audits of internal control over financial reporting in determining the procedures necessary for the current engagement.

3744.17 Factors that affect the risk associated with a control in a subsequent audit include:

    a. the nature, timing, and extent of procedures in previous audits,

    b. the results of testing of controls in previous audits, and

    c. whether or not there have been changes in the controls or processes since the previous audit.

3744.18 After considering the risk factors identified and results of past audits, the auditor may be able to assess risk lower than in previous years for subsequent audits.

3744.19 The auditor may also use the results of past audits as a benchmarking strategy for automated applications in subsequent audits.

3744.20 The auditor should also consider varying the nature, timing, and extent of testing of controls to respond to changes in circumstances and to introduce unpredictability into the testing process.

3745 Evaluating Identified Deficiencies

3745.01 The auditor must determine the severity of control deficiencies that come to their attention to determine whether, individually or in the aggregate, the deficiencies are material weaknesses as of the date of management's assessment.

3745.02 The severity of a deficiency depends on:

   a. whether the company's controls will fail to prevent or detect a misstatement of an account balance or disclosure and

   b. the magnitude of the potential misstatement resulting from the deficiency.

3745.03 The severity of a deficiency does not depend on whether a misstatement has occurred, but rather on whether there is a reasonable possibility that the company's controls will fail to prevent or detect a misstatement should it occur.

3745.04 Risk factors affect whether there is a reasonable possibility that a deficiency, or combination of deficiencies, will result in a misstatement in an account balance or disclosure not being prevented or detected. These factors include the following:

   a. The nature of the accounts, disclosures, and assertions

   b. The exposure of the related asset or liability to loss or fraud

   c. The subjectivity, complexity, or extent of judgment required in determining the amounts involved

   d. The relationship between the deficient control and other controls, including whether they are interdependent or redundant

   e. The interaction between the deficient controls

   f. The future consequences of the deficiency

3745.05 Factors that influence the magnitude of the potential misstatement resulting from the deficiency or deficiencies include:

   a. the financial statement amounts or total amount of transactions exposed to the deficiency and

   b. the volume of activity in the account balance or class of transactions exposed to the deficiency in the current period and future periods.

3745.06 When evaluating the magnitude of potential misstatements, the maximum amount of overstatement is typically the account balance or total of transactions. The amount of understatements is more difficult to determine.

3745.07 When evaluating the potential effect of a control deficiency or deficiencies, the auditor should also take into consideration compensating controls. To have an effect on the auditor's decision, the compensating control would have to mitigate the deficiency to a point that it would prevent or detect a material misstatement.

3745.08 Indicators of material weaknesses in internal control include:

   a. identification of fraud committed by senior management,

   b. restatement of previously issued financial statements to reflect the correction of a material misstatement,

c. identification of a material misstatement in the financial statements in the current year that would not have been detected by the internal control over financial reporting, and

d. ineffective oversight by the company's audit committee.

3745.09 When evaluating the magnitude of a deficiency, or combination of deficiencies, the auditor should consider the level of detail and degree of assurance that would satisfy prudent officials in the conduct of their own affairs that there is reasonable assurance that the financial statements were prepared in conformity with generally accepted accounting principles. If the auditor concludes that there is doubt, they should treat the deficiency, or combination of deficiencies, as an indicator of a material weakness.

3746 Wrapping Up

3746.01 The auditor should form an opinion on the effectiveness of internal control over financial reporting based on evidence obtained from the testing of controls, misstatements detected during the financial statement audit, and any identified control deficiencies.

3746.02 After forming an opinion, the auditor should evaluate management's presentation of internal control over financial reporting as required in its annual report.

3746.03 Should the auditor determine that management's presentation is incomplete or improperly presented, the auditor should modify the auditor's report to include an explanatory paragraph describing the reasons for this determination.

3746.04 The auditor can only express an opinion on the effectiveness of internal control over financial reporting when there have been no scope limitations. Should scope limitations exist, the auditor should express a disclaimer of opinion or withdraw from the engagement.

3746.05 Written representations from management to the auditor should include the following:

a. An acknowledgement for responsibility to establish and maintain effective internal control over financial reporting

b. A statement that management has performed an evaluation and made an assessment of the effectiveness of the company's internal control

c. A statement that management's assessment did not rely on the auditor's procedures as part of its assessment

d. A statement that management's conclusion regarding the effectiveness of internal control was based on the control criteria as of a specified date

e. A statement that management has disclosed to the auditor all deficiencies identified in its evaluation, including separately disclosing significant deficiencies it believes to also be material weaknesses

f. A statement describing any fraud resulting in a material misstatement to the financial statements or any fraud involving senior management or employees with a significant role in the internal control over financial reporting

g. A statement specifying whether control deficiencies identified and communicated to the audit committee during previous engagements have been resolved

h. A statement whether there were any changes in the internal control over financial reporting subsequent to the date being reported on that may have significant effect on internal control, including corrective actions with respect to significant deficiencies and material weaknesses

3746.06 The failure to obtain written representations from management, or management's refusal to provide them, is considered a scope limitation that will result in the auditor either disclaiming an opinion or withdrawing from the engagement.

3746.07 AU 333 specifies who should sign the letter, the period to be covered by the letter, and when to obtain the updated letter from management.

3746.08 Prior to issuing the auditor's report on internal control over financial reporting, the auditor must communicate, in writing, to management and the audit committee, all material weaknesses identified in the audit.

3746.09 If the auditor concludes that the oversight of the company's audit committee is ineffective, the auditor must communicate that conclusion, in writing, to the board of directors.

3746.10 The auditor should also consider whether there are any deficiencies, or combination of deficiencies, that are determined to be significant deficiencies and communicate such deficiencies, in writing, to the audit committee.

3746.11 The auditor should also communicate to management, in writing, all deficiencies in internal control over financial reporting that have been discovered during the audit. It is not necessary to repeat information about deficiencies already reported. The audit committee should be made aware of this communication.

3746.12 The auditor is not required to perform procedures to identify all control deficiencies. Rather, the auditor only communicates deficiencies in internal control over financial reporting that have come to their attention.

3746.13 As the audit of internal control over financial reporting does not provide the auditor with assurance that they have identified all deficiencies less severe than a material weakness, the auditor should not issue a report stating that no such deficiencies were noted during the course of the audit.

3746.14 Should the auditor become aware of fraud or possible illegal acts during the course of the audit, they should determine their responsibilities to report as determined under AU 316, AU 317, and the Securities Exchange Act of 1934.

3747 Reporting on Internal Control

3747.01 The auditor's report on the audit of internal control over financial reporting must include the following items:

    a. A title that contains the word *independent*

    b. A statement that management is responsible for maintaining effective internal control over financial reporting and for assessing the effectiveness of internal control over financial reporting

    c. Identification of management's report on internal control

    d. A statement that the auditor's responsibility is to express an opinion on the company's internal control over financial reporting based on their audit

    e. A definition of internal control over financial reporting

    f. A statement that the engagement was conducted in accordance with standards of the PCAOB

g. A statement that the standards of the PCAOB require the engagement be planned and performed by the auditor to obtain reasonable assurance about whether effective internal control over financial reporting was maintained in all material respects

h. A statement that an audit includes obtaining an understanding of internal control over financial reporting, assessing the risk that a material weakness exists, testing and evaluating the design and operating effectiveness of internal control based on the assessed risk, and performing such other procedures as the auditor considered necessary

i. A statement that the auditor believes the auditing procedures provide a reasonable basis for their opinion

j. A paragraph stating that, because of inherent limitations, internal control over financial reporting may not prevent or detect misstatements and that projections of any evaluation of effectiveness to future periods are subject to the risk that controls may become inadequate because of changes in conditions, or that the degree of compliance with the policies or procedures may deteriorate

k. The auditor's opinion on whether the company maintained, in all material respects, effective internal control over financial reporting as of the specified date, based on the control criteria

l. The manual or printed signature of the accounting firm

m. The city and state, or state and country, from which the report is being issued

n. The date of the auditor's report

3747.02 The company may issue a combined report or separate reports on the company's financial statements and on internal control over financial reporting. Examples of reports may be found in PCAOB Standard No. 5.

3747.03 The auditor should date the report no earlier than the date in which they obtained sufficient competent evidence to support the auditor's opinion. The report should be dated as of the same date as the report on the company's financial statements.

3747.04 If the auditor identifies deficiencies that, individually or in the aggregate, result in a material weakness, the auditor must issue an adverse opinion on the company's internal control over financial reporting.

3747.05 When expressing an adverse opinion, the auditor's report must include:

a. the definition of a material weakness and

b. a statement that a material weakness has been identified and identification of the material weakness described in management's assessment.

3747.06 The auditor should determine the effect of their adverse opinion on the internal control over financial reporting on their opinion on the financial statements, and disclose whether their opinion on the financial statements was affected.

3747.07 Changes in internal control over financial reporting or other factors that may significantly affect the effectiveness of the identified controls or the stated control objectives could occur after the date of management's assertion but prior to the date of the auditor's report. Therefore, the auditor should inquire about such changes or factors and obtain written representations from management regarding such matters.

3747.08 The auditor should inquire and examine the following items for the subsequent period:

    a. Internal audit reports

    b. Independent auditor reports (if other than the current auditor's) of deficiencies in internal control

    c. Regulatory agency reports on the company's internal control

    d. Any information regarding the effectiveness of the internal control over financial reporting obtained from other engagements

3747.09 The auditor may also inquire and examine other documents for the subsequent period. AU 560 provides guidance on subsequent events for a financial statement audit that may be helpful for an auditor performing an audit of internal control over financial reporting.

3747.10 Should the auditor become aware of subsequent events that materially and adversely affect the effectiveness of the company's internal control over financial reporting as of the date specified in management's assessment, the auditor should issue an adverse opinion. If the auditor is unable to determine the effect of the subsequent event, the auditor should disclaim an opinion.

3747.11 An auditor may become aware of a subsequent event that did not exist as of the date specified in management's assessment, but before the issuance of the auditor's report. If a subsequent event of this nature has a material effect on the company's internal control over financial reporting, the auditor should include in the report an explanatory paragraph describing the event and its effects.

3747.12 After the issuance of the auditor's report, the auditor may become aware of conditions that existed as of the report date that may have affected the auditor's report had they known of them. Should this occur, the auditor should evaluate the subsequent information as described in AU 561.

3750 PCAOB Auditing Standard No. 6, *Evaluating Consistency of Financial Statements*

3751 Consistency and the Auditor's Report on Financial Statements

3751.01 The purpose of PCAOB Auditing Standard No. 6 (AS6), *Evaluating Consistency of Financial Statements,* is to establish standards and provide guidance for auditors in evaluating the consistency of financial statements.

3751.02 Auditors should evaluate whether the consistency of the financial statements has been materially affected by changes in accounting principle or adjustments to previously issued financial statements.

3751.03 All periods covered by the auditor's report should be evaluated for consistency.

3751.04 The following matters relating to consistency should be recognized in the auditor's report if they have a material effect on the financial statements:

    a. Changes in accounting principle

    b. Correction of misstatements in previously issued financial statements

3752 Change in Accounting Principle

3752.01 A change in accounting principle involves a change from one generally accepted principle to another when there is more than one generally accepted principle or when the former principle is no longer accepted.

3752.02 A change in accounting estimate effected by a change in accounting principle should be treated the same as other changes in accounting principle.

3752.03 The change in accounting principle should be evaluated to verify:

    a. the accounting principle is generally accepted,

    b. the accounting for the effect of the change is in accordance with generally accepted accounting principles,

    c. disclosures for the change in principle are adequate, and

    d. the alternative accounting principle is preferable and has been justified by the company.

3752.04 If the criteria in section **3752.03** are met, the auditor should include an explanatory paragraph in the auditor's report as described in AU 508. If the criteria are not met, the matter is considered a departure from generally accepted accounting principles.

3753 Correction of a Material Misstatement in Previously Issued Financial Statements

3753.01 Changes due to the correction of a material misstatement in previously issued financial statements should be addressed in the auditor's report as described in AU 508.

3753.02 The financial statements should adequately disclose the restatements to correct misstatements in previously issued financial statements. Failure to adequately disclose the restatements can result in modification of the auditor's report as described in AU 431 and AU 508.

3754 Changes in Classification

3754.01 Changes in classification of previously issued financial statements do not require modification of the auditor's report unless the change also involves a change in accounting principle or a correction of a misstatement.

Index

A

Accounting and Review Services Committee, 3641
Accounting estimates (audits of), 3344
Accounting estimation model, 3463
Accounting records, 3311, 3338
Advanced computer systems (audits of), 3240
Adverse opinion, 3516
Agreed-upon procedures, 3683
Analytical procedures, 3339
Application controls (EDP), 3211.06 & .08–.09
Application of accounting principles (reports on), 3582
Appointment of the independent auditor, 3152
Assertions on financial statements, 3312, 3324, 3337
Attestation standards, 3681
Attribute sampling, 3422.02, 3440
    tables, 3443
Audit committees, 3143, 3615.07–.11
    communication with, 3540
Audit engagement
    compared to compilation and review, 3645
    steps in, 3151
Audit evidence, 3300
    competent, 3342.02, 3344.04
    nature of, 3310
    sufficiency, 3325
    types of, 3330
Audit hypothesis model, 3473
Audit objectives, 3112, 3155.08, 3353
    consistency, 3142.01
    economic activity, 3112.03
    errors, 3112.07
    examples of, 3353
    fairness, 3112.01
    full disclosure, 3112.02
    generally accepted accounting principles, 3112.04
Audit planning, 3155
Audit procedures, 3121, 3313, 3350–70
    accounts payable, 3371
    accounts receivable and revenues, 3363
    cash, 3361
    contingencies, 3343.01
    contingent liabilities, 3374
    examples of, 3354
    interest-bearing debt and related expense, 3373
    inventories and cost of goods sold, 3365
    long-term investments, 3367
    marketable securities and investment revenue, 3362
    notes receivable and interest income, 3364
    other current liabilities, 3372
    payroll, 3372
    planning the audit, 3155
    property, plant, and equipment: depreciation and depletion, 3366
    related parties, 3341
    stockholders' equity and dividends, 3375
Audit programs, 3200
    specialized, 3233.02–.07
Audited financial reports, 3500
Audit risk, 3131, 3412.01, 3472
    control risk, 3134.03, 3220, 3414
    detection risk, 3134.05, 3686.12
    inherent risk, 3134.03, 3686.12
    nonsampling risk, 3412.05–.07
    sampling risk, 3412.03–.04
Audit sampling, 3400, 3411.01
    attribute, 3440
    discovery, 3450
    in assessing control risk, 3414
    in substantive tests of details, 3413
    risk of sampling error, 3412.06
    selection of approach, 3415
    selection of sample, 3430
    statistical, 3420
    uncertainty, 3412
    variable, 3460–70
Audit trail, 3211.05–.06
Auditing, overview of examination, 3000
    abbreviations, 3014.01
    index of official pronouncements, 3014.02
    suggested readings and references, 3015
Auditing advanced computer systems, 3240
    advanced audit techniques, 3242
    unique controls, 3241
Auditing examination, 3010
    AICPA content specification outline, 3013
    general content, 3012
    suggested readings and references, 3015
Auditing procedures, 3121.02, 3350, 3360, 3370
Auditor reporting responsibilities, 3114, 3572
    regarding SEC reporting, 3660
Auditor's reports, 3126, 3127
Auditor's response to risk assessment, 3174
Auditor's standard report, 3510
    adverse opinions, 3516
    comparative financial statements, 3519
    consistency, lack of, 3523
    dating, 3534
    departures from GAAP, 3522, 3525
    disclaimer of opinion, 3517
    emphasis of a matter, 3527
    explanatory language, 3514
    going concern, 3526
    inadequate disclosure, 3524
    introductory paragraph, 3512.02

modifications, 3520
opinion paragraph, 3512.02
present fairly, 3513
qualified opinion, 3515
reissuing of, 3532.03
reliance on another auditor, 3521
scope paragraph, 3512.02
subsequent discoveries, 3532
summary of reports, 3518
uncertainties, 3525

B

Broad scope audits, 3671

C

Capital formation and flow, 3113.02
Central limit theorem, 3462.04
Client
    representation letter, 3336, 3355.01
    responsibilities, 3114
Client-reported documents, 3572.01
Comfort letters, 3662
Communication between predecessor and successor accountants, 3648
Communication between predecessor and successor auditors, 3153
Communication with audit committee, 3540
Comparative financial statements (reports on), 3519, 3646
Competent evidence, 3342.02
Compilation and review of financial statements, 3642
    review engagement, 3644
Compilation engagement, 3643
    pro forma financial information, 3653
    reports on, 3647, 3652.05, 3653.09
    specified elements, accounts, or items of a financial statement, 3652
Compliance attestation, 3686
Compliance auditing (government), 3345
Compliance with contractual or regulatory requirements, reports on, 3624–25
Computer processing, 3211
Condensed financial statements, 3581
Confidence level, 3442.01
Confirmations, 3333
Consistency, 3124.02, 3523
Contingencies, 3343.01
Contingent liabilities, 3374
Control environment, 3213.04
Control procedures, 3211.05, 3211.09, 3414.03–.06
Control risk, 3134.02, 3686.12
    and audit sampling, 3414
Cost-benefit, 3424.01

CPA examination, 3012
    auditing content, 3012.02

D

Dating the report, 3534
    reissuance, 3532.03
    subsequent events, 3531
Departures from GAAP, 3522
Derivative instruments, audits, 3347
Detection risk, 3134.05–.06, 3686.12
Disclaimer of opinion, 3126.01, 3152.02, 3517
Disclaimer (unaudited), 3631
Disclosure, 3124.04
    assertion, 3314
    inadequate, 3515.08, 3524
Discovery sampling, 3422.02, 3450
    tables, 3452
Distribution of sample means, 3462.05
    normal, 3462.03
Division of responsibility, 3521.01
Dollar unit sampling, 3434
Due care, 3144

E

Economy and efficiency audits, 3671.02
EDP accounting control procedures, 3211
    application controls, 3211.08
    general controls, 3211.07
EDP auditing, 3200, 3230
    around the computer, 3231
    through the computer, 3232
    with the computer, 3233
EDP effect on audit, 3211, 3212, 3213
EDP effect on auditor's assessment of control risk, 3220
Emphasis of a matter, 3527
End of audit procedures, 3355
Engagement letters, 3154, 3642.08–.09
Error analysis, 3425.02, 3442.06–.07
Evidence, 3310, 3320, 3330
    accounting records, 3311.06
    confirmations, 3333
    corroborating evidence, 3343.04
    documentary, 3334
    fieldwork standards, 3123
    internal, 3331
    oral, 3335
    sufficient, 3323
    visual, 3332
"Except for" report, 3515.01, .05, & .07–.08
Existence, 3173.06, 3312.02
Explanatory language, 3514
Explanatory paragraph, 3515.03–.07
    adverse opinion, 3516.02–.03

departure from GAAP, 3515.06–.07, 3522
disclaimer, 3517.05
qualified opinion, 3515.05, .07, & .08

F

Fairness, 3142.01
Fieldwork standards, 3123
Financial forecasts and projections, 3684
Flowcharts, 3342
Foreign countries (reporting), 3583
Fraud
    assessment of risk, 3174
    communications about, 3176, 3615.09, 3642.09–.10
    description of, 3171
    documentation of, 3177
    risk factors, 3172, 3173
Full disclosure, 3664.03

G

GAAP, 3112.04, 3513.03–.07
    departure from, 3522
    hierarchy, 3513.03–.07
GAAS, 3120
    fieldwork standards, 3123
    general standards, 3122, 3140
    reporting standards, 3124
GAS programs, 3233.08–.13
General audit procedures, 3350
    audit objectives, 3353
    permanent files, 3352
    preliminary steps, 3351
General controls (EDP), 3211.07
General standards, 3122, 3140
    due care, 3144
    independence, 3142
    quality control, 3146
    technical training and proficiency, 3141
Generally accepted accounting principles (GAAP), 3112.04, 3513.03–.07
    departure from, 3522
    hierarchy, 3513.03–.07
Generally accepted auditing standards (GAAS), 3120
    fieldwork standards, 3123
    general standards, 3122, 3140
    reporting standards, 3124
Going concern, 3526
Government auditing standards, 3670
    broad scope audits, 3671
    compliance audits, 3345
    economy and efficiency audits, 3671.02, 3674.07
    examination and evaluation standards, 3673
    financial and compliance audits, 3345, 3674.06
    general standards, 3672
    program results audits, 3671.03
    reporting standards, 3674

H

Hedging activities, 3347
Homogeneity, 3441.04

I

Illegal acts by clients, 3153.04, 3345.02, 3642.09–.10
Inadequate disclosure, 3524
Independence, 3122.02, 3142
Independent audit
    defined, 3111
    objectives, 3112
    public benefit, 3113
Independent calculations, 3337
Index of official pronouncements, 3014
Industry conditions, 3137.04
Inherent risk, 3134.03
Inquiry of a client's lawyer, 3343
Integrated test facility, 3232.07
Interim audit work, 3155.06, 3324.08–.10
Interim financial information, 3610
    client's representation, 3614.09, 3615.05
    reporting, 3616
    review procedures, 3614
Interim reviews, 3610
    communication with audit committees, 3615
    objective, 3612
    procedures, 3614
    report, 3616
Internal auditor, 3333.06
Internal control, 3331, 3740
    documentation, 3331
    EDP systems, 3211.05
    fieldwork standard, 3123
    flowcharts, 3342
Internal control checklists
    accounts payable and other current liabilities, 3371, 3372
    cash, 3361
    inventories and cost of goods sold, 3365
    investments, 3367
    long-term liabilities, 3374
    payroll, 3372
    plant, property, and equipment, 3366
    receivables and sales, 3363
    stockholders' equity, 3375
Introductory paragraph, 3512.02, 3519.09, 3521.01
Inventory, 3152.03, 3365
Investments, 3347, 3362, 3367

L

Lawyer, inquiry of client's, 3343
Letters for underwriters, 3662

M

Management representations, 3336
Management responsibilities, 3114.01
Management's discussion and analysis, 3687
Marketable securities and investment revenue, 3362
Material error, 3113.04, 3412.01
Materiality, 3130, 3322.09, 3346
Maximum tolerable rate, 3442.04, 3443.02
Mean, 3462.01
  estimation, 3463.01–.02

N

Negative assurance, 3624.01, 3662.06, 3674.06, 3683.09, 3685.07
Nonindependence disclaimer, 3632, 3633.03
Nonpublic companies
  association, types of, 3633
Nonsampling risk, 3412.02 & .05–.07
Nonstatistical sampling, 3410, 3411.02, 3421.02
Normal distribution, 3462.03–.05
Notes receivable and interest income, 3364

O

Obligations, 3347.08
OCBOA (other comprehensive basis of accounting), 3622
Omitted procedures, 3533
Opinion paragraph, 3512, 3515
  adverse, 3516
  disclaimer, 3517
  "except for," 3515
  standard, 3512
Opinions on specified items, 3623
Oral evidence, 3335
Other comprehensive basis of accounting (OCBOA), 3622

P

Payroll, 3372
PCAOB No. 1, 3714
PCAOB No. 3, 3720
PCAOB No. 4, 3730
PCAOB No. 5, 3740
PCAOB No. 6, 3750
PCAOB Rule 3100, 3714.01, 3721.05
PCAOB Rule 3501, 3502, 3520–24, and 3526, 3700
PCAOB Rule 3525, 3700
PCAOB Rule 3526, 3700

Personal financial statements
  review of, 3649
Planning the audit, 3123.01, 3155
  audit planning, 3155.01–.07
Population, 3413.02, 3431.03, 3463
Predecessor accountant, 3648
Predecessor auditor, 3153
Prescribed forms, 3626
Present fairly, 3513
Presentation, 3339.08, 3347.08
Presumptively mandatory requirements, 3127.02, 3681.05
Pro forma reporting, 3653, 3685
Probability proportional to size (PPS), 3434
Professional judgment, 3131.04, 3135.01, 3146.20, 3412.08, 3424.02, 3425
Professional skepticism, 3333.03, 3344.02
Projected error, 3413.09–.11, 3463.02
Pronouncements index
  auditing, 3014
Public companies
  association, types of, 3633
  nonindependence disclaimer, 3632
  unaudited disclaimer, 3631
Public Company Accounting Oversight Board (PCAOB), 3700
Public interest, 3113

Q

Qualified opinions, 3515
Quality control standards, 3146

R

Random number table, 3432
Ratio analysis, 3157
Reissuing of report, 3519.07, 3532.03, 3543, 3646.03–.06 & .11–.14
Related parties
  audits of transactions, 3341
Reliability factor, 3463.02
Reliability level, 3442, 3443.02–.04
Reliance on another auditor, 3521
Reporting standards, 3124, 3511, 3600, 3674
Reports
  application of accounting principles, 3582
  condensed financial statement, 3581
  financial statements for use in other countries, 3583
  review of interim financial statements, 3616
Reports on audited financial statements, 3500
Representation letter, 3336
Representative sample, 3430, 3431.02
Responsibilities
  to public, 3113

Restricting the use of an accountant's report, 3642.16–.19
Restricting the use of an auditor's report, 3584
Review engagement, 3644
Review of interim financial information, 3610
    objectives, 3612
    procedures, 3614–15
    reports, 3616
Review services, 3640
    compared to audit and to compilation, 3645
    engagement, 3644
    objective, 3642.01
    report, 3642.15
Rights, 3112.06, 3312.02, 3347.08
Risk (see also Audit risk)
    assessment, 3213.05
    nonsampling, 3412.05–.07
    of assessing control risk too high (underreliance), 3412.10 & .11
    of assessing control risk too low (overreliance), 3412.10 & .11, 3414.01, 3442.02
    of incorrect acceptance, 3412.09, 3471.02
    of incorrect rejection, 3412.09, 3471.01
    sampling, 3412.03
    ultimate, 3472

S

Sample size (n), 3413.05, 3433.01, 3434.03–.05, 3435.01, 3436, 3437, 3443, 3451.01, 3452, 3463.02, 3471.01, 3472.04, 3473.02
Sampling (see also Audit sampling), 3400
    frame, 3431.04
    PPS, 3434.01–.05
    probability proportional to size, 3434
    representative, 3431.01 & .02
    risk, 3412.03
    systematic, 3433
    with replacement, 3431.05, 3463.02
    without replacement, 3431.06
Scope limitations, 3515.04, 3525
Scope paragraph, 3512.02
SEC reporting, 3660
Securities Act of 1933, 3661
    accountant's responsibility, 3663
Securities Exchange Act of 1934, 3664
    10–K, 3664.02–.03
    10–Q, 3664.02–.03
    8–K, 3664.02–.03
    proxy, 3664.02–.03
    regulation S-X, 3664.04
Segregation of duties, 3166.02, 3167.06, 3414.02
Service auditor, 3696
Service centers, 3211.02
Service organizations, 3696
Special reports, 3620
    compliance with contractual or regulatory comprehensive basis other than GAAP, 3624
    opinions on specified elements, 3623
    prescribed form, 3626
    requirements, 3624–25
    types, 3621
Specialists (using work of), 3342
Standard deviation (SD), 3462.02, 3463.02
Standard error (SE), 3463.02
Standard report, 3510, 3512
Statements on attest engagements, 3680, 3682–83, 3685–87
Statements on Auditing Standards (SAS), 3014
    No. 1, 3141–42, 3144, 3363, 3365, 3367, 3521, 3522, 3523, 3524, 3531, 3534
    No. 8, 3550
    No. 12, 3343
    No. 25, 3145
    No. 26, 3630, 3633
    No. 29, 3570
    No. 32, 3524
    No. 35, 3683
    No. 37, 3664
    No. 39, 3400
    No. 42, 3581
    No. 43, 3513, 3514
    No. 46, 3533
    No. 48, 3200
    No. 50, 3582
    No. 51, 3583
    No. 52, 3513, 3560
    No. 54, 3600
    No. 56, 3339
    No. 57, 3344
    No. 58, 3510, 3520, 3622
    No. 59, 3526
    No. 61, 3540
    No. 62, 3620
    No. 64, 3510, 3521, 3526
    No. 65, 3130
    No. 67, 3333
    No. 69, 3513
    No. 70, 3696
    No. 72, 3662
    No. 73, 3342
    No. 74, 3345
    No. 76, 3662
    No. 77, 3150, 3526, 3620
    No. 79, 3525
    No. 80, 3300
    No. 83, 3154, 3600
    No. 84, 3153
    No. 85, 3336
    No. 86, 3662
    No. 87, 3584
    No. 88, 3523, 3696

No. 89, 3174, 3540
No. 90, 3540, 3615
No. 91, 3513
No. 92, 3347
No. 93, 3510, 3520
No. 95, 3120
No. 96, 3314
No. 97, 3582
No. 98, 3510, 3696
No. 99, 3170
No. 100, 3610
No. 101, 3346
No. 102, 3120
No. 104, 3144
No. 105, 3120
No. 106, 3330
No. 107, 3130
No. 108, 3155, 3156
No. 109, 3160
No. 110, 3320
No. 111, 3400
No. 113, 3120
No. 114, 3540
No. 115, 3697
No. 116, 3610
Statements on Financial Accounting Standards
    No. 5, 3333, 3336.03, 3343.01
Statements on Quality Control Standards (SQCS)
    No. 7, 3146
Statements on Standards for Accounting and Review Services (SSARS), 3640
    No. 1, 3642–45
    No. 2, 3646
    No. 3, 3647
    No. 4, 3648
    No. 6, 3649
    No. 7, 3641–42
    No. 8, 3643
    No. 9, 3648
    No. 10, 3644
    No. 11, 3641
    No. 12, 3646
    No. 13, 3652
    No. 14, 3653
    No. 15, 3642–45
    No. 16, 3654
    No. 17, 3642–45
    No. 18, 3610
Statements on Standards for Attestation Engagements (SSAE)
    No. 10, 3682–87, 3690
    No. 11, 3682
    No. 12, 3682
    No. 13, 3681
Statistical sampling, 3410, 3420
    advantages, 3423

    defined, 3421
    disadvantages, 3424
    professional judgment, 3425
    stratified sampling, 3436
    types, 3422
Statistical sampling models, 3422
    attribute sampling, 3422.02, 3440
    discovery sampling, 3422.02, 3450
Statistical terms, defined, 3462
Stratified sampling, 3436
Study suggestions for audit exam, 3013
Subsequent discoveries, 3532
    dating, 3534
Subsequent events, 3531, 3542
Substantive tests, 3350, 3360, 3412.09, 3413
    and audit hypothesis model, 3473.02
    and audit sampling, 3413, 3422.04
    examples of, 3350, 3360
Successor auditor, 3153, 3648
Sufficiency, 3325
Supervising the audit, 3156
Supplementary information, 3560
Systematic process, 3112.01

T

Tagging, 3242.01
Technical training and proficiency, 3122.02, 3141
Test deck, 3232.01–.05
Tests of controls, 3412.10, 3414, 3422.04
Tolerable error, 3413.03
Tolerable rates, 3414.06, 3442

U

Ultimate risk, 3472
Unaudited financial statements of public companies, 3630
Uncertainty, 3412, 3525
Unconditional requirements, 3127.01, 3681.04
Unqualified opinion, 3512

V

Variable sampling, 3422.03, 3460
    accounting estimation approach, 3460
    audit hypothesis approach, 3470
Visual evidence, 3332

W

Workpapers, 3314
    permanent file, 3352